SCOTTISH
THEOLOGY

SCOTTISH
THEOLOGY

From John Knox to John McLeod Campbell

THOMAS F. TORRANCE

T&T CLARK
EDINBURGH

T&T CLARK LTD
59 GEORGE STREET
EDINBURGH EH2 2LQ
SCOTLAND

First published 1996

ISBN 0 567 08532 5

British Library Cataloguing-in-Publication Data
A catalogue record for this book is available
from the British Library

Typesetting by Trinity Typesetting, Edinburgh
Printed and bound in Great Britain by Hartnolls Ltd, Bodmin

To New College, Edinburgh,
With Thanksgiving and Prayer

Quantum in nobis est, pacem colamus,
illaesa tamen veritate, et salva charitate

John Forbes of Corse

Contents

Preface

For many years I have collected old Scottish books in the hope that one day I might be able to write a history of Scottish Theology from 1560 to 1850, if only to supplement those that have already appeared: James Walker, *The Theology and Theologians of Scotland, chiefly those of the Seventeenth and Eighteenth Centuries* (Edinburgh, 1888), and John Macleod, *Scottish Theology In Relation to Church History Since the Reformation* (Edinburgh, 1943). Hitherto that has not proved possible as I have been heavily engaged with Christian dogmatics, Patristic theology, and with the relation between Christian theology and science. Then after I had completed what I thought to be my last book, *The Christian Doctrine of God, One Being Three Persons,* my old purpose was renewed. I had been asked to prepare a chapter on Scottish theology from the Reformation to the Disruption for the volume being published in commemoration of the 150th anniversary of New College, Edinburgh. When I agreed to do this I turned back to my collection of old Scottish theology, and read and studied again books I had not read for many years, and some I had not read at all. I found that in order to write the short chapter asked of me, I had to reinform myself very fully. In order to get a proper grip on it all I had to write much more than was needed for New College. In this way I became caught up in preparing a small volume for publication, but when I worked over it again and again, it grew under my hand, and I found myself producing this book. I was encouraged to do this by my son Iain who has inherited my fascination for Scottish theology and lectures on it at the University of Aberdeen. I am most grateful to him for many valuable suggestions and also for his help with the proofs.

This book is not really a history, but comprises brief soundings in the thought of some of the most notable and influential theologians in the Kirk. There are notable churchmen and scholars whom I have not taken into consideration – I think of churchmen like Alexander Henderson, George Gillespie, and William Carstares, and the Aberdeen Doctors, apart from John Forbes of Corse. Nor have I taken into account the rich literature of expository theology, both in the many biblical commentaries which took their origin with Robert Rollock and James Durham as well as David Dickson, and the many volumes of sermons published by Scottish preachers over two centuries. Again I have given little attention to the controversial writings in which Scottish theology abounds, not least the host of pamphlets that appeared in the seventeenth and eighteenth centuries. In preparing this work I have, for the most part, used books from the limited collection on my own shelves, so that its survey of theological literature is limited.

The chapters that follow are more or less independent of one another, and do not follow in argument from one another. There are indeed basic theological questions running through the course of Scottish theology which, while meeting with different approaches in the checkered history of the Kirk from the Reformation, and through the Enlightement to modern times, do help to give it a distinct continuity, but it is a continuity of agreement in difference and difference in agreement. However, since the same basic questions keep cropping up provoking different reactions, they have had to be considered and discussed again and again. This means that there is inevitably some repetition, but not without fresh aspects of old controversies and truths being brought to light.

In Chapter One on John Knox and the Scottish Reformation, I have offered a general account of the deep doctrinal change that took place, but in the succeeding chapters I have tried to focus on the main issues that arose as a result of the adherence of the Church of Scotland to the *Westminster Confession of Faith*. Following upon the teaching of the great Reformers there developed what is known as 'federal theology', in which the place John Calvin gave to the biblical conception of the covenant was radically altered through being schematised to a framework of law and grace governed by a severely contractual notion of covenant, with a stress upon a primitive 'covenant of works', resulting in a change in the Reformed understanding of the 'covenant of grace'. This was what Protestant scholastics called 'a two-winged', and not 'a one-winged' covenant, which my brother James has called a bilateral and a unilateral conception of the Covenant. The former carries with it legal stipulations which have to be fulfilled in order for it to take effect, while the latter derives from the infinite love of God, and is freely proclaimed to all mankind in the grace of the Lord Jesus Christ. It was the imposition of a rigidly logicalised federal system of thought upon Reformed theology that gave rise to many of the problems which have afflicted Scottish theology, and thereby made central doctrines of predestination, the limited or unlimited range of the atoning death of Christ, the problem of assurance, and the nature of what was called 'the Gospel-offer' to sinners. This meant that relatively little attention after the middle of the seventeenth century was given to the doctrine of the Holy Trinity and to a trinitarian understanding of redemption and worship. Basic to this change was the conception of the nature and character of God. It is in relation to that issue that one must understand the divisions which have kept troubling the Kirk after its hard-line commitment to the so-called 'orthodox Calvinism' of the Westminster Standards, and the damaging effect that had upon the understanding of the Word of God and the message of the Gospel. It must be added that a study of the vicissitudes of the Kirk reveals that commitment to the National Covenant and the Solemn League and Covenant had the effect of politicising theology in a rather misleading and unhelpful way – this is a matter from which the Church of Scotland and the Free Churches of Scotland still suffer.

Throughout this book I have usually kept to the spelling of the Scots vernacular in citations from the sixteenth and seventeenth centuries, and also to the punctuation and sometimes even to the syntax of writers, for example, in the works of John Knox and James Fraser of Brae. I hope this will not be too distracting for readers who are not familiar with the old Scots tongue. It may convey vividly something of the distinctive character of Scottish theology, and the problems that recur throughout its tradition and are still with us, which are evident in our unhealed Church divisions. There are what I consider rather divisive elements and unfortunate features in Scottish theology which must not be glossed over. These are due a) to the way in which biblical and Reformed theology has suffered from the imposition of a logico-causal framework of thought developed by Protestant scholastic thinkers in their reaction to the Counter-Reformation, and b) to subscription to the National Covenant and the Solemn League and Covenant, in the misguided attempt to impose a Roman-like uniformity of religion on the United Kingdom. This led in different ways and at different times in Scotland to a politicisation of theology with serious detriment to the evangelical mission and the spiritual welfare of the Kirk. Nevertheless I find that Scottish theology, as represented in the leading theologians with whom I have been concerned, is rich with great treasure, much of which is still untapped, especially in great Latin tomes which have never been translated into English. It is my hope that this study will encourage others to forage more deeply in the religious and theological literature of Scotland, and allow it to bear effectively upon moves toward the evangelical and theological renewal of which we are in such great need today.

St Andrew's Day, 1995,
Edinburgh

1

John Knox and the Scottish Reformation

'The theology of Scotland begins with the Reformation, and the first of our great theological writers is John Knox himself.'[1] There were, of course, Scottish theologians of note in the pre-Reformation Church, Richard of St Victor, John Duns Scotus, and John Major, to mention only three, but there is no doubt that John Knox made a unique contribution to the character and shape of the theology of the Reformed Church of Scotland. This was certainly to see changes and modifications over the centuries between the Reformation and the Disruption, but underlying them all and affecting them was the original mould contributed by John Knox and the *Scots Confession* of 1560.[2]

Of particular note is the Preface of the Confession. Matthew 24.14 was first cited on its frontispiece. 'And this glad tydings of the kingdom shalbe preached throught the hole world for a witness to all nations and then shall the end come.' Then the Preface follows with the sentence:

> The Estaitis of Scotland with the Inhabitants of the same professand *Christ Jesus* his haly Evangel, to their natural Countrymen, and unto all uther realmes professand the same Lord *Jesus* with them, wish Grace, Mercie and Peace fra God the Father of our Lord *Jesus Christ*, with the Spirit of richteous Judgement, for Salvation.

This is quite startling for, in contrast to every other confessional statement issued during the Reformation, it gives primary

---

[1] James Walker, *The Theology and Theologians of Scotland, Chiefly of the Seventeenth and Eighteenth Centuries*, 2nd edn Edinburgh, 1888, p. 1.
[2] See the edition by G. D. Henderson, 1937, and the fascinating evaluation of it by Karl Barth, *Knowledge of God and the Service of God*, London, 1938.

1

importance to the missionary calling of the Church.[3] This was
certainly in line with the outlook of John Calvin, but in sharp
contrast to the teaching of Theodore Beza who, in his debate with
Hadrian à Saravia over the missionary command of Christ reported
in Matthew 29.19–20, insisted that it applied only to the covenanted
and the elect![4] Of course, the missionary task to which Knox and
his fellow Reformers devoted themselves was the proclamation of
'the sweet savour of the Evangel' to people in Scotland – that was
surely the origin of our 'Home Mission'.

How far was John Knox a theologian? Here are some of his
statements about himself in this respect.

> Consider, Brethren, it is no speculative theologian which
> desires to give you courage, but even your Brother in
> affliction.[5]

> The time is come that men cannot abyde the Sermon of
> veritie nor holesome doctrine.

> For considering my selfe rather cald of God to instruct the
> ignorant, comfort the sorrowfull, confirme the weake, and
> rebuke the proud, by tong and livelye voyce in these corrupt
> dayes, than to compose bokes for the age to come, seeing
> that so much is written (and that by men of singular
> condition), and yet so little well observed; I deemed to
> containe my selfe within the bondes of that vocation,
> whereunto I found my selfe especially called...[6]

> It hath pleased his mercy to make me not a lord-like Bishop,
> but a painful Preacher of his blessed Evangel...[7]

John Knox himself was essentially a *preacher-theologian*, one who
did not intend to be a theologian, but who could not help being a
theologian in the fulfilment of his vocation. He regarded his

---

[3]   Cf. Henry Cowan, *The Influence of the Scottish Church in Christendom*, London,
      1896, p. 29.
[4]   See the dissertation by Luke B. Smith, *The Contribution of Hadrian à Saravia
      (1531–1613) to the Doctrine of the Nature of the Church and its Mission*, 1965, New
      College Library.
[5]   'Epistle to the Congregation of the Castle of St Andrews', 1548, *The Works of
      John Knox*, Collected and Edited by David Laing, Edinburgh 1846–64, Vol. 3,
      p. 10.
[6]   Preface to the sermon on 1 Timothy 4, *Works*, Vol. 6, p. 229.
[7]   Letter to John Wood, 1567/8, *Works*, Vol. 6, p. 559.

vocation: a) as a preacher of the Gospel, someone burdened with the lively Word of God, which he had to proclaim in a correspondingly lively manner; b) as a steward of the mysteries, or 'a steward of the mystery of redemption' (one of his favourite expressions).

> The price of Christ Jesus, his death and passion is committed to our charge, the eyes of men are bent on us, and we must answer before the Judge, who will not admit everie excuse that pleaseth us, but will judge upryghtly, as in his words he hath before pronounced ... Let us be frequent in reading (which allace, over many despise) earnest in prayer, diligent in watcheing over the flock committed to our charge, and let our sobrietie and temperate lyfe eshame the wicked, and be example to the godly...[8]

The desperate earnestness with which Knox took his calling demanded theological earnestness: i.e. a theology in the service of evangelism and preaching, in which 'arguments and reasons serve only instead of handmaids, which shall not command but obey Scripture pronounced by the Voice of God'.[9] We have only one theological treatise from him, that on *Predestination*,[10] but his letters and pamphlets, his controversial writings, his service book, sermons, his *Book of Common Order*, his contribution to *The Book of Discipline,* and his *History of the Reformation*,[11] reveal profound discernment and shrewd theological judgment. Again and again, he put his finger upon the really crucial issues, and the way he handled them indicates how his theological insights affected his vocation. This is particularly evident in his little work *A Declaration on the True Nature and Object of Prayer.*[12]

In this Reformation theology of John Knox and his colleagues there took place a radical shift from the medieval set of mind, away from an abstract theology of logically ordered propositions to a lively dynamic theology, addressed not primarily to the salvation of the individual soul, but to the nation as a whole. It involved a

---

[8] *Works*, Vol. 6, p. 425.
[9] *Works*, Vol. 5, p. 61; cf. also 3, pp. 126; Vol. 6, pp. 175ff, 205, 425.
[10] *Works*, Vol. 5.
[11] *Works*, Vols. 1 & 2. For *The Book of Common Order of the Church of Scotland, Commonly known as John Knox's Liturgy,* see the edition by G. W. Sprott, Edinburgh, 1901.
[12] *Works*, Vol. 3, pp. 89–105; cf. also 'Exposition of the Sixth Psalm of David', 1554, pp. 119–56.

radical change in the doctrine of God. This is very evident in the
first article of the Confession on the doctrine of the Holy Trinity:
'ane onlie God ... ane in substance, and zit distinct in thre
personnis, the Father, the Sone, and the holie Gost'. Thus in the
Scots Confession as in John Knox's *Genevan Liturgy*, the doctrine of
the Trinity is not added on to a prior conception of God – there is
no other content but the Father, the Son and the Holy Spirit.[13]
There was no separation here between the doctrine of the One
God (*De Deo Uno*), and the doctrine of the triune God (*De Deo
Trino*), which had become Roman orthodoxy through the definitive
formalisation of Thomas Aquinas. This trinitarian approach was
in line with *The Little Catechism* which Knox brought back from
Geneva for the instruction of children in the Kirk. 'I believe in
God the Father, and in Jesus Christ his Son and in the Holy Spirit,
and look for salvation by no other means.'[14] Within this trinitarian
frame the centre of focus in the Confession and Catechism alike is
upon Jesus Christ himself, for it is only through him and the Gospel
he proclaimed that God's triune reality is made known, but
attention is also given to the Holy Spirit. Here once again we have
a different starting point from other Reformation Confessions.
Whereas they have a believing anthropocentric starting point, such
as in the *Heidelberg Catechism*, this is quite strongly theocentric and
trinitarian. Even in Calvin's *Institute*, which follows the fourfold
pattern in Peter Lombard's *Sentences*, the doctrine of the Trinity is
given in the thirteenth chapter within the section on the doctrine
of God the Creator. Calvin's *Genevan Catechism*, however,
understandably followed the order of the *Apostles' Creed*. The
trinitarian teaching in the *Scots Confession* was by no means limited
to the first article for it is found throughout woven into the
doctrinal content of subsequent articles.

The doctrine of God

John Knox's doctrine of God, nowhere more vividly declared than
in his prayers, in the context of worship, stands out in remarkable
contrast to medieval Roman theology. This is in every sense a *living*

---

[13] *Works*, Vol. 3, p. 440.
[14] See my edition in *The School of Faith, The Catechisms of the Reformed Church*,
London, 1959, p. 239.

doctrine of the ever-living and ever-acting Lord God. Its very language reflects something of the passion and conviction produced by the lively voice of God heard in the Holy Scriptures of the Old and New Testaments. In the words of Knox one hears the trumpet blasts of the mighty Word of God – and yet in the midst there is no mistaking the still small voice of God in his incredible mercy and compassion which penetrates and transcends the thunder.

'God' is no mere doctrine. Knowledge of God is not something thought out but is heard, confessed and acknowledged on the ground of his own self-witness, and is conveyed to people through godly attention to the teaching of the Holy Scripture, not in formal propositions but only by words in motion, words of passion which proclaim the Gospel of salvation and through which there resounds the majesty of God. Yet in the midst of such an encounter with the living God, the doctrine itself as formulated for example in the *Scots Confession* of 1560 is crystal clear in its derivation from 'the infallible Word of God' and God's revelation of himself in Jesus Christ.

1) *The uniqueness of God*

God is 'the one only God', absolutely unique.[15] It is to him only that we must cleave, and him only that we must serve and worship, and in him alone put all our trust. It was in these terms that the *Scots Confession* opened its articles of faith. That needed to be said, and Knox was never weary of saying it – God is alone in his ineffable majesty and can lend majesty to no one. It belongs to God as God to be utterly unique in the exaltation of his Being and nature. God is only like God, and will have no other gods before him, and no images of God can have any place in our knowledge and worship of him. The unique God can only be confessed and acknowledged. It was John Duns Scotus, the hero of John Major, who said (as well as Aquinas) 'God is not in a genus' (*Deus non est in aliquo genere*) – which means that we cannot know him in any general way or speak of him in general terms. The unique God can be known only through himself in the light of his own majesty and glory.

'There is one God only to whom we must cleave, to serve him and worship him, who is also our only trust and refuge.'[16] This

---

[15] *Scots Confession*, Art. 2, edition by G. D. Henderson, Edinburgh, 1937, pp. 43f; *Works*, Vol. 6, pp. 361f.

[16] *Works*, Vol. 6, p. 361.

God cannot be known at a distance, abstractly or dispassionately or without feeling his impact upon the knower. Only in that condition of the knower can there be true knowledge of God. That is one of the points that strikes one again and again about Knox's language, especially in prayer. It hurts to know God – the man who really knows God suffers from him, is marked by God, is smitten down to the dust and only then stands on his feet to know and talk to God. But for one to know God in such a way is to be renewed, and transformed into the image and likeness of God after which man was originally created.

Knowledge of the one and only God, as far as it is true knowledge, enshrines the mystery of God, and so is confessed and acknowledged as God eternal, infinite, immeasurable, incomprehensible, omniscient, invisible. This God whom we know cannot be fitted into *our* knowledge. God cannot be commanded by our reasons – cannot be comprehended by our minds. It is certainly to our minds that God reveals himself but only in such a way that he remains eternal, infinite, incomprehensible, etc. Knowledge of God cannot be put into precise words. God's majesty defies definition or description – all theological language is apocalyptic in so far as it is genuine. That is true above all of the Trinity – knowledge of this God is infinitely open. Thus in faith the human reason is opened wide to the infinite and incomprehensible being and majesty of God as the Father, the Son and the Holy Spirit.

2) *The Holy Trinity*
The Confession of Faith and the liturgy, and the catechisms that followed, explicitly affirm the Ecumenical Faith, Apostles Creed, Nicene, 'Athanasian' Creeds of the ancient Catholic Church, in explicit affirmation of all catholic orthodoxy.[17] These creeds were held to give expression to God's 'eternal verity', born again in the faith of the Scottish people and thus were given a place in regular public worship of God in the Reformed congregations. It is clear in the *Scots Confession*, as in Knox's *Genevan Liturgy*, that the doctrine of the Trinity is not added on to a prior conception of doctrine of God, but belongs to the basic and essential content of the doctrine of God – there is no other content but Father, Son and Holy Spirit.[18]

---

[17] Cf. also *The Treatise of Balnaves on Justification by Faith, The Works of John Knox*, Vol. 3, p. 440.

[18] *Works*, Vol. 3, p. 440; Vol. 6, pp. 343, 361.

This clearly reflects the approach of John Calvin in chapter 13 of the first book of his *Institute of the Christian Religion*.[19]

(a) It is as a Trinity that the majesty and sublimity of God are made known. As Holy Trinity God is revealed to be intrinsically personal. God is Person precisely as he is triune, so that intimate personal relationship is involved in acknowledgment of the one only God, cleaving to him, serving him, worshipping and trusting personally in him as Father, Son and Holy Spirit. The majesty of the one only God and the transcendent mystery of the eternal God as such do not produce the personal communication between God and man – that belongs to the personal self-revelation of God as Holy Trinity. God is Father, Son and Holy Spirit, and remains what he is in his eternal Self even when he gives himself to be known by us in such personal ways.

(b) It is the *triune God* who is known as Father, Maker, Pastor and Redeemer.[20] It is the Trinity who creates, appoints, governs all things in heaven and earth, visible as well as invisible. God the Father Almighty can be known only through the Son, as the Incarnation of God and of his work for our redemption. Fatherhood is defined in terms of redeeming grace toward us and free adoption of us as his children. 'We call him Father not so much because he has created us, but by reason of his free adoption by which he has chosen us in Jesus Christ.'[21]

(c) It is as the triune God, Father, Son and Holy Spirit, that God relates himself to all creation, visible and invisible. His relation to creation is supremely as personal will – but the purpose and glory of that relation is Jesus Christ. There are here distinct elements of cosmic redemption, in God's concern for all creation and of all his handiwork, but what all that means will be revealed only at the last day. This strictly trinitarian theology means that Knox regarded God's relations with all creation exclusively in terms of personal will, and exclusively in the light of Christ's redemption and saving purpose.

---

[19] See my account of 'Calvin's Doctrine of the Trinity', *Trinitarian Perspectives*, Edinburgh, 1994, pp. 41–76; cf. also pp. 21–40.
[20] *Works*, Vol. 6, p. 306.
[21] *Works*, Vol. 6, p. 317.

3) *Paradox of immutability and active intervention*
John Knox never wearied of affirming the immutability of God.
He ever remains the same God, true and faithful to his 'joyful
promise' to Adam that the seed of the woman would break down
the serpent's head.[22] This took the form of an *ordinance of grace* in
which God provided a way within the history of mankind for
deliverance and redemption. It is indeed upon the ordinance of
grace that the whole order of creation depends, for it remains the
same in the midst of the world's turmoil and man's enmity to God.
In the midst of man's sin, and in spite of it, the ordinance of grace
assumed the character of a promise. The promise involves
judgment – the seeking out of man, his calling, his rebellion and
conviction of sin, but throughout all judgment and wrath, through
all calamity and disaster, God's purpose for mankind was being
worked out. In the first instance this took historical form in the
calling of Israel to be the medium of God's self-revelation to
mankind, and it is that ordinance which proved to be the centre
around which all things revolve and in relation to which they
cohere.[23] He is the God who brought Israel out of Egypt and
destroyed Pharaoh in the Red Sea, who sent the Jews into exile,
and brought them back as a remnant into Palestine. God is
immutable and his ancient Word still holds sway – his ancient ways
still appear in his dealings with man. But this is no immutability
conceived in philosophical categories – it is the immutability of
God's purpose, will and action, for God is above all the living God
who is at work in his creation, whose hand disposes nations and
kingdoms. His divine ordinance of grace took historical shape in
his covenanted relations with the people of Israel through whom
a way was prepared for its ultimate fulfilment in the Incarnation
and in the inauguration of the Church.[24] No theologian has had a
more vivid and dramatic or a more powerful realisation of direct
divine action in history than Knox, and of its ultimate soteriological
character. It is here that his theology stands out in such contrast to
medieval teaching – its dynamic outlook indicates that there had

---

[22] *Scots Confession*, Art. 4, G. D. Henderson, pp. 45f.
[23] See the Sermon preached by Knox on Isaiah, xxvi. 13–21, *Works*, Vol. 6, pp.
233–73.
[24] 'For as our God in his owne nature is immutable, so remayneth his love
towardes his elect alwaies unchangeable (Eph. I); for as in Christ Jesus he
hath chosen his church before the beginning of al ages, so by him will he
mayntayne and preserve the same unto the end.' *Works*, Vol. 6, p. 267.

taken place a radical move away from the rather static categories of the medieval frame of mind. This is vividly evident in his acceptance of the influence of the Old Testament and its significance for his own times in Scotland. The very same God of whom we learn in the Old Testament Scriptures, not least through the great prophets, and in the New Testament Scriptures in the original mission of the Church, now deals with men and nations through the mighty acts of his saving Word.

God is the Lord of history and its Judge. All creation is related to God directly through his personal will which commands and gives it its order. Disordered creation is therefore constantly under God's personal and direct overruling and discipline. 'Discipline' is one of the great words of Knox. It speaks of the activity by which form and order are imposed upon disorder to bring worldly and spiritual affairs and states into conformity to the divine will. In the Church, and among the nations, that discipline is carried out through God's Word.

When Knox thinks of Scotland, he sees the whole of its history under the hand and personal direction of God through his 'gentle chastening' – which is gentle even in the midst of dire calamities because in them God is working out his purpose of redemption. Here the Old Testament Scriptures supply Knox with vivid and dramatic examples of the divine Word at work – righteous conformity to God's will exalts a nation but the nation that rebels against God, and falsely transfers to its own sovereignty divine majesty, inevitably falls under the wrath of God. However, this Old Testament teaching is interpreted in the light of the New Testament in terms of the death and resurrection of Christ which supplies the true and final norms to which all divine action in history conforms. Justification by the blood of Christ governs nations as well as individuals. Judgment and mercy are seen together in intimate and inseparable conjunction. There is no doubt that for Knox the supreme purpose of divine love and mercy prevails over all temporal chastisement and outpouring of divine wrath – the way of mercy and love is not apart from judgment.

It may be noted in this connection that John Knox regarded the Ascension as one of the great saving events along with the death and resurrection of Christ.[25] The Christ who died for our sins,

---

[25] See Ch. XI, of the *Scots Confession, Works,* Vol. 2, pp. 103f, & G. D. Henderson, pp. 57f.

vanquished death and hell, rose again as the first fruits of the new
creation, has ascended to the throne of the divine Judgment and
from there rules over the world. It is also the throne of divine mercy
– it is the merciful Christ, the Saviour, by whom God will judge the
world. That means that all history has soteriological and
eschatological purpose – and its inner meaning will be fully
unveiled at God's great Judgment, but may be revealed even today
because divine judgment is being carried out through the Word
of the Gospel. God is even now at work among the nations in
judgment unto salvation in anticipation of the final judgment –
his will and Word work both ways. Of particular note in this
connection was the preaching of Knox – while he laid considerable
stress on God's judgments, it was above all a proclamation of the
Gospel to the Scottish Nation full of passionate pleading on behalf
of the divine mercy.

God answers prayer. God is free in faithfulness to himself to work
out his purposes, and through his providence to turn evil into
good.[26] The Christian has no right to complain, as Knox himself
refused to do of the harsh treatment he received in the French
galleys – it was God's doing! And God's purposes will not be
thwarted – hence the great comfort and secret of prayer lies in the
fact that God will prevail.[27] That was one of John Knox's most
masterful convictions.

The Person and work of Christ

In the theology of the Scottish Reformation the Old Testament
story of the people of Israel was regarded as the prehistory of the
Incarnation, reflecting in itself already the essential pattern of the
death and resurrection of Jesus Christ. In the Old Testament
messianic community the divine 'ordinance of grace' becomes
embodied in history and moves toward its focus and completion
in the Incarnation. This saving activity of God exhibited by the
messianic community in history is the meaning of *election*. But now
we see that the election, at once corporate and individual, at once
eternal in origin and yet active within history for its fulfilment, is
consummated in Jesus Christ. Jesus Christ is the eternal election

---

[26] *Works*, Vol. 2, pp. 35f, 172ff, 350f; see the *Declaration on Prayer*, Vol. 3, pp. 90f.
[27] *Works*, Vol. 1, pp. 228f.

of God working itself out in the midst of the estrangement of the human race from God.

That is the context in which the *Scots Confession* regarded the Person and Work of Christ.[28] It was not concerned here with scholastic dogma, but with the concrete action of God in history, and specifically in the life and deeds of Jesus Christ. All is interpreted in terms of God's incarnate activity, not in terms of a metaphysical but of a personal (or hypostatic) union of two natures, Godhead and manhood. It is here most clearly that we see a difference between the *Scots Confession*, and indeed all Reformed confessions, and the ecumenical creeds of the Patristic period at least as they have often been interpreted. At Nicaea and Chalcedon, for example, the Church was concerned to formulate aright, and in such a way as to avoid damaging heresies, the relation between God and man in Jesus Christ. That was a magnificent achievement, and the guiding light was the absolute significance of the full Deity of Christ for Christian worship and salvation, together with the rejection of any docetic denial of our Lord's manhood and earthly existence. In the later tradition of the Church, however, the christological dogmas formulated by the Ancient Fathers often tended to be interpreted mainly in rather static terms and categories. That represented a failure to understand how the divine action against the powers of darkness deliberately involved the death of Jesus. Greek and Latin Fathers were sometimes almost apologetic about the death of Jesus, as though it was but one of the unfortunate if inevitable features of the eschatological war between the Kingdom of Light and the kingdom of darkness. They thus failed to give sufficient attention to the fact that it was precisely through the death of Jesus as the incarnate Son of God that God *himself* in Christ had come amongst us to make atonement for our sin and triumph over all evil, and that the Person and work of Christ are to be interpreted from the perspective of his death, and his accomplishment in death and resurrection for our salvation. Of course there were great fathers like Athanasius, Gregory Nazianzen, and Cyril of Alexandria who approached and interpreted the Incarnation from a strong soteriological perspective, while many of the Latin Fathers tended to detach their understanding of the atoning death of Christ from the whole course of his incarnate life. Unlike the Church Fathers, however, Knox took up the

---

[28] *Scots Confession*, Art. 6–11, G. D. Henderson, pp. 49ff. See also 'Ane Exposition of the Creed', *Works*, Vol. 6, pp. 317ff.

teaching of Calvin upon the *Triplex Munus*, or threefold Office of
Christ as king, priest, and prophet.[29]

It was certainly characteristic of the theology of the Scottish
Reformation that the great bastion of salvation was held to be the
atoning and redeeming action of God in mighty triumph over the
powers of evil, against anti-Christ. That battle, however, is waged
in the heart of humanity and humanity's enmity to God. The sharp
focus of the *eschatological* drama in the *apocalyptic* conflict between
God and the devil, heaven and earth, light and darkness, is found
in the Incarnation, death, resurrection, ascension and *parousia* of
Jesus Christ. They are the mighty acts of God, the actual salvation
events in God's ordinance of grace which invades the history of
mankind and brings about complete and final victory over the
forces of evil and darkness. Thus all that John Knox preached about
the living mighty God of history reached its climax in the sacrificial
death and triumphant resurrection and ascension of Jesus, and it
is in its light that we are to understand his doctrine of Christ's
Person and work.

(1) *The Incarnation*

The doctrine of the Incarnation is governed throughout by the
message of salvation.[30] There was no speculation about whether
there would have been an Incarnation if man had not fallen,
whether the Incarnation was a necessary act or device or a divine
after-thought, or an inevitable event in the relation between God
and man. It is the way freely taken by the grace of God in the midst
of man's enmity to God. Although man has separated himself from
God, God will not let him go, and sends his own Son to enter into
man's estrangement and to be *Immanuel*, God with us, in the midst
of our existence, God and man perfectly united. In him true God
has become true man, yet without ceasing to be God, in order to
fulfil within humanity the eternal purpose of God's love and grace.
The Incarnation is itself, therefore, an act of salvation, not alone
by itself, but an act of salvation integral to the whole purpose of
redemption.

In this way the Incarnation involves more than the completion
of God's purpose of creation. All that was lost in Adam is here

---

[29] *Works*, Vol. 6, pp. 319f.
[30] *Scots Confession*, Art. 6, G. D. Henderson, pp. 49f; *Works*, Vol. 2, pp. 146f; Vol. 3,
pp. 93f, 6ff; cf. Vol. 3, p. 454; Vol. 6, pp. 363f.

fulfilled, but here creation is transcended, and a higher and closer relation between God and man is wrought out on the basis of the Incarnation rather than just on the basis of creation. Here for example God is *Father*, and Christ is our *Brother*, but we may now think of God as *our* Father, not so much on the basis of creation as on the basis of redemption. While Christ is himself by nature, Son of God, we are made children of God by grace. And so through the Incarnation man has become a joint-heir with Christ of the eternal heritage in God the Father.

Care was taken to point out that the incarnate Son is the eternal Wisdom of God, the eternal Word that was with God from the very beginning, by whom all things were created and are conserved and kept in being. He was the creator Word, without whom there is no creaturely being, the source and meaning of all creation, who became incarnate, so that in the Incarnation creation and redemption are held together. The work of the incarnate Word is not only to forgive sin and annul death, destroy guilt, but to inaugurate a new creation, to create a new humanity, but now a humanity in the closest relation and union with God.

This Incarnation, then, involved a perfect union between perfect natures, Godhead and manhood – God and man joined in one Person through what the *Scots Confession* calls 'this maist wondrous conjunction betwixt the God-head and the man-head in *Christ Jesus* (which) did proceed from the eternal and immutable decree of God, from quhilk al our salvatioun springs and depends.'[31] This God-man partakes of our flesh of the seed of David, of the lost seed of Adam, yet is born without sin by the operation of the Holy Spirit. There is here both continuity and yet discontinuity. It is a Virgin Birth by the operation of the Holy Spirit: great stress was laid on this in Knox's liturgy, and in the two liturgical confessions as well as in the *Scots Confession*.

The classical dogmas of the ecumenical creeds were asserted and affirmed, and the heresies of Arius, Marcion, Eutyches, Nestorius, and others were condemned as damnable and pestilent. In particular the Confession condemned those which deny the eternity of Christ's Godhead, or the verity of his human nature, and either confound them with one another or divide them from one another.

---

[31] *Scots Confession*, Art. 7 – G. D. Henderson, p. 51.

(2) *The election and God-manhood of Christ*

The relation between the eternal decrees and the wondrous conjunction between Godhood and manhood in Jesus Christ was given particular prominence in the *Scots Confession* by its isolation as a separate article.[32] No more explanation is given – this is one of the places in Christian faith where the mind is opened upward in sheer wonder.

The doctrine of election is *christologically conditioned*. Election proceeds certainly from the eternal decree of God from which all salvation springs and on which it depends, but this eternal decree of election assumes in time once and for all the form of the wondrous conjunction of God and man in Christ. It is significant that at the heart of the mystery of election there is the hypostatic union of God and man, two perfect natures united and joined in one Person. The usual problem of election is how to distinguish and relate the two poles of activity: 'You have not chosen me, but I have chosen you.' How are we to relate God's action to our faith? The secret of that is seen only in the God-manhood of Christ, for that is the very heart of election, and the pattern of *our* election, and is visible only there since it is election in Christ.

(3) *Election and mediation*

The coming of God and man together in Christ takes place amid the conditions of enmity and sin, and the union of God and man is a union fulfilled within sinful flesh.[33] Christ is himself the Elect One – in him election becomes and operates as atoning mediation. Thus mediation is the specific form which election assumes in sinful history. That means that the union of God and man in Jesus Christ is not thought of as somehow ontologically complete at Bethlehem. It begins there by entry into the enmity between the justice of God and our sin, but it is completed in the death, resurrection and ascension of Christ. It is particularly noteworthy that election, and predestination, are expounded in terms of Christology, for they have to be understood as the activity of God *in Christ*. This was made very clear by the *Scots Confession* in the way that it interposed the article on election between those on the mediatorial union of God and man in Christ and that on Christ's death, passion and

---

[32] *Scots Confession*, Art. 8, G. D. Henderson, pp. 51f.
[33] This was how, as we shall see, it was understood by Hugh Binning in his *Sermons on Romans* 8.1–10.

burial. In the term predestination, of course, the emphasis falls upon the truth that God has chosen us in Christ *before* the foundation of the world (Ephesians 1.4), which has to be linked with the truth that Christ as the Lamb of God was slain before the foundation of the world. There was here no thought of an election or eternal purpose of God taking place apart from Christ or behind his back, as it were, for he is himself eternally very God of very God. The 'eternal veritie of his God-head and the veritie of his human nature' united indivisibly together constitute the supreme truth upon which everything in the Gospel depends.[34]

Objectively, our election is consummated as the wondrous conjunction between God and man in Christ, established in the midst of our enmity and sin, secured in the resurrection and completed by the ascension of Christ as God and man to the right hand of God the Father. That is to say, hypostatic union and atoning union are held together as the obverse of one another, for the Person and the work of Christ cannot be separated from one another. *Subjectively*, our election is consummated when this 'most holy fraternity' between God and man is restored to us. It is therefore not enough simply to believe in this, said Knox, for it must be applied to us.[35] That takes place when Christ dwells in us by the power of the Holy Spirit, the very Christ who as God and man is our Advocate before the face of the Father ever interceding and entreating on our behalf.

It is noteworthy that in the *Scots Confession of Faith* itself the concept of election was explained and set out in terms of Christology, in such a way that at the heart of it emphasis was laid on a conjunction and union of the elect with Christ which was grounded on the saving conjunction and union of Godhead and manhood in Christ himself. The problems that had been raging on the Continent over the concept of predestination were deliberately avoided in a confessional document of that kind. But in 1560 John Knox himself published a lengthy work on the subject, 'An answer to a great number of blasphemous cavillations written by an Anabaptist, and aduersarie to Gods eternall Predestination'.[36] This was a detailed and carefully argued refutation of ideas that called in question a doctrine which Knox felt to be necessary for

[34] *Scots Confession*, Art. 7 & 8.
[35] Ed. G. W. Sprott, p. 12.
[36] *Works*, Vol. 5, pp. 19–468.

the Church of God, for without it Christian faith could not be truly taught or established in humility before God and joy in his unbounded mercy.

What was at stake, Knox felt, was the absolutely unconditional nature of God's grace. In it Knox presented a resolutely Augustinian doctrine of predestination, with help drawn from John Calvin.[37] Like Calvin he stressed that predestination has to be understood strictly *in Christ alone*, and that in the last resort faith must rest in the eternal, incomprehensible and immutable counsel of God. God's will knows no 'Why'.[38] In face of the fact that some people are saved and some are damned, Knox took up Calvin's Pauline point that the preaching of the Gospel is a savour of life unto life and of death unto death, that is to say, that the ultimate 'cause' of reprobation (as distinct from the 'evident' cause due to unbelief[39]), is the very same grace of God by which the elect are saved – there is no 'no' and 'yes' in God but only the 'Yes' of his purpose of love for us.[40] In spite of the fact that some people are saved and some are damned, which might appear to indicate that there are two wills in God, there is only one will of God which is 'secret and hid from us, reserved in his eternal wisdom, to be revealed at the glorious coming of the Lord Jesus'.[41] He refused to commit himself to the idea that 'God's absolute ordinance is the *principal cause* of reprobation, of sinne, and damnation.'[42] The problem that faced Knox, then, is the fact that damnation cannot but be traced back in some way to the eternal will of the eternal God, for there is only one will in God; he did not take up Calvin's point that people's rejection of God's grace and their reprobation by God can be understood by us only as something rationally inexplicable: reprobation is to be regarded, then, as happening *per accidens*, or *accidentaliter*, as Calvin said. Knox, however, did commit himself to saying that the sovereign mercy of God is not common to the

---

[37] According to J. S. McEwen, 'Knox's views on Predestination are a balance of opposite extremes; a fact which the careless and hurried reader of his work is apt to miss.' *The Faith of John Knox*, London, 1961, p. 66. These extremes, however, were held together by Knox within his corporate conception of 'election in Christ'.

[38] *Works*, Vol. 5, pp. 38f, 42, 103f.

[39] *Works*, Vol. 5, pp. 41f, 103, 168, etc.

[40] *Works*, Vol. 5, pp. 21, 99, 382f, 387; Vol. 2, p. 96.

[41] *Works*, Vol. 5, pp. 113 & 313.

[42] *Works*, Vol. 5, pp. 112f.

reprobate but only to the flock of Christ Jesus.[43] The main purpose of his work was quite evidently to uphold against all cavil the truth that we are saved by grace alone and not of ourselves, i.e. the evangelical tenet of *the utter freedom and unconditional nature of God's grace in the Lord Jesus Christ and his Gospel*. Later on, unfortunately, when the doctrine of double predestination was championed and logically elaborated in Scottish theology, it was done in such a way that the doctrine of the unconditional nature of grace was obscured or set aside, and assurance became a haunting and desperate problem. Properly understood, 'election is the true ground of assurance'[44] for it is election, that is, election by grace alone in Christ, that is the objective ground of faith and assurance. That was the issue that cropped up in the Marrow controversy and cropped up again in the deposition of John McLeod Campbell.

(4) *The significance of Godhead and manhood in Christ*

The evangelical significance of this emphasis on the 'Godhead' of Christ lies in the fact that only God can save man. It is God himself who is here at work in Christ, and no other. The evangelical significance of the 'manhood' of Christ lies in the fact that it is our very humanity that God has assumed in Christ, otherwise what God has done in Christ does not affect us. It is of quite central importance for our salvation, therefore, that in the humanity which Christ shares with us God has acted for our sakes and on our behalf.

> It behoved the Messiah and Redeemer to be very God and very Man, because he was to underlie the punishment (*poenas esset pensurus*) due for our transgression, and to present himself in the presence of the Father's Judgment, as in our person, to suffer for our transgression and disobedience, by death to overcome him that was the author of death.[45]

In his manhood Christ suffered for our sin in obedience and under judgment – in his Godhead he triumphed, and was victorious over all wickedness.[46] It is, then, in Christ that God's saving action for man has been grounded in our humanity. Hence it is in the very

---

[43] *Works*, Vol. 5, p. 87.
[44] J. S. McEwen, *The Faith of John Knox*, London, 1961, p. 71. 'Assurance of election can lie in nothing else than in the simple fact that we do believe in the mercy of God in Jesus Christ.' *Op. cit.* p. 74.
[45] *Scots Confession*, Art. 9 – G. D. Henderson, p. 53.
[46] See also *The Book of Common Order*, *Works*, Vol. 6, pp. 302f.

humanity of Christ which he took from us, in his oneness with us, that our salvation is lodged, secured and pledged. 'He was appointed by God to be our pledge'.[47]

(5) *The death of Christ*

As we have already noted the concept of Christ as Mediator has a specially important place in John Knox's understanding of salvation, for it is as Mediator who is himself God and man in his one Person that Christ mediates between Holy God and sinful mankind. When we ask what it is that Christ does in bringing this mediation about, Knox speaks of it as the self-offering of Christ as a voluntary *sacrifice* to his Father for us.[48] In our place and in our stead and for our sake, Christ took our lost cause upon himself in submitting to the judgment of God upon our sin that we might be absolved from our guilt at the tribunal seat of God. The sacrifice Christ offered was a painful sacrifice, but painful not just because he suffered the contradiction of sinners and endured the cruel death of the Cross, but because innocent though he was in being wounded and plagued for our transgressions he suffered the wrath of God. His condemnation in the presence of an earthly judge was but the counterpart of his judgment at the tribunal of God, and thereby, while remaining the only well-beloved and blessed Son of the Father, 'he made full satisfaction for the sins of his people'.[49] It is because Jesus Christ is himself God that the sacrifice he offered has infinite worth and significance. By its very nature this complete vicarious sacrifice offered for all and once for all excludes the possibility of any other sacrifice for sin – to affirm any other would be blasphemous against Christ's death.[50]

Several comments on this understanding of Christ's sacrifice may be in place. While traditional forensic language is used, the atoning sacrifice is not to be understood as fulfilled by Christ merely as man (which would imply a Nestorian Christology), but of Christ as the one Mediator between God and man who is himself God and man in one Person. This means that 'the joyful atonement made between God and man by Christ Jesus, by his death, resurrection and ascension'[51], is not to be understood in any sense

---

[47]   *Works*, Vol. 6, p. 310.
[48]   *Scots Confession*, Art. 9.
[49]   *Scots Confession*, 9 & *The Book of Common Order, Works*, Vol. 6, pp. 319f, 364f.
[50]   *Works*, Vol. 6, p. 363.
[51]   *Works*, Vol. 5, p. 23.

as the act of the man Jesus placating God the Father,[52] but as a propitiatory sacrifice in which God himself through the death of his dear Son draws near to man and draws man near to himself. It is along these lines also that we must interpret the statement of the *Scots Confession* that Christ 'suffered in body and soul to make the full satisfaction for the sins of the people', for in the Cross God accepts the sacrifice made by Christ, whom he did not spare but delivered him up for us all,[53] as satisfaction, thereby acknowledging his own bearing of the world's sin guilt and judgment as the atonement. As Calvin pointed out in a very important passage, God does not love us because of what Christ has done, but it is because he *first* loved us that he came in Christ in order through atoning sacrifice in which God himself does not hold himself aloof but suffers in and with Christ to reconcile us to himself.[54] Nor is there any suggestion that this atoning sacrifice was offered only for some people and not for all, for that would imply that he who became incarnate was not God the Creator in whom all men and women live and move and have their being, and that Jesus Christ our Lord and Saviour was not God and man in the one Person, but only an instrument in the hands of the Father for the salvation of a chosen few. In other words, a notion of limited atonement implies a Nestorian heresy in which Jesus Christ is not really God and man united in one Person. It must be added that the perfect response offered by Jesus Christ in life and death to God in our place and on our behalf, contains and is the pledge of our response. Just as the union of God and man in Christ holds good in spite of all the contradiction of our sin under divine judgment, so his vicarious response holds good for us in spite of our unworthiness: 'not I but Christ'.[55] Here another aspect of Christ's mediatorial office has to be taken into account, his high-priestly intercession for us, which has a special place in John Knox's doctrine of the Eucharist expounded in the light of the Seventeenth Chapter of John's Gospel.

---

[52]   In the Latin translation by Adamson, however, the term *pacificator*, not found in the original Scots text, was used to speak of the mediatorial role of Christ. G. D. Henderson, *Scots Confession*, p. 52.

[53]   Romans 8.32.

[54]   John Calvin, *Institute*, 2.16.4–5.

[55]   Galatians 2.20.

(6) *The resurrection*

John Knox called the resurrection 'the chief article of our faith'. The emphasis in the Scots Confession,[56] is on its stark actuality confirmed by 'the senses and judgments of the Apostles and others', and confirmed even by Christ's 'very enemies', testifying to the sheer reality of his bodily resurrection. A docetic conception of the resurrection was completely rejected and set aside.

Knox thought of the resurrection in the closest association with the death of Christ – death and resurrection are one whole event. If the negative side of Christ's saving work is stressed in his death, e.g. the cancelling of guilt, destroying of the powers of evil, the positive is stressed in the resurrection of the body of Christ from the dead 'for our justification'.[57] By justification here is meant not simply that we are forgiven but that we are declared righteous. It is in the resurrection that the finality of death is visible, and we are made to partake of the positive content of the divine salvation in renewal. 'The which death, albeit it did sufficiently reconcile us to God, yet the Scriptures do commonly attribute our regeneration to his resurrection; for as by rising again from the grave the third day, he conquered death, even so the victory of our faith stands in his resurrection.'[58] The relation of the death to the resurrection is realised by believers in justification and regeneration, and so the Confession in *John Knox's Liturgy* runs: 'I confess that Jesus Christ did not only justify us by covering all our faults and iniquities, but also renews us by his Spirit and that these two points can not be separate, to obtain pardon for our sins, and to be reformed into a holy life.'[59]

Justification is regarded as importing new humanity. The resurrection means that our redemption, our salvation by the death of Christ, is carried through death and hell into the new realm, into the Kingdom where there is no possibility of defeat, decay or destruction. As believers in the death of Christ we believe that we are forgiven, while we remain in the world of sin and decay. But the Resurrection of Christ assures us that the death of Jesus, that the atonement, is not involved in any passing world of decay. Our atonement *is* Christ and he has by his resurrection passed beyond the reach of any defeat – hence the complete finality of atonement

---

[56]   Article 10.
[57]   Romans 4.25.
[58]   *Works*, Vol. 4, p. 170.
[59]   *Works*, Vol. 6, p. 364.

and salvation. This resurrection imports more than the victory over death and damnation, for it establishes the fact that just as in his Incarnation the Son of God was really made man as one of us, so we are united with him in his risen humanity and may therefore ever live before God as those whose humanity has been recreated and renewed. We died when Christ died, but we rose again when he rose again. That is surely the content of the sacrament of Baptism.

(7) The ascension of Christ

Knox laid unusually strong emphasis on the ascension of Jesus Christ in the self-same body which was born of the Virgin Mary, and was crucified, dead and buried and which rose again, and very rightly. It is one of the most neglected doctrines of the Faith. Ascension is not just an addendum to the story of Jesus, a ringing down of the curtain on his earthly life, but it is one of the great essential salvation events. The ascension of the Lord Jesus is the inauguration of the Kingdom of God over the whole creation, but as centred in Christ it is the Kingdom of Christ. What did the ascension do?

(1) It was the completion of the Incarnation event.[60] He who descended also ascended. The very same body which had been born of the Virgin Mary, was crucified, and died and was buried, ascended into heaven, for the accomplishment of all things. Thus the saving work of Christ reaches up into eternity, into the ultimate mystery of God.[61]

(2) The union of God and man in Christ was assumed into the immediate presence of God the Father on his throne – there Christ wears our human life, and it is in our name that he is there at the right hand of God the Father Almighty, standing in for us.

(3) In our name and for our comfort he ascended to take possession of his Kingdom, to inaugurate it and enlarge it.[62] There he is given and receives all power in heaven and on earth – there the crucified Christ sits at the right hand of power and glory.

---

[60] Cf. Philippians 5 & Ephesians 4.
[61] *Works*, Vol. 4, pp. 170f; Vol. 6, pp. 320f, 363f.
[62] *The Confession of Faith used in the English Congregation at Geneva*, see *The Book of Common Order*, ed. G. W. Sprott, p. 9. Edinburgh, 1901.

(4) The Heavenly Session of Christ speaks of the fact that he ever lives to make intercession for us as our Advocate and High Priest and only Mediator, and prays and intercedes for us. This is the teaching of the Epistle to the Hebrews, and plays a central role in Knox's doctrine of the Lord's Supper.

(5) In his ascension Christ opened the heavens into which we may appear in him before the throne of the Father's mercy. Christ's ascension is the ground of our comfort and assurance. It is the ascended Christ who sends us his Spirit, the Comforter. Thus the full meaning of the ascension is to be discerned in relation to the outpouring of the Holy Spirit upon the Church. It is in this light that the Church of Christ is to be understood, as 'the blessed society which we the members have with our Head and only Mediator Christ Jesus, whom we confess and avow to be the Messiah promised, the only Head of his Kirk, our just Lawgiver, our only High Priest, Advocate and Mediator.'[63]

(8) *Pentecost*
The resurrection and ascension of Jesus Christ mean the final completion of our salvation in the objective sense, for Christ alone among his brethren possesses glory, honour and prerogative till all his enemies be made his footstool, which we undoubtedly believe they will be at the final judgment, as the *Scots Confession* expresses it. In consummation of all this the Lord Jesus will return visibly as he was seen to ascend, when the time of refreshing and restitution of all things will come, and all God's promises will be fulfilled. But the ascension implies two other things:

(1) The suspension of final judgment until Christ comes again. Christ alone possesses all power and glory. He possess that in our name, but he has withdrawn himself visibly from us, until he comes again. The full execution of his judgment and salvation is therefore yet to come. That leaves the world throughout the ages time for repentance and for faith. This is therefore the age of grace, the age when Christ will enlarge his Kingdom, which he does by pouring forth his Spirit, withholding his final bodily presence which would mean the final judgment. The Spirit convicts the world of sin, righteousness and judgment, and acts upon the Church making

---

[63] *Scots Confession*, Art. 11.

its members participate in the life of the resurrection, and leading them into all truth.

The doctrine of the Holy Spirit is therefore the doctrine of 'realised eschatology', but the Holy Spirit points forward to the Second Advent, which implies a doctrine of 'future eschatology'. Thus Knox:

> We do assuredly believe in the Holy Ghost, whom we confess to be God equal with the Father and the Son; by whose working and mighty operation our darkness is removed, our eyes spiritual are illuminated, our souls and consciences sprinkled with the blood of Jesus Christ, and we retained in the truth of God, even to our lives end.[64]

(2) The ascension also means that Christ's Person, with his presence in power and glory, is withdrawn from our sight, so that we are sent back to contemplate him, not primarily in the mystery of his Being in eternity, but as *Jesus* who was born, lived, and taught, was crucified and rose again. Christ deliberately withdrew himself from our sight so that our minds might be sent back to the Cross. And as we turn to the Gospel testimony of the Cross, the Holy Spirit is poured out upon the Church, and makes that testimony the Word of our salvation. There is no way to Jesus, no contact with the risen Lord, but by way of the crucified – no *theologia gloriae*, but first a *theologia crucis* and then on that basis a *sursum corda* following the movement of the ascension. Hence the Eucharist raises us up in thanksgiving from the Cross to the Heavenly Session of Christ our Mediator and High Priest at the right hand of Power. It is at the Eucharist where our participation in the crucified, risen and ascended Christ is unceasingly renewed, that we learn to live as those whose life is hid with Christ in God, and who here and now enjoy 'that blessed society which we the members have with our Head and our only Mediator Christ Jesus'.[65]

(9) *The Second Advent*

'We do constantly believe that he shall come from the right hand of his Father, when all eyes shall see him; yea, even those who have pierced him; and then shall be gathered as well those that shall

---

[64] *Works*, Vol. 6, p. 322; cf. Vol. 4, p. 170.
[65] *Scots Confession*, Art. 11.

then be found alive, as those that before have slept.'[66] Knox referred to this final Advent of the Lord as the day of refreshing and restitution of all things, in which those who from the beginning have suffered violence, injury and wrong, for righteousness sake, shall inherit that blessed immortality promised from the beginning.[67] It is the day when all secrets will be revealed, God's great work will be unveiled, and a separation will take place between the obedient and the disobedient, believers and unbelievers.

Final divine judgment and salvation were completed in the death and resurrection of Christ, but with the ascension there was a delayed action in fulfilment as far as history is concerned until the Final Advent. The Church in history lives between the times, the time of patience and waiting: proclamation of the Gospel and prayer. The sense of Christ's Advent presence was strong in the consciousness of Knox and the Scottish Reformers, in which attention was directed away from themselves to Christ.

> As we willingly spoil ourselves of all honour and glory of our own Creation and Redemption, so do we also of our regeneration and Sanctification, for of ourselves we are not sufficient to think one good thought, but he who has begun a good work in us, is only he that continues us in the same, to the praise and glory of his undeserved grace.[68]

The orientation of faith toward the risen, ascended and advent Christ imported for believers at the Reformation a deep sense of objectivity in looking away from themselves and their own spiritual experience even of redemption and regeneration and sanctification to Christ. It is in Christ, in the body of his Son, that the Father looks upon us, and accepts our imperfect obedience, as if it were perfect, and covers our works which are defiled by many spots, with the justice of his Son. This turning of the Scottish Reformers to the risen and advent Christ away from themselves spelled the end not only of the kind of works-righteousness, self-justification and trust in church tradition that prevailed in pre-Reformation Scotland, but the end of all pietism.

The *Scots Confession* devoted several articles to 'good works', that is to disciplined Christian living and service, but nevertheless the emphasis fell upon the fact that it is *Jesus Christ himself* who is the

[66] *Works*, Vol. 6, p. 321.
[67] *Scots Confession*, Art. 11.
[68] *Scots Confession*, Art. 12.

true centre and indeed the very substance of daily Christian life. That Christ-centred objectivity spelled the end of concern for self-righteousness and reliance on work-righteousness; yet far from dampening the need for disciplined godly living and daily goodness, by turning Christian people away from pietistic inwardness, it actively kindled and encouraged good works, as we can see particularly in the emphatic concern for the poor and needy throughout the realm. This legacy of the Scottish Reformation, 'the veritie is not in us',[69] left a permanent mark on the tradition of Scottish theology and spirituality.

(10) *The triplex munus: Christ as King, Priest and Prophet*
The tradition stressing the threefold Office of Christ was carried over from Calvin into Scottish Theology.

> The name Jesus, which signifies a Saviour, was given unto him by the Angel, to assure us that it is he alone that saves his people from their sins. He is called *Christ*, that is to say, Anointed, by reason of the offices given unto him by God his Father; to wit, that he alone is appointed *King, Priest, and Prophet*. *King*, in that all power is given unto him in heaven and earth; so that there is none other but he in heaven or earth, that has just authority and power to make laws to bind the consciences of men; neither yet is there any other that may defend our souls from the bondage of sin, nor yet our bodies from the tyranny of man. And this he does by the power of his Word, by which he draws us out of the bondage and slavery of Satan, and makes us to reign over sin, while we live and serve our God in righteousness and holiness of our life. A *Priest*, and that perpetual and everlasting, we confess him, by reason that by the sacrifice of his own body, which he once offered up upon the cross, he has fully satisfied the justice of his Father in our behalf; so that whosoever seeks any means besides his death and passion, in heaven or in earth, to reconcile them unto God's favour, they do not only blaspheme, but also, so far as in them is, renounce the fruit and efficacy of that his only sacrifice. We confess him to be the only *Prophet*, who has revealed unto us, the whole will of his Father in all things pertaining to our salvation.[70]

---

[69] Cf. *Scots Confession*, Art. 11.
[70] *Works*, Vol. 6, p. 319.

There is little doubt that the offices of King and Prophet soon came into public prominence in the Scottish Church, due largely to the long strife between the Kirk and the Crown, but the Priestly office of Christ retained a strong place both in worship, and in the conception of the Holy Ministry. Of not a little significance here was, I believe, Calvin's *Commentary* (or *Homilies) on The Minor Prophets* which reached John Knox in Scotland at the beginning of the Reformation, when doubtless the prayers with which Calvin concluded his Homilies left a deep impression on him. In them the High Priesthood of Christ our only Mediator is given prominence in the prayer and worship of the Church, but in that context marked attention was given several times to the belief that some people are set apart 'to perform the solemn office of priesthood'.[71]

The doctrine of the Church

It was fundamental for the Scottish Reformation that the doctrine of the Church is an article of faith.

> As we believe in one God, Father, Son and Holy Spirit; so do we most constantly believe that from the beginning there has been, and now is, and to the end of the world will be, one Kirk, that is to say, one company and multitude of men chosen of God, who rightly worship and embrace him by true faith in Jesus Christ, who is the only Head of the Kirk, which always is the body and spouse of Christ Jesus, which Kirk is called catholic, that is universal, because it contains the Elect of all ages, of all realms, nations and tongues, be they of the Jews, or be they of the Gentiles, who have communion and society with God the Father, and with his Son Christ Jesus, through the sanctification of the Holy Spirit: and therefore it is called the communion, not of profane persons, but of Saints, who as citizens of the heavenly Jerusalem, have fruition of the most inestimable benefits, to wit, of one God, one Lord Jesus Christ, one faith, and one baptism, out of which Kirk, there is neither life nor eternal felicity.[72]

---

[71] John Calvin, see especially the concluding prayers to comments on Malachi 1.6–10; 2.1–5, 6–9; 3.4–8.
[72] *Scots Confession*, Art. 16.

This teaching about the *de fide* nature of the Church was brought out clearly in Knox's refutation of the Jesuit of Tyrie and his letter on the Church of Scotland. As we shall see, Knox pointed out to him that his views on the Church required an alteration in the Apostles' Creed, from *Credo sanctam Ecclesiam* to *Video sanctam Ecclesiam.* 'If there be no kirk upon the face of the earth but that which is visible, and that which may be shown first by certain notes external, then superfluous and vain it were to say, I believe the Holy Kirk Universal, but confidently affirm "I see the Holy Kirk".' Knox insisted on the *Credo Sanctam Ecclesiam*, for the Church like the Trinity belongs to the essential articles of faith, and it is as such an object of faith that he expounded the doctrine of the Church, not as an object of sight.[73]

The Church as article of faith means that the Church belongs to salvation. And so Knox himself was ready to uphold the historic Cyprianic statement, *extra ecclesiam nulla salus.* 'We affirm, that without the society and bosom of the true Kirk, never was, is, nor shall be, salvation unto man. In this and like general heads we disagree not from the Papists; but the difference and doubt stands in the specials, to wit, what faith is, and what ground it has...'[74] As the Body of the risen and ascended Lord the Church is known only by faith, and faith is the evidence of things not seen, the substance of things hoped for. That was the basis of the doctrine of the Kirk visible and invisible in Scottish Reformed theology.

It was another tenet of Knox's doctrine of the Church that it has a succession which stretches from creation to the Second Advent of Christ in unbroken continuous being. As the counterpart of the ordinance of grace the Church is marvellously preserved throughout the ages in the pattern of the Incarnation: the death and resurrection of Christ, and is constantly called into being out of death into life. As such the life and pattern of the Kirk preserved in the history of the people of Israel was regarded as pointing ahead to the Incarnation for it bodied forth continuously in its history the promise which at last was fulfilled in its midst by the incarnate Advent of the Son of God. As the Body of the incarnate Son the Church is empowered by him and sent out into the world to proclaim the Gospel, and waits for the Second Advent of the ascended Christ.

---

[73] This was actually in line with the *Tridentine Catechism*, X. qq. xviii & xix!
[74] *Works*, Vol. 6, p. 486.

It is this setting of the Church in the heart of the eschatological drama between the Cross and the final *parousia* that enables the Church to preserve its essential pattern as the blessed Society which bears about in its body the dying and the rising of the Lord Jesus. All that goes on in history, all the achievement of men, all the tradition of the Church, come under the judgment of the Cross and the final judgment. The true order, the essential form of the Church, is revealed only in the resurrection of Jesus Christ, and in his appearing again in glory. The face of the Kirk is the face of Jesus Christ the crucified, risen and ascended Lord who will come again. And therefore if people are to restore the Kirk to its true face they must look both to the cross and the resurrection of Jesus, and to his coming again in glory.

Throughout the theology of the Scottish Reformation, there is the strongest sense of the continuity of the Christian Church with Israel, the Old Testament people of God, for it is the same mighty living God who acts in both. But there is a difference marked by the Incarnation.

First, the Old Testament Church was tied to the temple, its cult, and its institutions, although the destruction of the tabernacle and then of the temple was an indication from God that the Church has its real existence beyond. But that was not evident until New Testament times. The New Testament Church has its being and ground in Jesus Christ. He is 'the Glory of the sacred temple', but the temple here is not tied to place or to the institutions of history. It is the blessed society which was wondrously joined to Jesus Christ. It is the Church as *community* which takes the place of the Old Testament temple. The Christian Church is enshrined in Christ, and as such has a freedom from locality and lineal succession. The Christian Church is not subject to the bondage of succession and tradition in history. Reformation understanding of the Kirk 'out of which there is neither life nor eternal felicity',[75] meant that there was no room for the kind of individualism that characterised some kinds of medieval monasticism or that which arose later in Protestantism. Far from being a merely private matter, religion is bound up with the corporate life and activity of the Church as a divine community concorporate with the crucified, risen and ascended Christ. The Church as the Body of the Lord Jesus Christ constitutes the place and form in which Christian life exists and Christian activity is carried out.

---

[75] *Scots Confession*, Art. 16.

Second, in the New Testament the ordinance of grace assumed the form of the incarnate Word. It is through the Word proclaimed in the Gospel, therefore, that the Christian Church is continually called into being from death to life. But as grounded in the Word the Church has its being not in itself but above and beyond itself, and so is called to transcend the patterns of history in ever being re-formed in its life according to the Word and its true form in Jesus Christ. It is just because the Church has its being in the Word, who is eternal, that the true Church in so far as it conforms to the Word surmounts the past and all antiquity. The Church of the Word is the most ancient Church, and goes back behind everything, e.g. the Church of Rome and the Old Testament temple, to God himself. It is no 'new found Kirk'![76]

Third, the Church of the New Testament is certainly the Church of the last day – the last day beginning with the Evangel of Christ and reaching to his coming again.

> The last dayes continew from the first appearing of Jesus Christ in the flesh, until his returning unto judgment. So that the last dayes do not onely include the first publicatioun of the Evangel, but also the defection from it; yea, and the restitutioun of it again unto the world, be the brightness whereof, that man of sin should be revealed and destroyed. Whereof we conclude, that if the last dayes do yet continew, whereof the Prophet maketh mention, the things promysed to be performed in them are not yet altogether compleit, but are in their progress, and shall so proceed till that all be finished that is foirspoken be the holie Prophets and Apostles of Jesus Christ. And so may Jesus Christ this day be working in Scotland, albeit that papists rage against his Evangell, as in those days he wroght in Jerusalem when the preastes and the hole visible Kirk (for the most part) raged against the same.[77]

However, as Knox pointed out, ever since the advent of the incarnate Word into the midst of history there is ferment and upheaval, there is judgment, the last days are already upon the world, the shadow of the final judgment is already cast over the world. The New Testament Church exists in that critical situation,

---

[76] *Works*, Vol. 6, p. 492.
[77] *Works*, Vol. 6, p. 495.

but it exists in it, for all its blood and agony, as the Community of
the Resurrection, the Community which has its citizenship beyond
in heaven and in the new creation. Indeed it is just because the
Church is an alien Body within the world, that the existence of the
Church as the Resurrection Church creates ferment and upheaval,
yet that very upheaval is the sign of the breaking up of the old
world and the birth of the new.[78]

The secret and mystery of the Kirk is the real presence of Jesus
Christ in its midst.

> Our Maister Christ Jesus appointed us to no one certane
> place, wher we shallbe assured of his presence; but rather
> forbidding the observatioun of all places, he sendes us his
> own spirituall presence, saying "Wheresoever two or three
> are gathered in my name, there am I in the middest of them"
> (Matt. 18). And in another place, "Behold I am with you to
> the end of the world" (Matt. 28). We, being grounded upon
> these promyses, have good hope through Jesus Christ, that
> in our congregationis we have the favourable presence of
> Jesus Christ, as wel in his Word as in his holy Sacramentes.
> For in his Name alone convene we; by him alone we call upon
> God our Father; and by him alone we are assured, through
> the power of his Holy Spreit, to obtain our requests made
> according to his wil.'[79]

This Church continues in our midst through the Holy Spirit and
the Word and sacraments, and the Church is the true Church as it
meets in the name of Christ, listens to his voice and keeps covenant
with him.

The Presence of Christ in Word and sacraments is bodied forth
in history (in a 'mystical' not a legal way) in an ordered community
of people who are members of each other and members of Christ
as his Body. He is the only Head and Pastor, the only Bishop and
King of the Church. The Church is a membered community
involving internal relations, inter-personal communications, and
historical and doctrinal form. We give the Word and the sacraments
to one another – that is essential, to the membership of the Church
in this membered community. As such the Church is the Body of

---

[78]   *Works*, Vol. 6, p. 505 – two Kirks in Rome!
[79]   *Works*, Vol. 6, p. 496; cf. also Vol. 3, pp. 73ff.

Christ, the Spouse of Christ, bonded with him in a sacred marriage yet to be consummated.

> We confess that it is ane holie actioun, ordaynit of God, in the whilk the Lord Jesus, by earthlie and visibill thingis sette befoir us, lifteth us up into hevinlie and invisibill thingis. And that when he had prepareit his spiritual banket, he witnessit that he him self was the lyvelie bread, whairwith our saullis be fed unto everlasting lyfe.[80]

The notes of the true Kirk are three: Word, sacraments and discipline: first, the true preaching of the Word of God in which God has revealed himself unto us; second, the right administration of the sacraments of Christ Jesus, which are annexed to the Word and promise of God to seal and confirm them in our hearts; last ecclesiastical discipline uprightly administered, as God's Word prescribes, whereby vice is repressed and virtue nourished.[81] In the observation of these notes the true face of Jesus Christ appears. *We* cannot make the face of Jesus Christ appear. Nevertheless, Jesus Christ himself, made known through Word and sacraments, is the true ordinance governing the life, form, and activity of the Church. We believe in Christ in the midst of those who meet in his name and by faith hear the voice of his Spirit speaking in and through the Scriptures and obey him. We see him in the Sacraments, and walk in holiness according to the leading of the Spirit of Jesus Christ. There the true Church manifests itself in the power of the presence of Christ the sole Head and Lord of the Church – there it steps forth before us, and distinguishes itself from any Church that usurps his authority. It was the way that Knox laid emphasis upon 'discerning the Body of Christ' in Word and Sacrament, that governed his attitude to the Roman Church.[82] All-important, of course, was the attention to be given to whether the *Evangel* is proclaimed and people are fed and nourished with Christ the bread of life. And therefore the true and faithful Kirk will always be open to continual renewal and reformation under the impact of the ordinance of grace and the guidance of the voice of God heard in

---

[80] *Works*, Vol. 3, p. 73. Cf. James S. McEwen's remarks about this passage, *The Faith of John Knox*, London, 1962, p. 56.

[81] *Scots Confession*, Art. 18, G. D. Henderson, p. 75; see also *Works*, Vol. 4, pp. 71f.

[82] *Works*, Vol. 6, pp. 497 & 490.

the Holy Scriptures of the Old and New Testaments. The Scriptures
are not to be followed, however, as interpreted by private or public
persons, but as they are understood and interpreted within the
worshipping and faithful congregation of God's people ordered
according to the ordinances of Christ's Church.

The Church visible and invisible. Credo sanctam Ecclesiam, not *Video
sanctam Ecclesiam.* Knox gave special attention to this distinction in
his debate with Master Tyrie.

> For if there be no Kirk upon the face of the earth, but that
> which is visible, and that which may be shawen first be certane
> notes external, then superfluous and vain it wer to say, I
> believe the holy Kirk universall; but confidently we might
> affirme, I see the holy Kirk. If Maister Tyrie will say, We may
> both see and beleve, and be our sight our faith be
> strengthened; for Thomas saw the wounds in the handes,
> feet, and syde of Christ Jesus, and beleved; and so we may
> see the Kirk and yet beleve it.... But the question is, If that
> we are not bound to beleve those things which sometymes
> ar utterly removed from the external senses of men? Maister
> Tyrie will acknowledge no Kirk except that which hes been,
> and is visible. We, in the contrare, acknowledge and
> reverence the spous of Christ Jesus, sometymes exyled from
> the world (Apoc. 12) receiving sometymes the wynges of an
> egle that she may fle to the wilderness, whereof God, and
> not of man, she hath her place prepared. We reverence her
> which doeth complane, that she hath bene desolate, barrane,
> a captive, and a wanderer to and fro. That spouse of Jesus
> Christ brages so lytle of her succession, visible to mannes
> eyes, but she is rest in admiration, who should have nurished
> her children during the tyme of her baniwement (Isaiah 49).[83]

Knox went on to add that it is not without great cause that the
Holy Ghost has taught us to say 'I *believe* the Kirk universal', because
sometimes the Kirk Militant is so afflicted, and its beauty obscured,
that the synagogue of Satan usurps the title of the true Kirk, and
Babylon is preferred to Jerusalem; so that the elect are compelled
to complain and say: 'We see not our own signs, now is there no
prophet any more amongst us' (Ps. 74). For his part, however, Knox
strongly affirmed that the true Church of Jesus Christ is visible.

---

[83] *Works*, Vol. 6, pp. 501f.

He claimed that is now the case with the Church in Scotland, and that it is as beautiful in all her ornaments within the realm of Scotland as ever it was in Corinth, Galatia or Philippi, or even in Rome itself.[84]

It was much the same line that Knox took in his argument for the true succession of the Kirk in Christ, in contrast to mere lineal succession,[85] but that was expounded by him in terms of the ordinance of grace. The Church in history is fully visible, but it is mixed up with hypocrites and obscured. The true Church has a public face, for it is the *imago Christi*, but this is thought out in relation to the true notes of the Kirk, where doctrine, godly discipline and mission have primary place in the discernment of the Church of Christ.[86]

The Church as One, Holy, Catholic and Apostolic.

(1) *One.* As there is one God, one faith, one Baptism so there is one Kirk, one company of people chosen of God who rightly worship and embrace him by true faith in Jesus Christ, who is the only Head of the Kirk, which is the Body and Spouse of Christ.[87]

(2) *Holy.*
The Church is Holy because it receives free remission of sinnes, and that by faith only in the blood of Christ. Secondly, because it being regenerat, it receiveth the Spirit of sanctification and power to walke in newness of lyfe, and in good works, which God has prepared for his chosen to walk in. Not that we think the justice of this Church, or of any member of the same, ever was, is, or yet shall be so ful and perfect, that it nedeth not to stoupe under mercie; but that because the imperfections are pardoned, and the justice of Jesus Christ imputed unto such as by true faith cleave unto him.[88]

(3) The Kirk is commonly called *Catholic.* 'The name of the Kirk is common and is taken as well for the wicked as for the assembly of the godly... The term Catholick, signifies Universal.' It is not Catholic because it overflows the whole earth.

---

[84] *Works*, Vol. 6, p. 494.
[85] *Works*, Vol. 6, pp. 487f & 497f; Knox claimed repeatedly that the cause of the Church of Scotland was one with that of 'the primitive Kirk', Vol. 4, pp. 301, 304, 306, 310, 338.
[86] *Scots Confession*, Art. 18.
[87] *Scots Confession*, Art. 16.
[88] *Works*, Vol. 6, pp. 322f.

We must have a better assurance of that Kirk, to which we aucht to joyne our selfis, then that it is Catholick or universall: to wit, it must be holy and the communion of sanctis; for in the Confession of our Faith we say not, 'I beleve the Kirk universal", but "I beleve the holy Kirk universal, the communion of sanctis'.[89] Holiness and Catholicity go together, and are to be interpreted in terms of each other.

Which Church we cal Universal, because it consisteth and standeth of all tongues and nations; yea, of all estates and conditions of men and women, whome of his mercy God calleth from darknes to lyfe, and from bondage and the thraldome of synne to his spiritual service and puritie of life. Unto whom also he communicates his Holy Spirit, giving unto them one Faith, one Head and soveraygne Lord, the Lord Jesus, one Baptisme and right use of Sacraments; whose hearts also he knitteth together in love and Christian concorde. To this Church, holy and universal we acknowledge and believe three notable gifts to be graunted; to wit, remission of sinnes, which by true faith must by obteined in this life. Resurrection of the flesh, which all shal have, albeit not in equal condition; for the reprobate shal rise but to fearful judgement and condemnation; and the just shall rise to be possessed in glory...The juste shall receive the life everlasting which is the free gift of God given and purchased for his chosen by Jesus Christ, our only Head and Mediator: to whom with the Father and the Holy Ghost, be all honor and glory, now and for ever.[90]

The doctrine of the sacraments

The definitive statement was given in the Scots Confession:

As the Fathers under the Law, besides the veritie of the Sacrifices, had twa chiefe Sacramentes, to wit, Circumcision and Passover, the despisers and contemners whereof were not reputed for Gods people; sa we acknawledge and confesse

[89] *Works*, Vol. 6, p. 489 – see also p. 496.
[90] *Works*, Vol. 6, p. 323.

that we now in the time of the Evangell have twa chiefe
Sacramentes, onelie instituted be the Lord *Jesus*, and
commanded to be used of all they that will be reputed
members of his body, to wit, Baptisme and the Supper or
Table of the Lord *Jesus*, called the Communion of his Body
and his Blude. And thir Sacramentes, as well of Auld as of
New Testament, now instituted of God, not onelie to make
ane visible difference betwixt his people and they that wes
without his league: Bot also to exerce the faith of his
Children, and, be participation of the same Sacramentes, to
seill in their hearts the assurance of his promise, and of that
most blessed conjunction, union and societie, quhilk the
elect have with their head *Christ Jesus*. And thus we utterlie
damne the vanitie of thay that affirme Sacraments to be
nathing else bot naked and baire signes. No, wee assuredlie
beleeve that be Baptisme we are ingrafted in *Christ Jesus*, to
be made partakers of his justice, be quhilk our sinnes are
covered and remitted. And alswa, that in the Supper richtlie
used, *Christ Jesus* is so joined with us, that he becummis very
nourishment and fude of our saules. Not that we imagine
anie transubstantiation of bread into *Christes* body, and of
wine into his naturall blude, as the *Papistes* have perniciouslie
taucht and damnablie beleeved; bot this union and
conjunction, quhilk we have with the body and blude of *Christ
Jesus* in the richt use of the Sacraments, wrocht be operatioun
of the haly Ghaist, who by trew faith carryis us above all things
that are visible, carnal, and earthly, and makes us to feede
upon the body and blude of *Christ Jesus*, quhilk wes anes
broken and shed for us, quhilk is now in heaven, and appearis
in the presence of the Father for us: And zit notwithstanding
the far distance of place quhilk is betwixt his body now
glorified in heaven and us now mortal in this eird, zit we
man assuredly beleve that the bread quhilk we break, is the
communion of *Christes* bodie, and the cupe quhilk we blesse,
is the communion of his blude. So that we confess, and
undoubtedlie beleeve, that the faithful, in the richt use of
the Lords Table, do so eat the bodie and drinke the blude
of the Lord *Jesus*, that he remaines in them, and they in him:
Zea, they are so maid the flesh of his flesh, and bone of his
bones; that as the eternall God-head hes given to the flesh
of *Christ Jesus* (which of its awin conditioun and nature wes
mortal and corruptible) life and immortalitie; so dois *Christ*

Jesus his flesh and blude eattin and drunkin be us, give unto
us the same prerogatives...'[91]

Two points in particular may be noted here: the overall
trinitarian frame, and the christological pattern, in which the two
sacraments of the Gospel are described. Both Baptism and the
Lord's Supper are first and foremost acts of God himself through
Christ and in the Holy Spirit; and both Baptism and the Lord's
Supper convey and seal to the believing participant conjunction
and union with Christ. Baptism is the sacrament whereby we are
ingrafted into Christ and his righteousness, and the Lord's Supper
is the sacrament whereby believers partake so really of the bread
and the wine that inexplicably the bread we eat is the communion
of Christ's Body and the wine we drink is the communion of Christ's
Blood. The two sacraments complement one another but in
different ways both of them have the same content, *Christ Jesus
himself*. The union and conjunction with Christ given in the
sacrament of Baptism is effectually followed by the sacrament of
Communion in which faithful participants have conjunction with
Christ which it is beyond the capacity of the human mind to grasp.
Baptism is concerned with the beginning of the Christian life in
the Church, while the Lord's Supper is concerned with the
continuance of that life in the Church. Both Baptism and the Lord's
Supper or Communion mediate a 'blessed fraternity' with Christ
in which the faithful in their own appropriate way share in the
'blessed union and conjunction' of God and man in the one Person
of Christ.

The doctrine of Baptism

John Knox thought of Baptism particularly as the sacrament of
the Father's love, for in it we are directly related to God as our
Father. Baptism puts us in mind of the 'league and covenant made
between God and us, that he will be our God and we are his people.
He is our Father and we are his children'. It is the sign of our first
entrance into the Kingdom of God.[92] Thus considered Baptism is
the sacrament of the New Covenant that corresponds to
circumcision as the sacrament of the Old Covenant, but in this
sacrament we are admitted to God's family by adoption through
Christ, God's only beloved Son, and through ingrafting into his

---

[91]   *Scots Confession*, Art. 21.
[92]   *Works*, Vol. 4, p. 123.

Body.[93] Hence the baptismal service begins with the question, 'Do you present this child to be baptized, earnestly desiring that it may be ingrafted in the mystical Body of Jesus Christ?' Baptism initiates into this covenant which God the Father maintains in utter faithfulness, so that as he has given us the sign of his children, he continues to 'acknowledge us as of his heavenly household'.[94]

Because 'the effect and signification of Baptism is that of his free grace, we are received into the household of God',[95] it is right and natural that the children of those already members of Christ and of the New Covenant should also be baptised and given the sign of God's children. Indeed we must baptise them if we are to obey the command 'to preach and baptise all without exception'.[96]

> He has promised that he wilbe our God, and the God of our children unto the thousand generation ... doing us therby to wyt, that our children appetteyne to him by covenant, and therefore oght not to be defrauded of those holy signs and badges whereby his children are knowen from Infidells and Pagans.[97]

Because this is the primary fact about Baptism 'it is not requisite that all who receyve this Sacrament have the use of understanding and faythe; but chiefeley that they be conteyned under the name of God's people; So that remission of synnes in the bloode of Christ Jesus, doth appertaine to them by God's promise.' Because Baptism is the sacrament of God's fatherly love and his reception of children into his household, it follows that he will take them under his 'tuition and defence', and bring them to share in his fatherly provision for his household. From all this Baptism cannot be separated. Baptism by its very nature stands at the beginning of it, and is the sacrament and seal of God's bounteous promise of such provision, especially for the gift of the Holy Spirit who makes effectual these divine promises extended to us in Baptism.

The Book of Common Order or *John Knox's Liturgy* substantiates this doctrine of the baptismal initiation of children on the ground also that they were admitted by our Saviour Christ to his presence, when

---

[93] *Works*, Vol. 6, p. 96; cf. Vol. 4, pp. 123f, 187f.
[94] *Works*, Vol. 4, p. 187; *The Book of Common Order* (ed. G. W. Sprott), pp. 134ff.
[95] *Works*, Vol. 4, pp. 123f.
[96] *Works*, Vol. 4, pp. 187f.
[97] *Works*, Vol. 4, p. 187.

he embraced and blessed them (Mark 10; Matt. 19; Luke 18), and
on the ground that the Apostle declared that children begotten of
parents, one of whom was a believer, to be clean and holy. 'These
testimonies of the Holy Ghoste assure us, that infants be of the
number of God's people; and that remission of synnes doth
apperteyne to theim in Christ. Therefore, wythout injurie they
cannot be debarred from the common signe of God's children.'[98]

The Sacrament of Baptism is related directly to the Person and
work of God's Son, as the sign of our ingrafting into him, and of
our participation in all the saving benefits which flow from union
with him. In the little catechism used to examine the children
before they were admitted to Holy Communion the answer given
to the question, 'What is meant by Baptisme?' runs, 'First, it
signifieth that we have forgiveness of our sinnes by the blood of
Christ; secondly, it setteth before our eyes our regeneration or new
spiritual birth.'[99] The fruit of Baptism flows to us from Christ
himself, and it is only through being ingrafted into him, or being
united to him, that we can become partakers of what he has already
wrought out and accomplished in our name and on our behalf in
himself. This ingrafting has two special elements. (1) It involves a
translation out of our natural state and inheritance into newness
of life and a heavenly inheritance in Christ. 'For as by Baptisme
once receyved is signified that we (aswel infants as others of age
and discretion) being straungers from God by originall synne, are
receyved into his familie and congregation, with full assurance,
that althoghe this roote of synne ly hyd in us, yet to the electe it
shal not be imputed.'[100] (2) Baptism means that we are clothed
with Christ and endowed with his righteousness, that is, 'made
partakers of his justice by which our sins are covered and
remitted'.[101] Baptism is both the seal of justice and the sign of
regeneration.[102] Thus while Baptism is the sacrament of God's
Fatherly love and of union with Christ, it is also the sacrament of
justification by grace.[103]

---

[98] *Works*, Vol. 4, p. 187; *The Book of Common Order*, ed. Sprott, p. 135.
[99] *Works*, Vol. 6, pp. 344f.
[100] *Works*, Vol. 4, p.172.
[101] *Scots Confession*, Art. 21.
[102] *Works*, Vol. 4, p. 120.
[103] *Scots Confession*, Art. 21. Refer to *Interim Report of the Special Commission on Baptism*, submitted to the General Assembly of the Church of Scotland in May, 1958, pp. 12f.

The doctrine of the Lord's Supper or the Eucharist

By nature Knox was greatly attracted to what he called 'the glistering beauty of ceremonies', and doubtless it was because he was so susceptible in that way that he felt the power of the Roman Mass upon him. In defence against that power Knox appealed again and again to the words of Deuteronomy 12.32 as a guide to the ordering of Church worship. 'Not that which appeareth good in thine eyes shalt thou do to the Lord thy God, but what the Lord thy God hath commanded thee, that shalt thou do: add nothing to it, diminish nothing from it.'[104] It was thus that Knox felt led under the impact of the Holy Scriptures to frame a form of worship for the Kirk agreeable to the Word of God.

The Roman Mass was regarded as the Church's counterpart to a *timeless* sacrifice in the form of a temporal repetition – through the transubstantiation of the bread and wine into the Body and Blood of Christ, the Church's celebration of the Mass participated in the timeless reality of the eternal sacrifice. This gave the Church through the celebration of the Mass formidable control over the living and the dead, which it did not hesitate to exercise in its daily relations with people in Scotland.

In tune with Calvin, Knox's attack upon the Mass, and his Reformation of it, took three main lines:

1) The restoration of the doctrine of the sole mediatorship of Jesus Christ, and his once-for-all atoning sacrifice on the Cross. This involved a new emphasis upon the man Jesus in atonement and worship as our sole Mediator and High Priest before God.

2) The restoration of the historical perspective to the Lord's Supper, and the reformation of the liturgy according to what took place in the upper room on the night in which Jesus was betrayed. In some respects this return to history was the most radical change – liturgically it meant the recovery of the historical warrant, as delivered by St Paul in 1 Corinthians 11.

3) The preface of Knox to the celebration of the Supper indicates that in the Reformed Rite the proper substance of the sacrament was held to be restored, and the proper place of Christ was restored along with it.[105] That is, the emphasis upon the *whole Christ* as the proper 'substance' or 'matter' of the sacrament: the Christ who

---

[104] *Works*, Vol. 1, p. 515.
[105] *Works*, Vol. 4, pp. 191ff; Vol. 6, pp. 324ff.

was crucified, but also the Christ who is risen, has ascended, and is coming again. More than any other of the Reformers Knox emphasised here the *Ascension and Advent* of Christ, which he referred to as chief articles of the faith. They are restored to the place originally occupied in the eucharistic liturgy, e.g. in the Nicene Liturgies of St Mark and St James. The importance of the ascension and advent meant this: *ascension* introduced the 'distance' between the symbols of bread and wine on earth and the ascended Christ, but nevertheless a 'distance' bridged by the real presence of the risen and ascended Christ through the Spirit. Hence the place of the *sursum corda* in the heart of the Reformed Eucharistic Rite – the ascension with Christ became of primary importance again: we are made to sit with Christ in heavenly places.[106] *Advent* introduced the element of judgment, judgment upon the actual worldly symbols used in the Eucharist as nothing in themselves, but as pointing to a fulfilment in the Advent, not merely to a fulfilment here and now, but in the resurrection. Expressed otherwise, the real presence or *parousia* of Christ here and now in Holy Communion was not held apart from but as closely bound up with the real presence or *parousia* of Christ when he comes again. This introduced into the doctrine of the real presence a strong eschatological perspective which deepened and personalised the reality of his presence to faithful communicants.

The elements of bread and wine, in relation to the Body and Blood of Christ, were not thought of in terms of a change in their physical substance as bread and wine, that is in terms of transubstantiation or a fusion with the actual Body and Blood of Christ.

> We confesse, and undowttedlye beleve, that the faithfull, in the rycht use of the Lordis Table, so do eatt the body, and drynk the bloode of the Lord Jesus, that he remaneth in thame and thai in him: yea, that thai ar so maid flesche of his flesche, and bone of his bones, that as the Eternall Godheid hath gevin to the flesche of Christ Jesus (whiche of the awin conditioun and nature was mortall and corruptible) lyfe and immortalitie, so doeth Christ Jesus his flesche and bloode eatten and drunken by us, give to us the same prerogatives: Whiche albeit we confesse, are neather gevin unto us at that onelie tyme, neather yit by the propir power

[106] *Works*, Vol. 2, pp. 113ff & Vol. 3, pp. 73f.

and vertew of the Sacramentis onelie; yit we affirme, that the faithful in the rycht use of the Lordis Table hes sick conjunction with Christ Jesus, as the naturall man can not comprehend: yea, and farther we affirme, that albeit the faithfull oppressed be negligence, and manlie infirmitie, doth not profit so mekill as thei wold att the verray instant actioun of the Supper, yit shall it after bring furth frute, as livelie seid sawin in good ground; for the Holy Spreit, which can never be devided from the rycht institutioun of the Lord Jesus, will not frustrat the faythfull of the fruit of that misticall actioun. But all this, we say, cumis by trew fayth, whiche apprehendeth Christ Jesus, who onelie maikis his Sacramentis effectuall unto us; and thairfoir, whosoever slandereth us, as that we affirmed or beleved Saramentis to be onelie naiked and bair signes, do injurie unto us, and speak against a manifest treuth. But this liberallie and francklie we most confess, that we maik ane distinctioun betwix Christ Jesus, in his natural substance, betwix the elementis in the Sacramentall signes; so that we will neather worship the signes in place of that which is signifeid by thame; neather yit do we dispyse and interprete thame as unprofitable and vane; but do use thame with all reverence, examyning our selfis diligentlie befoir that so we do, becaus we ar assured by the mouth of the Apostle, 'That sick as eat that bread and drynk of that cupp, unworthelie, are guyltie of the body and bloode of the Lord Jesus.'[107]

John Knox affirmed very firmly, then, that there is a *real presence*, and a real eating of the Body and a real drinking of the Blood of Christ, but in an *incomprehensible manner through the Spirit*, and to be received and understood in faith. This eliminated the notion of a *causal* relation (especially as expounded in Aristotelian terms) between sign and the thing signified, and introduced a dynamic relation through the Word and Spirit, and with it a *real relation* that was more than *signitive*, in which the signs of consecrated bread and wine *really convey* through the Spirit what they promise, but convey in the freedom of the Spirit in which he is not bound to the temporal action. The clearest way, perhaps, to put this might be to say that while we are given the real presence of Christ (*parousia*) in the Eucharist, it is not the same mode of real presence

---

[107] *Works*, Vol. 2, pp. 114f; *The Scots Confession*, G. D. Henderson, p. 87.

as we shall have at the final *parousia* although intrinsically bound up with it in Christ. So long as there is a difference in mode between the Advent *parousia* and the eucharistic *parousia*, the Reformed Church could not agree to a notion of transubstantiation.

Reconstruction of the doctrine of Knox

The major feature here is the restitution of the proper conception of the mediatorship of Christ as God and man – see the *Declaration of the true Nature of Prayer* (one of the most important documents for the understanding of the theology of the Scottish Reformation).[108] For Knox what Christ did on our behalf he did not only as Son of God, but as man 'that he might offer sacrifice'. The priesthood of the man Jesus is stressed very, very strongly by Knox and it is here that he overcomes the Roman sacerdotal notion of priesthood: for in this one historical man all priesthood is done away, except what he has and undertakes for us in his divine-human Person. Jesus Christ as man has offered once for all the perfect sacrifice; his sacrifice as man in man's place radically alters the basic concept of priesthood and sacrifice and does away with any other human act of priestly mediation and sacrifice. The important point here can be put like this: if what Christ did was an act only as God for us, then that demands an answer from man corresponding to it: hence the notion of a human priesthood to convey to man what God has done. But if Christ acted, not only as God, but as man, and has already once for all offered man's sacrifice, man's response to God, then our sacrifice is already made, and our response to God is already offered. This does not mean that we do not have to worship God in sacrifice and oblation, but it does mean a) that our sacrifice is mainly one of thanksgiving and praise (the meaning of 'Eucharist') for what has been offered on our behalf, and b) that whatever we offer, even by way of thanksgiving, praise, and prayer, ourselves in living sacrifice, etc., we offer only 'by the hand of Christ'. 'Christ is our right hand by whom we offer anything unto the Father' — cited by Knox from Ambrose.[109] This has an important consequence for Knox's understanding of 'Eucharistic sacrifice'.

Like all the Reformers Knox stressed the gift of grace in Holy Communion – God's free incarnate self-giving to us in Jesus Christ

---

[108] *Works*, Vol. 3, pp. 96f – the section on the Mediator.
[109] *Works*, Vol. 3, p. 97.

– and therefore the element of reception, as our answer (*gratitudo*) to Grace (*gratia*). The eucharistic action 'represents' the death of Christ, the self-giving of Christ to us unto death, and through the Cross. Here Knox uses the terms 'represent' and 'figure' to describe how the 'action' gives a (dramatic) representation of the death of Christ. All the gifts of 'Christ clothed with his Gospel' are here bestowed such as forgiveness and healing and renewal, but in the Lord's Supper it is particularly the maintaining of our 'league' and 'oneness' with Christ that is ever being bestowed upon us (implying Baptism, the other sacrament of our 'first entrance' into this 'league' and 'oneness' with Christ).[110]

Consequent upon Christ's self-giving to us is the stress upon our oneness with Christ crucified, risen and ascended.[111] It is at the Supper, therefore, where we have a testimony of the unity we have with Christ, which is also 'in deed and truly accomplished', that we are gathered into a visible unity and show forth what kind of people we are. This has as its corollary a doctrine of the Church as Communion.[112]

A characteristic stress of Knox here, however, was *prayer*. We do not only receive Christ and his gifts at the Supper, but in union with him we engage in prayer, and all that prayer at the Lord's Supper signifies. This is the point where Knox put forward his own doctrine of 'Eucharistic sacrifice'. Thus in his debate with the Abbot of Crossraguel Knox defined 'sacrifices called Eucharistic' as 'thanksgiving, the mortification of our bodies, and the obedience that we give to God in the same, is also called sacrifice. Prayer and invocation of the name of God hath also the same name within the Scriptures, liberalitie toward the poor, is also so termed' – and this he distinguished from propitiatory sacrifice. 'But there is one Sacrifice which is the greatest, and most of all called *Propitiatorium*, which is that sacrifice whereby satisfaction is made to the justice of God, being offended at the sins of man, etc.'[113] The strong emphasis on prayer as part of the eucharistic sacrifice was very characteristic, but this is linked in Knox's mind with John 17 where we read of Christ's sanctifying or consecrating himself for us that we might be consecrated in him. That was where Knox 'first cast his anchor', as he said when dying – John 17 was for him a favourite passage of

[110] *Works*, Vol. 4, p. 123.
[111] *Works*, Vol. 6, pp. 366f.
[112] *Works*, Vol. 2, pp. 74f.
[113] *Works*, Vol. 6, p. 198.

Scripture which he cited again and again, sometimes reflecting in the language he used that of John Calvin in his commentary on the passage.[114] 'The vertue of which prayer is perpetual, and at all times obtaineth mercy in the presence of his Father's throne for his Elect.' As Christ is the only priest, and it is by his right hand that we offer anything to God, our prayer at the Eucharist is offered by Christ, or put otherwise, his high-priestly prayer (which we overhear in John 17) stands behind and gathers up our prayer at the Eucharist, when we pray in his Name. Hence it is in prayer and in intercession at the Eucharist that Knox discerns the true 'priestly character' of the holy ministry, involving not only the prayer of thanksgiving but also of intercession in Christ. This carries with it a further element in 'Eucharistic sacrifice'.[115]

The emphasis upon intercession, and upon oneness with Christ and with one another, at the Supper, carried with it in Knox's mind, the stress upon care for the poor. This reflected a revolt by Knox against the Roman use of the Mass to dominate over people, and which did in fact have the effect of grinding the faces of the poor in Scotland, but it was also by way of acting out or showing forth the oneness with Christ which we receive at the Supper, and by way of fulfilling already the care for others in our intercessions at the Supper. It was this element that Knox sought to work out radically in the first *Book of Discipline*, and which threatened such economic revolution in Scotland that it provoked severe reaction headed by the Queen and Maitland. It was, however, the spiritual and theological outcome of Knox's doctrine of the Holy Supper in which we all share equally in the gifts of Christ and in which we all break bread one with another.[116] That action at the celebration, and rising out of the 'action' of thanksgiving (*actio gratiarum* = *eucharistia*) is still part of the eucharistic sacrifice. This is why in the tradition of Scottish sacramental parlance 'the Action' was often a name for the celebration of Holy Communion, while sermons delivered at the celebration of Holy Communion came to be called 'action sermons'.

With Knox stress upon the sacraments involved not only what he called 'that most blessed conjunction, union and society which

---

[114] *Works*, Vol. 6, pp. 643 & 659.
[115] Consult my contribution to the *Festschrift for Peter De Klerk*, 'Legal and Evangelical Priests: The Holy Ministry as Reflected in Calvin's Prayers', Leiden, 1996, pp. 57–67.
[116] *Works*, Vol. 2, p. 187, etc.

the elect have with their head',[117] but also our participation in the new humanity of Christ which was one of John Calvin's important contributions to the Reformed Faith. The same teaching was given, and nowhere better given, in the *Catechism* of John Craig, who was one of Knox's colleagues and his successor as minister in St Giles. But strangely this was the very element in the thought of John Calvin (he did not like to mention 'Knox'!) which William Cunningham attacked as a blot upon Calvin's reputation as a Reformed theologian! However, it is still this emphasis upon the *vicarious humanity* of Christ which we lack. If the emphasis is upon the fact that *God* has acted for us in Christ, then our human response is by way of cooperation, because an act on the part of *man* is required in addition to and complementary to the act of God. Hence Protestantism often teaches, or tends to teach, that we are all co-workers and 'co-redeemers' with Christ and God! But for Calvin and Knox that error is obviated in their teaching about the vicarious and priestly nature of the human Jesus. It was in the Eucharist that their stress upon that came out most strongly. It was through union with Christ in his vicarious humanity nourished in sacramental communion that the concern of the Reformed Kirk with human and social care in the lives of people was grounded.

Bibliography

Barth, Karl, *The Knowledge of God and the Service of God, Recalling the Scottish Confession of 1560,* London, 1938.

Burleigh, John H. S., *A Church History of Scotland,* London, 1960.

Calderwood, David, *The History of the Church of Scotland,* Wodrow Society, 8 vols., Edinburgh, 1842–49.

Calvin, John, *Institutio Christianae Religionis,* Geneva, 1559, tr. Thomas Norton, London, 1561.

Cameron, James K., 'John Knox', *Theologische Realenzyklopädie* Bd XIX, Lieferung 1/2, pp. 281–7.

Cowan, Henry, *John Knox, The Hero of the Scottish Reformation,* London, 1905.

Cowan, Ian B. *The Scottish Reformation: Church and Society in Sixteenth Century Scotland,* London, 1982.

[117] Here again John 17 was his main source – 'that they may be one' – see *Scots Confession,* Art. 21.

The Confession of Faith used in the English Congregation at Geneva, Received and Approved by the Church of Scotland in the Beginning of the Reformation, With Proofs from the Scriptures, Edinburgh, 1725.

Donaldson, Gordon, *The Scottish Reformation,* Cambridge, 1960.

Donaldson, Gordon, *Scottish Church History,* Edinburgh, 1985.

Fleming, David Hay, *The Reformation in Scotland,* London, 1910.

Hazlett, W. I. P., 'The Scots Confession 1560: Context, Complexion and Critique', *Archiv für Reformationsgeschichte,* 78, 1987, Gütersloh, pp. 287–320.

Kirk, James, *The Scottish Reformation: Church and Society in Sixteenth Century Scotland,* London, 1982.

Knox, John, *The Works of John Knox,* Collected and ed. by David Laing, Edinburgh, Vol. I, 1846; II, 1948; III, 1854; IV, 1955; V, 1858; VI, 1864.

Knox, John *et al., Scots Confession (Confessio Scoticana),* 1560, with Introduction by G. D. Henderson, Edinburgh, 1937.

Lindsay, Thomas M., *A History of the Reformation,* Volume II, *In Lands Beyond Germany,* Edinburgh, 1907 & 1908.

Lorimer, Peter, *John Knox and the Church of England,* London, 1875.

M'Crie, Charles Greig, *The Confessions of the Church of Scotland, Their Evolution in History,* Edinburgh, 1907.

MacEwen, Alexander R., *A History of the Church in Scotland,* Vol. II, 1546–1560, London, 1918.

McEwen, James S., *The Faith of John Knox,* London, 1961.

Maxwell, W. D., *John Knox's Genevan Service Book,* 1556, Edinburgh 1931.

Percy, Lord Eustace, *John Knox,* London, 1937.

Peterkin, Alexander, Editor, *Booke of the Universall Kirk of Scotland,* 3 vols., Edinburgh, 1839.

Ridley, Jasper, *John Knox,* Oxford, 1968.

Sefton, Henry R., *John Knox,* Edinburgh, 1993.

Shaw, Duncan, *The General Assemblies of the Church of Scotland, 1560–1600,* Edinburgh, 1964.

Sprott, G. W., *The Book of Common Order of the Church of Scotland, Commonly known as John Knox's Liturgy, With Historical Introduction and Illustrated Notes,* Edinburgh, 1901.

Torrance, Iain R., "Patrick Hamilton and John Knox: A Study in the doctrine of Justification by Faith", *Archiv für Reformationsgeschichte,* Jahrgang 65, 1974, Gütersloh, pp. 171–84.

Torrance, T. F., *The School of Faith, The Catechisms of the Reformed Church,* London, 1959.

Torrance, T. F., *et al.*, *Church of Scotland Reports on Baptism*, Edinburgh, 1961; the 'Interim Report of the Special Commission on Baptism', Edinburgh, 1958; *The Doctrine of Baptism*, Edinburgh, 1962.

Watt, Hugh, *John Knox in Controversy*, Edinburgh & London, 1950.

Wotherspoon, H. J., and Kirkpatrick, J. M., *A Manual of Church Doctrine, according to the Church of Scotland*, second edn, revised and enlarged by T. F. Torrance and Ronald Selby Wright, London, 1960.

Wotherspoon, H. J., *The Second Prayer Book of King Edward the Sixth (1552)*, with Historical Introduction and Notes, and *The Liturgy of Compromise used in the English Congregation at Frankfort*, George W. Sprott, Edinburgh, 1905.

2

The Older Scottish Tradition
1581–1647

John Craig, John Davidson and Robert Bruce

The Reformed theologians who immediately followed Knox shared with him his commitment to the teaching of John Calvin in the evangelical non-scholastic way in which it had been understood and handed on through the *Scots Confession* and the *Book of Common Order.* Particular mention should be made of John Craig, John Davidson and Robert Bruce. They were fully committed to the biblical stance of the Reformation and to the creeds of the Ancient Catholic Church, with their trinitarian and christological affirmations. This was reflected in the trinitarian doxologies of the fourth century appended to the psalms in *The Psalm Book,* or *The Book of Common Order,* commonly known as 'John Knox's Liturgy'.[1] In line with the new dynamic approach made prominent by Knox they gave central place to the mediatorial role and redemptive work of Christ, of our union and communion with him through the Holy Spirit, and of our participation in his saving and sanctifying humanity. The incarnate constitution of the Person of Christ, the Mediator, belongs to the inner substance of his atoning reconciliation; that is to say, the atonement has to do not only with the *act of God* in Christ, but with the *whole course of his life and obedience* from his birth to his death and resurrection.[2] If by his sacrificial death on the Cross Christ saves us from actual sins, through his conception and birth of the Virgin Mary he saves us from our original sin.

---

[1] See *John Knox's Liturgy,* and the account of it by Robert Edward, *The Doxology Approven,* Edinburgh, 1683 & 1731. Cf. also The Church Service Society edition of *The Book of Common Order of the Church of Scotland,* G. W. Sprott, Edinburgh, 1901.

[2] John Calvin, *Institute,* 2.16.5.

The evangelical and theological heart of this old Scottish tradition was taught in the catechisms of John Craig (1512–1600) and John Davidson (1549–1604), central to both of which was the union of God and man in Christ and our spiritual and sacramental union with him, which were expressed not in scholastic but in biblical terms in the light of the history of redemption.[3] It was within the frame of the incarnate self-revelation of God in Jesus Christ, and particularly in connection with the union and communion of the faithful with Christ as Mediator and Redeemer, that John Craig expounded the saving beliefs of the Church confessed in the Creed.[4] He spoke of Christian doctrine in terms of the way we honour God and render to him our thanksgiving. Like John Knox, John Craig gave powerful attention to the mediatorial and priestly office of Christ, and in the *Negative Confession* of 1581[5] distinguished Reformation theology sharply from that of the Roman Church (which he had earlier served in the Dominican Order). His teaching was characterised by a strong trinitarian emphasis on 'the love of the Father, the death of Christ and the power of the Holy Spirit' as working together, and of the Church as 'the good work of the three Persons'.[6] Within this perspective he gave central attention, not to the Covenant, but to Christ, and to the work of the Holy Spirit in the Church. It is Christ himself, he held, who is 'the substance' of the Covenant.[7] John Craig had a high doctrine of the Church as the Communion of those who are united to Christ and united mutually to one another in Christ as his Body. He regarded the Church as essentially a worshipping community filled with praise and thanksgiving to God for the Gospel and for the new life in Christ which is freely offered to all.

In his catechetical teaching Craig devoted 'the Second part of our Belief' to the doctrine of Christ as king, priest and prophet,

---

[3] For John Craig's *Catechism* of 1581 (and his *Short Catechism* of 1592), see Horatius Bonar, *Catechisms of the Scottish Reformation*, London, 1886, pp. 177–285, and my edition in *The School of Faith*, London, 1959 pp. 97–165 & 243f. For John Davidson's *Catechism* of 1602, see H. Bonar, *op. cit.* pp. 324–53. Mention should also be made of the *Metrical Catechisms* in English and Latin, Horatius Bonar, *op. cit.* pp. 301–23; the prose Latin Catechism of 1595, *Summula Catechismi, Rudimenta Pietatis*, by Andrew Simpson, 1590, H. Bonar, *op. cit.* pp. 287–98 and see T. F. Torrance, *The School of Faith*, pp. 285–90.

[4] *The School of Faith*, pp. 106ff.

[5] See the edition by G. D. Henderson, appended to his edition of the *Confessio Scoticana*, pp. 103–11.

[6] See *The School of Faith*, pp. 119 & 107.

[7] *The School of Faith*, p. 105.

the offices for which Christ was anointed by the Spirit, and which expressed how Christ saved us.[8] Special attention was given to his priestly office in which he gave unusual place to the obedience and praying of Christ as part of his atoning passion offered for us in satisfaction of God's wrath.[9] Like Calvin he held that Christ died for all, suffering for us in soul as well as body, sustaining the person of guilty men, taking upon himself their punishment, and their curse, thereby bringing upon them the blessing of God. Of particular note is the question and answer: 'What comfort do we have in the person of the Judge? Our Saviour, Advocate, and Mediator only shall be our Judge',[10] for it marks the vast difference between Craig's radically christocentric doctrine of God and of Christ's atoning satisfaction offered once for all, on the one hand, and on the other hand, the federal concept of God as primarily the omnipotent lawgiver who required to be appeased if we are to be saved.[11] Thus with John Craig there was no concept of God as Judge behind the back of Christ.

Distinctive also is the fact that Craig regarded election as bound up more with adoption into Christ, with union with him, and with the communion of the Spirit, than with an eternal decree. The union of people with Christ exists only within the communion of the redeemed and in the union they conjointly have with Christ the Head of the Church. 'All who are united with Christ are joined with the Church. Which of these two unions is the first and cause of the other? The mystical and spiritual union with Jesus Christ. For we are all saints of God, because we are joined first with Christ in God.'[12]

Union with Christ and faith are correlative, for it is through faith that we enter into union with Christ, and yet it is upon this corporate union with Christ that faith and our participation in the saving benefits or 'graces' of Christ rest.[13] John Craig held that there was a twofold union which he spoke of as a 'carnal union' and a 'spiritual union'.[14] By 'carnal union' he referred to Christ's

---

[8]   *The School of Faith*, pp. 110ff.
[9]   *The School of Faith*, pp. 110ff, & 114.
[10] *The School of Faith*, p. 115.
[11] *The School of Faith*, pp. 115f.
[12] *The School of Faith*, pp. 160f. See also *Interim Report on the Special Commission on Baptism*, presented to the Church of Scotland in May, 1958, p. 18.
[13] Thus Craig's *Short Catechism*, Part III, QQ 22f.
[14] *Craig's Catechism, 1581* – see my edition, *The School of Faith*, London, 1959. pp. 113 & 124f, and the Introduction, pp. cvi ff.

union with us and our union with Christ which took place in his birth of the Spirit and in his human life through which he sanctifies us. The foundation of our union with Christ, then, is that which Christ has made with us when in his Incarnation he became bone of our bone and flesh of our flesh; but through the mighty power of the Spirit all who have faith in Christ are made flesh of his flesh and bone of his bone. It is only through this union, through ingrafting into Christ by faith and through communion with him in his Body and Blood, that we may share in all Christ's benefits – outside of this union and communion there is no salvation, for Christ himself is the ground of salvation.[15] Hence, as Craig pointed out, the Creed speaks of the remission of sins within the credal article on the Spirit and the Church.[16] While he laid emphasis on the work of the Spirit in effecting union and conjunction with Christ, Craig insisted also that God uses three main instruments to bring us into union and to maintain us in it: the Word, the sacraments, and the ministry of men.[17]

The sacraments are regarded as communicating the divine mysteries to the faithful, and in union with the Word they offer Christ to all. They require faith for their reception, but at the same time they nourish that faith and build it up, as ordinances serving union with Christ. The sacraments are regarded, therefore, as effectual instruments in the hands of Christ, in which he offers himself in his wholeness to us. Craig did not understand grace in the Roman or Augustinian sense. Grace is the fatherly favour of God extended to us through the gracious acts of Christ. Thus Baptism brings us into the family of the heavenly Father, through our adoption in Christ the Son and union with him who was incarnate in our flesh and bore our sin, and stood under the judgment of God for us – as such Baptism signifies our death and resurrection in Christ, the forgiveness of sins and our regeneration. The washing with water corresponds to our washing in Christ's Blood, which is effected by the power of the Spirit in our hearts and consciences. So our guilt is removed and we share in Christ's humanity.[18] Because of this we feel forgiven, and dying to sin, advance in love toward God and man. While Baptism mediates to us the forgiveness of sins in the sacrament of the Lord's Supper

---

15   *The School of Faith*, p. 121.
16   *The School of Faith*, p. 122.
17   *The School of Faith*, pp. 113, 120ff, 150ff, 160f.
18   *The School of Faith*, pp. 152–4. See again the *Interim Report on Baptism*, p. 18.

our souls are fed with the Body and Blood of Christ, and we are spiritually joined with Christ's Body, so that through this union with him we enjoy his saving benefits. Craig made a point of saying that we 'receive his very substantial body and blood by faith'. His natural body is in heaven, yet we receive it on earth by faith, through the wonderful working of the Spirit.[19]

With John Craig a new tendency entered Scottish theology, the *feeling* of being forgiven and regenerated in Christ which is continuously nourished and deepened in us through the sacraments of Baptism and the Lord's Supper.[20] However, in spite of what we may feel, and in spite of the doubts that may 'arise out of our flesh', we rely not upon our feeling but upon the objective reality of salvation and the divine promise of our inheritance in the Kingdom of Heaven sealed to us in Word and sacrament.

The catechism of John Davidson was important for the strong evangelical convictions that were developed in the parish ministry. Its teaching was characterised by a remarkable concentration on the Person and work of Christ.[21]

The salvation of man is so fully wrought, and perfitely accomplished by Christ in his awn person, that nothing is left to bee done or wrought by us in our persons, to bee any cause of the least part of it? That is most certaine. For as his blude purgeth us from all sinne, and his perfite righteousness becommes oures, so in him wee are compleit.[22]

In becoming one with us, Christ took our cause so fully upon himself that all parts of our salvation and sanctification were fulfilled *in him* as the incarnate Son of God so that they become ours through union and conjunction with him.[23] Thus the doctrines of reconciliation, justification, and regeneration were expounded not just in imputational terms but in terms of their actual fulfilment and embodiment in Christ who through his conjunction with us in his birth, life, death and resurrection became so profoundly 'ane with us' that we are made 'ane with him' and are therein made

---

[19] *The School of Faith*, pp. 154–7.
[20] *The School of Faith*, pp. 103, 108, 137, 163.
[21] See the edition of *Davidson's Catechism* by Horatius Bonar in the Appendix to his *Catechisms of the Scottish Reformation*, London, 1866, pp. 324–57.
[22] *Davidson's Catechism*, Bonar edn, p. 336.
[23] *Davidson's Catechism*, pp. 336–41, 343, 350f.

partakers of his righteousness and of God's election of us already made sure in Christ in whom we believe.

In Davidson's teaching faith and union with Christ are so closely intertwined that they were held to be the obverse of one another, our faith being the counterpart of what Christ has fulfilled for us and in our place in himself, while what Christ has done for us and is in his own Person in his conjunction with us is the ground and heart of faith. It is through faith in Christ sealed in our hearts by the Holy Spirit that we have assurance of redemption and salvation.

> Whereby is this union and straite coniunction made between Christ crucified and us? ... By Faith onely; as the onely instrument whereby we receave him to dwell in our heartes ... Then there is no parte of our righteousness left, without the apprehension or grip of Faith, seeing it is all whollie in the person of Christ apprehended by Faith? It is so ... What is this Faith that is the onely instrument of this strait coniunction betweene Christ crucified and us? ... It is the sure perswasion of the heart, that Christ by his death and resurrection hath taken away all our sinnes, and clothing us with his awin righteousnesse, has throughly restored us to the favour of God.[24]

> Our justification is only wrought by him in himselfe, without us, sa that how soone we freely believe, we are justified, counted righteous, and get the right of life everlasting through the death and resurrection of Christ.[25]

All through his Catechism Davidson laid the strongest emphasis upon what has taken place in the Person of Christ apart from believers, and never upon the persons of those who believe. This was coupled with his emphasis upon the prevenient love of God, from which salvation flowed, without any suggestion that God had to be placated or appeased in order to love and be gracious toward sinners.[26]

It was to Davidson's statement that 'Faith is ane heartie assurance that our sinnes are freely forgiven us in Christ',[27] that appeal was

---

[24] *Davidson's Catechism*, p. 350.

[25] *Davidson's Catechism*, p. 345.

[26] *Davidson's Catechism*, pp. 334f.

[27] *Davidson's Catechism*, p. 340; for similar statements by Craig, see his *Short Catechism*, Q. 22, and *The School of Faith*, pp. 103 & 106.

to be made again and again in Scottish theology in face of the lack of assurance that came with the change in the doctrine of God brought about by federal theology and the idea that God had to be appeased in order to be gracious to us. With Davidson, however, the assurance of salvation which is identical with faith is ultimately grounded in 'the tender mercy and grace of God, who loving us when we were his enemies, provyded our salvation to bee wrought onely by his wellbeloved Sonne Jesus Christ, made Man of the Virgine Marie without sinne.'[28] That is to say, it was from the ultimate love of God the Father in freely giving his Son to be our Mediator, Redeemer and Saviour, that all parts of our salvation are fully accomplished in such a way in Christ that nothing on our part can 'deface the assurance of our salvation'. This is the assurance which is divinely sealed for us and in us in the sacrament of Baptism and reiterated in the sacrament of the Lord's Supper.[29]

Through this teaching John Davidson became with John Knox and John Craig a leader of the persistent Scottish tradition which wedded evangelical passion with the sacramental life of the Church. In this respect his influence extended to some of the Covenanting divines such as Thomas Boston and James Fraser of Brae. The sacraments were regarded as essentially evangelical ordinances, and even 'converting ordinances', annexed to the preaching of the Gospel. They are specially appointed 'to offer Christ crucified … to the rest of the senses as the Word does to the ear and hearing.'[30]

It was on this same Christological and soteriological ground that Robert Bruce (1554–1631) expounded his rich doctrine of Baptism and the Lord's Supper and of the union and communion of believers with one another in the Church as the Body of Christ.[31] 'It was largely under Bruce's leadership that the Scottish Reformation found stability.'[32]

---

[28] *Davidson's Catechism*, p. 335.

[29] *Davidson's Catechism*, Bonar's edition, pp. 336ff.

[30] See the 1753 edition of *Davidson's Catechism*, pp. 31f; and Bonar's edition, pp. 340f. The idea that the sacrament of the Lord's Supper was a converting or regenerating ordinance was later rejected by George Gillespie, *Aaron's Rod Blossoming*, Edinburgh, 1644.

[31] Robert Bruce, *The Mystery of the Lord's Supper*, 1589, and his sixth Sermon on Isaiah 38 published in 1591. See the Introduction to my edition of *The Mystery the Lord's Supper*, 1958, pp. 33f.

[32] Iain R. Torrance, 'Robert Bruce', N. M. de S. Cameron *et al.* (eds), *Dictionary of Scottish Church History and Theology*, Edinburgh, 1993, p. 104.

As Bruce's teaching was very influential, we may present it more fully. In discussing the salvation that Christ has wrought for us as God and man, the only Mediator between God and man, Bruce had this to say:

> *First*, he delivered us from the sins which we call actual, by the perfect satisfaction whereby he satisfied fully, in suffering hell in his soul, and death in his body on the Cross, and so freed us from our actual sins, and their punishment. In this work he is perfect Mediator.

This is the aspect of Christ's work which Reformed theologians spoke of as his *passive obedience*. Then, in the third place, Bruce went on to speak of Christ's *active obedience*.

> Now in the *third place*, also, he is perfect Mediator, for he not only satisfied for our sins, but he fulfilled the whole Law for us, and indeed more than the Law required, for the Second Table requires only that we love our neighbour as ourselves. But Christ did more than this, for no one so loves his neighbour that he will willingly die for him. Christ, in dying for us, showed that he loves us more than the Law requires. Therefore, not only has he fulfilled the Law for us, but done more than the Law demanded. Now this perfect righteousness of his intervenes between us and the Father, and covers our rebellion and disobedience; otherwise, we would not be free from condemnation here either.

These are the two aspects that cover the atoning work of Christ in scholastic Calvinism, his passive and active obedience on our behalf. But Bruce, following Calvin himself, was not content with that, and so between these two he expounded another, and no less essential, aspect of Christ's atoning reconciliation.

> *Secondly*, he delivered us from the disorder and rotten root from which we proceed. For, as you see, Christ Jesus was conceived in the womb of the Virgin, and that by the mighty power of his Holy Spirit, so that our nature in him was fully sanctified by that same power. And this perfect purity of our nature in his Person covers our impurity, for he was not conceived in sin and corruption as we are, but by the power of the Holy Spirit, who perfectly sanctified our nature in him, even in the moment of his conception. Thus in that he was thoroughly purged, his purity covers our impurity.

If Bruce thought of the atoning satisfaction of Christ as freeing us from our actual sins, it is clear that he thought of his perfect purity in Incarnation and birth as covering our original sin, or sanctifying our human nature. This stress upon incarnational redemption in Christ Jesus was sandwiched by Bruce in between his accounts of Christ's passive and active obedience, for it belongs to the very heart of his saving work. And so he summed it up by saying that all these, namely, perfect satisfaction, perfect purity, perfect righteousness are to be found in Christ perfectly. It is in this 'whole Christ' that we are given to participate in the sacrament of the Lord's Supper, and therefore we are given to share not only in the benefits of his death on the Cross and in his righteous fulfilment of the will of God, but also in his sanctified human nature so that we are sanctified in the purity of his Incarnation through union with him in his humanity. In this doctrine of saving and sanctifying union with Christ, Bruce was of course in line with the *Scots Confession*, and the catechisms authorised by the Kirk before they were unfortunately replaced by the Westminster Divines.

These theologians, Craig, Davidson and Bruce, also laid considerable stress like all the Reformers on the sovereignty and grace of God, but they did not understand it in the causal Augustinian/Thomist sense of Roman theology. They thought of election as taking place in Christ and as bound up with adoption in him more than with an abstract eternal decree of predestination.

Several doctrinal points in these early decades after the Reformation were to become crucial issues for the Church of Scotland in the next two centuries.

(a) The place of the active and passive obedience of Christ in his mediatorial role. The active obedience of Christ gave expression to the profound interrelation between the Incarnation and the atonement, whereas the passive obedience, understood as his obedience under and to the law, carried with it the implication that the Person and sacrifice of Christ were to be interpreted in a judicial and instrumentalist way. The latter carried with it a depreciation of the humanity of Jesus, with a suspicion of a Nestorian dualism between his divine and human natures.

(b) The interrelation between union with Christ, justification and faith.[33] In the teaching of people like Knox, Bruce, Craig and

[33] See the address given to New College Theological Society by Thomas Gregory on 'Union to Christ the Ground of Justification', p. 40, published with 'Christ the Centre of Christianity' by Alexander Martin, Edinburgh, 1883.

Davidson, union with Christ and faith were strictly correlative, for it is through faith that we have union with Christ, and yet it is upon this union with Christ that faith rests as its inner bond. All this presupposes the hypostatic union of God and man in the one Person of Christ, the incarnate Son of God, for it is only by our being ingrafted into Christ through the Holy Spirit that we may partake of all his saving benefits. The stress here is upon the objectivity of grace, not upon faith itself, for in faith we look to Christ and away from ourselves and our own believing.

As John Welch, John Knox's son-in-law taught, it is not the measure of faith that saves us, but the blood of Christ it holds to that saves – the grasp of faith is itself held in the mighty grasp of Christ.[34] 'It is not the measure of faith that saves us, but the strength of Christ's hold upon us', as is revealed in the covenant of grace which is 'all of condescension and all of love', a covenant which is sealed and extended to us in Baptism. Here Welch likens faith to the weak fingers of little children who are unable to 'grip and fathom' the purse of gold which their father holds out to them.[35] It is Christ the object of faith who holds on to us and saves us even when our faith is so weak. The Christ in whom we believe far exceeds the small measure of our faith, and so the believer finds his security not in his poor believing grasp of Christ but in the gift of grace that exceeds his expectations and his capacity to grasp it. Galatians 2.20: 'not I but Christ' was of critical significance.[36] Here we have the old Scots conception of faith as 'affiance', as our involvement in Christ's alliance with us in his Incarnation and atoning sacrifice, so that we can no more be torn away from Christ than Christ can be divested of the very flesh he assumed from us, as Welch expresses it. Faith, no matter how weak, is our implication in the covenanted faithfulness of Christ, in his obedient humanity and in his self-offering to God in our name and on our behalf. Faith is not simply belief in and acceptance of the active and passive obedience of Christ imputed to us. It is an actual participation in his faithful obedience as the incarnate Son of the Father. It is not therefore upon the strength of our faith that we rely but upon the

---

[34] John Welch, *Forty-Eight Select Sermons*, Glasgow Edition, no date, pp. 358ff, 446, 451.

[35] Sermon X on John 5.24 and 6.39; XLI on Isaiah 42.3; XLIII on John 3.16; and XXVII. *Forty-Eight Select Sermons*, preached by that Eminent and Faithful Servant of Jesus Christ, Mr John Welch, Edinburgh, 1744.

[36] *Ibid.* Sermon XXVIII, on Galatians 2.20.

faithfulness of Christ. 'Now Christ is the gift, and weak faith may hold him as well as strong faith may hold him; and Christ is as truly thine when thou hast a weak faith, as when thou hast come to these triumphant joys through the strength of faith.'

In spite of this teaching by Welch and others, the question of the assurance of salvation began to be thrust forward into prominence, for due to the teaching of Theodore Beza assurance was detached from faith. He felt constrained to compose an answer to people troubled about their predestination, but it proved to be in vain.[37] What was at stake here was the sole sufficiency of Christ who was incarnate in our flesh and offered himself in atoning sacrifice for us and in our place, so that in faith we look away from ourselves to him. It is in him alone that we are freely offered and find forgiveness and regeneration. Theologians and preachers like Robert Bruce pointed here to the sacraments and their saving promise, or rather to the objective reality of God's saving grace which is sealed to us in them, for Baptism and the Lord's Supper direct believers away from themselves and their feelings to Jesus Christ. As it has already been noted, this was Davidson's definition of faith, firmly linked to a doctrine of union with Christ, as an assurance that our sins are freely forgiven us in Christ.[38] This was to play an important role in the theological debates that followed in the Kirk, when a federal and forensic doctrine of election and justification took over, and faith and assurance, or faith and confidence, tended to be torn apart from each other. For generations of people in the Kirk faith was deeply disturbed and shaken by the doctrine thundered from the pulpits that Christ did not die for all but only for a few chosen ones – assurance of their salvation withered in face of the inscrutable decree of divine predestination.

In the years that followed the Reformation, it was opposition to Roman Catholicism that helped to give cohesion to Scottish theology in spite of different views of Church and State, not least through concentration on the Person and work of Christ as Mediator. The Reformed theological position of the Presbyteries and the Assembly was powerfully affirmed by the so-called *Negative*

---

[37] This was given by way of an answer to D. Andreas at the Colloquy at Mompelgart in a statement translated and attached to the work of William Perkins on *The Golden Chaine*, London, 1592.

[38] See the edition of Davidson's Catechism by Horatius Bonar in the Appendix to his *Catechisms of the Scottish Reformation*, London, 1866, pp. 340 & 329.

Confession of 1581[39] which was commissioned by the King and drawn up by John Craig, in order to consolidate the Protestant stance of the Kirk in the face of the Counter-Reformation based on the Council of Trent. While reaffirming the *Scots Confession*, this new Manifesto of the Reformed Kirk included several sections calling for a covenanted commitment to the doctrine and discipline of the Kirk that were later to be become the basis of the National Covenant.

When Theodore Beza succeeded John Calvin in Geneva, a rationalistic supralapsarian form of Calvinism arose under his influence which was to leave its mark on Scottish Theology.[40] During the counter-Reformation Du Moulin the younger staged a series of remarkable debating triumphs over Jesuit opponents by expounding the teaching of Calvin in the form of logically impeccable syllogisms.[41] This helped to give rise to a rigidly scholastic and rationalistic form of Calvinism in which logico-causal relations tended to replace ontological relations. The Synod of Dort (1618–19) gave Du Moulin a gold medal, for what he had been doing was fully in line with its own rejection of Roman and Arminian teaching and its own way of strict logico-causal thinking. This was the kind of Bezan Calvinism which, with the stringent articles of the Synod of Dort, was held to express true Calvinist orthodoxy, and which was to leave its mark on Scottish theology not least through Samuel Rutherford. Moreover, a new situation arose in Scotland when the Church found itself opposing an Erastian prelacy along with episcopacy and an Arminian notion of grace, both of which, it was felt, challenged the sovereignty of Christ as the sole Head of the Kirk and Mediator of our salvation. In this development Andrew Melville played a crucial role both in the relation of the Kirk to the Crown, and in the introduction of Aristotelian philosophy and Ramist dialectics into the Scottish Universities, particularly evident in the application of logical analysis in the commentaries of Charles Ferme[42] and Robert

---

[39] The text of the *Negative Confession* is given by G. D. Henderson at the end of his edition of the *Scots Confession*, Edinburgh, 1937, pp. 101–11.

[40] See Theodore Beza, *Summa Totius Christianismi, sive descriptio et distributio causarum salutis electorum et exitii reproborum, ex sacris literis, collecti*, Geneva, 1555.

[41] See Leslie Gordon Tait, *Pierre du Moulin (1568–1658) Huguenot Theologian*, 1955, Dissertation, New College Library.

[42] Charles Ferme, *Analysis Logica in Epistolam Apostoli ad Romanos*, Edinburgh, 1651, Wodrow, 1850.

Rollock.[43] On the one hand, a form of a two kingdoms theory put forward by John Davidson, together with a rejection of episcopacy in any form, was sharpened into an instrument to oppose the claim by the King to have authority over the Assemblies. This was in its own way no less 'Erastian' than the position advocated by the King and his bishops. Moreover, at that time a federal theology was imported which changed the general framework of Reformed Theology,[44] and involved a strange return to the Medieval attempt to impose ecclesiastical uniformity upon the Church, and even to magnify the claims of the Church in extending its jurisdiction over matters beyond Christian doctrine and spiritual discipline.

Robert Rollock (1555–99)

For Calvin and Knox the substance of both the Old and New Testaments was the same, Jesus Christ and the Gospel of grace and redemption. With Andrew Melville[45] and Robert Rollock,[46] however, instead of one covenant of grace and redemption with differing dispensations, there were held to be two different covenants, one of nature and works, and one of grace.[47]

> The covenant of God generally is a promise under some one condition. And it is twofold; the first is the covenant of works; the second is the covenant of grace ... The covenant of works, which may also be called a legal or natural covenant, is founded in nature, which by creation was pure and holy, and in the law of God, which in the first creation was engraven

---

[43] Cf., for example, his *In Epistolam S. Pauli Apostoli ad Romanos, Commentarius, analytica methodo conscriptus*, 1595, or *Analysis Logica in Epistolam Pauli Apostoli ad Galatas*, 1603.

[44] For the origins of federal theology, see David A. Weir, *The Origins of Federal Theology in 16th-Century Reformation Thought*, Oxford, 1990; and J. B. Torrance, 'The Concept of Federal Theology – Was Calvin a Federal Theologian?' *Calvinus Sacrae Scripturae Professor*, ed. W. H. Neuser, Grand Rapids, 1994, pp. 15–40.

[45] See his *Commentarius in Divinam Pauli Epistolam ad Romanos*, Edinburgh, Wodrow, 1889, pp. 385–514.

[46] *Select Works of Robert Rollock*, ed. W. M. Gunn, Wodrow Edn, Edinburgh, 1849.

[47] The rise and development of federal theology in Britain was due in large measure to William Perkins, particularly to his work *Golden Chaine, Or The Description of Theology, containing the order of the causes of Salvation and Damnation, according to God's Word*, Eng. tr. London, 1592, Chap. 19.

in man's heart.[48] For after that God created man after his own image, pure and holy, and had written his law in his mind, he made a covenant with man, wherein he promised him eternal life, under the condition of holy and good works, which should be answerable to the holiness and goodness of their creation, and conformable to his law.[49]

Rollock went on to say that the covenant of works was *not grounded in Christ, or the grace of God in Christ,* and in it there was no mediator between God and man, and claimed that it was given formal expression in the Mosaic Law. Here the biblical notion of covenant which was essentially a one-way covenant or unilateral (μονόπλευρον) covenant was changed into a two-way conditional contract, the fulfilment of which depends on the completion of certain stipulations.[50] It was then in that sense unfortunately that 'covenant' came to be understood, and with it a misunderstanding of justification by faith.[51] The general effect of all this was that faith was intellectualised, theology was logicalised, and the Christian life was moralised. These tendencies, the federal scheme of salvation, the moralising of the Christian life, and the intellectualising of faith, the logicalising of theology, passed into Scottish theology, and made it possible for the acceptance by the Kirk of the puritanised Calvinism of the *Westminster Confession of Faith,* and its demand for ecclesiastical uniformity.

There was another side, however, to Robert Rollock as 'Minister of the Evangel of Jesus Christ' as he preferred to be called even when Principal of the College of Edinburgh. This was his concern for biblical exposition which he introduced into Scottish universities, and, not least his regular preaching of the Gospel in line with the tradition of John Knox and Robert Bruce. The importance he gave to biblical exposition was very evident in his commentaries on the epistles of St Paul, to the Romans,[52] Galatians

---

[48] On the concept of the *foedus naturale* or covenant of nature, see J. B. Torrance, *op. cit.* pp. 23ff.

[49] Robert Rollock, *Tractatus De Vocatione Efficaci,* Edinburgh 1597; Eng. tr. *A Treatise of God's Effectual Calling,* Wodrow Edition, Edinburgh, 1849, p. 34.

[50] Robert Rollock, *A Treatise of our Effectual Calling, Works,* Wodrow Society, Edinburgh, 1849, p. 34.

[51] See James B. Torrance, 'Covenant or Contract? A Study of the Theological Background of Worship in Seventeenth-Century Scotland', *Scottish Journal of Theology,* 23.1, Edinburgh, 1970, pp. 51–76.

[52] *In Epistolam S. Pauli ad Romanos,* Geneva, 1595.

and Ephesians,[53] Colossians, Thessalonians, Philemon, and the Epistle to the Hebrews,[54] but also his expository *Lectures upon the History of the Passion and Resurrection, and Ascension of the Lord Jesus Christ, Beginning at the eighteenth Chapter of the Gospel, according to S. John.*[55] The evangelical character of Rollock's preaching may be gathered from a volume of his sermons in the Scots vernacular published in the year he died.[56]

> Believe me it is not a thing of small importance to preach the Word: it is not the same thing as to expound the text of Plato and Aristotle, or to set forth a harangue bedaubed with the colours and allurements of rhetoric. The preaching of the Word depends on holiness, humility, and the efficacious demonstration of the Spirit. God knows how highly I have ever prized it.

Before long a bifurcation took place in Scottish theology, between the federal Calvinism of Samuel Rutherford, George Gillespie, David Dickson and James Durham, and the teaching of Calvin himself and of people like James Fraser of Brea (or Brae) and Robert Leighton, which continued to have its place in the parishes of the Kirk where the older Reformed theology was held and taught in a 'Knoxian' and more evangelical way. There were some very able theologians, mild Calvinists of deep evangelical convictions, however, who sought to preserve a more christocentric emphasis concerned with the interrelation of the Incarnation and atonement, like Robert Boyd who had a deep interest in patristic doctrine, and Hugh Binning who was one of the finest spirits in the Kirk but who died very early, and there were others like John Forbes of Corse and John Cameron, who sided with the views of Knox and Calvin and were close to the Nicene teaching of the ancient Church. While they were definitely Calvinist they rejected

---

[53] *Analysis Logica in Epistolam Pauli Apostoli ad Galatas, In Epistolam S. Pauli ad Ephesios*, Geneva, 1593 & 1596.

[54] *In Epistolam Sancti Pauli Apostoli ad Colossenses Commentarius*, Geneva, 1592; *In Epistolam Pauli Apostoli I & II Ad Thessalonicences, & Analysis Logica Epistolae Pauli Apostoli Ad Philemonem*, Geneva, 1598; & *Analysis Logica in Epistolam ad Hebraeos*, Geneva, 1605.

[55] Edinburgh, 1626; reprinted in *Select Works of Robert Rollock*, Vol. 2, Edinburgh, 1844.

[56] *Certaine Sermons Upon Several Places of the Epistles of Paul, Preached Be M. Robert Rollock, Minister of the Euangell of Jesus Christ at Edinburgh*, Edinburgh, 1599.

the anti-episcopal and anti-missionary teaching of Theodore Beza which was reinforced by Article 2 on limited atonement formulated by the Synod of Dort, that Christ died *sufficienter* for all, but *efficaciter* for the faithful. That 'common solution', as it was called, had already been rejected by Calvin.[57] He was followed in this view by John Cameron,[58] who like him held that God loved the *world*, and that Christ died for *all mankind*.[59] While he held an Augustinian and Calvinist doctrine of election, the primary premise with which he operated was, not an abstract divine decree, but the eternal and prevenient love of God for all his creation. He rejected the interpretation of John 3.16 that 'God so loved the world' means that he loves only those who believe in his only begotten Son. Christ certainly died for all, and made satisfaction for all, but his death makes blessed only those who embrace him with true faith. The sun shines its light upon all, but he who sleeps or shuts his eyes receives no light.[60]

John Cameron (1579–1625)

John Cameron was for several years Principal of Glasgow University, and later for a short time of Edinburgh University. He was an independent thinker and scholar, who grounded Christian doctrine on careful exegesis in which he deployed great linguistic learning. It was due to his biblical orientation that he was somewhat critical of the federal system of thought for he disliked its hard contractual character. While he spoke of a threefold conception of the covenant, in which he allowed for a 'covenant of nature' in line with the teaching of Robert Rollock, he preferred the main biblical contrast between the 'old legal covenant' and the covenant of grace, between works and grace, and gave particular attention to the relation between the divine promise of grace and its fulfilment in

---

[57] *Concerning the Eternal Predestination of God*, tr. by J. K. S. Reid, London, 1961, IX.5, p. 148.

[58] Thus *Ioannis Cameronis Opera*, c. 534.2: 'Rectius faciunt qui Christum pro impiis *sufficienter* (ut loquuntur) satisfecisse docent (quae mea sententia est) efficaciter autem pro solis piis: quanquam *sufficientiae* vocabulum mihi amplius quiddam videtur in hoc argumento significare quam nonnulli arbitrantur.'

[59] See Calvin, *Institute*, 2.16.1–3; and *De praedestinatione*, IX.5.4.

[60] *Ioannis Cameronis Opera*, Geneva, 1628 & 1642, c. 532.2. See the whole correspondence between Cameron and Capel, cc. 529–35, especially cc. 532ff.

the Gospel.[61] He gained a great reputation on the Continent as essentially a biblical scholar noted for his very careful and accurate interpretation of the Scriptures. This became very clear in debates with Roman theologians in France, where he served as a Professor at Bordeaux, Sedan and Saumur, over his famous exposition of 'You are Peter'.[62] This biblical fidelity was evident all through his lectures or *praelectiones*, as well as in his exegesis of the Gospel of St Matthew, the Epistle to the Hebrews, and his excursus on the Word of God and the Church.[63] For example, in regard to the questions on the efficacy of grace and the exercise of freewill, in which he disagreed with Andrew Melville, he would not allow abstract notions of God's irresistible power to detract from faithful interpretation of the Scriptures.[64]

John Cameron was a moderate Calvinist, critical alike of the hyper-Calvinist views of Theodore Beza and of Arminian conceptions of grace and freewill.[65] He was not a 'universalist', however, for he did not believe that all people will necessarily and eventually be saved, for it conflicted with God's eternal election of some only to everlasting life. While holding, with 'the teaching of the whole Church' that God loved the world and that Christ is the Saviour of the world, he rejected the idea that God's love for the 'world' (John 3.16) can be interpreted to mean that God loves only those who believe in his only begotten Son. At the same time he sought to put forward a mediating view of atonement, according to which while we say that Christ died absolutely (*absolute*) for the faithful, it may be said that he died conditionally (*conditionate*) for all.[66] In his discussion of the disputed statement of St Paul in

[61] *De Triplici Dei cum Homine Foedere Theses, Ioannis Cameronis Opera*, cc. 544–551.
[62] *Ioannis Cameronis Opera*, cc. 1–26.
[63] *Ioannis Cameronis Opera*, cc. 107ff & 416ff.
[64] *Ioannis Cameronis Opera*, cc. 330ff; cf also cc. 530ff over the interpretation of Isaiah 5.4.
[65] *Ioannis Cameronis Opera*, 1628 & 1642, *Amica Collatio de Gratiae et Voluntatis Humanae Concursu in Vocatione*, cc. 606–708. He referred to Beza rather derisively as 'that most learned commentator'! 'He might well have been called Bezae-mastix (Beza's scourge)' – H. M. B. Reid, *The Divinity Principals of the University of Glasgow, 1545–1645*, Glasgow, 1917, pp. 176f.
[66] *Ioannis Cameronis Opera* , 1628 & 1692, cc. 389f, 531ff. This was a view rejected by James Fraser of Brae, *A Treatise on Justifying Faith*, Edinburgh, 1749, pp. 162 & 175f: 'To say that Christ redeemed Reprobates upon Condition of their Believing is to say in Effect, he redeemed them not at all ...' 'I judge it to be derogatory to the Wisdom of God to send his Son to shed his Blood upon a Condition which he certainly knows shall never be performed.'

1 Timothy 2.4 Cameron pointed to a similar distinction between absolute salvation (*absoluta*) and hypothetical salvation (*hypothetica*), which he interpreted to hold conditionally (*cum conditione*)[67] This must be thought out in the light of what the Scriptures say of 'God's antecedent love (*Dei amorem antecedentem*)'.[68] God loves the world, gave Christ for the life of the world, and will have all men to be saved and come to the knowledge of the truth, and calls them to repentance. It is on the ground of that *antecedent love that God gives faith*. This is shown by a no less celebrated passage than, 'No one comes to me except the Father draw him' (John 5.44). That is to say, in spite of his claim that in the Holy Scripture there is not a single promise that all men will be saved, John Cameron was determined to be faithful to the New Testament teaching about the antecedent love of God for the world in giving his only begotten Son to be the Saviour of all who believe in him, and thus about God's will that all people should come to a knowledge of the Gospel.[69]

Robert Boyd (1578–1627)

Robert Boyd the son of James Boyd, the Reformed Archbishop of Glasgow, was a person of moderate views on presbytery and episcopacy but with strong objection to the imposition by the King of bishops on the Kirk. He had studied in the University of Edinburgh when Robert Rollock was Principal, without becoming a Ramist in his philosophy or a hard-line federalist in his Calvinism. He was also a friend of Robert Bruce and of John Welch, the banished outspoken son-in-law of John Knox, and shared their views on faith and assurance.[70] After graduating from Edinburgh he spent a number of years in France, but in 1614 at the request of King James to return to Scotland he was appointed Principal of

---

[67] This was in line with his distinction between an absolute covenant (*foedus absolutum*) and a hypothetical covenant (*foedus hypotheticum*). *Ibid*. c. 544.1.

[68] *Ioannis Cameronis Opera*, c. 551.2.

[69] *Ioannis Cameronis Opera*, cc. 453f & 532f.

[70] On his friendship with Bruce, see H. M. B. Reid, *The Divinity Principals of the University of Glasgow, 1545–1654*, Glasgow, 1917, pp. 117 & 144. For his friendship with John Welch see the correspondence between them edited by David Laing, *The Miscellany of the Wodrow Society*, Volume I, Edinburgh, 1844, pp. 545–63.

Glasgow University and Minister of Govan. He was later appointed Principal of Edinburgh University and became minister of Greyfriars, but resigned in 1623 in defiance of 'The Five Articles of Perth'.

In his twofold ministry as Professor of Theology and Parish Minister, Robert Boyd developed a remarkable combination of biblical and systematic theology and gained a considerable reputation on the Continent as in Scotland for scholarly erudition. Wodrow pointed out that 'He always observed this rule, to fetch his divinity from the fountain of the sacred scripture'. This was very evident in his massive *Ad Ephesios Praelectiones*, Lectures or Commentary on the Epistle to the Ephesians, published unfortunately only in Latin, which restricted its use.[71] In faithful biblical interpretation he was able to give a powerful account of the Lord Jesus Christ, together with the promises about him made in the Gospel, as 'the proper object of saving faith' (*fidei salutaris objectum proprium*). That was the christocentric emphasis which governed all his academic presentation of Christian doctrine. At the same time, with his parishioners clearly in mind, Boyd gave memorable form to the truth that 'all our love by which we are related to God is a reflection and reciprocation of God's love toward us' (*noster omnis amor, quo in Deum ferimur, amoris erga nos Dei reflexio quaedam ac reciprocatio*).[72] It is because God has *first* loved us that in a movement of mutual love we are brought to love him in a reciprocal way. That is to say, in our union with God in Christ actualised by the Spirit, our love, like faith, is the *reflex* or *effect* of God's love toward us manifested in Christ. 'Herein is love', he cited, 'not that we have loved God but that he has loved us and sent his Son to be the propitiation for our sins' (1 John 4.10). This mutual or reciprocal movement of love is what is actualised through the Spirit in our union with God in Christ.[73] That was a way of understanding and of expressing God's electing love in Christ which was to be taken up by Hugh Binning and Robert Leighton in countering the doubt and difficulties for faith generated in people's minds by the harsh legalist form of predestination.

It was doubtless because of problems about predestination in people's minds that Robert Boyd devoted a long excursus to the

---

[71] Robert Boyd, *In Epistolam Pauli Apostoli Ad Ephesios Praelectiones*, Geneva, 1661.
[72] *Praelectiones*, cc. 138.2 – 139.1.
[73] *Praelectiones*, c. 138; cf. also cc. 648–9.

subject which is properly to be understood in the light of what he had to say about redemption, although this was presented for the most part in connection with other doctrines of the faith, and his emphasis upon the prevenience of God's eternal love upon which they all rest. He drew a relative distinction between election and predestination: election has to do with the gratuitous act of divine grace and its bearing upon reconciliation and adoption in Christ, whereas predestination has to do more with the means whereby election is brought about. Again election is not properly applied to the reprobate for they are not elected to be damned.[74] Boyd raised, very understandably and rightly, the question whether the doctrine of predestination was a subject for public proclamation to the faithful, and not rather a matter to be propounded in the Schools.[75] Election, however, is a saving doctrine, he said, and should be taught, for it has to do, not with foreseen merit, but with the gratuitous kindness and eternal love of God mediated to us in and through Christ, promised by him, and freely proclaimed to us in the Gospel, as in John 3.16.[76] That is to say, election is a powerful term for salvation by grace alone.

In line with the teaching of Calvin, and the teaching of 'orthodox doctors', such as Polanus, Boyd spoke of election as taking place first in Christ, and then in all those who are united to Christ – As the Mediator, who is God and Man, or indeed God-Man (θεανθρωπός), he is the Cause (*Causa*) and the Foundation (*Fundamentum*) of election, and the Head of the elect (*Caput electorum*).[77] It is in the Person of Christ, the *Theandros* (God-Man) Mediator, that election takes place. 'There is such a connection between Christ and the elect that it may properly be said that as the Mediator Christ himself is the one who has been principally elected.' Boyd speaks of Christ the *Theandros* as 'the productive Head of all the Elect (*ut caput quoddam foetum omnibus electis*).'[78] He is the One elected, the Head of the Elected, and we are elected in and through him, the incarnate Son of God, and are his 'mystical Body'.[79] Those elected (*electi*) in Christ are those who are loved

---

[74] *Praelectiones*, cc. 11.1f; cf. 54.1 & 59.1.
[75] *Praelectiones*, cc. 54.1F, *et seq.*; cf. c. 18.2B.
[76] *Praelectiones*, cc. 16.2; 18.2; 69.1–2.
[77] *Praelectiones*, cc. 63–67.
[78] *Praelectiones*, c. 65.IA.
[79] See his massive excursus, *de aeterna Sanctorum Praedestinatione sive Electione, Methodica Tractatio, op. cit.* cc. 54–135.

(*dilecti*) by him and brought into union with him, for divine election and divine love are one and the same, and as such constitute the Church, the community of those who love one another with the love with which they are loved by Christ.[80] As with Knox (who is not mentioned) election and union with Christ (grounded on his personal or hypostatic union as the one medium of our union with God) constitute the spiritual structure and form of the Church as the living and organic Body of Christ.[81] Robert Boyd certainly held, in line with the Augustinian and Calvinist tradition, that only some people, not all, are elected, for Christ did not give himself over to death for all men in expiation of their sins, but only for the faithful. Yet for Boyd that is not to preclude the Church from publicly proclaiming the Gospel in which the grace of Christ is promiscuously offered to all (*promiscuè offertur omnibus*) irrespective of their race and condition.[82] However, while the vicarious sacrifice of Christ in suffering and dying for us (*pro nobis*), the Just for the unjust, was certainly of sufficiency (αὐτάρκεια – *sufficientia*) for all, Boyd thought it pointless to ask whether this is to be considered for all and every sinner (*pro omnibus & singulis peccatoribus*).[83]

It is particularly important to note that Boyd pointed behind the fact that Christ loved us and gave himself for us (*pro nobis*), delivering himself to God as an oblation and victim for our salvation, to the fact that God the Father loved us so much that 'He did not spare His own Son, but delivered him up for us all – how shall he not with him freely give us all things?' (Romans 8.32). He cited along with this John 3.16: 'God so loved the world that he gave his only begotten Son that whoever believes in him should not perish but have everlasting life.' This means that what is attributed to Christ as Mediator is to be attributed to the Father in the first place and is grounded in his eternal goodwill and mercy – the Father and the Son share one and the same will and the same love toward sinners. There is no distinction in love and grace between the Father and the Son although they take effect in time in the sacrifice of Christ as Mediator. But Boyd went on to emphasise that while the act of Christ in giving himself up for our sakes was common to the Father and the Son, it was first of all

---

[80] *Praelectiones*, cc. 648–9.
[81] *Praelectiones*, cc. 170.2; 538.1 & 2, *et seq.*
[82] *Praelectiones*, cc. 752.2E *et seq.*
[83] *Praelectiones*,. cc. 651.1A – 651.2A; cf also c. 75.1B–C.

(*omnium primo*) the act of the Father in delivering up his own Son. Our redemption is thus grounded in the decree of gratuitous mercy put into effect by Christ in his complete obedience to the Father.[84]

For the theologian, Boyd's *Praelectiones* are of special importance in the history of Scottish theology. In them he advanced an evangelical understanding of the Gospel, with a close relation between the Incarnation and redemption. As the incarnate Son of God, the one Mediator between God and man, who is himself both God and man, Christ gave himself freely in atoning sacrifice or 'ransom for all' (ἀντίλυτρον ὑπὲρ πάντων, 1 Tim. 2.6).[85] He saves all who believe in him through his obedient life and death on the Cross – here active and passive obedience were held together.[86] However, this did not imply for Boyd, what was called 'universal redemption', for it cannot be held that all men have been saved or will be saved.[87] Immense stress was laid on atoning mediation and redemption,[88] and on the sovereignty of grace in opposition to Arminianism.[89]

Throughout the *Praelectiones*, Boyd made relatively few references to Calvin and Athanasius, but his citations from Basil, Gregory Nazianzen, Cyril of Alexandria, Chrysostom, Ambrose, Augustine and Jerome abound. While he was essentially a biblical theologian whose thought was steeped in and shaped by the apostolic foundation of the Church and the Faith once delivered to the saints, his powerful dogmatic presentation of the doctrines of Christ and the Blessed Trinity was deeply indebted to Nicene and Chalcedonian Christology. This is perhaps where Boyd's theological importance for Scottish theology lies.

In some respects the highlight of Boyd's remarkable dogmatic *Praelectiones* is to be found in his *Christology* in which we are given a very precise and accurate account of the incarnate Person of Christ and his eternal Deity as it was given classical formulation by the Orthodox Fathers of the Church at the great Ecumenical Councils in refutation of Arian and Nestorian heresies.[90] Thus Boyd affirmed the Deity of Christ as 'coeternal and consubstantial with the Father

---

[84] *Praelectiones*, cc. 650.1A – 651.2A.
[85] *Praelectiones*, c. 752.2Ef.
[86] *Praelectiones*, cc. 796–797.
[87] *Praelectiones*, c. 752.2Ef.
[88] *Praelectiones*, See especially cc. 297–319 & 818.2 *et seq.*; cc. 1081 *et seq.*
[89] *Praelectiones*, cc. 213.1 – 227.2.
[90] See especially *Praelectio* CII, cc. 482–90.

(Patri συνίδιον & ὁμοούσιον)' in accordance with the Council of Nicaea, and affirmed the two natures Christ, God-man and Mediator, as 'united in one Person without confusion, without change, without division, and without separation (ἀσυγχύτως, ἀτρέπτως, ἀδιαιρέτως, ἀχωρίστως)', in accordance with the Council of Chalcedon.[91] What is particularly interesting is that Robert Boyd then went on to speak of how the *personalis unio* (the hypostatic union, ἕνωσις ὑποστατική, ἕνωσις καθ' ὑπόστασιν) in Christ is to be understood, in which he deployed the twin terms *anhypostatic* (ἀνυπόστατος) and *enhypostatic* (ἐνυπόστατος) to show how in the Incarnation of the Son or Logos there did *not* take place in Christ an assumption of a separately existing or independent human *hypostasis* or personal subsistence (which would have been adoptionist heresy); but that nevertheless, *in* the incarnate Logos or Son of God the human nature of Christ was given an *hypostasis* or real personal subsistence, so that his Person was not other than the Person of the divine Son. Thus while the human nature of Christ was ἀνυπόστατος in itself, it became ἐνυπόστατος *in* the pre-existent Son, and so the divine and human natures of Christ constituted in their union one indivisible subsistent Person.[92] This coupling of the expressions 'anhypostatic' and 'enhypostatic' to speak of the hypostatic union of the divine and human natures in Christ ultimately derives from the *Contra Theodoretum* of Cyril of Alexandria, but Boyd made no reference to him in regard to this. He was evidently following one of the Reformed scholastic dogmaticians at this point.[93] This is also evident in his use of St Basil's expression 'mode of being', ὁ τῆς ὑπάρξεως τρόπος, to speak of the distinctive personal mode of the Son's subsistence, but unlike Basil he spoke of him as begotten 'from the *substance* of the Father (*ex Patris substantia*)' in line with the Council of Nicaea.

In explaining how he understood the way in which the divine and human natures, and their different 'actions' or 'energies', are

---

[91] *Praelectiones*, c. 484.1F–2C.
[92] *Praelectiones*, cc. 486–7, especially 487.2B.
[93] He may have had before him the work of Amandus Polanus (whom he cited elsewhere), *Syntagma Theologiae Christianae*, Hanover, 1624, which became a textbook for theological students in Scotland. For the relevant teaching of these Reformed Dogmaticians see Heinrich Heppe, *Reformed Dogmatics* (tr. G. T. Thomson, Edinburgh, 1950), pp. 427ff. The *Christianae Theologiae Compendium* of Johannes Wollebius, published at Basel in 1626, was also used in Scotland. It was translated into English by Alexander Ross, 3rd edn, London, 1660.

to be understood within the personal union of Christ as *Theandros* or God-man, Boyd referred to the patristic doctrine of the communication of properties (ἰδιωμάτων ἀντίδοσις vel κοινωνία) between the divine and human natures of Christ.[94] It is in this way, he claimed, that one may interpret the statement that God has redeemed the Church 'with his own blood'. It is to be understood 'economically' (οἰκονομικῶς, *dispensatione*), as the Greek Fathers said, not in terms of any change or exchange in nature, for in their union with one another divine nature and human nature act mysteriously together without denial of their essential difference.[95] There is a communion or sharing of operations in the theandric union of divine and human natures in Christ the incarnate Mediator who, as God-Man, is God *and* Man. It is very admirable and astonishing that Robert Boyd had such a clear and detailed grasp of the great truths and dogmas of the Early Church, and employed them unerringly within his exposition of classical Patristic and Reformed theology.

Boyd did not give the same detailed attention to the doctrine of the Holy Trinity, when he commented on Ephesians 2.18: 'Through him we both have access by one Spirit to the Father'.[96] There he was concerned with expounding the threefold way in which we have access to the Father, and the threefold 'mode and order' of God's saving activity toward us.[97] Boyd then turned briefly to speak of the *opera* of the Trinity in the light of the fact that 'the fulness of the Godhead dwells in Christ bodily' (Col. 2.9). It was not the Father nor the Spirit, but the eternal Son of God who became man, the only begotten Word who became flesh, Jesus Christ. In him God himself has put on and is clothed with humanity, the humanity of the incarnate Son. It is then in that humanity of Christ, which through the hypostatic union subsists personally in him, that he imparts himself to us.[98]

Such is the great work and 'sublime mystery ' of the Trinity, to which nothing is comparable in heaven and earth (Eph. 3.20–21). Boyd referred here first to the purely internal works of the Holy

[94] Cf. Gulielmus Bucanus, *Institutiones Theologiae*, II.20, Geneva, 1609.
[95] *Praelectiones*, cc. 488–9; see also the reference to the *De fide orthodoxa* of John of Damascus at cc. 484.2C, and 629.2F.
[96] *Praelectiones*, cc. 309.2 *et seq.*
[97] *Praelectiones*, c. 313.2B & C.
[98] *Praelectiones*, c. 486.1A. The Latin here is rather involved and difficult to construe simply!

Trinity (*opera trinitatis merè interna*), which are what they are in their eternal movement within 'the Glorious and Sacrosanct Trinity' irrespective of any relation to creaturely realities. Then he turned to speak of the purely external works of the Trinity (*opera merè externa*) which are not restricted to any one Person of 'the Blessed Triad', whether of creation and providence or of redemption, with particular reference to the 'special work of economy' (*opus oeconomiae specialis*) in which divine wisdom has to do with the salvation of man.[99]

Robert Boyd did not offer detailed discussion of the doctrine of the Trinity, as he had of the doctrine of Christ. However, it is very clear from what he did write about it in the course of his Christology, particularly regarding the assumption of Christ's human nature into the Second Person of the Holy Trinity, his ascension into heaven and session as God-man (θεανθρωπός) at the right hand of the divine Majesty,[100] that he was concerned to uphold the teaching of 'the whole Orthodox Church' (*tota orthodoxa ecclesia*), in rejecting heresies regarding the divine and human natures of Christ and any cavilling against the doctrine of the mutual and coinherent relation, or ἐμπεριχώρησις, of the three Divine Persons with one another.[101] The perichoretic relation applies also to the operations of the whole Trinity, even when one Person, the Father, the Son, or the Holy Spirit, is immediately concerned, for each divine Person with his distinctive properties or characteristics is who he is as Person in relation to the other Persons.

In the midst of this discussion Boyd gave his reflections about the proper mode of personal subsistence in contrast to the mode of singular or individual being.[102] He referred to the fact that the subsistence proper to individual substance (*substantiae singulari*), and inseparable from it, is other than or different from 'personality' (*personalitatem*), i.e. the mode of subsistence proper to a person. Although an individual being subsists through itself in the mode

[99] *Praelectiones*, c. 486.1A–C.
[100] *Praelectiones*, cc. 488.1F *et seq.*
[101] *Praelectiones*, c. 486.2C: *ne quis de S. Sanctae Trinitatis personis, earumque mutua* ἐμπεριχώρησις, *cavilletur.* For an account of περιχώρησις or ἐμπεριχώρησις, which Boyd may have had before him, see Polanus, *Syntagma Theologiae Christianae*, III.8, Hanover, 1624.
[102] *Praelectiones*, cc. 486.2 – 487.1. What follows is a cut-down and somewhat telescoped version of Boyd's argument.

of substance (*per se subsistat ad modum substantiae*), yet it does not subsist through itself in the mode of person (*non tamen per se subsistit ad modum personae*). That is to say, persons are what they are as persons in relation to one another – the relations between persons belong to what persons really are. A person does not exist separately or apart from communion or fellowship with the other (*non separatim et extra alterius communionem consortiumque*). Moreover, as each person is who he is as a person in relation to the other, so he acts in mutual relation with the others, each from the other (*ab alio*). While Boyd had learned what 'personality' (the personal mode of being) actually is from reflecting on the way in which the human and divine natures of Christ are united in his one Person, and from reflecting on the way in which the three Divine Persons are perichoretically related to one another with their differentiating characteristics as Father, Son and Holy Spirit, he uses this reflex insight into what persons and inter-personal relations ontically are, to help him grasp more incisively the personal nature of the three divine Persons and their personal coinherence and communion with one another. Although Robert Boyd did not go on to develop his doctrine of the Holy Trinity further, it is nevertheless very evident in his understanding of the Holy Liturgy (*Leiturgia sacra*); but it was also evident in the Trinitarian doxologies with which he concluded each of his *Praelectiones*.[103]

Hugh Binning (1627–53)

Like Robert Boyd Hugh Binning too once held an appointment in the University of Glasgow and served the parish of Govan at the same time, before he died at the early age of twenty-six. He was essentially a biblical theologian, who objected to the analytical and logical way of presenting the teaching of the Holy Scriptures, but expounded them with an evangelistic intention in an open call to sinners to respond to the full invitation of Christ to come to him and believe his promise of salvation.[104] In an early memoir it was said:

---

[103] *Praelectiones*, c. 491.1A–B.
[104] *The Works of the Pious, Reverend and Learn'd Mr. Hugh Binning*, Edinburgh 1735; See also *The Works of The Rev. Hugh Binning*, With a Life of the Author, and Notes, by James Cochrane, Glasgow, 1839.

That he was among the first in Scotland, that began to reform Philosophy from the barbarous terms, and unintelligible Distinctions of the Schoolmen, and the many vain Disputes and trifling Subtilties, which rather perplexed the Minds of the Youth, than furnished them with solid and useful knowledge.

He had such a large stock of usefull Knowledge, as to be *philologus, philosophus, & theologus eximius,* and might have been an ornament in the most famous and flourishing University in Europe.

He was no stranger to the rules of Art, and knew well how to make his Method subservient to the Subject he handles.

But the main object of his pious and devout contemplations was God in Christ reconciling the world to himself: For God who commanded the Light to shine out of darkness, hath shined into his heart to give him the Light of the Knowledge of God, in the Face of Jesus Christ.[105]

Hugh Binning had no compunction about proclaiming the free grace of the Gospel, for the Lamb of God bears away the sins of the world, and is himself the propitiation for the sins of the world. 'The full invitation of the Gospel is nothing else but – Come unto me, and have rest.'[106] He spoke of 'the ground-work' of all a Christian's hope and consolation as

Jesus Christ himself, the eternal Son of God and Saviour of the world, one able to save to the uttermost, all that put their trust in him, so that every soul that finds itself, and not able to subsist, nor abide the judgment of God, may repose their confidence in him, and lay the weight of their eternal welfare upon his death and sufferings, with assurance to find rest and peace in him in their souls. He is such an one as faith may triumph in him over the world, and all things beside.

It is significant that in making such a statement, Binning did not add, as some of his hyper-Calvinist colleagues would have done, a

---

[105] 'The Life of Hugh Binning, sometime Minister of the Gospel at Govan', *Works*, pp. vii, ix, xxi & xxiii. See also the appreciation by Patrick Gillespie, reprinted in the 1839 edition of Binning's *Works*, Vol. I, pp. iii–v.
[106] Sermon on Matthew 11.28, *Works*, 1840 edn, Vol. III, p. 226.

rider to the effect that this applies only to the few people eternally elected to be saved.

Binning was very critical of Arminian and Antinomian ideas. He attacked what he called a 'mistake in the very nature of faith' that led to current perplexities and doubts about assurance, and thus stood very close to John Welch, and anticipated Robert Leighton.

> It is not so much the Inevidence of Marks, and Fruits, that makes them doubt, as the Misapprehension of the Thing itself; for as long as they mistake it in its own Nature, no Sign, no Mark can satisfie it. You take faith to be a Perswasion of God's Love, that calms and quiets the Mind. Now such a Perswasion needs no Sign to know it by, 'tis manifest by its own Presence as Light by its own Brightness.[107]

Binning called in question the habit, even by those who rejected Arminianism, of seeking supplementary evidence for faith in inward religious experience and the sanctified notions of the heart. It belonged to the very ground of faith that we are taken outside of ourselves and find our refuge in Christ who is able to save to the uttermost all who come to him.[108]

Binning adopted a mild form of the federal theology. He had problems about the use of the concept of 'covenant', for

> if we speak properly, there cannot be a covenant between God and man, – there is such an infinite distance between them such unequal parties, our obedience and performance being absolutely in his power ... Yet it pleased his Majesty to propound it in these terms, and to stoop so low unto man's capacities, and, as it were, come off the throne of his sovereignty, both to require such duties of men, and to promise unto them a free reward.[109]

Moreover in regard to the so-called covenant of works, 'do this and live', he declared 'there was some in-breakings of grace and free condescendency of God; for it was no less free grace and undeserved favour, to promise life to his obedience, than now to promise life to our faith.'[110] He hesitated to think of the covenant

[107] *Works*, p. 38.
[108] Sermon II on Romans 8.1, *Works*, pp. 165f.
[109] *Works*, p. 136.
[110] *Works*, p. 34.

of grace as a pact or a conditional contract between God and man, and regarded the role of 'covenant' in theology in a way that was closer to the teaching of John Calvin than of Robert Rollock.

Central to his theology was the doctrine of the incarnate Mediator who gave himself a sacrifice 'one for all' in propitiation not only for our sins but for the sins of the whole world, which Binning regarded as 'the marrow of the Gospel'.[111] While like Calvin Binning could sometimes use placatory language in a doctrine of atonement,[112] he nevertheless took care to emphasise that it is *God* in his love who freely brings about the redemption of sinners and provides the propitiation in and through which God himself draws near to them in his love.

> He finds to himself a ransom to satisfy his justice, Job. xxxiii.24. He finds a propitiation to take away sin, a sacrifice to pacify and appease his wrath. He finds one of our brethren, but yet his own Son in whom he is well pleased; and then holds out all this to sinners, that they may be satisfied in their own consciences, as he is in his own mind. God hath satisfied himself in Christ; you have not to do this. He is not now to be reconciled to us, for he has never really been at odds, though he covered his countenance with frowns and frets, since the fall, and hath appeared in fire, and thunders, and whirlwinds, which are terrible, yet his heart had always love in it to such persons; and therefore he is come near in Christ, and about reconciling us to himself.[113]

> Herein is the atonement and propitiation set forth ... Now it is not so much God reconcilable to sinners, as God in Christ reconciling sinners to himself, 2 Cor. v.21.[114]

> 'God is love; and in this was the love of God manifested, that God sent his only begotten Son into the world, and he that loveth is born of God, and knoweth God; but we love God,

---

[111] Sermon on 1 John 2.2; 'Here is the strength of Christ's plea, and ground of his advocation, "that *he is the propitiation*". The advocate is the priest, and the priest is the sacrifice; and such efficacy this sacrifice hath, that the propitiatory sacrifice may be called the very *Propitiation* and *Pacification* of sin. Here is the marrow of the gospel.' *Works*, p. 478.

[112] E.g. *Works*, pp. 478 & 481.

[113] *Works*, p. 35.

[114] *Works*, 1839–40 edn, Vol. III, p. 255.

because he loved us first, and if God so loved us, we ought
also to love one another,' 1 John iv. This is the very substance
of the gospel, a doctrine of God's love to man, and of man's
love due to God.[115]

Thus the affection of love in the followers of Christ, Hugh Binning
could say, is 'the reflex of the love of God'.[116] His essay on *Christian
Love* from which these citations come is a theological and spiritual
gem.

Like the Scottish Reformers he laid great stress on union and
communion with Christ as grounded in the hypostatic union of
divine and human natures in him, and also his reconciling
fellowship with us; and like Calvin he spoke of this as 'the blessed
exchange' which the incarnate Mediator effected between sinners
and himself.[117] Of particular importance was the account he gave
in his exposition of the eighth chapter of Romans, of the *bond of
union* which Christ forged between us when in his Incarnation he
took upon himself our sinful flesh, the flesh of sinners, and without
sinning himself condemned sin in the flesh, sanctifying himself
for us that we may be sanctified in him, and thus forged 'the
wonderful interchange' through which we are redeemed and made
partakers of the Holy Spirit.[118] Binning expounded this also in
relation to the teaching of St Paul in Galatians 2.20, 'I yet not I,
but Christ', in a way that was later to be echoed in the teaching of
James Fraser of Brae.

Along with Robert Boyd and John Forbes of Corse, Hugh
Binning was one of the few Scottish theologians to have given
attention to the doctrine of the Trinity. While it is upon Jesus Christ
the eternal Son of God and Saviour of the world that faith is
immediately focused, properly speaking, he declared,

> our salvation is not the business of Christ alone but the whole
> Godhead is interested in it deeply, so deeply, that you cannot
> say, who loves it most, or likes it most. The Father is the very
> fountain of it, his love is the spring of all – "God so loved the

---

[115] From *A Treatise of Christian Love*, first printed at Edinburgh in 1743, *Works*,
1839–40 edn, Vol. III, p. 409.

[116] *Ibid.* p. 411.

[117] *The Works of Hugh Binning*, 1735 edn, pp. 10f, 161, 267f, 296f, 301f, 323, 392ff.

[118] See especially the Sermons 10, on Romans 8.3: *Works*, pp. 215ff; 24, on Romans
8.9, pp. 209ff; 25 on Romans 8.9, pp. 296ff; 37 & 38 on Romans 8.14–15,
pp. 345ff, 348ff; and Sermon on 1 John 1.3, pp. 389ff.

world that he hath sent his Son". Christ hath not purchased that eternal love to us, but it is rather the gift of eternal love … Whoever thou be that wouldst flee to God for mercy, do it in confidence. The Father, the Son, and the Holy Ghost, are ready to welcome thee, all of one mind to shut out none, to cast out none. But to speak properly, it is but one love, one will, one council, and purpose in the Father, the Son, and Spirit, for these Three are One, and not only agree in One, they are One, and what one loves and purposes, all love and purpose.

Binning then cited the well-known passage from Gregory Nazianzen: 'I cannot think upon one, but by and by I am compassed about with the brightness of three, and I cannot distinguish three, but I am suddenly driven back unto one.'[119] This trinitarian perspective for our understanding of the Gospel is supremely important, for it means that the Incarnation and the atoning sacrifice of Christ are to be understood as flowing freely from the ultimate and unlimited Love of God the Father, which is precisely what was wanting in federal Calvinism and its contractual concepts of salvation and limited atonement purchased from the Father for the elect by the suffering Christ.

John Forbes of Corse (1593–1648)

John Forbes of Corse was one of the ablest and most learned theologians whom Scotland produced between the Reformation and the Disruption. He was ordained by a Scots Presbytery in Holland, appointed to the first Chair of Divinity in Aberdeen, and although a cousin and friend of Andrew Melville was deposed in 1641 for declining to accept the National Covenant of 1638. In his general theological position he was a mild Calvinist, and stood close to Bruce, Boyd and Binning, without adhering to federal theology. Like Boyd he was deeply committed to the trinitarian and Christological teaching of the Orthodox Fathers of the Ancient Catholic Church, and was an irenical theologian with deep sacramental and practical concern for the life and mission of the Kirk.

---

[119] *Works*, pp. 89f. See also pp. 81ff.

While John Forbes shared much of the teaching of continental
scholastic Calvinists he was different from them in two main
respects. (1) He did not offer a doctrine of salvation schematised
by double predestination. He was much closer to Calvin in his
understanding of the interrelation between the Incarnation and
the atonement. (2) Like Calvin he held that it is through union
with Christ that we are made partakers of all his saving and
sanctifying benefits. For Forbes the Church was not so much 'the
Church of the born again' with emphasis upon the evidence of
election in inward feelings of divine grace and regeneration. His
emphasis was much more on the Word of the Gospel and the
covenant-community of those who are in union and communion
with Christ and are made one Body with him through the Spirit.

His great work published at Amsterdam in 1645 was entitled
Instructiones Historico-Theologicae de Doctrina Christiana.[120]
Unfortunately he died before he could write the second part which
he had planned. But as it stands it is a work of monumental
importance in the history of theology, for in bringing together the
interpretation of the Scriptures, the teaching of the Orthodox
Fathers, and the Ecumenical Councils (Nicaea, Constantinople and
Chalcedon particularly), he laid the foundation for Christian
dogmatics, and initiated the pursuit of Reformed Patristics. This
was in continuation of the work of John Calvin, but, as he indicated
in his Prefaratory Epistle to the King, his 'historico-theology' was
indebted to the works of the great Greek Fathers, Athanasius,
Nazianzen, Cyril of Alexandria, and Chrysostom especially, while
in areas concerned with the doctrine of the Church in the West
he turned for help to Augustine.

In the *Libri* that follow exposition of the articles of faith is given
in accordance with the canonical teaching of the Apostles' Creed,
the Antiochene Symbol, the Nicene-Constantinopolitan Creed with
the Council's Encyclical Epistle, and the Athanasian Symbol. While
in some respects the *Instructiones Historico-Theologicae* may be said
to be a scholastic work, it was very different from the rationalistic
scholasticism of the medieval schoolmen or of Lutheran and
Calvinistic Protestantism. Throughout, Forbes was concerned with
soteriological and ontological, rather than logical, connections –

---

[120] Amsterdam, 1645. See also Arnoldi Montani, *Forbesius Contractus, sive
compendium instructionum historico-theologicarum*, Amsterdam, 1667. And his *Opera
Omnia*, 2 vols., Amsterdam, 1702–3.

a form of theological thinking which some of his contemporaries and his Calvinist successors in Scotland and Holland failed to appreciate. Moreover, he did not allow ecclesiastical affiliation or prejudice to push his thought into extremes.

After introductory sections in which he presented the gist of the teaching of several of 'the most ancient fathers', Ignatius, Justin, Athenagoras and Irenaeus, Forbes cited the Apostles' Creed, and the text of the four Symbols of the Faith, the *Antiochenum, Nicaenum, Constantinopolitanum,* and *Athanasianum,* and together with them, the Encyclical Epistle of the Council of Constantinople to Damasus, the *Expositio Fidei* of Athanasius, and excerpts from his *De decretis* and *De Synodis,* and *Contra Arianos.*[121] On this basis Forbes started right away as in the *Scots Confession* with the doctrine of the Holy Trinity, *Unus Deus Trinitas,* which is not added on to the doctrine of the One God but is given as its very substance and inner heart. This is a doctrine of 'Trinity in Unity and Unity in Trinity'.[122] Only then did he move on to Christology and soteriology.[123]

Forbes' account of the Trinity is drawn mostly from the works of Athanasius, Basil, Nazianzen, Epiphanius, and Hilary, with a section given to the *Filioque* clause.[124] Forbes supported this presentation both from the teaching of the New Testament, and from the liturgies of the Nicene and post-Nicene periods, with use of the ancient trinitarian canticles and doxologies. Forbes began with a citation from the *Expositio Fidei* of Athanasius (but attributed to Justin), and then quoted a sentence from Ephiphanius which characterised Forbes' whole approach: 'Trinity in Unity, One God, the Father, Son and Holy Spirit' (Τρὶας ἐν μονάδι, καὶ εἷς θεὸς, πατὴρ, υἱος, καὶ ἄγιον πνεῦμα), with reference to their consubstantial relations with one another.[125] Athanasius is then cited to explain the proper significance of the term consubstantial or ὁμοούσιος, as meaning from the very essence of God.[126] This is supported especially by lengthy citations in Greek from several of the Orations of Gregory Nazianzen.[127]

---

[121] *Instructiones,* I.IV. 1.

[122] *Instructiones,* I. 15–16; 1.17, 7; 18.6, 23; 33.2 & 15.

[123] *Instructiones,* II. 1–13.

[124] *Instructiones,* I.6.2–6.

[125] *Instructiones,* I.5, c. 14.1: Epiphanius, *Anchoratus,* 2 & 6.

[126] Athanasius, See *De decretis,* 19–22.

[127] *Instructiones,* I.5.4–5: Gregory Nazianzen, *Orations* 29, 39, 32, 35 & 24. References are also made to Ambrose, Basil and Hilary.

The Father is the Father, and is Unoriginate, for he is of no one; the Son is Son, and is not unoriginate, for he is of the Father. But if you take the word Origin in a temporal sense, he too is Unoriginate for he is the Maker of Time, and is not subject to Time. The Holy Spirit is truly Spirit, coming from the Father indeed, but not after the manner of the Son, for it is not by Generation but by Procession (since I must coin a word for the sake of clarity).[128]

It would not be right to speculate about these inner trinitarian relations of the Son and the Spirit to the Father, or to think of them in terms of sensible or corporeal images. However, as Nazianzen pointed out, whatever the Father has, apart from being Cause or Principle, the Son has, and whatever the Son has also belongs to the Spirit, apart from sonship.

It was on that basis that John Forbes offered an explanatory discussion of the procession of the Spirit from the Father and the Son.[129] Appeal was made to the teaching of Christ in the Gospel according to St John, especially with reference to John 15.26 and 16.13–15, and the teaching of St Augustine both in his work *On the Trinity* and his *Tractates on the Gospel of St. John.* He took into account the statement of Epiphanius that

the Spirit proceeds from the Father and receives from the Son. The Spirit is not alien to the Father and the Son, but is of the same Substance and the same Deity, eternally subsisting with the Father and the Son as the Holy Spirit, Divine Spirit, Spirit of Glory, Spirit of Christ, Spirit of the Father.[130]

In explaining the difference with the Greeks Forbes noted that in their view of the procession of the Spirit from the Father they took account of the fact that the Spirit is 'consubstantial and coequal with the Father and the Son'. John Forbes himself, then, in view of the implications of the Nicene *homoousion* for an understanding of the inner trinitarian relations and the coequality of the three divine Persons, adopted a mediating position between East and West. Then with reference to Philippians 3.15–17, he concluded:

---

[128] Gregory Nazianzen, *Oratio* 39.12.
[129] *Instructiones*, I.6.1–6.
[130] *Instructiones*, I.6.3, with reference to Epiphanius, *Contra Sabellianos*, 4.

'As far as it is possible let us cultivate peace, but without harming truth, and preserving charity.'[131]

The most distinctive character of Forbes' trinitarian theology was the place that he gave to *doxology*, for the Blessed Trinity (*Sanctissima Trinitas*) is more to be adored and worshipped, and invoked in prayer, than made the subject of doctrinal propositions. This doxological and indeed liturgical approach is very manifest in the theological attention he gave to the *Trisagion*[132] and the *Gloria Patri*.[133]

In *De Hymno Trisagio* Forbes recalled the words of Athanasius about

> the Cherubim and Seraphim who with veiled faces extol the glory and majesty of God, with untiring lips doing nothing else but glorifying the divine and ineffable nature with the Trisagion ... For the Triad praised, reverenced, and adored is one and indivisible and without degrees. It is united without confusion, just as the Monad is distinguished without division. In that they offer their praises three times, saying, 'Holy, Holy, Holy', they show that the three divine Hypostases are perfect, just as with one voice they say 'Lord', thereby declaring his One Being.[134]

Forbes recounted some of the disputes about the trinitarian interpretation of the *Trisagion*, about whether it referred to Christ alone or to the Three Persons of the Trinity but that was settled at the Council of Chalcedon and through it developed into the *Tersanctus* or Thrice-Holy Hymn taken up in the liturgies of Basil and Chrysostom:

> Holy God, Holy and Mighty, Holy and Immortal, have mercy on us (thrice). Glory to the Father, and to the Son, and to the Holy Ghost, Both now, and always, and unto the ages of the ages. Amen. Holy Immortal, have mercy upon us. Holy God, Holy and Mighty, Holy and Immortal, have mercy on us.

---

[131] *Et Quantum in nobis est, pacem colamus, illaesa tamen veritate, & salva charitate. Instructiones,* I.6.6, c.17.2.

[132] *Instructiones,* I.16. cc. 29.31.

[133] *Instructiones,* I.22, cc. 38–39.

[134] Athanasius, *In illud Omnia mihi tradita sunt a Patre, &c., Instructiones,* cc. 29–3–0 – cited from the Paris edition of the *Opera Athanasii,* 1627, pp. 154–5.

For the theological import of this Forbes referred particularly to
John of Damascus, and his citations from Gregory the Theologian
(Nazianzen).[135] The passage from John of Damascus reads:

> We hold the words 'Holy God' to refer to the Father, without
> limiting the title of divinity to him alone, but acknowledging
> also as God the Son and the Holy Spirit: and the words 'Holy
> and Mighty' we ascribe to the Son, without stripping the
> Father and the Holy Spirit of might; and the words 'Holy
> and Immortal' we attribute to the Holy Spirit, without
> depriving the Father and the Son of immorality. For indeed
> we apply all the divine names simply and unconditionally to
> each of the subsistences in imitation of the Apostle's words,
> Rom, xi.36. And we follow Gregory the Theologian, when
> he says, 'But as to us there is but one God, the Father, of
> whom are all things, and one Lord Jesus Christ, through
> whom are all things, and one Holy Spirit in whom are all
> things; for the words 'of whom' and 'through whom' and
> 'in whom' do not divide the natures, but they characterise
> the properties of one simple nature. And this becomes clear
> from the fact that they are once more gathered into one, if
> only one reads with care these words of the same Apostle,
> 'Of him and through him and in him are all things: to him
> be the glory for ever and ever'.

Forbes followed up this doxological discussion with a chapter
De hymno glorificationis,[136] in which he gave close attention to the
crucial importance of *Gloria Patri* for the doctrine of the Trinity in
the Post-Nicene Church: 'Glory to the Father, the Son and the Holy
Spirit.' Several versions of it were being used with different
prepositions 'with', 'through' and 'in' which implied differences
in the doctrine of the Trinity, not least over ambiguous recognition
of the Deity of the Son and of Holy Spirit, which Arianising
Churchmen exploited. This was theologically important, for the
Orthodox doctrine of the Trinity was at stake, and liturgically
important, for the doxological formulae appended in the Nicene
era to the singing of the Psalms.[137] Thus used the *Gloria Patri et*

---

[135] *Instructiones*, I.16.8–12 – John of Damascus, *De Fide Orthodoxa*, 10.3.10, and
Gregory Nazianzen, *Orationes*, 43.7 & 45.4.

[136] *Instructiones*, I.22.1–10.

[137] *Instructiones*, XX.II.7, c.1.

Filio et Spiritui Sancto gave definite trinitarian character to the Liturgy. The problem was dealt with at length by St Basil in AD 375, in his book *On the Holy Spirit*, to which Forbes referred right away, for Basil used more than one version, '*with* the Son *together with* the Holy Spirit' and '*through* the Son *in* the Holy Spirit'.[138] Basil explained that in the way he used the *Gloria Patri* equal and the same Glory was attributed to the Son and the Spirit with the Father – what was important, he said, was not the syllables and words, but the reality itself which they, intimated.[139] Full and unambiguous recognition was given to the Deity of the Son and of the Holy Spirit. With reference to Basil's book Forbes wrote: 'This hymn was diligently retained in the Church, for the custody of Nicene Doctrine against the Arians.' The doctrine of the Holy Trinity was settled at the Council of Constantinople. 'There is one Godhead, power and being of the Father and of the Son and of the Holy Spirit, equal in honour and dignity and coeternal in sovereignty in three most perfect Hypostases, that is in three perfect Persons.'[140] Following the Council, as Forbes learned from John of Damascus, the form used was: *Gloria Patri & Filio & Spiritui Sancto: Sicut erat in principio, & nunc, & semper, et in secula seculorum, Amen.*[141] It was eventually the Alexandrian form of the *Gloria Patri* which influenced the oblatory formulary of the old Roman Order: 'Through him and with him and in him is to thee God the Father Almighty, in the unity of the Spirit, all honour and glory.'

Forbes followed up this account with discussion of the place of prayer to the Father 'through' the Son and 'in' the Spirit within the 'one undivided adoration and invocation, and praise of the most Blessed Trinity'. Here once again he took his guidance from the great Orthodox Fathers like Athanasius, Nazianzen, Nyssen, Epiphanius, Cyril of Alexandria, and from the Council of Constantinople, as well as from the pre-Nicene Liturgy of St Mark, and the post-Nicene Liturgy of St Chrysostom.[142] But he also turned to the Latin Fathers, Prudentius, Fulgentius, and Augustine among others. He pointed out that in the celebration of the Eucharist,

---

[138] See my discussion of this in *Theology in Reconciliation*, London, 1975, pp. 189ff; and J. A. Jungmann, *The Early Liturgy To the Time of Gregory the Great*, Notre Dame, 1959, pp. 193f.

[139] Forbes' reference here, c. 38.1, is to the *De Spiritu Sancto*, ch. 25 & 27.

[140] Theodoret, *Ecclesiastical History*, 5.9.

[141] *Instructiones*, I.22.7, c. 39.1.

[142] *Instructiones*, I.23.1, *et seq.*, & I.24–32; cf. also I.18.1–11.

while 'our prayers are sometimes directed to Christ and sometimes to the Father, it is the holy and undivided Trinity who is addressed, for the adoration of one Person is the adoration of the three Persons.'[143]

It is evident from these lengthy chapters of his *Instructiones* that John Forbes' appreciation of the doctrine of the Holy Trinity and its central importance for all Christian theology was reached mainly through doxological worship, for it was in that way that his mind and heart were lifted up really to know and adore God as intrinsically triune in the communion of his eternal Being. It was thus that he understood the essential nature of the Gospel message of reconciliation through the mediation of Christ as reconciliation with the divine Trinity of which the Apostle speaks in 1 Tim. 25: 'There is one God and one mediator between God and man, the man Christ Jesus.'[144] And so in view of the Apostle's statement, 'God was in Christ reconciling the world to himself' (2 Cor. 5.19), Forbes devoted a special chapter to the question why it was fitting that the whole work of reconciliation through the Mediator should be attributed to the Father. Expressed the other way round this means that when we are told that God the Father saves and redeems us through Christ, there is implied the fact that the whole undivided Trinity was and is at work.[145] In the following section Forbes spoke about a useful rule regarding statements about the divine Trinity: when one of the three divine Persons is mentioned, the whole work of the Trinity is to be understood. God is intrinsically Trinity, for Trinity is the very essence of his very Being as God. It is as *Deus Trinitas*, that God acts, reveals and saves.[146] That became very evident to Forbes in his examination of the doxological canticles which we have just discussed.

It was in this light that John Forbes proceeded to write about *the Mystery of the Incarnation*. He began with a historical account of the errors refuted by various ecumenical councils, particularly Adoptionist, Arian, Sabellian, Eutychian, Apollinarian, Monothelite and Pelagian heresies, to which he added the Socinian heresy.

---

[143] *Instructiones*, I.23.32, c.44.1. The margin reads: *Unius personae invocatione invocatur Trinitas.* Later on in his *Instructiones*, in a brief chapter on 'the object of doxology and supplication', I.31.1–8, Forbes referred readers to the teaching of St Paul in 2 Corinthians 1.3; & Ephesians 1, 3.17 & 3.14.

[144] *Instructiones*, I.19.2.

[145] *Instructiones*, I.20.1–6.

[146] *Instructiones*, I.15.1–6; I.21.1–5.

Then, rather interestingly, he discussed Mohammedanism which he refuted by adapting anti-gnostic arguments in the early Church. In offering a summary expression of the 'Orthodox Antithesis', he cited one of the theological poems of Gregory Nazianzen, and then expounded the Letters of Cyril of Alexandria against Nestorius and his refutation of Theodoret. It was in the midst of these discussions that Forbes gave an account of the Incarnation of the Son in the humble form of a servant, as the reconciling movement in which Christ who, though he was rich, made himself poor for our sakes that we might be made rich in him. Thus it is in Christ, the incarnate and obedient Son of God, that we are justified. He appealed to patristic doctrine, taken not least from Cyril of Alexandria, about this way of thinking of justification and union with Christ together.[147] His emphasis was on the Person and work of the Mediator, at once priest and victim and temple, who is God and man in one Person, and who reconciles us to the Trinity – this was not the act of the Mediator alone for, although it was only the Son who became incarnate, the whole Trinity engaged in the work of reconciliation in distinctive ways appropriate to each Person.[148]

A noteworthy characteristic of Forbes' theological method is that it was only at this point in his *Instructiones* that he devoted specific doctrinal attention to 'The God and Father of our Lord Jesus Christ', and then proceeded to give formal expression to dogmatic statements about 'unity and distinction' in the One Triune God (*Unus Deus Trinitas*) and on that basis to offer some theses on the nature of God, and of the interrelations of the three divine Persons within the unity and simplicity of God. While he appeals again and again for help from the Fathers of the Church, he stresses that here before the transcendent mystery of the Triune God (*Deus Trinitas*) all that we may truly think and say derives from God's self-revelation alone.[149]

With regard to New Testament texts about the fact that Christ died for all, tasted death for every man, and gave himself a ransom for all, Forbes held that our understanding of this universality has to be qualified by the fact that the precious Blood of Christ cannot be thought of as having been shed in vain (*inane et vacuum*) – so that in the last resort Christ cannot be thought of as the Mediator and reconciler of 'infidels' but only of the faithful. Christ died

---

[147] *Instructiones*, VIII.23–24.
[148] Cf. again, *Instructiones*, I.19–20; VIII.23–24.
[149] *Instructiones*, I.29–35.

primarily for the elect, for those who believe in him, but there are other sheep who do not belong to his flock. The Blood of Christ effects the salvation of all people who believe in him.[150] In view of the immense price paid for redemption in the blood of Christ, redemption applies to the whole of the whole human race, but those who do not believe end up alienated from redemption. John Forbes does not, therefore, argue that the Gospel is not to be preached to the heathen. He was undoubtedly influenced particularly by the teaching of Augustine, but declined to press the issue at stake to its logical extreme in the idea that God had eternally predestinated some people to damnation.[151]

Of special note is Forbes' corporate view of election which he calls 'the *compredestination* of Christ and the elect in Christ'.[152] Compredestination means not only that God has elected and adopted us in Christ before the foundation of the world, but that he has elected Christ himself in whom he is well pleased, and elected us in Christ, predestinating us in love as those who are redeemed through the precious Blood of Christ as of a Lamb without blemish and spot. He has elected us not on the ground of any holiness or belief on our part, but in order that we may believe. Christ himself is the primary object of election and as such the ground of our election. He is predestinated in a bond (*in sponsum*) with his Church which is compredestinated in him as the Head of the body, as the Redeemer of those who are to be redeemed, the Saviour of those who are to be saved.[153] It is on that corporate union of the Church in Christ that Forbes goes on to offer extensive accounts of the sacraments as signs and seals of the saving grace of Christ given to the Church to preserve and deepen its union with Christ and the participation of its members in all his benefits in regeneration and sanctification. The sacraments are instituted not as seals of election but as seals of the covenant (in its biblical and not federal sense) through which we are linked to Christ in his election and his inclusive compredestination with us.

As with Calvin it is in the Reformed doctrine of the Eucharist that some of his more significant teaching about redemption and our participation in it is presented. In celebrating the mysteries,

---

[150] *Instructiones*, XI.13.7.
[151] See the discussion of this issue, *Instructiones*, VIII.15–16.
[152] *Instructiones*, VIII.30.1–4. He has here Ephesians 1.4–10, John 3.16, and 17.23 & 16, specially in mind.
[153] *Instructiones*, VIII.30.2.

he says, heed must be given to the warning *sursum corda*.[154] Like
Calvin, and also like Knox, he introduces the *epiclesis* from the
Alexandrian and Nicene Liturgical tradition,[155] and like them he
offers a realist doctrine of the real presence of Christ in the
Eucharist with help from Cyril of Alexandria. At the same time
Forbes gives a powerful refutation of the Roman Catholic teaching
about transubstantiation and propitiatory sacrifice in which he
adduces in support seven arguments from the Greek Fathers of
the ancient Catholic Church,[156] and then appeals to Pope Gelasius
(enthroned in 494), the author of books on the two natures of
Christ against Eutyches and Nestorius, which he adduces against
Bellarmine.[157] This was a powerful argument against transubstantiation from the doctrine of the hypostatic union of two natures
in Christ which remained unchanged and in the one Person of
Christ. As Christ's human nature was not changed in the hypostatic
union so the bread and wine remain unchanged under the impact
of the real presence of Christ. Forbes added to his refutation of
the Roman sacramental doctrine an account of the origin and
development of the error of transubstantiation, and of the three
evil fruits which resulted from it: adoration, mutilation of the
Eucharist, and the propitiatory sacrifice of the Mass, with reference
to Tridentine teaching.[158] The idea of there being any mediator
between us and Christ, such as a sacrificing priest in the Roman
Church, is in the nature of the case quite impossible.

Then after rejecting, again with patristic support, the Lutheran
notion of the corporal presence and ubiquity of the Body of Christ,
Forbes provides a 'compendium' of Calvin's doctrine of the
sacrament of the Eucharist.[159] Through our participation in the
Eucharist we are given to partake of the very substance of Christ
in such a way that we coalesce in one Body with him. While this is
brought about by the Spirit there takes place a real and substantial
communication of the Body and Blood of the Lord. Christ himself
descends to us by the external symbol and lifts us up to himself by

---

[154] *Instructiones*, XI.8.19.

[155] *Instructiones*, XI.10.6.

[156] *Instructiones*, XI.9–15.

[157] *Instructiones*, XI.15.14 & 16.1f.

[158] *Instructiones*, XI.19.1ff.

[159] *Instructiones*, XI.22.1–21. This is significantly omitted by W. L. Low in his account
of John Forbes' doctrine of the Eucharist, *The True Catholic Doctrine of the Holy
Eucharist*, Edinburgh, 1923.

his Spirit (hence *sursum corda*) in such a way that he truly vivifies us by his Flesh and Blood. Through the secret conjunction with Christ effected by the agency of the Spirit we do not simply receive the fruit or effect which believers derive from eating the Flesh of Christ, but *Christ himself* who is the matter of the Supper. By partaking of the whole Christ in this way through whose sacrifice and death our sins are expiated, we are cleansed by his Blood, and are raised by his resurrection to the hope of eternal life. Forbes held that the flesh of Christ in the mystery of the Supper is no less a spiritual matter than eternal salvation. Whence he concludes that all who are devoid of the Spirit of Christ can no more eat the flesh of Christ than drink wine without taste.

John Forbes fully endorsed the objectivity and realism of John Calvin's eucharistic doctrine: feeding upon the very substance of Christ in which through a wondrous conjunction of the Spirit believers are made one Body with him. This accorded with Forbes's stress throughout the *Instructiones* upon real rather than upon formal or canonical relations, upon ontological rather than logical or forensic relations, in his understanding of Christ and his saving and justifying work and of the nature of Christian devotion and worship. It was on these grounds that he upheld the universality and unity of the Apostolic and Catholic Church as grounded in and united to Christ. *Totus Christus caput et corpus est*, he cited from Augustine.[160] He had an abhorrence of heretical and schismatic movements, and refused to sign the National Covenant[161] which he felt fostered divisions not only between people in Britain but between the Reformed Church of Scotland and Reformation Churches on the Continent. It was in this spirit that he published his famous *Irenicum* in 1629 in which he supported the Five Articles of Perth, 1618, about kneeling at the celebration of the Eucharist, private celebrations of Communion and Baptism, etc. In it Forbes sought to bridge differences between presbyterian and episcopal practices.[162] Along with his biblically and patristically grounded 'historico-theology', this must be reckoned an anticipation of the ecumenical spirit of modern times.

---

[160] *Instructiones*, XIV.6.21.

[161] See his *Peaceable Warning, to the Subjects in Scotland*, Aberdeen, 1638.

[162] See also E. G. Selwyn, *The First Book of the IRENICUM of John Forbes of Corse*, Cambridge, 1923. See also Forbes' 'Spiritual Exercises', *Vitae Interioris sive Exercitiorum Spiritualium Commentaria*, *Opera Omnia*, Vol. 1, Amsterdam, 1702, pp. 92–165.

Bibliography

Binning, Hugh, *The Works of the Pious, Reverend and Learn'd Mr. Hugh Binning*, Edinburgh, 1735; and the edition by James Cochrane, 3 vols., Glasgow, 1839.

Bonar, Horatius, *Catechisms of the Scottish Reformation*, London, 1866.

Boyd, Robert, *In Epistolam Pauli Apostoli Ad Ephesios Praelectiones*, Geneva, 1661.

Bruce, Robert, *The Mystery of the Lord's Supper*, 1589, & ed. T. F. Torrance, London, 1958.

Bruce, Robert, *The Way to True Peace and Rest*, delivered in Edinburgh in 16 sermons on the Lord's Supper, Hezekiah's Sickness and other select scriptures, London, 1617.

Calvin, John, *Concerning the Eternal Predestination of God*, tr. J. K. S. Reid, London, 1961.

Cameron, John, *Ioannis Cameronis Opera*, Geneva, 1628 & 1642.

Edward, Robert, *The Doxology Approven*, Edinburgh, 1683 & 1731.

Ferme, Charles, *A Logical Analysis of the Epistle of Paul to the Romans*, Edinburgh, Latin edn 1651, Wodrow edn 1850.

Forbes, John, of Corse, *The First Book of the Irenicum of John Forbes of Corse*, tr. E. G. Selwyn, Cambridge, 1923.

Forbes, John, of Corse, *Instructiones Historico-Theologicae de Doctrina Christiana*, Amsterdam, 1645.

Forbes, John, of Corse, *Opera Omnia*, 2 vols., Amsterdam, 1702–3.

Forbes, John, of Corse, *Peaceable Warning, to the Subjects in Scotland*, Aberdeen, 1638.

Gillespie, Patrick, *The Ark of the Covenant Opened: Or, A Treatise of the Covenant of Redemption between God and Christ, as the Foundation of the Covenant of Grace*, London, 1677.

Heppe, Heinrich, *Reformed Dogmatics*, tr. G. T. Thomson, Edinburgh, 1950.

Macmillan, D., *The Aberdeen Doctors*, London, 1909.

Mitchell, A. F., *Catechisms of the Second Reformation*, London, 1886.

Patrick, Millar, *Four Centuries of Scottish Psalmody*, London, 1949.

Patrick, Millar, *The Scottish Collects From the Scottish Metrical Psalter of 1595*, Edinburgh.

Perkins, William, *The Golden Chaine*, London, 1592.

Polanus, Amandus, *Syntagma Theologiae Christianae*, Hanover, 1624.

The Psalmes of David in Metre According as they are sung in the Kirk of Scotland, Together, with the Conclusion, or Gloria Patri, eftir the Psalme: and alsua ane Prayer eftir everie Psalme, agreing with the meaning thairof, Edinburgh, 1595.

Reid, H. M. B., *The Divinity Principals of the University of Glasgow,* 1545–1654, Glasgow, 1917.

Reid, H. M. B., *The Divinity Professors of the University of Glasgow,* 1640–1903, Glasgow, 1923.

Rollock, Robert, *Certaine Sermons Upon Several Places of the Epistles of Paul,* Edinburgh, 1599.

Rollock, Robert, *In Epistolam S. Pauli ad Romanos,* Geneva, 1595.

Rollock, Robert, *Analysis Logica in Epistolam Pauli Apostoli ad Galatas, In Epistolam S. Pauli ad Ephesios,* Geneva, 1593 & 1596.

Rollock, Robert, *In Epistolam Sancti Pauli Apostoli ad Colossenses Commentarius,* Geneva, 1592.

Rollock, Robert, *In Epistolam Pauli Apostoli I & II ad Thessalonicenses, & Analysis Logica Epistolae Pauli Apostoli Ad Philemonem,* Geneva, 1598.

Rollock, Robert, *Analysis Logica in Epistolam ad Hebraeos,* Geneva, 1605.

Rollock, Robert, *De Vocatione, A Treatise of God's Effectual Calling, Works,* Wodrow Society, Edinburgh, 1849.

Rollock, Robert, *Select Works,* ed. W. M. Gunn, Wodrow edn Edinburgh, 1844–9.

Snow, W. G. Sinclair, *The Times, Life, and Thought of Patrick Forbes, Bishop of Aberdeen* 1618–35, London, 1952.

Torrance, I. R., *Christology After Chalcedon, Severus of Antioch & Sergius the Monophysite,* Norwich, 1988.

Torrance, J. B., 'Covenant or Contract? A Study of the Theological Background of Worship in Seventeenth-Century Scotland', *Scottish Journal of Theology,* 23.1, Edinburgh, 1970, pp. 51–76.

Torrance, J. B., 'The Concept of Federal Theology – Was Calvin a Federal Theologian?' *Calvinus Sacrae Scripturae Professor,* ed. W. H. Neuser, Grand Rapids, 1994, pp. 15–40.

Torrance, T. F., *The School of Faith,* London, 1959.

Weir, David A., *The Origins of Federal Theology in 16th-Century Reformation Thought,* Oxford, 1990.

Welch, John, *Forty-Eight Select Sermons,* Edinburgh, 1744, & Glasgow, no date.

3

The High Calvinists

Samuel Rutherford (1600–61)

Samuel Rutherford was undoubtedly one of the great and most influential theologians in the Calvinist and Presbyterian tradition of the post-Reformation Kirk. His knowledge of historic classical, patristic and medieval theology, Reformed and Lutheran scholastic theology, and not least contemporary theology in England and Scotland, was astonishing. In his interpretation of the Holy Scriptures he made considerable use of Hebrew, Syriac and Greek, as well as Latin. The general character of his thought was a logicalised form of Calvinism in which he quarried from an arsenal of medieval and post-medieval argumentation, and which he used to great effect in his debates particularly with Arminians and Antinomians. He was thoroughly orthodox in Nicene and Chalcedonian Christology (referring frequently, for example, to Christ as 'the consubstantial Sonne' of the Father, and also to 'the union personall' (or hypostatic union between Christ the man and God),[1] although he was clearly more indebted to the great post-Reformation Reformed and Lutheran theologians for his knowledge of patristic theology than to the Greek Fathers themselves. All his thinking was cast within a framework of strict federal and predestinationist principles, which meant that his formulation and presentation of doctrine was governed throughout by rigid forensic and logically necessary relations, and was characterised by a concentration on individual election and particular redemption. In characteristic Scottish fashion this was combined with a strong emphasis upon union and communion with Christ influenced by Calvin, and an overwhelming sense of

---

[1] *Christ Dying and Drawing Sinners to Himselfe. Or A Survey of our Saviour in his soule suffering, his lovelyness in his death, and the efficacie thereof.* London, 1647, pp. 74 & 133.

the majesty and mercy of God the Father, whose love is poured out freely and lavishly upon the Church through Jesus Christ.

At the same time his writing and preaching manifested a passionate devotion to Christ crucified and his 'matchless grace',[2] and a spiritual inwardness emotionally expressed in language indebted to the Song of Solomon and to St Bernard.[3] This was his way of expressing the intensity of what he called 'evangelical conviction' as opposed to 'legal conviction'.[4] While he was committed to the logical development of federal theology as it had come from Robert Rollock, he also thought of it in a more 'evangelic' way concerned with 'the Covenant of Life', in which law and Gospel from the very beginning were regarded as complementary, not contrary, to one another.[5] This meant that Rutherford's doctrine of God was ultimately of a merciful and gracious God, rather different from that of the harsh 'Law-Giver' of the doctrinaire federalists – for him the covenant, of works as of grace, flowed from the prevenient love of God revealed in Christ who as God and man is himself the covenant.[6] The covenant is God's love to man, the fruit and effect of his love, 'a sure and eternal covenant, bottomed upon infinite love', in which Christ is the Mediator and Surety who is not to be thought of as 'a loose nail in the covenant'.[7] Nor is Christ to be thought of as more merciful than the Father, for he and the Father are one ... 'Infinite love and infinite majesty concur both in Christ.'[8] Rutherford clearly had a thoroughly Christ-centred doctrine of God, which modified the federal conception of God as Law-Giver and Judge. In his doctrine of God mercy and judgment, grace and law coincided, which led him to object strongly to any antinomian understanding of the Gospel – there is a proper place within the covenant of grace

---

[2] See above all *Christ Dying and Drawing Sinners to Himselfe.*
[3] See particularly *Letters of Samuel Rutherford,* two vols. ed. A. A. Bonar, 1863. John Buchan referred to this rather aptly as 'the oriental lusciousness of Samuel Rutherford' – *Montrose,* Edinburgh, 1928, p. 62.
[4] *The Covenant of Life Opened: Or, A Treatise of the Covenant of Grace,* Edinburgh, 1655, p. 70.
[5] *The Covenant of Life,* pp. 3f, 7f. Cf. his account of law and Gospel in the teaching of Luther, *A Survey of the Spiritual Antichrist. Opening the Secrets of Familisme and Antinomianisme,* London, 1648, and his 'Survey of Antinomianism', *ibid.* Part 2, pp. 7ff.
[6] *The Tryal and Triumph of Faith,* London, 1645, pp. 46f.
[7] *The Tryal and Triumph,* pp. 63 & 64.
[8] *The Tryal and Triumph,* pp. 68f.

for obedience to God's law and for evangelical works.[9] Properly
understood Law and Gospel belong together. There is a 'Gospel-
obedience' which flows from grace. 'A believing faith must be a
working faith.'[10]

Due to the theological conflicts that arose in England and
Scotland in which Rutherford took a keen part before and after
the Westminster Assembly, it was the *doctrine of atonement* that was
thrust into the centre, to which we must give primary attention,
for it was particularly relevant to the development of Scottish
theology, and also to his own pastoral concern and practical
approach. He did not devote a monograph to the atonement, so
that his many statements about it have to be sifted out from books
that were concerned with clearing away damaging errors, detached
from their immediate context in the argument and connected
coherently together. Two of these works are especially revealing:
*Christ Dying and Drawing Sinners to Himselfe. Or A Survey of our Saviour
in his soule-suffering, his loveliness in his death, and the efficacie thereof,*[11]
and *The Covenant of Life Opened: Or, A Treatise of the Covenant of
Grace.*[12] To these may be added *A Survey of the Spiritual Antichrist.
Opening the Secrets of Familisme and antinomianisme...*[13]

Rutherford's doctrine of the atonement was of course ultimately
rooted in the teaching of John Calvin about Christ as the Mediator,
in which he was especially indebted to the stress of Irenaeus,
Athanasius, Hilary, and Cyril of Alexandria on the interrelation
between the Incarnation and the redemptive work of Christ.[14] In
his doctrine of the Mediator, however, which he allied closely to
the priestly office of Christ, Calvin operated with a more Western
conception of atoning satisfaction, but with greater stress upon
the whole course of Christ's vicarious obedience, as satisfying divine
judgment and paying the penalty for the sin and guilt of mankind.
There were two sides to Calvin's teaching: one in which he stressed
the idea that by his atoning sacrifice Christ appeased the Father
on our behalf,[15] and one in which he insisted that in his love God

---

[9] *The Covenant of Life*, Ch. XIX, pp. 153ff.
[10] *The Covenant of Life*, p. 159.
[11] London, 1647.
[12] Edinburgh, 1655.
[13] London, 1648.
[14] See Calvin's *Institute*, especially chapters 12, 15 & 16, and his *Commentary on the
     Epistle to the Hebrews*.
[15] *Institute*, 2.12.1–4.

the Father goes before and anticipates our reconciliation in Christ, thus rejecting the idea that it is only after we were reconciled to him through the blood of Christ that God began to love us.[16] It is significant that Rutherford did not offer a doctrine of the atonement as appeasing the wrath of God, but did hold that Christ's Incarnation and dying were not 'the cause of that love and free-grace of God which moved God to send his Son in the flesh but posterior unto, and later than that love: for because he loved us he sent his Son in the flesh to die for us.'[17] He refutes 'strange divinity' about 'reconciling God to man instead of a reconciling of man to God.'[18] He made the same point in one of his famous *Communion Sermons:*

> If God should begin at any point in time to love sinners, His love would have had a beginning, Christ himself would have had a beginning, because love with him is one with his essence and nature ... and therefore we are said in Scripture 'to be reconciled to God', and not God to be reconciled unto us. His love is everlasting.[19]

Of Christ himself, he said in another sermon, 'Christ loves you better than His life, for He gave His life to get your love.'[20] He could have spoken similarly of God the Father who, in refusing to spare his only Begotten Son (to which Rutherford referred again and again), revealed that he loves us more than he loves himself!

Unlike Calvin, however, as we have noted, Rutherford's theology was set firmly within the structure of the federal system with its distinction between a covenant of works and a covenant of grace, which was grafted on to Calvin's teaching along with the rationalism that came with Theodore Beza and was given approval by the Synod of Dort with its promulgation of the absolute decrees of predestination and reprobation, and of limited atonement. With the scholastic brand of Calvinism that arose in this way the Anselmic concept of satisfaction for the infinite gravity of sin was allied to a doctrine of divine punishment conceived in terms of contractual and governmental law, and synodal authority was given to this concept of atonement in the strict terms of penal substitution.

---

[16] *Institute*, 2.16.3–5.
[17] *The Covenant of Life*, p. 231.
[18] *Christ Dying*, pp. 378f.
[19] *Fourteen Communion Sermons*, ed. A. A. Bonar, 2nd edn Glasgow, 1877, p. 236.
[20] *Fourteen Communion Sermons*, XII, p. 285.

Within that tradition Rutherford's conception of the evangelical nature of what he called 'The Covenant of Life', that is, of works as well as of grace, was put forward in a necessitarian way. The atoning death of Christ and the extent of divine redemption were thought out at every point in accordance with two far-reaching premises concerned a) with what God had originally intended, and b) with what was effectually and finally accomplished. That is to say his teaching about atonement was governed by the eternal decrees of election and reprobation on the one hand, and by the fact that many people have actually been damned on the other hand.[21] Yet Rutherford's 'restrictive' view of redemption was expressed with emphatic teaching about the everlasting covenant love of God who so loved us that he 'sparred not his Sonne, but gave him to the death for us all'.[22]

He spoke of the atoning blood of Christ as a ransom (λύτρον, ἀντιλύτρον), in which Christ gave himself for us, in our place, or in our room.[23] It was a ransom, he declared, of infinite worth, citing from Anselm, 'as a redeemed one I owe my self and more than my self to thee, because thou gavest thy self who art so farre more than my self, for me, and then promised thy self to me.'[24] It is noteworthy that Rutherford, like Calvin, did not think of this ransom as restricted to Christ's death, for we are saved by his life as well as by his death,[25] and through his intercession at the right hand of God – Christ's praying for us like his vicarious obedience was an essential ingredient in his atoning and redeeming activity.[26] He who offered himself without spot to God, ever lives to make intercession for us. That does not mean that in heaven Christ acts as a sacrificing priest, to expiate our sins and satisfy for them, for he has already done that on the Cross once for all. Nevertheless he continues to be a Mediator for sinners, and pleads as High Priest and Advocate for those who believe in him.[27]

> True he is a Mediator and intercessor now, *applicatione, non expiatione,* by applying his blood, but not by shedding of it:

[21] Thus, for example, *Christ Dying*, pp. 382, 409f, 416.
[22] *Christ Dying*, pp. 17 & 72f; *The Covenant of Life*, pp. 231 & 309.
[23] *The Covenant of Life*, pp. 228, 239, 254, 350.
[24] *The Covenant of Life*, p. 23 : Anselm, *Monologion*, 40, *Opera Omnia*, Vol. I,. p. 40. See again *Christ Dying*, pp. 125f, 128, etc.
[25] *Christ Dying*, pp. 419, 435; cf. Calvin, *Inst.* 2.16.5.
[26] *The Covenant of Life*, pp. 226ff, 331, 348; cf. also pp. 196–200 & 349ff; *Christ Dying*, pp. 399f, 418, 436.
[27] See *Christ Dying*, pp. 379ff.

And he is an *Advocate*, but called δικαίος, Jesus the
Righteous, and an Advocate as just and righteous, supposeth
a right and just cause, that sufficient satisfaction and
payment is given to God for the sins of these for whom *Christ*
intercedes.[28]

The Lord Christ appears for us now in heaven in that body
and nature in which he once suffered before God, for the
acquiescing of Justice for ever in the once payed ransome.

And it is as such that he remains for ever the substantial and natural
Head of all for whom redemption has been purchased.[29]

In a profound sense the whole Trinity, the Father and the Spirit,
as well as the Son, participated in the work of redemption, for it
was in fulfilment of the special agreement between them within
the Covenant; nevertheless the satisfaction which Christ made was
properly and voluntarily his own.

The Lord the Creditor, and Christ, the Cautioner did strike
hands together. Christ put himselfe in our room, as an
hostage, pledge and surety to dye for us, and paid the first
and second death, the sum that we were owing, according
to a paction between the Lord and Christ, and we requested
not Christ to be surety, only by beleeving, we thank him, and
subscribe an Amen to what he has done.[30]

The Son was incarnate. The Son offered himself his own life,
his own blood to God for our sinnes. Neither the *Father* nor
the *Spirit* at all is *God* incarnate, neither the *Father* nor *Spirit*
offered his own life, his own blood to God.[31]

However, since the ransom paid by the Son in our place, was paid
by him as God as well as Man, as 'the Mediator God-Man', it was of
infinite value.[32]

Rutherford thought of this ransom paid by Christ for us in a
penal way as the *punishment* due to sinners under divine Law,
inflicted by God on him, not as a single man, but by

---

[28] *The Covenant of Life*, pp. 365f.
[29] *The Covenant of Life*, p. 366.
[30] *The Covenant of Life*, p. 248.
[31] *The Covenant of Life*, p. 196.
[32] *The Covenant of Life*, pp. 228, 239, etc.

a special paction if he shall lay down his life, and work his work, and suffer for our sins that which we should have suffered he shall receive his wages and see his seed.[33]

He punished Christ, who was not inherently, but only by imputation the sinner, with no hatred at all, but with anger and desire of shewing and exercising revenging justice, but still loving him dearly as his only Son. But on this account Christ must stand in our room.[34]

The Lord punished Christ for us to declare the glory of his justice in punishing sin in his own Son, who was the sinner by imputation...[35]

Since sin against God is infinite in its gravity, the price of ransom required to be infinite,[36] but that meant that the punishment inflicted upon Christ had to be and was infinite – 'he gave himself an infinite ransome' and 'endured infinite wrath for us.'[37] Thus 'by his death he not only exhausted the infinite punishment due to us ... but purchased to us an infinite and eternal weight of glory, by the worth of his merit.'[38]

However, Rutherford pointed out, there was much more to Christ's death than we can easily conceive. That applies to the kind of satisfaction he paid through his physical death, 'Law-debted satisfaction', which he found somewhat deficient.[39] Atoning satisfaction for sin was much profounder than the satisfaction of justice – it was what took place in the inner Person of Christ, the spiritual 'soule-suffering', which was the underlying theme of his book *Christ Dying and Drawing Sinners to Himselfe*. It is here that Rutherford made his really important contribution to the doctrine of atonement, in his understanding of

Christ's greatest Soule-trouble as a Sonne (for that he was essentially), was in that his holy soule was saddened and made *heavie even unto death*, for sinne, as sinne, and as contrary to

---

[33] *The Covenant of Life*, p. 253.
[34] *The Covenant of Life*, p. 251; cf. pp. 20ff.
[35] *The Covenant of Life*, p. 32.
[36] This was Anselm's principle that satisfaction ought to be proportionate to guilt, *Cur Deus Homo*, 1.20, *Opera Omnia*, Vol. II, p. 88.
[37] *Christ Dying*, pp. 127 & 136.
[38] *Christ Dying*, pp. 126f.
[39] *The Covenant of Life*, p. 235.

his Father's love. The Elect sinned against the *Lord*, not looking to him as either *Lord*, or *Father*: but *Christ* payed full deare for sinne; eying *God as Lord, as Father*. Wee looke neither to *Lord*, to *Law*, nor to *Love*, when we sinne; *Christ* looked to all three, when he satisfied for sinne. *Christ* did more than pay our debts.[40]

What Rutherford had in mind here was a conception of atonement which satisfied the Father and his love, a satisfaction that had to do with sin as sin against the Love of God, and not just as an infringement of divine law, and it was a form of satisfaction which he offered from out of the depths of his own soul in union with his Godhead.

Later Rutherford went on to explain how he understood this vicarious soul-suffering of Christ in a passage in which he discussed the active and passive obedience of Christ, and spoke of Christ in his union with us in these words: '*Christ repententh for us, and obeyeth for us, he being the end of the Law to everyone that believeth ... Christ* doth all for us, *Christ* weeped for my sinnes, and that is all the repentance required in me,'...[41] This vicarious repentance in the profound sorrow and soul-suffering of Christ which is echoed in us by the Spirit calls for a corresponding response of *Amen* in sorrow and repentance on our part. That 'Amen' on our part is grounded in an 'Amen' of the crucified Christ, of which he does not repent.

All the Saints are in *Christs* debt, of infinite love. When we *grieve the Spirit* purchased by Christ, we draw blood of his wounds afresh, and so testifie, that wee repent that *Christ* suffered so much for us. The *Father hath sworn, and will not repent, that he is an eternal Priest*, and stands to it, that his bloud is of eternal worth; and when the Father sweareth this, *Christ* is the same one *God* with him, and sweares, that he thinketh all his bloud well bestowed, and will never give over the bargaine, *his Bride* is his *Bride*, though deare bought, and his intercession in heaven speaketh his hearty *Amen*, and fullest consent of love to our Redemption.[42]

It must be noted, however, that the atoning soul-suffering of Christ and the satisfaction it renders to the Father's Love avail only

---

[40] *Christ Dying*, p. 21; cf. p. 43.
[41] *Christ Dying*, p. 79; cf. pp. 136f, 244f.
[42] *Christ Dying*, p. 137.

for the elect, in spite of its infinite nature. This is where the two major premises in Rutherford's theological system, noted above, impose definite limitation on the range of the sufficiency of Christ's atoning satisfaction. God decreed both the end and the means of salvation – he did not intend to save all people, and did not make effectual grace universally available, so that finally only a limited number of people will actually be redeemed, enough, as Anselm had argued, to make up for the fallen angels.[43] This was the teaching Rutherford persistently advocated against Arminians and Semi-Arminians who in different ways sought to take seriously the fact that in his death Christ came to draw *all* men unto him.[44] He insisted relentlessly that the intrinsical sufficiency of Christ's atoning satisfaction availed only for the elect; there was no 'universal grace' for the heathen.[45] 'The heathen have no right to God as their God and Father.'[46] 'Christ did not die for Pagans.'[47] Even when Rutherford spoke of the covenant generally as a 'simple way of saving sinners', he remarked that while considered formally, or *in abstracto*, it applies to all within the visible Church, but considered *in concreto*, 'the Lord carries on the covenant in such and such a way commensurably with the decrees of Election and Reprobation.'[48] This meant in restrictive practical terms, for example, that infants 'being without the Covenant ... cannot be chosen and predestinate in Christ to salvation.'[49]

It was in this way that Rutherford sought to explain the limitation of atonement to his congregation at Anwoth.

> Christ offers in the Gospel life to all, so that they believe, but God mindeth to bestow life on a few only ... There is no greater mystery, than this, 'Many are called, but few are chosen.' So Christ's sending with his commission, cometh under a twofold notion: one is, in the intention of the Evangel; the other is, in the intention of him who proposeth the Evangel to men – I mean, God's intention to give faith and effectual grace. The former is nothing but God's moral

[43] Anselm, *Cur Deus Homo*, 1.16f, *Opera Omnia*, Vol. II, pp. 74f.
[44] *Christ Dying*, Part III, pp. 364ff.
[45] *Ibid.* pp. 11ff.
[46] *Christ Dying*, p. 122.
[47] *The Covenant of Life*, p. 228.
[48] *The Covenant of Life*, p. 94. In line with this Rutherford drew a distinction between 'external covenanting' and 'internal covenanting.' *Ibid.* pp. 118ff.
[49] *The Covenant of Life*, p. 96.

complacency of grace, revealing an obligation that all are to
believe if they would be saved; and upon their own peril be
it, if they refuse Christ.[50]

In another sermon Rutherford argued in a similar way.

It is true, the Gospel excepteth no man from pardon, and
all that hear the gospel are to be wearied and laden, and to
receive Christ by faith, as if God intended to save them. But
the promises of the gospel are not simply universal, as if God
intended and purposed that all and every one should be
actually redeemed and saved in Christ, as Arminians teach;
and so God excepteth in his own hidden decree, not a few,
though he reveal not in the gospel who they are, yet he
revealeth in the gospel the general, that 'many are called,
but few are chosen.' I grant that there is no ground for any
one man not to believe upon this ground, because some are
reprobated from eternity, and it may be that I am one of
those, for the contrary is a sure logic; many are chosen to
life eternal and it may be that I am one of those. It is most
untrue that Christ belongeth to sinners as sinners, for then
Christ should belong to all unbelievers, how obstinate soever,
even to those who sin against the Holy Ghost. Nay, Christ
belongeth only to sinners elected to glory, as elected to glory
in regard of God's gracious purpose, and He belongeth only
to unbelieving sinners, as believing, in regard to actual union
with Christ (Eph. iii.17, Gal. ii.20.).[51]

As Rutherford realised these arguments were hardly a satisfactory
explanation of the mystery, which forced him to return to the
problem again and again.

When Rutherford sought to present his federal theology in a
less doctrinal and more popular form, as he did in his sermons,
he often spoke of the personal relation of the believer to Christ in
terms of a marriage contract, but no less frequently adopted the
language of the market and commerce in which he described the
covenant of grace as a bargain, as a striking hands with God and
spoke of its saving benefits as purchased through the Blood of

---

[50] *The Tryal and Triumph*, pp. 92f. See also his *Fourteen Communion Sermons*, 2nd
     edn Andrew A. Bonar, Glasgow, 1877, p. 70.
[51] *Fourteen Communion Sermons*, pp. 111f.

Christ.[52] It was this more popular presentation of federal theology that was taken up by his friends David Dickson and James Durham in *The Sum of Saving Knowledge* which was widely disseminated throughout the Kirk and gave rise to a rather moralistic and indeed a semi-pelagian understanding of the Gospel.

In his federal thinking Rutherford operated with the covenant of life in terms of two covenants, the covenant of nature and works contracted by God with Adam, and the covenant of grace contracted by God and Christ on behalf of the elect, and offered freely to the elect as a testament which he had sealed with his blood and left to them as a legacy with all the blessings of the covenant. Christ himself, the Mediator who is God and man in one Person, is 'the substantial covenant', who is offered in the Gospel to sinners on the condition of 'saving and true faith'. Yet in faith, Rutherford emphasised, it is not upon faith itself that believing sinners rely but upon Christ the object of faith, so that in faith they go out of themselves and rest on Christ alone. 'Faith is a palsied-hand under Christ to receive him. It is an evangelical act.'[53] With faith obedience also is a condition of salvation and justification, yet 'condition' must not be taken in the wrong sense, for it is not upon himself that the sinner is called to rely but upon the justifying obedience of Christ.[54] Rutherford understood this in terms of his 'active' as well as his 'passive obedience'.[55] He thought of the active obedience as related to 'the whole course of Christ's obedience from his birth to the grave by doing and suffering',[56] and of his passive obedience as related to his actual death on the Cross including 'his soul trouble', all that he 'did and suffered in his state of humiliation'.[57] By faith we are united to Christ and are possessed of him, who dwells in us so that it is by living in him that we believe (Eph. 3.17, John 11.26, & Gal. 2.20). Rutherford took care to point out that faith is not to be understood in any causative way or instrumental way, that is in accordance with the functioning of causes in nature. He could, however, speak of 'grace as the cause of grace', where cause is used in another sense of divine activity. 'Grace worketh more from an

[52] See the Sermons on Canticles ii.14, 17, pp. 248ff & ii.8–12, pp. 315ff. *Fourteen Communion Sermons*, 2nd edn Andrew A. Bonar, Glasgow, 1877.

[53] *The Tryal and Triumph*, p. 59.

[54] Cf. *The Covenant of Life*, p. 196.

[55] Cf. *Christ Dying*, p. 79.

[56] For 'the whole course of his obedience', see Calvin, *Institute*, 2.16.5.

[57] *Christ Dying, passim;* and *The Covenant of Life*, Part II, pp. 226f.

intrinsecall cause, and more spontaneously than nature', yet he understood this 'grace', nevertheless, in terms of 'omnipotency'.[58] Our right to Christ flows from his merits and from the grace of predestination – it rests on the 'objective grace' of his Incarnation and dying in our room and place.[59]

This teaching was evidently a reflection not only of the teaching of John Calvin, but of the emphasis of Robert Bruce on the whole incarnate life of Christ from his birth to his resurrection as the vicarious substance of his redemptive activity. The Cross and atonement were nevertheless conceived in strictly juridical terms: we are justified and saved through a free forensical act of God deriving from eternity but pronounced in time in the Gospel, and applied to us now, yet not until we believe. 'We cannot be justified before we believe.'[60] In one of his Communion sermons Rutherford said : 'I observe two times when we are justified before God and set free from the condemning power of the law as a covenant of works. 1. When Christ died and rose again for our justification. 2. When we believe in Christ dying and rising again, and resting and relying on him alone for salvation.'[61]This corresponds to what elsewhere he called 'objective and subjective grace'.[62] In his survey of antinomianism, Rutherford drew a similar distinction, between grace in Christ and in God, and its fruit, a created grace which inheres in us subjectively.[63]

Rutherford sometimes spoke of a form of the covenant as 'the Covenant of Redemption' which Christ as God and man fulfilled on both sides. He was not just a witness to confirm the covenant relations between God and man, but was himself its author, its surety and Mediator.[64] He thought of the covenant of redemption in two ways: '1. As transacted in time between *Jehovah* and *Christ*, in his actual discharge of his office as King, Priest, and Prophet. 2. As it is an eternal transaction and compact between Jehovah and the Second Person, the *Son of God*, who gave personall consent that he should be the Undertaker, and no other.'[65] He could also

[58] *Christ Dying*, pp. 158f.
[59] *The Covenant of Life*, pp. 230ff, 236ff.
[60] *The Covenant of Life*, pp. 59 & 62.
[61] *Communion Sermons*, Sermon XIV on Canticles ii.8–12, p. 359.
[62] *The Covenant of Life*, pp. 230f.
[63] *A Survey of the Spiritual Antichrist*, Part 2, p. 52.
[64] *The Covenant of Life*, Part II, Ch. V, pp. 282–308. See further pp. 355ff.
[65] *Ibid.* pp. 302f, 380f, 399; for the *triplex munus*, see pp. 418f; also *Covenant of Life*, pp. 300f, 316f, 341, 348.

speak of it as 'the Covenant of Reconciliation' for that was the form in which Christ completed his saving work in time. However, in its distinction from the covenant of grace fulfilled in Christ as its testator, the covenant of redemption did not play a significant role in Rutherford's Christology and soteriology, except perhaps to emphasise the freeness of God's saving grace embodied and proclaimed in Christ who had fulfilled all its conditions. The covenant of redemption was not included in his Catechism.

It should be noted that Rutherford's doctrine of election or predestination was not thought of as grounded in the incarnate Person of Christ, as it was with John Calvin and John Knox, but in a strictly federal or contractual 'bargain' between him and God, and was interpreted in necessary, causal, and forensic terms. The rigidly logical and determinist lines of thought which he used in his controversy with Jesuits and Arminians over the doctrine of grace,[66] forced his thinking into line with the teaching of Beza and the Synod of Dort about the limited extent of the atonement, so that, as we have noted, he rejected the idea that the Gospel is to be preached to the heathen, for redemption applies only to those for whom it has been bought, and to no others.[67] Christ did not die for all men, or for the sins of all humanity.[68] While he traced the Incarnation and dying of Christ to the free grace of God which moved him to send his Son in the flesh,[69] he qualified that by arguing that 'God's love is infinite in its act, but not in its object.'[70] Because he thought in terms of a strictly causative relation between God's eternal decrees and their end, he could not but think of the reprobate or the damned as those for whom Christ had not died – had he died for them they would all inevitably be saved. There is no biblical evidence, he claimed, that Christ died for all with the 'effectual intention' or 'efficacious intention' of bringing them to God,[71] but this appears to imply, in spite of his own argument about effects flowing necessarily from causes, and the concatenation of the means and the end, in God's saving and providential acts,[72]

---

[66] *Exercitationes Apologeticae pro Divina Gratia, contra Jesuitas & Arminianos*, Frankfurt, 1651; and *Christ Dying*, pp. 262ff, 305ff, 318ff, 328ff.

[67] *The Covenant of Life*, p. 17.

[68] See part III of *Christ Dying*, 1647, pp. 364ff; *The Covenant of Life*, Part II, Ch. III, pp. 236–56.

[69] *The Covenant of Life*, Part II, Ch. II, pp. 230f.

[70] *The Tryal and Triumph*, 1645, p. 16.

[71] *The Covenant of Life*, pp. 237–9 & 376; *Christ Dying*, pp. 378–81.

[72] *Ibid.* pp. 231 & 239; and *The Tryal and Triumph*, London, 1645, pp. 75f.

that Rutherford himself argued from final effects to original ends!

As with other theologians holding a rigid federal system, Rutherford had problems with a straightforward interpretation of New Testament statements such as John 3.16, beloved by the Arminians. He tried to get over the difficulty by making use of a distinction between the covenant as preached and the covenant as fulfilled. He granted that Christ undertook that the Gospel should be preached to 'reprobates', that is, to those who were found among the members of the visible Church inevitably mixed as it was with many hypocrites, but he did not undertake to stand for them as their surety or to pray for them as High Priest.[73] Elsewhere Rutherford argued that

> the promises of the Gospel are holden forth to sinners, as sinners, hath at twofold sense: 1. As they be sinners, and all in a sinfull condition to whom the promises are holden forth. This is most true and sound. The Kingdom of grace is an hospital and Guest-house of sick ones, for the art and mercy of the Physician Christ. 2. So as they are all immediately to believe and apply Christ and the promises, who are sinners.[74]

Here once again Rutherford objected that 'Christ should be holden forth to all sinners, Americans, Indians, and sinners who never by the least rumor, heard one word of Christ.'[75] To help him with his problem Rutherford resorted to a distinction between a 'permissive will' or 'forbidding will', and a 'commanding will' or 'approving will'.[76] 'In a permissive decree God appointed the Crucifying of the Lord of Life ... but he did never will the Crucifying of his Son.'[77] That is to say, while Christ permitted the Gospel to be preached to reprobates, he would not and did not lay down his life to save them as he did for the elect. Part of Rutherford's problem was his understanding of the Gospel of grace in terms of a covenant with its definite 'conditions and properties' that had to be fulfilled by

---

[73] *The Covenant of Life*, pp. 339–41.
[74] *Christ Dying*, p. 258.
[75] *Christ Dying*, p. 238.
[76] Cf. Calvin's *Commentary on Ezekiel*, on 18.23, *CTS*, tr. T. Myers, Edinburgh, 1850, pp. 246ff, & *Commentary on 1 Timothy*, 2.3–5, tr. T. A. Smail, Edinburgh, 1964, pp. 208f.
[77] *The Covenant of Life*, p. 343.
[78] *The Covenant of Life*, pp. 118ff.

them, which left no place for open-ended mission in a proclamation of the Gospel preached outside or beyond the visible Church to the heathen. Salvation could take place only within a forensically predetermined covenant-structure – God had made no covenant of grace applicable to all mankind like the covenant of works, as Amyrald and the Arminians thought when they extended the Lord's command to preach the Gospel to all nations to apply to all and every man.[78] That was a more restrictive way of thinking than the Roman *extra ecclesiam nulla salus* accepted by Calvin and Knox.

Nevertheless, Rutherford's faithfulness to the Gospel message could be stronger than his logic – Christ clothed with the Gospel is greater than the covenant! Thus, as we have noted, in his famous *Communion Sermons* where his understanding of the atonement was governed by the New Covenant in Christ's Body and Blood, and not so much by federal theology, Rutherford could write: 'We are said in Scripture 'to be reconciled unto God' and not God to be reconciled unto us. His love is everlasting ... so that sin could not change God's mind.'[79] That was a very significant point for Rutherford to make in tune with the teaching of John Calvin.[80] However, he was not consistent for he followed Beza and the Synod of Dort rather than Calvin who rejected the proposition of Alexander of Hales that Christ suffered sufficiently for all, but efficaciously only for the elect.[81] For Rutherford, as for the *Westminster Confession*, the atoning satisfaction made by Christ was *purchased* from the Father, so that a sufficient act of redemption by Christ on the Cross could not but be necessitarian in its actuality and exclusive in its application – it was held that an all-sufficient atonement meant that every one would actually and necessarily be saved, which conflicted with Rutherford's strict notion of limited election.

In his argument with the Arminians bearing on the words of Christ 'I will draw all men', Rutherford showed that a serious conception of universal atonement would mean that Christ died 'for all' with the deliberate purpose and intention of drawing all men to himself, so that they would actually be saved.[82] The

[79] *Fourteen Communion Sermons*, p. 236. See again *The Covenant of Life*, p. 231.
[80] John Calvin, *Institute*, 2.16.3–4.
[81] See again Calvin, *De aeterna praedestinatione*, IX.5.
[82] See Rutherford's long argument against the Arminian doctrine of 'universal atonement', *Christ Dying*, Part III, 'All Men', pp. 364ff.

argument that followed is clear from the following headings alone: 'A Redemption purchased, and never applied, is comfortless'[83] – 'The end of Christ's dying not a possible, but an actual reconciliation'[84] – 'Universal conversion, no lesse in scripture than universal atonement'[85] – 'The love of God in Christ peculiar to the elect'.[86] Elsewhere he made the emphatic statement that 'Christ is never called the Head of all men, Elect and Reprobate, but the Head of the Body the Church.'[87] The decided rejection of any notion of the universal extent of Christ's atoning death called for still further attention to biblical passages seeming to favour universal atonement. He claimed to show, for example, that the 'world' in John 3.16 did not mean literally 'all men' but only 'the believing world', and that statements referring to the salvation of 'all men' meant 'all who are saved', so that 'all' was to be interpreted restrictively in line with cited instances of Hebrew and Greek usage to mean 'many', and not 'all' in the strict sense of 'every one'. It was in the same way that Rutherford understood the statement that Christ 'tasted of death for every man' (Heb.2.9).[88] The Biblical use of 'all', he claimed, is to be understood figuratively as a '*Senecdoche, of All, for many*'.[89] He thus interpreted 1 Tim. 2.6, for example, in accordance with Matt. 20.28, backing it by an appeal to common use in Syriac.[90] On the other hand it must be pointed out that the 'Semitism' 'for many' in Matt. 20.28 (or Mark 10.45) was clearly understood and interpreted by St Paul himself to mean 'for all'! It is difficult not to hold that Rutherford was interpreting crucial biblical passages about the extent of the atonement in a forced way, in what Thomas Chalmers was later to call 'an unnatural sense', in order to fit them in with his federal system of thought, instead of allowing his preconceptions to be called into question by straightforward New Testament teaching.

There is no doubt that in his affirmation of the National Covenant and the Solemn League and Covenant at the Westminster Assembly, which helped to politicise his ecclesiology, Rutherford's

---

[83] *Christ Dying*, pp. 376ff.
[84] *Christ Dying*, pp. 396ff.
[85] *Christ Dying*, pp. 402–8.
[86] *Christ Dying*, pp. 409–19.
[87] *The Covenant of Life*, p. 233.
[88] *Christ Dying*, p. 431.
[89] *Christ Dying*, p. 408, & pp. 404ff.
[90] *Ibid.* pp. 419–38, & *The Covenant of Life*, pp. 254f.

fierce presbyterian opposition to all forms of Erastianism and Prelacy, Arminians, Libertines and Antinomians,[91] helped to force his thinking into extreme hyper-Calvinist positions which he tried to justify by casting them into strict syllogistic form. This led him into adopting arguments that would have horrified Calvin. 'If Christ died for all, so that they may perchance suffer for their sins in hell, God shall be unjust in punishing Christ for their sins and in punishing those same sinners in hell.'[92] Particularly difficult was his logicalised view of sin which God used as a means (not an accidental means but a means in itself) to an end which he could not otherwise accomplish.[93] This logical approach to sin led Rutherford to diverge from the view of Calvin, expressed by him several hundred times in his works, that we cannot but think of the event of a sinner's rejection of grace or of reprobation, as happening *per accidens* or *accidentaliter*, in face of the Gospel operating as a savour of life unto life and of death unto death.[94]

Rutherford's preaching and pastoral ministry were governed by an overwhelming sense of the majesty, love and mercy of God the Father, whose grace is poured out lavishly upon his Church through Jesus Christ and indwells its members through the presence of the Holy Spirit. While Rutherford taught that the elect are irresistibly drawn to Christ,[95] he laid great stress on faith, indwelling effectual grace, and inward religious experience in spiritual communion with Christ.[96] Yet he insisted that faith cannot add anything to the

---

[91] Thus, for example, *A Survey of the Spiritual Antichrist; or A Free Disputation Against pretended Liberty of Conscience*, London, 1648. The politicisation of his thought is also very evident in his ecclesiological writings, *The Due right of Presbyteries, Or, A Peaceable Plea for the Government of the Church of Scotland*, London, 1644; *The Divine Right of Church Government and Excommunication*, London, 1648; as also in *Lex Rex: The Law and the Prince, A Dispute for the just Prerogative of King and People.* London, 1644.

[92] *The Soume of Christian Religion*, or *Catechism*, ed. A. F. Mitchell in *Catechisms of the Second Reformation*, London, 1886, p. 188.

[93] Rutherford's *Catechism*, ed. A. F. Mitchell, pp. 170f; cf also *The Covenant of Life Opened*, pp. 146f; and p. 145: 'the greatest part of men breake their teeth, in biting the neerest link of the chaine of second causes, but they arise never up to *God*, the first Mover.' Rutherford was unable to distinguish between the contingent and the adventitious.

[94] Cf. the comments by James Walker, *The Theology and Theologians of Scotland*, 1888, pp. 49ff, 60f; and my comments on Calvin's doctrine of election, *Kingdom and Church*, Edinburgh, 1956, pp. 106f.

[95] Thus *Christ Dying*, pp. 262f, 305f, 310, 314, etc.

[96] This was a theme running through *Christ Dying*.

sufficiency of Christ's atoning satisfaction for us. No act of obedience can perfect the satisfaction of Christ – but this is not to say that there are no conditions. God accepts the satisfaction of Christ without any condition on our part, but out of his grace which is absolutely free, God works in us the 'condition of believing'. What Rutherford was concerned to inculcate in statements of this kind was the utter objectivity of grace.

> When we believe conditionally '*if I believe, I am saved*', faith relies not fiducially upon the '*I believe*', or upon the condition: it is a weak pillar to the sinner to stay his unquiet heart upon, to wit, his own believing, but faith rests on the connexion, as made sure in the Lord, who of grace gives the condition of believing, and of grace the reward conditioned, so that faith binds all the weight upon God only, even in the conditional Gospel-promises.[97]

> Believing adds nothing to the intrinsical sufficiency of satisfaction, as not believing diminishes nothing from the sufficiency thereof.[98]

And so Rutherford insisted again and again that in turning to the promises of God we must look out of ourselves, and look to Christ alone; if we look for any ground of believing in ourselves and in our own acts of sanctification, we will never have the assurance we want.

However, in spite of this stress on the objectivity of grace and of faith, the kind of hyper-Calvinism which Rutherford advocated with its concept of an atonement limited only to the elect coupled with a doctrine of double predestination through irresistible divine decree, had the effect of stirring up and intensifying the problem of assurance in the Kirk, which did not arise in the evangelical approach of the older Scottish theology in which faith and assurance belong inseparably together in an objective apprehension of Christ. This is what Rutherford himself held: 'Faith is essentially a persuasion and assurance of the *love of God* to me in *Christ* ... It is a relying, and fiducial acquiescing and recumbencie on *Christ* for salvation. It is granted in this sense, that faith is a

---

[97] *The Tryal and Triumph*, 1655, p. 17.
[98] *The Covenant of Life*, p. 12.

bottome to our assurance of our being in Christ.'[99] No matter how weak and wanting the response of our faith may be, it is upon Christ himself that we rely. It was on the ground of this objective concept of faith that Rutherford rejected the notion of assurance held by the Arminians in which the sinner on the ground of a general notion of salvation is thrown back upon himself and his own acts in responding to Christ.[100] In spite of this teaching, the insistence on what he once called 'the two absolute decrees of Election and Reprobation, from eternity',[101] together with particular redemption, undermined Rutherford's view of faith as essentially a persuasion of the love of God in Christ *'to me'*, and aggravated a state of affairs in the Kirk where the human heart cried out for a rather different understanding of the Gospel. That was precisely what was at stake in 'The Marrow Controversy' when 'the Marrow men' returned to the evangelical teaching of John Davidson of Saltoun and Prestonpans, although they too could not shake themselves free from the narrow predestinationist views of the *Confession of Faith.*

The Sum of Saving Knowledge:

David Dickson (1583–1663) and James Durham (1622–58)

David Dickson and James Durham, both of whom engaged in expository activity, collaborated in compiling *The Sum of Saving Knowledge*,[102] on the basis of sermons delivered by Dickson at Inveraray. It was composed, Wodrow tells us, 'so as it might be most useful to vulgar Capacities'.[103] In that respect it was certainly very successful, for it supplied ordinary people with a simplified and formalised account of the plan of salvation according to the federal system of theology, expressed in the common language of the market-place. However, in this way the dynamic content of the Gospel was fused with the contractual means of putting into effect

---

[99] *Christ Dying*, p. 85.
[100] *Christ Dying*, pp. 424ff.
[101] *Christ Dying*, p. 311; see pp. 382 & 410f.
[102] Robert Wodrow, *Analecta*, Vol. III, Edinburgh, 1843, p. 10.
[103] From 'A Short Account of the Life of Mr David Dickson', in the 1764 edition of *The Sum of Saving Knowledge*, p. xviii.

the eternal decrees held to issue from the Council of the Trinity, while the inclusion of 'Kirk-government' among the means of grace injected a strong presbyterian ecclesiasticism into theology. Ever since its publication in 1650, *The Sum of Saving Knowledge* has had an immense influence on the thinking of the Kirk by members and ministers alike. Although it was not officially authorised by the General Assembly it was long printed together with the Westminster Standards and associated with their authority. David Dickson who had composed a Latin Commentary on the *Westminster Confession of Faith*, known as *Truth's Victory over Error*,[104] and of the widely used *Therapeutica Sacra*,[105] was the main contributor, but James Durham, his favourite pupil and friend, exercised a moderating influence in its attempt at giving the essential doctrines of the faith an acceptable form for popular use.

It will be best if *The Sum of Saving Knowledge*, in its main text, is given in full, for it provides us with a rather remarkable, and remarkably clear, picture of the understanding of Scottish Theology as it was being taught and was taking shape in the parishes of the land.[106]

The Sum of Saving Knowledge may be taken up in these four heads:- 1. The woeful condition wherein all men are by nature, through breaking the covenant of works. 2. The remedy provided for the elect in Jesus Christ by the covenant of grace. 3. The means appointed to make them partakers of this covenant. 4. The blessings which are effectually conveyed unto the elect by these means – Which four heads are set down each of them in some few propositions.

---

[104] David Dickson, *Praelectiones in Confessionem Fidei*, tr. from Dickson's MS by George Sinclare, and published as *Truth's Victory over Error: Or, The True Principles of the Christian Religion*, by G. S., Edinburgh, 1684; republished under Dickson's name, Glasgow, 1752, 1764 & 1787.

[105] David Dickson, *Therapeutica Sacra, The Method of Healing the Diseases of the Conscience Concerning Regeneration*, Latin edn, London, 1656, and English edn, Edinburgh, 1664.

[106] The text of *The Sum of Saving Knowledge: Or A Brief Sum of Christian Doctrine*, is readily available in the volume: *The Subordinate Standards and Other Authoritative Documents of the Free Church of Scotland*, Edinburgh, 1894, and later, pp. 251–64. See also John Macpherson, *The Sum of Saving Knowledge*, main text with commentary published as one of the Hand-Books for Bible Classes and Private Students, Edited by Marcus Dodds and Alexander Whyte, Edinburgh, 1886.

HEAD I.

Our woeful condition by nature, through breaking the covenant of works.
Hos. xiii. 9. O Israel thou hast destroyed thyself.

1. The almighty and eternal God, the Father, the Son, and the Holy
Ghost, three distinct persons in one and the same undivided
Godhead, equally infinite in all perfections, did, before time, most
wisely decree, for his own glory, whatsoever cometh to pass in time;
and doth most holily and infallibly execute all his decrees, without
being partaker of the sin of any creature.

2. This God, in six days, made all things of nothing, very good in their
own kind: in special, he made all the angels holy; and he made our
first parents, Adam and Eve, the root of mankind, both upright and
able to keep the law written in their hearts. Which law they were
naturally bound to obey under pain of death; but God was not bound
to reward their service, till he entered into a covenant or contract
with them, and their posterity in them, to give them eternal life, upon
condition of perfect personal obedience; withal threatening death in
case they should fail. This is the covenant of works.

3. Both angels and men were subject to the change of their own
free will, as experience proved (God having reserved to himself the
incommunicable property of being naturally unchangeable): for
many angels of their own accord fell by sin from their first estate,
and became devils. Our first parents, being enticed by Satan, one of
these devils, speaking in a serpent, did break the covenant of works,
in eating the forbidden fruit; whereby they, and their posterity, being
in their loins, as branches in the root, and comprehended in the
same covenant with them, became not only liable to eternal death,
but also lost all ability to please God; yea, did become by nature
enemies of God, and to all spiritual good, and inclined only to evil
continually. This is our original sin, the bitter root of all our actual
transgressions in thought, word, and deed.

HEAD II.

The remedy provided in Jesus Christ for the elect by the covenant of grace.
Hos. xiii. 9. O Israel thou hast destroyed thyself; but in me is thine help.

1. Albeit man, having brought himself into this woeful condition,

be neither able to help himself nor willing to be helped by God out of it, but rather inclined to lie still, insensible of it, till he perish; yet God, for the glory of his rich grace, hath revealed in his word a way to save sinners, viz. by faith in Jesus Christ, the eternal Son of God, by virtue of and according to the tenor of the covenant of redemption, made and agreed upon between God the Father and God the Son, in the council of the Holy Trinity before the world began.

2. The sum of the covenant of redemption is this: God having freely chosen unto life a certain number of lost mankind, for the glory of his rich grace, did give them, before the world began, unto God the Son, appointed Redeemer, that, upon condition he would humble himself as far as to assume the human nature, of a soul and a body, unto personal union with his divine nature, and submit himself to the law, as surety for them, and satisfy justice for them, by giving obedience in their name, even unto the suffering of the cursed death of the cross, he should ransom and redeem them from all sin and death, and purchase unto them righteousness and eternal life, with all saving graces leading thereunto, to be effectually, by means of his own appointment, applied in due time to every one of them. This condition the Son of God (who is Jesus Christ our Lord) did accept before the world began, and in the fulness of time came into the world, was born of the Virgin Mary, subjected himself to the law, and completely paid the ransom on the cross. But by virtue of the aforesaid bargain, made before the world began, he is in all ages, since the fall of Adam, still upon the work of applying actually the purchased benefits unto the elect; and that he doth by way of entertaining a covenant of free grace and reconciliation with them, through faith in himself; by which covenant he makes over to every believer a right and interest to himself and to all his blessings.

3. For the accomplishment of this covenant of redemption, and making the elect partakers of the benefits thereof in the covenant of grace, Christ Jesus came clad with the threefold office of Prophet, Priest, and King: made a Prophet, to reveal all saving knowledge to his people, and to persuade them to believe and obey the same; made a Priest, to offer up himself a sacrifice once for them all, and to intercede continually with the Father, for making their persons and services acceptable to him; and made a King to subdue

them to himself, to feed and rule them by his own appointed ordinances, and defend them from their enemies.

HEAD III.

The outward means appointed to make the elect partakers of this covenant, and all the rest that are called, to be inexcusable. Matt. xxii.14. Many are called.

1. The outward means and ordinances, for making men partakers of the covenant of grace, are so wisely dispensed, as that the elect shall be infallibly converted and saved by them; and the reprobate, among whom they are, not to be justly stumbled. The means are specially these four – (1) The word of God. (2) The sacraments. (3) Kirk-government. (4) Prayer. In the word of God, preached by sent messengers, the Lord makes offer of grace to all sinners, upon condition of faith in Jesus Christ; and whosoever do confess their sins, accept of Christ offered, and submit themselves to his ordinances, he will have both them and their children received into the honour and privileges of the covenant of grace. By the sacraments, God will have the covenant sealed for confirming the bargain on the foresaid condition. By kirk-government, he will have them hedged in, and helped forward unto the keeping of the covenant. And by prayer, he will have his own glorious grace, promised in the covenant, to be daily drawn forth, acknow-ledged, and employed. All which means are followed either really, or in profession only, according to the quality of the covenanters, as they are true or counterfeit believers.

2. The Covenant of grace, set down in the Old Testament before Christ came, and in the New since he came, is one and the same in substance, albeit different in outward administration: For the covenant of the Old Testament, being sealed with the sacraments of circumcision and the paschal lamb, did set forth Christ's death to come, and the benefits purchased thereby under the shadow of bloody sacrifices and sundry ceremonies; but since Christ came, the covenant being sealed by the sacraments of baptism and the Lord's Supper, doth clearly hold forth Christ already crucified before our eyes, victorious over death and the grave, and gloriously ruling heaven and earth for the good of his own people.

HEAD IV.

The blessings which are effectually conveyed by these means to the Lord's
elect, or chosen ones. Matt. xxii.14. Many are called, but few are chosen.

1. By those outward ordinances, as our Lord makes the reprobate
inexcusable, so, by the power of his Spirit, he applies unto the elect,
effectually, all saving graces purchased to them in the covenant of
redemption, and maketh a change in their persons. In particular,(1) He doth convert or regenerate them, by giving spiritual life
to them, in opening their understanding, renewing their wills,
affections, and faculties, for giving spiritual obedience to his
commands.(2) He gives them saving faith by making them, in the
sense of deserved condemnation, to give their consent heartily to
the covenant of grace, and to embrace Jesus Christ unfeignedly.
(3) He gives them repentance, by making them, with godly sorrow,
in the hatred of sin and love of righteousness, turn from all iniquity
to the service of God. (4) He sanctifies them, by making them go
on and persevere in faith and spiritual obedience to the law of
God, manifested by fruitfulness in all duties, and doing good works,
as God offereth occasion.

2. Together with this inward change of their persons, God changes
also their state; for, so soon as they are brought by faith into the
covenant of grace, (1) he justifies them, by infusing into them that
perfect obedience which Christ gave to the law, and the satisfaction
also which upon the cross Christ gave unto justice in their name.
(2) He reconciles them, and makes them friends to God, who were
before enemies to God. (3) He adopts them, that they shall be no
more children of Satan, but children of God, enriched with all
spiritual privileges of his sons. And last of all, after their warfare in
this life is ended, he perfects the holiness and blessedness, first, of
their souls at their death, being joyfully joined together again in
the resurrection at the day of his glorious coming to judgment,
when all the wicked shall be sent away to hell, with Satan whom
they have served; but Christ's own chosen and redeemed ones,
true believers, students of holiness, shall remain with himself for
ever, in the state of glorification.

****

Under the first 'Head', this remarkable document begins unusually and very properly with the doctrine of the Trinity, but not as it is revealed in and through the historical self-revelation of God in the Gospel. 'The Trinity' here is an abstract concept, in line with that of the *Westminster Confession of Faith*, the importance of which at the head of this document lies in the fact that it was within the Council of the Holy Trinity, that the eternal contract or covenant with mankind and its conditions was made. In the first instance this was 'the covenant of works'. This binding and unalterable contract constitutes the ultimate axiom or dogmatic principle in accordance with which what follows is logically ordered – which reminds one of the nature and rational structure of Scots Law which is based on Roman Law, an axiomatic system in which different laws are logically derived from first principles. Thus the *Sum of Saving Knowledge* is a system of doctrinal propositions arranged in a fourfold structure, within which saving knowledge is presented.

There is no doubt that here we have to do with the core of traditional Reformed theology, including the active and passive obedience of Christ, and union with him on the ground of his personal union with God, etc., but pared down to a basic skeletal structure which hardly measures up to the evangelical content of the Gospel – it is a sum of doctrines didactically set out rather than kerygmatically presented as saving knowledge. In its first 'Head', as in a number of post-Reformation formularies of belief, the *Sum* deals with the fall of mankind, and original sin, the depravity of nature. This is described apart from the Gospel of redemption, although it is only in the light of the Gospel that the fallen condition of man is properly to be understood – evil looked at in itself is always distorting.

A major premise in the 'reasoning' of the *Sum* is, not the infinite love of God revealed in Christ, but the restrictive concept of eternal predestination of some only 'for life', the elect. It is noteworthy, however, that there is no suggestion of a predestination of some 'for death', no divine decree relating to the damned or the reprobate.[107] God is in no sense the author of evil, or the partaker of the sin of any creature, although with his creation of angels and human beings endowed with reason and will, it is recognised that the possibility of disobedience and sin was given. This is not easy to construe with the rather deterministic view of God who while 'holily' nevertheless 'infallibly executes all his decrees'.

---

[107] Cf. John Macpherson, *The Sum of Saving Knowledge*, p. 64: 'There is a decree of election, but no decree of reprobation.'

Under the second 'Head' the *Sum* spoke of the remedy provided in Jesus Christ for the elect by the covenant of grace, a way to save sinners by faith in Jesus Christ. This covenant rests upon a prior covenant, 'the covenant of redemption' eternally agreed between the Father and the Son, to the effect that the Son would be the Redeemer of a certain number of lost mankind, *provided* that he fulfilled certain conditions: he must humble himself to assume human nature, submit himself to the law, as a surety for the elect and satisfy justice by giving obedience in their name, suffering the cursed death on the cross, thereby ransom and redeem them all from sin and death, and 'purchase' unto them righteousness and eternal life with all saving graces. It was only through fulfilment of this 'bargain' in the 'covenant of redemption' that the 'covenant of free grace and reconciliation' could be put into effect. In accepting these conditions Christ became incarnate as the second Adam, invested with the threefold office of prophet, priest and king, to reveal God's saving grace, to offer himself up a sacrifice for them all, intercede continually with the Father for them, and to subdue and rule over them. It is on the ground of this finished work that the Gospel is offered to all 'on no other condition but faith'.[108] In the 'Practical use of Saving Knowledge', it is added: 'The sum of the gospel or covenant of grace and reconciliation is this: If thou flee from deserved wrath to this true Redeemer, Jesus Christ (who is able to save to the uttermost all that come to God through him) thou shalt not perish, but have eternal life (Rom. x. 8, 9, 11).'[109]

In the section 'Warrants to Believe', the *Sum* points out that the special motive to embrace Christ, and believe in him, is 'the earnest request that God maketh to us to be reconciled to him in Christ; holden forth, 2 Cor. v.19, 20, 21.' It is significant, however, that although it cites 'God was in Christ reconciling the world unto himself', it lays all the emphasis *not* on *God's reconciling act* but on the repeated injunction *to be reconciled to him*.[110] This was in line with the omission at the start to trace everything back to the infinite, aboriginal, prevenient Love of God, and accordingly to relate atoning satisfaction made by Christ to 'justice', rather than to the holy Love of God the Father. On the other hand, after asserting that God requires 'no other conditions but faith', the *Sum* puts

---

[108] 'The Practical use of Saving Knowledge', IV, *Sum*, p. 253.
[109] *Sum*, p. 254.
[110] *Sum*, p. 259.

into the mouth of God by way of paraphrasing biblical statements, 'If ye will believe me, and be reconciled to me, I will, by covenant, give unto you all saving graces in him.' And then adds: 'Consider that this general offer in substance is equivalent to a special offer made to every one in particular; as appeareth by the apostle's making use of it, Acts XVI.31. *Believe on the Lord Jesus Christ and thou shalt be saved, and thy house.* The reason of which offer is given, John III.16. *For God so loved the world, that he gave his only begotten Son, that whosoever believeth in him should not perish, but have everlasting life.*'. Then after speaking of the dire consequences of unbelief reference is made to several texts of a minatory nature, to 'convince a man of the greatness of this sin of not believing in Christ', in line with the threat of death and damnation in the covenant of works.[111]

It was clearly of evangelistic importance for Dickson and Durham that in *substance* the Gospel offer made to all men is the *same* as that made to 'true believers', the few elect who will actually be saved.[112] In the section 'Warrants to Believe', which follows 'The Practical Use of Saving Knowledge', they express this 'Gospel offer' in popular mercantile terms, which appears to have had the effect of undermining any suggestion as to the unconditional nature of saving grace, as in the citation from Isaiah 55.1–5, 'Ho every one that thirsteth, come ye to the waters, and he that hath no money, come ye, buy, and eat...' Here it is stated, the Lord

> maketh open offer of Christ and his grace, by proclamation of a free and gracious market of righteousness and salvation, to be had through Christ to every soul without exception, that truly desires to be saved from sin and wrath, 'Ho everyone that thirsteth', saith he ... He craveth no more of his merchant, but that he be pleased with the wares offered, which are grace, and more grace; and that he heartedly consent unto, and embrace the offer of grace, that so he may close a bargain, and a formal covenant with God; 'come, buy without money ... Come buy wine and milk without money and without price'.[113]

In its third 'Head' the main text of the *Sum* was devoted to 'the outward means and ordinances, for making men partakers of the

---

[111] *Sum,* p. 255.
[112] Cf. David Dickson's Commentary on the Confession of Faith, *Truth's Victory over Error,* pp. 118 & 163.
[113] *Sum,* pp. 257f.

covenant of grace, are so wisely dispensed, as that the elect shall be infallibly converted and saved by them; and the reprobate, among whom they are, not to be justly stumbled.' Thus while the elect are thereby made partakers of the covenant, all the rest that are called are rendered 'inexcusable'. This is a difficult statement, but it might be taken in accordance with the way in which Calvin, with reference to 2 Cor. 2.15, spoke of the twofold effect of the preaching of the Gospel as a 'savour of life' to those who are saved, but as 'a savour of death' to those who perish. Here he claimed that the proper function (*proprium officium*) of the Gospel is to be distinguished from (so to speak) its accidental one (*ab accidentali*).[114] But that would seem to be ruled out by the *Sum* in its statements about the 'infallible execution' of God's decrees in respect of whatsoever comes to pass in time. It is rather in this way that we may understand the statement at the beginning of 'Head' IV, that by those outward ordinances 'our Lord makes the reprobate inexcusable'.

The fourth section of the *Sum of Saving Knowledge* was devoted to the blessings which are effectually conveyed by the means of grace to the Lord's elect, or chosen ones. The first paragraph dealt with the conversion or regeneration of the elect, and the inward change of their persons wrought effectually in them by the power of the Spirit in respect of faith, repentance and sanctification. The second paragraph dealt with the objective ground of that change in justification, reconciliation, and adoption in Christ, and the final end of 'Christ's own chosen and redeemed ones, true believers'. But the question arose, prompted by the emphasis throughout on election and predestination: how do people know that they are chosen, redeemed, and true believers? It was clearly in view of that worrying question that Dickson and Durham added to the main text of their account of saving knowledge three sections on its practical use, in which detailed attention was given to how believers in Jesus Christ through the reasoning of faith about evidence, warrants, and motives, could be assured and strengthened in their convictions.

What they were concerned to do here, was to increase what they called '*the quality of the covenanters*', and to 'hedge them in' to righteous living and the teaching of the Kirk.

---

[114] John Calvin, *Commentary on 2 Corinthians*, 2.15 ; cf. *Inst.* 2.5.5f.

The chief general use of Christian doctrine is, to convince a man of sin, and of righteousness, and of judgment, John XVI.8, partly by the law or covenant of works, that he may be humbled and become penitent; and partly by the gospel or covenant of grace, that he may become an unfeigned believer in Jesus Christ, and be strengthened in his faith, upon solid grounds and warrants, and give evidence of the truth of his faith by good fruits, and so be saved.[115]

While many appropriate passages of the Scriptures are cited, the steady focus is not so much upon Christ himself as (a) upon 'doctrines', with attention given to *reasoning* out their inner connections with a view to deepening and clarifying believers' grasp of their truth on the solid ground of four 'warrants to believe',[116] and (b) upon probing into the ground and sincerity of personal convictions and testing whether they reveal evidences of true faith in the soul and of their personal reconciliation with God.[117]

All this was intended to meet and overcome the problems of doubt and lack of assurance that were increasingly rife due to the preaching not so much of the Word of God, but of doctrines, and of doctrines formulated in accordance with the strict tenets of covenanting theology, but actually it fell far short of achieving that end. On the other hand, this was balanced by the way in which Dickson and Durham, both of whom had been revivalist preachers of salvation from the wrath and judgment of God, presented 'the Gospel offer' of free grace to *all* sinners which is the same in *substance* as that made to the elect,[118] went far to help the actual ministry of the Gospel in the parishes of the land. At the same time, in spite of the fact that all the conditions of man's redemption had been fulfilled by Christ, the recurring stress at every point upon the conditional 'if' of the covenant of grace and reconciliation as well as of works, meant that the problems of assurance kept pressing for answers – in the last analysis believers were thrown back upon themselves.

---

[115] *Sum*, p. 254.

[116] *Sum*, pp. 257–61. For suggestions as to how penitent believers might 'reason' out doctrinal connections, *if this, then that,* for themselves, see pp. 356, 260, 261, 264.

[117] *Sum*, especially pp. 262–4.

[118] *Sum*, pp. 255, 257f.

In some respects *The Sum of Saving Knowledge* did not compare favourably with the well-known work of Patrick Gillespie, *The Ark of the Covenant Opened: Or, A Treatise of the Covenant of Redemption between God and Christ, as the Foundation of the Covenant of Grace*.[119] Chapter VII of that work, entitled 'Of the Grounds of assurance and comfort, and supports of Faith, resulting from the Covenant of Suretiship, unto all those who are in the Covenant of Reconciliation and Grace', was rather more effective. While all through his book Patrick Gillespie referred unremittingly to the covenant, it had a powerful christocentric, christological and soteriological, orientation through the primacy it gave to the Person of Christ as the Mediator of the New Covenant and the condescending love of God redemptively embodied in him as 'the Covenant of Suretiship'.

Although *The Sum of Saving Knowledge* was meant to help people understand and follow the teaching of the Kirk, its actual impact while undoubtedly immense was not altogether fortunate. As C. G. M'Crie pointed out, the effect of this formalisation of the plan of salvation in the language of the market-place was to mislead.

> The *Sum* is objectionable in form and application. Detailed descriptions of redemption as a bargain entered into between the first and second Persons of the Trinity in which conditions were laid down, promises held out, and pledges given, the reducing of salvation to a mercantile arrangement between God and the sinner, in which the latter signifies contentment to enter into a relation of grace, so that ever after the contented, contracting part can say, 'Lord, let it be a bargain', – such presentations have obviously a tendency to reduce the Gospel of the grace of God to the level of a legal compact entered into between two independent and, so far as right or status is concerned, two equal parties. The blessedness of the mercy-seat is in danger of being lost sight of in the bargaining of the market-place; the simple story of salvation is thrown into the crucible of the logic of the schools and it emerges in the form of a syllogism.[120]

---

[119] London, 1677, 'Written by a Minister of the New-Testament'.

[120] C. G. M'Crie, *The Confessions of the Church of Scotland*, Edinburgh, 1907, pp. 72f.

Bibliography

Anselm, St, *Opera Omnia*, ed. F. S. Schmitt, Edinburgh, 1946.

Calvin, John, *Commentary on the Epistle to the Hebrews*, tr. W. B. Johnston, Edinburgh, 1963.

Calvin, John, *Commentary on 2 Corinthians, Timothy, Titus & Philemon*, tr. T. A. Smail, Edinburgh, 1964.

Calvin, John, *Institutes of the Christian Religion*, tr. Henry Beveridge, Edinburgh, 1845.

Dickson, David, *Therapeutica Sacra, The Method of Healing the Diseases of the Conscience Concerning Regeneration*, Latin edn, London, 1656, and English edn, Edinburgh, 1664.

Dickson, David, *Praelectiones in Confessionem Fidei*, tr. from Dickson's MS by George Sinclare, and published as *Truth's Victory over Error: Or, The True Principles of the Christian Religion*, by G. S., Edinburgh, 1684; republished under Dickson's name, Glasgow, 1752, 1764 & 1787.

Dickson, David, with James Durham, *The Sum of Saving Knowledge*, reproduced in *The Confession of Faith; the Larger and Shorter Catechisms*, Edinburgh, 1894.

Gillespie, Patrick, *The Ark of the Covenant Opened: Or, A Treatise of the Covenant of Redemption Between God and Christ, as the Foundation of the Covenant of Grace*, London, 1661 & 1677.

Macleod, John, *Scottish Theology In Relation to Church History Since the Reformation*, Edinburgh, 1943.

Macpherson, John, *The Sum of Saving Knowledge*, Hand-Books for Bible Classes, Edinburgh, 1886.

M'Crie, C. G., *The Confessions of the Church of Scotland*, Edinburgh, 1907.

Mitchell, A. F., *Catechisms of the Second Reformation*, London, 1886.

Rutherford, Samuel, *Christ Dying and Drawing Sinners to Himselfe. Or A Survey of our Saviour in all his soule suffering, his lovelyness in his death, and the efficacie thereof*, London, 1647.

Rutherford, Samuel, *Fourteen Communion Sermons*, ed. A. A. Bonar, 2nd edn Glasgow, 1877.

Rutherford, Samuel, *The Covenant of Life Opened: Or, A Treatise of the Covenant of Grace*, Edinburgh, 1655.

Rutherford, Samuel, *The Divine Right of Church Government and Excommunication*, London, 1648.

Rutherford, Samuel, *Exercitationes Apologeticae Pro Divina Gratia*, Amsterdam, 1636, & Frankfurt, 1651.

Rutherford, Samuel, *A Free Disputation Against pretended Liberty of Conscience*, London, 1649.

Rutherford, Samuel, *Letters of Samuel Rutherford*, two vols., ed. A. A. Bonar, 1863; published first as *Joshua Redivivus; Or, Three Hundred and Fifty-two Religious Letters*, collected and edited by Robert McWard, Rotterdam, 1664.

Rutherford, Samuel, *Lex Rex: The Law and the Prince. A Dispute for the just Prerogative of King and People*. London, 1644.

Rutherford, Samuel, *The Due right of Presbyteries, Or, A Peaceable Plea for the Government of the Church of Scotland*, London, 1644.

Rutherford, Samuel, *The Soume of Christian Religion, or Catechism*, ed. A. F. Mitchell, *Catechisms of the Second Reformation*, London, 1886.

Rutherford, Samuel, *A Survey of the Spiritual Antichrist*, London, 1648.

Rutherford, Samuel, *The Tryal and Triumph of Faith*, London, 1645 & Edinburgh, 1845.

Strickland, David R., *Union with Christ in the Theology of Samuel Rutherford, an Examination of his Doctrine of the Holy Spirit*. Doctoral Thesis Edinburgh University, 1972. New College Library.

Walker, James, *The Theology and Theologians of Scotland, Chiefly of the Seventeenth and Eighteenth Centuries*, 2nd edn, revised, Edinburgh, 1888.

Wodrow, Robert, *Analecta: Or Materials for a History of Remarkable Providences; mostly relating to Scotch Ministers and Christians*, Vol. III, Edinburgh, 1843.

4

The Westminster Tradition
1647–1690

The *Westminster Confession of Faith* was the great confession of
Calvinist scholasticism which brought into quasi-credal form the
core of the systematised doctrine of the great Reformed
dogmaticians in the early post-Calvin era. It was undoubtedly a
magnificent achievement. It rested upon the teaching of
theologians of considerable stature. Many of them were well known
to the Assembly divines: particularly, Beza, Zanchius, Piscator,
Buchanus, Keckermann, Polanus, Wollebius, Ursinus, Amesius and
Wallaeus. In addition mention should be made of the *Leiden
Synopsis purioris Theologiae* (1581) and the Articles of the *Synod of
Dort* (1618). All of these works were in Latin, although the *Medulla
Theologiae* (1634) of William Ames, was translated and published
in English as *The Marrow of Sacred Divinity*, London, 1639. Of their
works on Reformed dogmatics, and of others that followed in the
next half century, Karl Barth wrote very appreciatively.

I found a dogmatics which had form and substance, oriented
upon the central indications of the Biblical evidences for
revelation, which it also managed to follow out in detail with
astonishing richness – a dogmatics which by adopting and
sticking to the main lines of the Reformation attempted alike
a worthy continuation of the doctrinal construction of the
older Church, and yet was also out to cherish and preserve
continuity with the ecclesiastical science of the Middle Ages.[1]

Among the English Commissioners at the Westminster Assembly
were James Ussher, Archbishop of Armagh, who had compiled the

---

[1] Foreword to Heinrich Heppe, *Reformed Dogmatics, Set out and Illustrated from the
Sources*, ed. Ernst Bizer, 1935, tr. G. T. Thomson, London, 1950, p. v.

Irish Articles of 1614 which had a significant influence on the
Westminster Confession of Faith,[2] William Twisse, the Anglican
Prolocutor of the Assembly, and Anthony Tuckney of Cambridge,
who was largely responsible for the *Larger* and *Shorter Catechisms*,
and also learned scholars like John Lightfoot of Ely. The
representatives appointed by the Church of Scotland were
Alexander Henderson, Robert Baillie, Robert Douglas (who did
not actually attend the Assembly), Samuel Rutherford, and George
Gillespie, together with several distinguished elders. 'The Scots
were not members and had not the right to vote, but they took a
prominent part in the debates and wielded an influence out of all
proportion to their numbers.'[3] Gillespie and Rutherford had read
widely in the works of the Continental theologians, as also those
of Anglican, puritan, and independent divines who were involved
in the debates at the Assembly.[4] Samuel Rutherford and George
Gillespie also made contributions through books of their own which
they published in London during the Assembly, but these had to
do more with church government than with dogmatic theology.
In 1636, however, Rutherford had published a work in which he
gave a hard-line Calvinist account of 'the orthodox doctrine' of
the divine decrees and the efficacious operation of grace, in
accordance with the scholastic theology of the Synod of Dort and
the Leiden Synopsis,[5] which anticipated the position adopted at
the Westminster Assembly.

Apart from being the product of a formidable Protestant
scholasticism, the *Westminster Confession* was also a socio-political
instrument designed to give rational doctrinal cohesion to the
participating Churches in the Commonwealth, both in order to
strengthen their Protestant stance over against the Church of
Rome, and to bring about a rather Rome-like uniformity of religion
in the British Isles – there must be only 'one face of the Kirk'.
That intention was undoubtedly reinforced, especially for the Scots,
by the ratification of the Solemn League and Covenant in 1643, a
definitely religio-political covenant, which has ever since had the

---

[2] During the Assembly James Ussher also published *The Principles of the Christian Religion, Summarily set down according to the Word of God*, London, 1645. See A. F. Mitchell, *Catechisms of the Second Reformation*, London, 1886, pp. 137–50.

[3] J. H. S. Burleigh, *A Church History of Scotland*, London, 1960, pp. 225f.

[4] See J. S. McEwen, 'How the Confession came to be Written', *The Westminster Confession in the Church Today*, ed. A. I. C. Heron, Edinburgh, 1982, pp. 6–16.

[5] *Exercitationes Apologeticae pro Divina Gratia*, Amsterdam, 1636.

effect of politicising theology in the Westminster tradition. Nevertheless the powerful intellectual coherence in theological outlook achieved in the *Westminster Confession* has given an enduring unified character to Scottish theology and culture ever since, even one that still spans the sad divisions in the Kirk.

In its formulation the *Westminster Confession of Faith* was mainly the product of Anglican and puritan Calvinists in England, heavily indebted, as indicated above, to the Irish Articles of 1615. It was not the product of Scottish theology although several ministers from the Church of Scotland contributed significantly to it at certain points. However, after it was adopted by the General Assembly of the Church of Scotland in 1647 it has ever since remained its principal doctrinal standard. Its acceptance, along with the *Larger Catechism* and the *Shorter Catechism,* by the Church of Scotland was not out of line with developments that had been taking place within it, but it did mean that a more legalistic Calvinism was authoritatively grafted on to the more evangelical Calvinism of the older Scottish tradition deriving from the *Scots Confession* and nourished by the pre-Westminster catechisms, notably those of John Craig and John Davidson, as well as those of John Calvin, and the Palatine (Heidelberg) Catechism, which were widely used. This older tradition had its main influence on the preaching and teaching in the parishes, but was also evident in theologians like Robert Blair with whom as with Robert Bruce and Hugh Binning the Incarnation and atoning redemption were held closely together. Its characteristic emphasis on the relation of theology to worship and of evangelical experience to sacramental Communion with Christ continued in the life and mission of the Kirk and erupted from time to time with significant results in periods of evangelical awakening.

The *Confession of Faith* does not manifest the spiritual freshness and freedom, or the evangelical joy, of the *Scots Confession* of 1560, and was not so much a 'Confession' as a rational explanation of Protestant theology composed in fulfilment of a constitutional establishment, reflecting the rigid dogmatism of the Synod of Dort, 1618.[6] Nevertheless it was and is an outstanding work of great

---

[6] Cf. the judgment of John McLeod Campbell about the Confession of Faith: while 'its statements are substantially true ... it is the fact, that from the living religion of the Reformation Church – from the indications of personal experience which we have in the Confessions of the early Church, there is an awful falling off in the Confession, we now have.' 'Speech Delivered at the Bar of the Very Reverend The Synod of Glasgow and Ayr', Greenock, 1831, p. 35.

theological substance and power, with an intrinsic authority of an impressive kind. Certainly in Scotland the Westminster Standards made a magnificent as well as a lasting impact on Scottish life and thought, particularly through their combination of high theology with worship and the glorification of God.[7] As George S. Hendry wrote:

> The Confession of Faith possesses great and undoubted merits. It could not have held its place in the Presbyterian Churches for so long were it not so. The time and care taken to its preparation, the systematic skill with which it handles the whole field of doctrine, the courage with which it faces the most difficult questions, the precision, elegance, and occasional nobility of the language it uses, combine to make it, in its way, a minor classic.[8]

Of particular note was the 'godly fear' or awesome sense of the Sovereign Majesty of God which left an enduring mark on Presbyterian worship, at least until the early twentieth century.[9]

The overall framework in which this Westminster Theology was expressed derived from seventeenth-century federal theology formulated in sharp contrast to the highly rationalised conception of a sacramental universe of Roman theology, but combined with a similar way of thinking in terms of primary and secondary causes. Moreover, it operated with a medieval conception of the *ordo salutis* (reached through various stages of grace leading to union with Christ), which reversed the teaching of Calvin that it is through union with Christ *first* that we participate in all his benefits.[10] Tied up with the federal theology this gave the *Westminster Confession* and *Catechisms* a very legalistic and constitutional character in which

---

[7] See David Dickson's Commentary on the *Westminster Confession of Faith*, posthumously published as *Truth's Victory over Error: Or, the True Principles of the Christian Religion*, 1684, 1752 & 1764, the English form of *Praelectiones in Confessionem Fidei*.

[8] G. S. Hendry, *The Westminster Confession for Today. A Contemporary Interpretation*, London, 1960; see James B. Torrance, 'Strengths and Weaknesses of the Westminster Theology', in Alasdair I. C. Heron, *The Westminster Confession in the Church Today*, Edinburgh, 1982, pp. 40–54; and also Holmes Rolston III, *John Calvin Versus the Westminster Confession in the Church Today*, Richmond, Virginia, 1972.

[9] See Ch. XXI of the *Confession*.

[10] On the revival of this medieval notion of *ordo salutis* through theologians like William Perkins, see J. B. Torrance, 'Strengths and Weaknesses of the Westminster Theology', pp. 45 & 52ff.

theological statements were formalised at times with 'almost frigidly logical definition'.[11]

In line with an increasing tendency in seventeenth-century biblicism the *Westminster Confession* devotes a long opening chapter to the Holy Scripture which, given by the inspiration of God, is very rightly stated to be 'the rule of faith and life'. Because the Holy Scripture derives from divine revelation, its authority depends wholly upon God who is truth himself, and is thus to be received as the Word of God and understood through the inward witness and illumination of the Holy Spirit. It is to be noted, however, that 'it was to divine revelation rather than to the writing of it that the inspiration belonged'.[12] The infallible rule of interpretation is the Scripture itself, and the supreme Judge by which all controversies are to be determined can be no other than the Holy Spirit speaking in the Scripture. This marks out very sharply the difference between the Reformed Church and the Roman Church, but the biblical support for its teaching is rather formal, and inadequate and sometimes rather misleading, for passages and texts are adduced to support notions held on other grounds.[13] The handling of the Scriptures is governed by a kind of biblical nominalism, for biblical sentences tend to be adduced out of their context and to be interpreted arbitrarily and singly in detachment from their spiritual ground and theological intention and content. Moreover, by giving the Holy Scripture thus handled priority of place over the fundamental doctrines of the Gospel, Westminster theology treats biblical statements as definitive propositions from which deductions are to be made, so that in their expression doctrines thus logically derived are given a categorical or canonical character. They are not treated, as in the *Scots Confession*, as having an open-structured character, pointing away from themselves to divine truth which by its nature cannot be contained in finite forms of speech and

---

[11] Thus A. F. Mitchell of the Shorter Catechism, *Catechisms of the Second Reformation*, p. xxvii.

[12] Thus rightly John Macpherson, *The Westminster Confession of Faith*, Edinburgh, 1881, p. 31.

[13] Rather fuller biblical support for the different articles of the Confession, with an 'Epistle to the Reader' by Thomas Manton, was given by A. Ker in a standard edition published along with *The Larger Catechism, The Shorter Catechism, The Sum of Saving Knowledge, The National Covenant, The Solemn League and Covenant, The Directory for the Publick Worship of God, The Form of Church-Government and of the Ordination of Ministers,* and *The Directory For Family-Worship.* Glasgow, 1757.

thought, although it may be mediated through them.[14] Nor does the *Westminster Confession* echo the humble readiness expressed in the *Scots Confession* to receive correction in the light of divine revelation.

> Protestand that gif onie man will note in this our confession onie Artickle or sentence repugnant to Gods halie word, that it wald pleis him of his gentleness and for christian charities sake to admonish us of the same in writing; and we upon our honoures and fidelitie, be Gods grace do promise unto him satisfactioun fra the mouth of God, that is, fra his haly scripture, or else reformation of that quhilk he sal prove to be amisse.[15]

In contrast the *Confession of Faith,* stamped with the authority of the Westminster Assembly and backed up by the General Assembly of the Church of Scotland, attained such a powerful and indeed definitive place in the tradition of the Kirk that the Holy Scriptures were often interpreted in the light of its teaching rather than the other way round. This was very apparent in the way sermons by leading Churchmen were often composed, not so much on the ground of biblical exegesis and interpretation, as under the prescriptive principles of the Westminster Standards – they were doctrinal rather than expository and evangelical sermons.

The Westminster way of beginning the Confession with a chapter on the Holy Scripture prior to and apart from the evangelical substance of the Faith tended to separate form from content. This feature was made acute by the character and structure of the following chapter, 'Of God, and the Holy Trinity'. Most of it was devoted to a relatively long and rather abstract account, mainly in adjectival terms and negative forms of thought, of what God is in his infinite power and sovereign nature,[16] but with only two condensed sentences on the Holy Trinity.

> In the unity of the Godhead there be three persons, of one substance, power, and eternity; God the Father, God the Son,

---

[14] Cf. Calvin's use of 'the analogy of faith' in interpreting biblical statements by referring them beyond themselves to 'God's eternal truth', *Institute,* 'Prefaratory Address to the King of France'.

[15] *Scots Confession, 1560,* edition by G. D. Henderson, Edinburgh, 1937, p. 41.

[16] Cf. David Dickson, who with reference to 'the most absolute, and most supreme Dominion, Sovereignty, and infinite Perfection' in God's Providence, wrote: 'He is in, and of himself, above all Law whatever, and under the command of none in heaven, or in Earth'. *Truth's Victory over Error,* p. 63.

and God the Holy Ghost. The Father is of none, neither begotten nor proceeding; the Son is eternally begotten of the Father; the Holy Ghost eternally proceeding from the Father and the Son.

The problem is not with the content, but with the fact that the doctrine of the Trinity appears as an addendum to the doctrine of God. This was very different from the teaching of John Calvin that there is no real knowledge of God except through his self-revealing and self-naming as Father, Son and Holy Spirit, in which we do not begin by asking what God is (*quid sit Deus*), but what kind of God is he (*qualis sit Deus*), and who God is (*quis sit Deus*).[17] Here, however, the doctrine of the Trinity was tacked on to a doctrine of God,[18] rather in line with medieval theology in its tractates 'On God' (*De Deo*) and 'On the Trine God' (*De Trino Deo*) in which statements about what God is are divorced from statements about who God is both as he is in himself and as he is toward us. This was a departure from the classical theology of the Nicene Church in that it gave priority to an abstract idea of the absolute sovereignty of God over his trinitarian nature as an eternal consubstantial communion of reciprocal personal relations and thus as essentially and intrinsically a God of love.

Had the *Confession of Faith* begun with the doctrine of the Holy Trinity and then presented its doctrine of God, the latter would have been very, very different. In speaking of the one Being of God as Father, Son, and Holy Spirit, the doctrine of the Trinity affirms the supreme truth that *Fatherhood, Sonship and Communion* belong to the essential nature of God as he is in himself, and that it is as such, and not otherwise, that God is omnipotent creator, lawgiver, and judge of all the earth. In the *Confession of Faith* itself God is said to be lawgiver and judge, but only said to be Father properly in his relation to those who are elected, justified and 'made partakers of the grace of adoption' and are thus 'enabled to cry Abba, Father'.[19] However, in making himself known to us as

---

[17] John Calvin, *Institute*, 1.2.1–2. Refer to 'Calvin's Doctrine of the Trinity' in my book *Trinitarian Perspectives. Toward Doctrinal Agreement*, Edinburgh, 1994, pp. 41f.

[18] Cf. Calvin who, in his *Geneva Catechism* of 1541, prefaced his account of the Apostles Creed with a section stating that 'the foundation of true reliance upon God is to know him in Jesus Christ' – *The School of Faith*, p. 7.

[19] *Confession*, Article 12.

Father through his Son and in the Holy Spirit God reveals to us that he is Spirit and that Fatherhood and Sonship characterise his essential nature as God, that his eternal Being is intrinsically an eternal Communion of Love, that God is *Father* and *is* Love in his ultimate Being, and that it is precisely as such that he is lawgiver and judge. Divine Love and divine Law are one and the same; it is in and through his presence and activity as a Communion of Love, as Father, Son and Holy Spirit, that God is the supreme lawgiver and judge.

Let it be said firmly, however, that in the *Westminster Confession* as a whole and in both *Westminster Catechisms*, the sheer sovereignty and majesty of God were allowed to shine forth in such a way that it left an indelible mark upon the Church of Scotland and its theology.

> God hath all life, glory, goodness, blessedness, in and of himself; and is alone in and unto himself all-sufficient, not standing in need of any of his creatures which he hath made, not deriving any glory from them, but only manifesting his own glory, in, by, unto, and upon them: he is the alone fountain of all being, of whom, through whom, and to whom, are all things; and hath most sovereign dominion over them, to do by them, for them, or upon them, whatsoever himself pleaseth. In his sight all things are open and manifest; his knowledge is infinite, infallible, and independent upon the creature, so as nothing is to him contingent and uncertain. He is most holy in all his counsels, in all his works, and in all his commands.[20]

> *What is God?* God is a Spirit, and in and of himself infinite in being, glory, blessedness, and perfection; all-sufficient, eternal, unchangeable, incomprehensible, everywhere present, almighty, knowing all things, most wise, most holy, most just, most merciful and gracious, long-suffering, and abundant in goodness and truth.[21]

This awesome sense of the sheer majesty of God was reflected not least in *The Directory for the Public Worship of God*, in the preparation

---

[20] *The Confession of Faith*, Ch. II.2.
[21] Cited from *The School of Faith*, pp. 185f.

of which the Scots particularly had a strong hand at the Westminster Assembly.[22]

Nevertheless, in failing to give primacy to the doctrine of the Holy Trinity, the *Confession of Faith* presents a doctrine of God as primarily omnipotent creator and judge of all the earth, who can only be Father to his creatures if the requirements of his Law are rigorously satisfied and God himself is thus satisfied. It is in this way that the Confession then goes on to present its articles of belief in God's eternal decrees, of creation and providence, in which he 'freely and unchangeably' ordained whatsoever comes to pass, the fall and punishment of mankind, and God's covenant with man, by which God was pleased to express 'some voluntary condescension' on his part.[23] Only then, and within that framework of God as judge and lawgiver, does the Confession come to the doctrine of the Mediator and his atoning satisfaction. This doctrine of God, not primarily as Father, but primarily as creator, lawgiver and judge, accentuated within the framework of a federalised and logicalised system of Calvinism, was to have problematic and deleterious effects in later Scottish theology. The tendency to trace the ultimate ground of belief back to eternal divine decrees behind the back of the Incarnation of God's Beloved Son, as in a federal concept of *pre*-destination, tended to foster a hidden Nestorian dualism between the divine and human natures in the one Person of Jesus Christ, and thus even to provide ground for a dangerous form of Arian and Socinian heresy in which the atoning work of Christ regarded as an organ of God's activity was separated from the intrinsic nature and character of God as Love. Perhaps it was in order to meet this problem that it could be said that it was the office of Christ as 'the mediatorial King', actually to contract and administer the covenant of grace.[24]

Apart from being methodologically erroneous and inadequate, the doctrine of God, thus presented within the framework of the Confession, is strictly not a fully *Christian* doctrine of God, that is, of God the Father made known to us definitively through Christ and his Spirit in the Gospel. Although in several later chapters of

---

[22] See *The Westminster Directory*, Edited, with An Introduction and Notes, by Thomas Leishman, Edinburgh & London, 1901.

[23] Chapter VII.1. See Samuel Rutherford, *The Covenant of Life Opened: Or, A Treatise of the Covenant of Grace*, Edinburgh, 1655, Ch. VI, pp. 15f.

[24] Thus A. A. Hodge in his comment on 'Article XII.3 of the Confession', *The Confession of Faith*, 1961 reprint, pp. 126–8.

the Confession mention is made of the Blessed Trinity in passing, notably in the chapter on creation, the Confession as a whole does not have a trinitarian or christological structure,[25] let alone a soteriological structure, which thereby affected people's understanding of the ultimate character of God.[26] George Hendry put his finger on the basic problem here.

> The Confession undoubtedly intends and professes to describe the God who is revealed in Christ, but, failing to discern the actual pattern of his being, it ends in describing another God, who is unrevealed, and who lacks the attributes of the God and Father of our Lord Jesus Christ. Thus it actually imperils the faith it asserts, that 'there is but one living and triune God,' because it fails to concentrate attention on the authentic image of himself which God has given us in Jesus Christ.[27]

In the Chapter on *God's Eternal Decrees* the Confession rightly warns: 'The doctrine of this high mystery of predestination is to be handled with special prudence and care, that men attending the will of God revealed in his word, and yielding obedience thereunto, may, from the certainty of their effectual vocation, be assured of their eternal election.' Here it is implied that in determining the ends God wants to accomplish he also determined the *means* by which his decrees would be accomplished. The effect of this, as J. B. Torrance has pointed out, was to subordinate grace to election.[28] That was to give rise to a limited way of thinking about redemption in which the fact that in the end some people will not actually be saved is read back into God's saving purpose and limits it.[29] Moreover, so far as the content of the doctrine of election is

---

[25] See J. B. Torrance, 'Strengths and Weaknesses of the Westminster Theology', *The Westminster Confession in the Church Today*, ed. A. I. C. Heron, Edinburgh, 1982, p. 45.

[26] It is significant that David Dickson in his comments on the first chapter returned to a definitely Christocentric and evangelical approach with stress on the uniqueness of Christ for salvation and knowledge of God, and followed it up with a more adequate biblically grounded account of the doctrine of the Trinity.

[27] G. S. Hendry, *The Westminster Confession for Today*, London, 1960, p. 47.

[28] 'Strengths and Weaknesses of the Westminster Theology', *op. cit.* p. 41.

[29] This was how it was interpreted by John Owen, who held that what was effectually fulfilled and accomplished by the death of Christ determines how we are to think of what God originally and actually intended by it! See Robert

concerned, no hint was given of the biblical principle governing
salvation history, of the election of one for the many either in
respect of Israel or of Christ, for in its teaching about God's eternal
unchangeable 'decrees' (a very unbiblical way of speaking[30]), the
emphasis is laid on a partitive and particularist nature of election,
with explicit statement to the effect that while some are
predestinated unto everlasting life, others are foreordained to
everlasting death. That implied a definite doctrine of reprobation.[31]
As David Dickson commented, the cause of reprobation and
election alike is 'the absolute will and good pleasure of God'.[32] On
the other hand, the Confession goes on to state that those who are
predestinated unto life, God 'has chosen in Christ unto everlasting
glory, *out of his mere free grace and love'.* In tracing everything back
to the grace and love of God[33] this reflects a milder form of
Calvinism than sometimes preceded it in Holland or often followed
in Scotland, although it nevertheless involves a Protestant form of
the Augustinian notion of 'irresistible grace', which is evident also
in the chapter on 'Effectual Calling' – 'while the elect come most
freely to Christ, they are made willing by his grace'. In hyper-
Calvinist mode it is the doctrine of God's 'eternal decrees', rather
than the one divine decree or purpose fulfilled in the incarnation,
which governs the following chapters on creation, providence, the
fall of man, sin and punishment, and God's covenant with man.
Only then does the Confession have a chapter 'Of Christ the
Mediator'. This is not to say that traditional doctrines of the
Reformed Faith are omitted in these chapters but that they suffer
from a methodological and analytical presentation which rather
distorts them.[34]

S. Franks, *The Work of Christ. A Historical Study of Christian Doctrine*, Edinburgh,
1962, p. 460.

[30] Cf. W. W. Bryden, *The Significance of the Westminster Confession of Faith*, Toronto,
1943, p. 12.

[31] This was contrary to the teaching of John Knox who declined to understand
or affirm 'that God's absolute ordinance is the principall cause of reprobation'.
The Works of John Knox, Vol. 5, p. 112. Cf. also p. 21.

[32] David Dickson, *Truth's Victory over Error*, p. 56. See also the Chapter X 'Of
Effectual Calling' which has to do with the elect and only the elect.

[33] As the *Larger Catechism* has it, 'out of his mere love, for the praise of his glorious
name' – Q. 13, *The School of Faith*, p. 186.

[34] This is also true of the Westminster Catechisms which are markedly less
Christological than their predecessors. See T. F. Torrance, *The School of Faith*,
pp. xviff.

The idea that the relations between God and mankind were governed by covenant had both a disadvantage and an advantage. On the one hand, through the notion of a covenant of works it not only altered the biblical notion of law (*torah*) and covenant (*berith*), but built into the background of Westminster theology a contractual framework of law (understood in the Latin sense as *lex*) that pervaded and gave a forensic and conditional slant even to the presentation of the truths of the Gospel.[35] On the other hand, the primary place given to the covenant of grace directed the focus of attention upon the fact that God calls people into fellowship with himself, addresses them personally and asks for their response in worship and love, within a covenanted correspondence of the whole universe to its creator. At the same time the way in which God's eternal decrees and the effectual calling of grace were conceived, in terms of election narrowed down to the selection of only some people for redemption,[36] meant that the relation between God and man was conceived in a particularist or individualist way without adequate attention to the corporate nature of salvation in Christ. While the doctrine of election rightly entailed a view of grace as objective and unconditional, the hard conception of double predestination was biblically and evangelically unfortunate. On the one hand, it rested on a mistaken Calvinist interpretation of the teaching of St Paul, 'Jacob have I loved, but Esau have I hated' taken out of its context of the doctrine of the remnant in Old Testament salvation history.[37] On the other hand, it introduced a deep-seated uncertainty into faith which was not adequately met by the later chapter 'Of Assurance of Grace and Salvation'.[38] As the history of theology in

---

[35] Cf. Rutherford who pointed out that the Covenant between God and man was 'of a far other nature than the covenant between man and man'. *The Covenant of Life Opened*, p. 40. On the other hand, the old Roman conception of law with which he operated in his work *Lex Rex: The Law and the Prince*, London, 1644, was rather different from that of the biblical *torah*.

[36] According to John McLeod Campbell 'the word *redemption* was not used by the Westminster Assembly in the sense in which holding *redemption limited* was a *limiting of atonement*'! *Memorials of John McLeod Campbell, D.D., Being Selections From His Correspondence*, edited by his son Donald Campbell, London, 1877, p. 79.

[37] Thus rightly George S. Hendry, *The Westminster Confession Today*, London, 1960, p. 52.

[38] Chapter XVIII. Cf. G. S. Hendry, *Westminster Confession*, pp. 51ff.

Scotland was to show again and again the lack of assurance in saving grace was due to the idea, as expressed by David Dickson, that 'Christ died only for his own sheep, viz. intentionally and efficaciously'.[39] The rigidly contractual concept of God as lawgiver together with a necessitarian concept of immutable divine activity allied to double predestination, with its inescapable implication of a doctrine of limited atonement, set the Church with a serious problem as to its interpretation of biblical statements about the offer of the Gospel freely to all people. Moreover, through a strictly forensic notion of justification in which a judicial relation substituted for an intimate union with Christ, faith failed to be grounded properly in the Person of Christ and inwardly linked in him with the assurance of salvation which he embodied.[40]

In the fine succinct Chapter XIII 'Of Christ the Mediator' we are given the evangelical heart of the Confession, presented in a trinitarian way faithful to Calvin and Nicene theology.

> It pleased God in his eternal purpose, to choose and ordain the Lord Jesus his only begotten Son, to be the Mediator between God and man; the Prophet, Priest, and King; the Head and Saviour of the Church; the heir of all things; and Judge of the world: unto whom he did from all eternity give a people to be his seed, and to be by him in time redeemed, called, justified, sanctified, and glorified.

He is 'the Son of God, the second Person of the Trinity, being very and eternal God, of one Substance and equal with the Father', who 'when the fulness of time was come did take upon him Man's Nature, with all the essential Properties and common infirmities thereof, yet without Sin, being conceived by the power of the Holy Ghost, in the womb of the Virgin Mary, of her substance'. In answer to the question 'Who is the Mediator of the covenant of grace?' the *Larger Catechism* ran:

> The only mediator of the covenant of grace is the Lord Jesus Christ, who, being the eternal Son of God, of one substance and equal with the Father, in the fulness of time became man,

---

[39] David Dickson, *Truth's Victory*, p. 57.
[40] Cf. the problematic comment of A. A. Hodge that full assurance is not of the essence of faith terminating directly upon Christ and his promise, *The Confession of Faith*, London reprint, 1961, pp. 244f.

and so was and continues to be God and man, in two distinct natures, and one person, for ever.[41]

Attention was given to the eternal purpose fulfilled in the Son's incarnate advent in time, and the hypostatic union of divine and human natures in his one Person, and not least the three-fold office of Christ as prophet, priest and king, the Head and Saviour of the Church, the heir of all things and the Judge of the world. All his saving and atoning work depended on the fact that 'Christ-God-Man' (as Dickson referred to Christ) was one Person. In him 'two whole, perfect and distinct Natures, the Godhead and the Manhood were inseparably joined together in one Person, without Conversion, Composition or Confusion.' Stress was thus laid upon the fact that it is upon *the oneness of his Deity with his Humanity* that the 'great value' of redemption rested.[42] This account of the Mediator was rightly presented in a dynamic perspective. Weight was laid by the Confession on the perfect obedience and sacrifice of Christ which through the eternal Spirit he offered to his Father in his incarnate, risen and ascended Person as Mediator.

This mediatorial work of Christ was expounded and complemented by the account given by David Dickson in which he explained the interrelation between the active and passive obedience of 'the whole Christ' in his vicarious life and death who was not given and born for himself but for us.[43] One misses here, however, the kind of place given to the redemptive activity of the incarnate Son in the *whole course* of his life and ministry from his birth to his resurrection and within the full movement of atoning mediation and reconciliation and the blessed exchange effected through Christ's identification with us in our sin and poverty that was so important for evangelical Calvinism. Appeal was frequently made here by the Reformed dogmaticians to Calvin himself.

When it is asked how, after abolishing sins, Christ removed the discord between us and God and acquired righteousness for us, it may be replied generally that he provided us with this by the whole course of his obedience.... From the

---

[41] *The School of Faith*, p. 191.

[42] Cf. David Dickson, *Truth's Victory*, pp. 72f. The Augustinian idea that Christ is Mediator only in virtue of his humanity, was rejected, p. 77.

[43] David Dickson, *Truth's Victory*, pp. 74ff. Cf. also A. A. Hodge, *The Confession of Faith*, London, 1961 reprint, pp. 150f.

moment he put on the form of a servant, he began to pay the price of liberation for our redemption.[44]

At this point the *Westminster Catechisms* had rather more to say about the humiliation which Christ suffered for our sakes in his birth, life, temptations, his subjection to the law, his ministry in the form of a servant, and his death and burial, which are more biblical and more in line with Calvin's teaching about the vicarious humanity of Christ in the form of a servant.[45] According to the *Confession of Faith* the Lord Jesus, through his perfect obedience under the law and self-sacrifice and endurance of the most grievous torments in his soul and most painful bodily sufferings, fully satisfied the justice of his Father and purchased reconciliation for us. This implied a transactional notion of atoning satisfaction in fulfilment of a divine requirement, on the ground of which the Father was induced to reconcile us, and was as it were 'bought off'. At this important point the *Westminster Confession* departed from the teaching of the New Testament in which there is no suggestion that reconciliation was bought *from* God; and it also departed from the teaching of Calvin about 'the love of God the Father which goes before and anticipates our reconciliation in Christ'. In support Calvin cited St Augustine: 'It was not after we were reconciled to God through the blood of his Son that he began to love us ... The fact that we are reconciled through Christ's death must not be understood as if his Son reconciled us to him that he might now begin to love those whom he hated.'[46] The truth of the prevenient love and grace of God in Christ was one of the primary principles of the Reformation. In the puritan form of federal theology (deriving from William Perkins and William Ames,[47] as well as from Zacharias Ursinus[48]) which influenced the Westminster

---

[44] John Calvin, *Institute*, 2.16.5. See Heinrich Heppe, *Reformed Dogmatics*, p. 459.
[45] *The Larger Catechism*, QQ. 36–40; *The Shorter Catechism*, Q. 27. *The School of Faith*, pp. 193f & 266.
[46] John Calvin, *Institute*, 2.16.3–4. Calvin's memorable words are: *Quia prius diligit, postea nos sibi reconciliati sumus.*
[47] See William Perkins, *Golden Chaine or The Description of Theologie, containing the Order of causes of Salvation and Damnation, according to God's word*, tr. from Latin, London, 1592; and William Ames, *The Marrow of Sacred Divinity, drawn out of Scripture and the Interpreters thereof, and brought into Method*, London, 1639; cf. also Wolfgang Musculus, *Loci Communes Theologiae Sacrae*, Basel, 1560.
[48] Zacharias Ursinus, especially his *Commentary on the Heidelberg Catechism*, 1598, but see also his *Catechesis, Summa Theologiae*, Heidelberg, 1612.

Divines, the Reformation principle of *sola gratia* evidently did not have a deep enough influence on their basic concept of God. However, in mitigation of a hard contractual conception of the Covenant the *Confession* inserted the following statement: 'This covenant of grace is frequently set forth in the scripture by the name of a Testament, in reference to the death of Jesus Christ the testator, and to the everlasting inheritance, with all things belonging to it, therein bequeathed.'[49] The point is that since the conditions of the covenant have been fulfilled in Christ, he himself embodied the covenant of grace which is now freely extended to sinners with all his benefits by way of a testament. As Patrick Gillespie expounded this:

> So is the covenant of grace a testament, because the same thing which the covenant requireth from its conditions to be performed on our part, the same things are bequeathed to us among Christ's goods, which by his testament and latter will he disponed and left to his people absolutely.[50]

Within the general structure which informs the *Westminster Confession of Faith*, however, this way of interpreting the covenant of grace as an absolute testament of grace appears somewhat ambiguous. The problem here, in part at least, arises from the fact that the chapter on the Mediator is preceded by that on providence in which use is made of a rational framework of God's relation to the world in terms of 'first cause' and 'second causes' understood in a qualified determinist way. Thus, in 'continuity with the ecclesiastical science of the Middle Ages',[51] a scholastic account of God's activity in his ordinary providential activity is given according to which he 'makes use of means, yet is free to work without, above, and against them, at his pleasure'. Along with the two-way contractual and conditional nature of the covenant of grace as well as of works, this helped to project into the Westminster tradition of Scottish theology a hard logico-causal understanding of the activity of God in redemption as well as in creation, thereby rationalising the doctrinal content of the Gospel.[52] Thus it is

---

[49] *The Confession of Faith*, VII.4.
[50] Patrick Gillespie, *The Ark of the Testament Opened*, London, 1661, p. 302.
[51] Thus rightly Karl Barth, Heppe, *Reformed Dogmatics*, p. v.
[52] Cf. the stress by William Perkins on 'the order of the causes of salvation and Damnation', in his *Golden Chaine*, which also had a decisive influence on David Dickson evident in his *Commentary on the Confession of Faith*, e.g. chapters III–VII.

implied that if Christ died for all people, then all people must be saved; but also if some people are damned, Christ could not have died for them. That was of course the teaching of the Synod of Dort which was upheld by the *Westminster Confession* and *Catechisms*. It was a logico-causal nexus of this kind that replaced in the relation of the atoning sacrifice of Christ to sinners the unique kind of divine activity by the Holy Spirit revealed in the Virgin Birth of Jesus and his resurrection from the dead.

It is highly significant that the Confession does not have a chapter on the Holy Spirit or indeed on the Gospel of God's infinite Love savingly incarnate in Jesus and proclaimed to all people alike, an omission that was made good by American Presbyterians in their edition of the *Westminster Confession of Faith*.[53] The same grave omission is found in the *Westminster Catechisms*.[54] The missionary outreach of the Gospel in obedience to Christ's commission to the Apostles (Matt. 28.19f & Mark 16.15f) was missing. A God who restricts his love to a fixed number of the elect is not a God who IS Love and therefore is not as infinitely loving as his infinite Being.

Apart from such a doctrine of God, salvation by grace alone, which Westminster Theology emphatically taught, becomes ambiguous and inconsistent as seems evident in the Confession's Chapter IX 'Of Free Will'. In it there is a proper recognition that every human being has free will in one sense, but it is also said that 'he has wholly lost all ability of will to any spiritual good accompanying salvation'. That was a distinction between *voluntas* and *arbitrium* with which Martin Luther was concerned in his great book *De servo arbitrio*, misleadingly translated as 'On Free-Will'. Everyone has free-will in the sense of *voluntas*, but no one has freedom in the sense of *arbitrium*, or control, over his/her free-will. Our free-will is a form of *self*-will from which we can no more escape than we can from our own selves. *Libera voluntas* is not *liberum arbitrium*. According to the Confession, when God converts a sinner and translates him into a state of grace, he frees him from his natural bondage. That is certainly the message of the Gospel. In the chapter 'Of Effectual Calling', on the other hand, the saving activity of God is presented not only in terms of a Gospel call to sinners, but as one which *makes* them willing. 'All those whom God has predestinated unto life, and those only, he is pleased effectually

---

[53] See G. S. Hendry, *Westminster Confession*, pp. 117ff and 121ff.
[54] See my Introduction to *The School of Faith*, pp. xcvff.

to call ... to grace and salvation by Jesus Christ.' By his almighty
power God determines them to what is good, 'effectually drawing
them to Jesus Christ, yet so as they come freely, being made willing
by his grace.' Thus in the last resort only those responding to the
Gospel call are really free to do so who have been predetermined
to do so by an inscrutable divine decree. This teaching about divine
election and effectual calling in which the sinner is 'altogether
passive', was certainly meant to establish the objectivity of saving
grace, but as expressed in this way, it had the effect of destroying
the sinner's confidence in Christ and damaging his assurance of
salvation.[55]

The lack of a christocentric framework in the *Confession of Faith*
made room for a moralistic notion of sin and the 'total depravity'
of human nature which has often been considered rather
pessimistic. Sin is certainly understood in the light of God's
righteous judgment, but the account given in the Confession of
the blinding and hardening of the ungodly in their sin is rather
different from the teaching of St Paul that the Gospel can blind
the unbelieving and that the law itself can be and is the strength
of sin. In the New Testament it is the Gospel, rather than the law,
however, that reveals both the real depth of sin and the universal
depravity of unregenerate human nature. This is made especially
clear in the Epistles of St Paul and St John: when seen from the
perspective of the *saving grace* of God in the Incarnation, atoning
death and resurrection of Christ, sin is exposed in its ultimate
nature as sin against God.[56] When understood from the
substitutionary death of Christ a person's being is seen to come
under the *total* judgment of Christ. Sin is then regarded in a much
more radical way than in the Westminster Theology, but it yields a
doctrine of sin which is formulated as a corollary of grace alone,
not as a lapse from original righteousness permitted by God 'who
was pleased, according to his wise and holy will, to permit, having
purposed to order it to his own glory.'[57] If Christ died for us, not
in a partial but in a total way, such that the whole of our being
comes under the judgment of the Cross, our good as well as our
evil, then it is in that light that a proper understanding of what the

[55] Cf. again G. S. Hendry, *Westminster Confession*, p. 131.
[56] Cf. James Fraser of Brea, 'Christ coming into the World to dy for Sinners, to
save them from Sin is a strong Demonstration, and speaks out very much of
the evil of Sin; what a real Marker was this?' *Meditations on Several Subjects in
Divinity*, Edinburgh, 1721, p. 150.
[57] Chapter VI.1.

Confession calls 'total depravity' is to be understood, not on moralistic grounds. Later on in the Confession, however, the conception of total depravity, in which we are said to be 'utterly indisposed, and made opposite to all good, and wholly inclined to all evil' is evidently modified.[58] Before the Cross of Christ, not least at Holy Communion when we partake of his Body and Blood, we cannot but feel ashamed for our whole being, for our good as well as our evil. This radical conception of our sinful nature is also evident in a proper understanding of justification by grace alone: by being freely put in the right with God we are thereby revealed to be wholly in the wrong in ourselves, so that we are ashamed not only of what we are in ourselves, but even of *our* faith and *our* repentance as unworthy in God's sight. But such a radical understanding of grace alone and the response of faith (such as was expressed in *Justifying Faith* by James Fraser of Brae), was not built into the Westminster tradition, in which evangelical Calvinists discerned hidden semi-Pelagian tendencies, or what they called neonomianism.

This way of thinking of sin and human behaviour may also be implied in a legalistic or judicial doctrine of justification by faith, which some Westminster theologians took care to point out.[59] As already noted, the evident intention of the rather paradoxical teaching on free-will and effectual calling is to stress the objectivity of saving grace. While attention is given to 'free-will', faith is regarded as the *passive* instrument of justification.

> Those whom God effectually calls, he also freely justifies, not infusing righteousness into them, but by pardoning their sins, and by accounting and accepting their persons as righteous; not for anything wrought in them, or done by them, but for Christ's sake alone; not by imputing faith, or any other evangelical obedience to them, as their righteousness; but by imputing the obedience and satisfaction of Christ alone unto them, they receiving and resting on him and his righteousness by faith; which faith they have not of themselves; it is the gift of God.

---

[58] Compare Chapters VI.4 and X.7.

[59] Cf. again David Dickson: 'The Gospel is so contrived by the Infinite Wisdom and Goodness of God, that there is a judicial transferring of our Sins, as a Debt on Christ the Cautioner, and a Translation of his Righteousness and Merit to be imputed to us, for our Justification, without the least Respect to our Works.' *Truth's Victory*, p. 123.

The Confession goes on to say that faith thus receiving and resting on Christ and his righteousness, is 'the alone instrument of justification; yet it is not alone in the person justified, but is ever accompanied with all the other saving graces, and is no dead faith, but works, by love.' This is in line with the chapters on 'Saving Faith' and 'Repentance unto Life'. As expounded by Scots theologians in this Westminster tradition, apart from its strange Roman use of 'graces' in the plural, this gave rise to two problems.

On the one hand, while this is followed by chapters on adoption and sanctification through the activity of the Holy Spirit, the Confession did not take the line of Calvin and Scots Reformation theology in which justification and union with Christ are held inseparably together, so that apart from brief sentences on 'Adoption', the notion of justification is construed mainly in terms of a forensic 'imputation' while union with Christ is understood as a 'judicial union', which must then be cultivated and deepened in a spiritual and sanctifying way through the help of 'indwelling grace'. On the other hand, within the contractual framework of the covenant, this concept of imputed righteousness rested on a notion of atonement in which 'Christ Jesus, by his obedience and sacrifice of himself which he through the eternal Spirit once offered up unto God, has fully satisfied the justice of the Father'. As David Dickson commented, he 'fully discharged the debt of all those who are thus justified and did make a proper, real and full satisfaction to the Father's justice in their behalf'.[60] That is to say, justification was regarded not only as the justification of the sinner but as the justification of the law of God and of God himself. This way of regarding the satisfaction of divine justice and the justification of God's eternal law had the effect of imprinting on Scottish theology a rather harsh view of God, one which became very marked in the preaching of many covenanting divines in their call for retribution on their political and ecclesiastical opponents. Moreover, this notion of justification as a legal fulfilling of the contractual requirement of the covenant in respect of God's eternal law, rather than as a gracious manifestation of the faithfulness of God embodied in the person of Christ, had a moralising effect upon the life and theology of the Kirk, which was particularly evident in the overwhelming attention given to the law, in comparison to the Gospel, and the call of the *Larger Catechism* for

---

[60] David Dickson, *Truth's Victory*, p. 91.

a detailed fulfilment of divine commandments.[61] On the other hand, Scottish ministers schooled in this moralistic form of Calvinism, as John Buchan once noted, 'gave to the Scottish people a moral seriousness, a conception of the deeper issues of life, and an intellectual *ascesis*, gifts which may well atone for their many infirmities.'[62]

Westminster Theology had a high doctrine of the Church, although it was not presented in connection with the chapters on Christology and soteriology. But along with the chapter 'Of the Communion of Saints', it continued the teaching of John Calvin in offering a theological account of the Church as the Body of Christ, realistically understood in its union with him, in departure from a 'two-bodied' (Calvin's expression) conception of the Church as a juridical institution and a mystical body found in Roman canon law. In Westminster Theology, then, the Church was identified with the Kingdom of the Lord Jesus Christ, the house and family of God, through which men are ordinarily saved and union with which was held to be essential to their best growth and service. A distinction was made between the invisible and the visible Church. As invisible the Church consists of the whole number of the elect gathered into one, under Christ the Head, and is 'the Spouse, the Body, the Fulness of him who fills all in all'. As visible, the Church consists of 'all those throughout the world who profess the true religion together with their children, and is the kingdom of the Lord Jesus Christ, the house and family of God, out of whom there is no ordinary possibility of salvation'. 'To this catholic, visible Church Christ has given the ministry, oracles and ordinances of God for the gathering and perfecting of saints in this life and to the end of the world, and does by his own Spirit, according to his promise, make them effectual thereunto.'[63]

It was in these terms as well as in terms of the one covenant of grace which, with different administrations and sacraments spanned the whole life of the people of God from Old Testament to New Testament times, that formulation was given to the ordinances of Baptism and the Lord's Supper in and through which Christ effectually applies and communicates his redemption to all for whom he died, interceding for them and revealing to them the mysteries of salvation.

---

[61] Cf. again *The School of Faith*, pp. xviif & 204ff.
[62] John Buchan, *Montrose*, Edinburgh, 1928, p. 63.
[63] *Confession of Faith*, XXV.1–3.

> Sacraments are holy signs and seals of the covenant of grace immediately instituted by God, to represent Christ and his benefits, and to confirm our interest in him, as also to put a visible difference between those who belong to the Church and the rest of the world; and solemnly to engage them in the service of God in Christ, according to his Word.[64]

It is worth noting that it was in this connection that David Dickson in his *Commentary on the Confession of Faith* could recall the command of Christ that the Gospel is to be preached to every creature.[65]

The *Westminster Confession of Faith* does not expressly teach a doctrine of limited atonement, and so the application of the covenant of grace and the proclamation of the Gospel to all people, it is sometimes argued, are not denied. But, as we have seen, its doctrine of a fixed number of the elect implies within its logicalised presentation of doctrine that it cannot be and is not actually effective for all men. If Christ had died for all people, then he would have died effectually for them! Neither the Confession nor the Catechisms speak of the sacraments as seals of the Gospel or as visible Word, inseparable from the audible Word proclaimed. Thus the evangelical character of the sacraments, so characteristic of the Reformation and the older Scottish Tradition, here tends to be depreciated. As George Gillespie contended, they are not to be understood or used as 'converting ordinances' but only as confirming ordinances.[66] The sacraments are not seals of the Word of the Gospel, but seals of faith in the Gospel. They are certainly seals of the covenant of grace, and therefore of its promises and 'warrants', but the evangelical character and range of that covenant are restricted. The sacraments confirm the interest of believers in Christ, and mark out those who belong to Christ and oblige them to obedience. Thus the term 'sacrament' is understood in its popular Latin sense as an oath taken by a soldier on enlistment – the ambiguous meaning deplored by Robert Bruce who preferred the biblical term 'mystery' or simply 'sign and seal'.[67]

---

[64] For an account of the Westminster doctrine of the sacraments, see *The Interim Report of the Special Commission on Baptism*, for 1958, pp. 31ff.

[65] David Dickson, *Truth's Victory*, pp. 118 & 163.

[66] See George Gillespie, *Aaron's Rod Blossoming, Or, the Divine Ordinances of Church Government Vindicated*, London, 1646, Chapters XII & XIII.

[67] See *The Interim Report of the Special Commission on Baptism*, Edinburgh, 1958, pp. 20ff & 32.

In every sacrament there is what the Confession calls 'a spiritual relation or sacramental union' between the sign and the thing signified, so that the names and effects of the one are applied to the other. This was in line with the teaching of Calvin, Knox, and Bruce. This relation or sacramental union between the signs or elements (water, bread and wine) and the reality signified (Christ with all his benefits) is regarded as governed by the nature of Christ on the one hand and of the elements on the other hands. It is both a 'spiritual' and a 'corporal' relation, which the older tradition thought of on the analogy of the union of the two natures of Christ as God and man, and therefore as a relation without separation and without confusion. Here, in the Westminster tradition, however, the relation is thought of more in an Augustinian way, as a relation between outward sign and inward grace. But there is no suggestion that the inward grace is causally conferred in the administration of the sacraments by any power in them, for the efficacy of the sacraments depends upon the work of the Spirit and the Word of their dominical institution. As the *Larger Catechism* expresses it: 'The Sacraments become effectual means of salvation, not by any power in themselves, or any virtue derived from the piety or intention of him by whom they are administered, but only by the working of the Holy Spirit, and the blessing of Christ, by whom they are instituted.'[68]

In the nature of the case there are and can be only two sacraments, of Baptism and Lord's Supper, due not only to the fact that Christ instituted them and only them, but to the fact that they alone have to do with the saving embodiment of Christ in our humanity, exhibited in his own participation in Baptism and the Holy Supper, thereby making his own Person their real content. Thus, as David Dickson expressed it, 'Christ was a co-partner and sharer of Baptism and the Lord's Supper which in his own Person he did sanctify and by them did testify and profess his Communion with his people of the New Testament.'[69] Through their grounding in Christ Baptism and the Lord's Supper are intrinsically related to one another, although one is the sacrament of what has taken place once for all in Christ, and the other is the sacrament of the continuing union and communion of the believers with Christ.

---

[68] Q. 161. *The School of Faith*, p. 224. Cf also Q. 91 of the *Shorter Catechism*, *The School of Faith*, p. 275.

[69] David Dickson, *Truth's Victory*, p. 231.

Holy Baptism. Baptism is both a sacrament of initiation, of children as well as adults, not just a declaration of a status or the bestowing of a warrant but an actual admission and ingrafting into Christ, and thus of their participation through the Holy Spirit in regeneration and remission of sins.[70] The *Larger Catechism* and the *Directory for Publick Worship* also speak here of 'adoption and resurrection unto eternal Life'. As a sign and seal of the covenant of grace, administered in the name of the Father, and of the Son and of the Holy Spirit, and thus as an ordinance of the faithfulness of God, Baptism reaches out effectively into the future, while the regeneration sealed in the sacrament is ultimately revealed only in the resurrection of the body. In this teaching the stress is not, as it was with John Knox, on Baptism as a sacrament of the Fatherhood of God,[71] for the emphasis of the *Confession of Faith* is on Baptism as a sign and seal of the *covenant* of grace (as defined by the Confession), which as such calls for the fulfilment of definite conditions.

In accordance with the prevailing federal theology the sacrament of baptismal union with Christ tended to be regarded as a contractual union demanding a contractual response, but in spite of the doctrine of effectual calling that lies behind this, the Confession makes a point of stating that 'grace and salvation are not so inseparably annexed unto it that no person can be regenerated or saved without it, or that all that are baptised are undoubtedly regenerated'. The emphasis in the sacrament of Baptism, however, is not on what we do but on what *God* does, for it is *he* who ingrafts, *he* who regenerates, *he* who remits sin, and *he* who calls and engages us to be the Lord's. 'Baptism is not the Sacrament of what we do, but a Sacrament of what God has already done in Christ, and therefore of what he offers us in the Gospel. It is a Sacrament of the Gospel and not of our response to the Gospel, although it requires response from us.'[72] As James S. Candlish expounded the teaching of the Church in the nineteenth century:

---

[70] *The Confession of Faith*, 30.
[71] This was later revived by John Warden of Gargunnock, *A Practical Essay on the Sacrament of Baptism*, Edinburgh, 1724, pp. 47f; and John Willison of Dundee, *The Practical Works of John Willison*, ed. W. M. Hetherington, London, 1844, p. 578. See again the 1958 Report of *The Special Commission on Baptism*, p. 45.
[72] H. J. Wotherspoon and J. M. Kirkpatrick, *A Manual of Church Doctrine According to the Church of Scotland*, revised and enlarged by T. F. Torrance and Ronald Selby Wright, London, 1960, p. 23.

Baptism is a token of our duty. But it is also a token of our being the Lord's, as bought with his blood, and of our consequent obligation of love, loyalty, and service to Him ... It is first and chiefly a pledge or token on the part of God in Christ to us; and only secondarily, though no less really, a pledge or token on our part of our allegiance to God.[73]

The Lord's Supper.[74] 'Our Lord Jesus, in the night wherein he was betrayed, instituted the sacrament of his body and blood, called the Lord's Supper, to be observed in his church unto the end of the world, for the perpetual remembrance of the sacrifice of himself in his death, the sealing of all benefits thereof unto true believers, their spiritual nourishment and growth in him, their further engagement in and to all duties which they owe unto him, and to be a bond and pledge of their communion with him, and with each other, as members of his mystical body.' In the *Larger Catechism* reference is made to the fact that in the Lord's Supper Christ's 'death is showed forth', and that communicants testify and renew their 'thankfulness'.[75] This was the 'eucharistic' aspect of the Lord's Supper to which John Knox gave such attention, and which was perpetuated in the common description of the celebration of the Lord's Supper as 'the Action' (*actio gratiarum*, or thanksgiving) – hence the common reference to Communion sermons as 'Action Sermons'.

If Baptism is the sacrament of our ingrafting into Christ who died for us and rose again so that by the power of the Holy Spirit we are once for all made members of the Body of Christ, and is therefore administered only once, the Lord's Supper is frequently to be celebrated as the sacrament of our participation in the Body and Blood of Christ given to us so that by the power of the Holy Spirit we enjoy continuous union and Communion with Christ 'as members of his mystical body', and therefore is constantly administered to the faithful. 'Worthy receivers, outwardly partaking of the visible elements in this sacrament, do then inwardly by faith, really and indeed, yet not carnally and corporally, but spiritually receive and feed upon Christ crucified and all the benefits of his death.' Of particular note is the place given to the *Epiclesis* –

---

[73] James S. Candlish, *The Christian Sacraments*, Edinburgh, 1895, pp. 62f.
[74] *Confession of Faith*, Chapter XXIX.
[75] QQ. 168–9. *The School of Faith*, p. 226.

ministers are appointed to 'bless the elements of the bread and wine, and thereby to set them apart from a common to an holy use'. This is also given a firm place in the *Directory for the Public Worship of God*. Strong emphasis was laid upon the real presence of Christ in the celebration of the Holy Supper, but there is no attempt to explain the nature of that presence. Hence notions of consubstantiation as of a repetition of the sacrifice of Christ are rejected.

The focus of attention is on the death of Christ, and thus on the Lord's Supper as a sacrament of holy remembrance of his atoning and unrepeatable sacrifice, but not as a 'memorial before God'. There is no indication of the import of the resurrection and ascension of Christ which had such a decisive effect on the understanding of the Eucharist in the Early Church, as also in the eucharistic teaching of Calvin and the old Scottish tradition, but place is given to the celebration of the sacrament as 'a spiritual oblation of all possible praise unto God'. Moreover, the celebration of the Lord's Supper is not understood to correspond to the descent of the Son of God to unite himself us and us to him in Incarnation and atonement, *and* to his ascent in resurrection and ascension to the throne of God as our Mediator and High Priest, presenting us in himself to the Father.[76] Nor is place given to the proclamation of the Lord's death until he comes again. The deficiency of the Confession at this point is not made good in the two last chapters of the Confession which are more concerned with the state of people after death, the resurrection of the dead, and the last judgment. Rather more attention was given in the *Larger Catechism*, to the resurrection, ascension, heavenly intercession and final advent of Christ.[77]

The Scottish Commissioners at the Westminster Assembly found that they were unable to gain acceptance of all that the Kirk would have wished, but agreed to the demands of their English colleagues in the hope of securing *uniformity* of religion, including Church Government.[78] However, the ratification of the Solemn League and

---

[76] See Wotherspoon and Kirkpatrick, *A Manual of Church Doctrine*, pp. 38–47.

[77] The *Larger Catechism*, 50–56. *The School of Faith*, pp. 194f.

[78] See the document written by Alexander Henderson at the request of the General Assembly, *The Government and Order of the Church of Scotland*, Edinburgh, 1641. Refer also to George Gillespie, *An Assertion of the Government of the Church of Scotland*, Edinburgh, 1641. On the principle of uniformity, see George Gillespie, *A Treatise of Miscellany Questions*, Edinburgh, 1649, Chapter XV, pp. 194–202.

Covenant in 1643 which bound together agreement between the Scots and English in religious and civil affairs meant that a more puritan form of Calvinism in thought and worship was imported and brought into use alongside that of the earlier confessions, catechisms, and service books of the Kirk. So far as the life and thought of Church members, elders and ministers were concerned, it was the Assembly's *Shorter Catechism* that contributed immensely and effectively to their thinking. It helped more than anything else to consolidate the public mind of the Kirk and regulate its instruction of the young. Through it Westminster Theology took deep root in Scotland, even during the period of the Second Episcopate.

With the Reformation there had developed a biblical theology which had an increasingly significant place in the parishes through the preaching and teaching of the Gospel by generations of ministers who had been trained to read the Scriptures in their original languages. As Thomas M'Crie pointed out it was Andrew Melville who laid the basis for this by introducing the teaching of Hebrew and Greek in the Universities in which not only professors but a number of ministers became very proficient.[79] Very soon there were published a number of commentaries on books of the Bible, such as those by Robert Rollock, David Dickson, James Durham, James Fergusson, George Hutcheson, and not least the saintly Robert Leighton, which were widely used by the ministry. As a result there developed an expository and biblical theology which had an increasing impact on the Church, moulding its basic theological outlook and reinforcing its evangelical commitment and mission. Particular mention must be made here of the Communion seasons, at which 'Action' or eucharistic sermons were preached in the tradition of Robert Bruce.[80] These Communion seasons were sometimes notable occasions of evangelical awakening and evangelistic fervour as at Shotts Kirk in June, 1630, during the preaching of John Livingstone.[81] Moreover the *Scots Confession* and

---

[79] Thomas M'Crie, *Life of Andrew Melville, The Works of Thomas M'Crie, D.D.*, 1856 edition, Vol. II, pp. 386f.

[80] Cf. John Macleod, *Scottish Theology in Relation to Church History Since the Reformation*, Edinburgh, 1943, pp. 96ff.

[81] See John Livingstone's own account of this, *Select Biographies*, Vol. 1, The Wodrow Society, 1845, p. 138f. See also the 'sacramental discourses' of John Livingstone and John Welch in *A Collection of Lectures and Sermons* (mostly by Covenanting Ministers), edited by John Howie, Glasgow 1779.

Reformation Catechisms continued to be in frequent use, even after the introduction of the *Westminster Catechisms*, which helped to give the Westminster Theology a strong Gospel slant in the understanding of ministers and congregations.

These biblical and evangelical trends in Scotland were understandably brought into relation to the prevailing covenant theology with its concepts of instrumental and conditional faith calling for formal commitment by way of what was called 'personal covenanting'.[82] In the course of this development adherence to the National Covenant could be linked to the New Covenant in the Body and Blood of Christ, as we find in the preaching of Alexander Henderson in which the pivotal point was sometimes upon faith in Christ rather than on Christ himself.[83] Within this covenanting movement some outstanding gems of evangelical spirituality were produced such as *The Christian's Great Interest* by William Guthrie of Fenwick which went through many editions.[84] His outlook was certainly christological and evangelical, but it was also rather subjective, for his emphasis fell upon faith as 'the condition of the covenant of grace' and upon 'personal covenanting' between God and man as a way of appropriating the grace of God with personal assurance. Thus he was never tired of calling upon sinners 'to close with Christ' and make him their own for sanctification and redemption, for 'then they become embodied in communion with him'.[85] While 'thousands of people are joined to Christ's Church through receiving the seal of the covenant, yet they do content themselves with an empty title of being in a sealed covenant with God.'[86] Hence Guthrie's personal call upon people to 'close with Christ' which met a great response. This represents an evangelical way of presenting the doctrine of the covenant in a form that reached multitudes of people in a direct and simple way that struck home to their spiritual needs. It is not surprising that

---

[82] See, for example, the two 'forms of personal covenanting' used by Thomas Boston, *The Whole Works of Thomas Boston of Ettrick*, Aberdeen, 1848, Vol. II, pp. 671–4.

[83] Alexander Henderson, *Sermons, Prayers and Pulpit Addresses*, ed. R. T. Martin, Edinburgh, 1867, p. 209, etc.

[84] William Guthrie, *The Christian's Great Interest, in Two Parts. I. The Trial of a Saving Interest in Christ. II. The Way how to attain it*. Glasgow, 1758; edition by William Dunlop, Edinburgh, 1763. Thomas Chalmers published another edition, with an introductory essay, Glasgow, 1825, reprinted in 1828.

[85] Second Sermon on Isaiah 55.1, 2.

[86] *The Christian's Great Interest*, 1952 edn, pp. 128f.

Thomas Chalmers said about Guthrie that 'he had long been the favourite author of our peasantry in Scotland', and that he himself regarded 'Guthrie's Triall of a Saving Interest in Christ' as 'the best book he had ever read'.[87] However we think of it, Guthrie's book must be placed alongside of Henry Scougal's deservedly acclaimed work, *The Life of God in the Soul of Man*, 1677.

It was in this deeply religious and evangelical spirit that there were found some of the finest and most godly people in the history of the Church of Scotland, who suffered martyrdom for their convictions, and for whom Christ meant more than anything else. On the other hand, the binding up of national or political covenanting with the New Covenant in the Body of Christ could give rise, and did unfortunately actually give rise, to a rather fanatical outlook among some of the Covenanters which provoked and bred a counter-fanaticism among their political and religious opponents. This has nowhere been more tellingly demonstrated than by John Buchan in his books, *Witch Wood* and *Montrose*.[88]

Bibliography

Ames, William, *The Marrow of Sacred Divinity, drawn out of Scripture and the Interpreters thereof, and brought into Method*, London, 1639.

Bryden, W. W., *The Significance of the Westminster Confession of Faith*, Toronto, 1943.

Buchan, John, *Witch Wood*, Edinburgh, 1927.

Buchan, John, *Montrose*, Edinburgh, 1928.

Burleigh, John H. S., *A Church History of Scotland*, London, 1960.

Calvin, John, *Institutes of the Christian Religion*, tr. F. L. Battles, Philadelphia, 1960.

Campbell, John McLeod, *Memorials of John McLeod Campbell, D.D., Being Selections From His Correspondence*, edited by his son Donald Campbell, London, 1877.

Campbell, John McLeod, 'Speech Delivered at the Bar of the Very Reverend The Synod of Glasgow and Ayr', Greenock, 1831.

Candlish, James S., *The Christian Sacraments*, Handbooks for Bible Classes, Edinburgh, 1895.

---

[87] Cited from the *Memoirs* of Dr Chalmers in the 1952 Glasgow edition *The Christian's Great Interest*, pp. xxiiif.

[88] John Buchan, *Witch Wood*, Edinburgh, 1927, & *Montrose*, Edinburgh, 1928.

Dickson, David, *Truth's Victory over Error: Or, the True Principles of the Christian Religion* (*Praelectiones in Confessionem Fidei*), English edn, 1684, 1752, 1764 & 1787.

Dort, Synod of, *Acta Synodi nationalis Dortrechti habitae*, Dordrecht & Leiden, 1620.

Franks, Robert S., *The Work of Christ. A Historical Study of Christian Doctrine*, London & Edinburgh, 1962.

Fraser, James, of Brea, *Meditations on Several Subjects in Divinity*, Edinburgh, 1721.

Gillespie, George, *Aaron's Rod Blossoming. Or, The Divine Ordinances of Church Government Vindicated*, London, 1646.

Gillespie, George, *An Assertion of the Government of the Church of Scotland*, Edinburgh, 1641.

Gillespie, George, *A Treatise of Miscellany Questions: Wherein Many usefull Questions and Cases of Conscience are discussed and resolved...*, Edinburgh, 1649.

Gillespie, Patrick, *The Ark of the Covenant Opened*, London, 1661.

Guthrie, William, *The Christian's Great Interest. In Two Parts. I. The Trial of a Saving Interest in Christ. II. The Way how to Attain it.* Glasgow, 1763. 6th edn, Glasgow, 1952.

Henderson, Alexander, *The Government and Order of the Church of Scotland*, Edinburgh, 1641.

Henderson, Alexander, *Sermons, Prayers and Pulpit Addresses*, ed. R. T. Martin, Edinburgh, 1867.

Henderson, G. D., *Scots Confession, 1560, and Negative Confession, 1581*, Edinburgh, 1937.

Hendry, G. S., *The Westminster Confession for Today. A Contemporary Interpretation*, London, 1960.

Heppe, Heinrich, *Reformed Dogmatics Set out and Illustrated from the Sources*, ed. Ernst Bizer, with a Foreword by Karl Barth, tr. G. T. Thomson, London, 1950.

Heron, Alasdair I. C., *The Westminster Confession in the Church Today*, Edinburgh, 1982.

Hodge, A. A., *The Confession of Faith*, 1869, reprint, London, 1958, 1961.

Howie, John, Editor, *A Collection of Lectures and Sermons*, Glasgow, 1779.

Ker, A., *The Larger Catechism, The Shorter Catechism, The Sum of Saving Knowledge, The National Covenant, The Solemn League and Covenant, The Directory for the Publick Worship of God, The Form of Church-Government and of the Ordination of Ministers*, and *The Directory For Family Worship*, Glasgow, 1757.

Leiden Synopsis Purioris Theologiae, Leiden, 1624.

Leishman, Thomas, *The Westminster Directory*, edited, with an Introduction and Notes, Edinburgh, 1901.

Macleod, John, *Scottish Theology in Relation to Church History Since the Reformation*, Edinburgh & London, 1943.

M'Crie, Thomas, *Life of Andrew Melville, The Works of Thomas M'Crie, D.D.*, 1855–6 edn, Vol. II, p. 386f.

Macpherson, John, *The Westminster Confession of Faith*, Edinburgh, 1881.

Mitchell, A. F., *Catechisms of the Second Reformation*, London, 1886.

Perkins, William, *Golden Chaine or The Description of Theologie, containing the order of causes of Salvation and Damnation, according to God's word*, tr. from Latin, London, 1592.

Peter Martyr, *Loci Communes*, Geneva, 1576.

Peterkin, Alexander, Editor, *Booke of the Universall Kirk of Scotland*, 3 vols., Edinburgh, 1839.

Peterkin, Alexander, *Records of the Kirk of Scotland, Containing the Acts and Proceedings of the General Assemblies from the Year 1638 Downwards, as Authenticated by the Clerks of Assembly, with Notes and Historical Illustrations*, Edinburgh, 1838.

Polanus, Amandus, of Polansdorf, *Syntagma Theologiae Christianae*, Hanover, 1624 & 1625.

Rutherford, Samuel, *The Covenant of Life Opened: Or, A Treatise of the Covenant of Grace*, Edinburgh, 1655.

Torrance, T. F., *The School of Faith*, London, 1959.

Torrance, T. F., et al., *The Interim Report of the Special Commission on Baptism, for 1958*, Edinburgh, 1958.

Torrance, T. F., *Trinitarian Perspectives*, Edinburgh, 1994.

Tweedie, W. K., *Select Biographies*, edited for The Wodrow Society, Vol. I, Edinburgh, 1845.

Ursinus, Zacharias, *The Summe of Christian Religion. Delivered by Zacharias Ursinus in his Lectures upon the Catechisme*. Tr. Henry Parry. Oxford, 1589.

Ursinus, Zacharias, *Explicationes Catechesios Palatinae*, Heildelberg, 1589.

Ursinus, Zacharias, *Opera Theologica*, Heildelberg, 1612.

Warden, John, of Gargunnock, *A Practical Essay on the Sacrament of Baptism*, Edinburgh, 1724.

Willison, John, *The Practical Works of John Willison*, ed. W. M. Hetherington, London, 1844.

Wotherspoon, H. J., and Kirkpatrick, J. M., *A Manual of Church Doctrine according to the Church of Scotland*, revised and enlarged by T. F. Torrance and Ronald Selby Wright, London, 1960.

5

Robert Leighton (1611–84), Episcopalian Calvinist

Robert Leighton was the son of the Rev Dr Alexander Leighton, a Master of Arts of St Andrews and a Doctor of Medicine of Leyden, who was ordained as a preacher in the English Church at Utrecht, but was soon dismissed for his puritan views on worship. He returned to England where he was prohibited from practising medicine, but served as a puritan preacher and lecturer. In 1630 information was laid against him as 'a Scotchman and Doctor of Divinity' for opposing Prelacy. He was accused of 'blowing the bellows of sedition' and sentenced by the Star Chamber in the reign of Charles I, for writing a book called *Zion's Plea against Prelacy*. He was degraded from his clerical office and condemned to fearful torture by branding and mutilation which he endured with incredible courage. In 1641 Parliament condemned his imprisonment and torture as illegal, and he was exonerated and awarded damages.[1] He returned to Edinburgh that year and supported his son Robert who had studied philosophy and divinity at the University of Edinburgh (where Aristotle was the favourite philosopher),[2] and now in his thirtieth year was ready to follow his father in the ministry of the Kirk. In 1642, in succession to Alexander Dickson, a son of David Dickson, Robert Leighton was presented by the Earl of Lothian to the Parish of Newbattle, and ordained by the Presbytery of Dalkeith.[3] In the following year, supported by his father, he signed the National Covenant and the Solemn League and Covenant.

Robert Leighton was evidently not altogether happy in the Presbytery of Dalkeith, where he objected to the habit of his fellow presbyters in descanting on the Covenant from their pulpits when

---

[1] For a full account see D. Butler, *The Life and Letters of Robert Leighton*, London, 1903, pp. 15ff & 31ff.
[2] *The Whole Works of Robert Leighton, D.D.*, new edn, London, 1830, vol. IV, pp. 309, 323, 352. It was Andrew Melville who introduced Aristotle into the Scottish Universities.
[3] See D. Butler, *The Life and Letters of Robert Leighton*, p. 138.

they should have been preaching the Gospel. When he was reprimanded by them for not 'preaching up to the times', he rejoined, 'If all of you preach up the times, you may surely allow one poor brother to preach up Christ Jesus and eternity'.[4] In spite of being a Covenanter and the son of a Covenanter, Leighton found the intolerance of his fellow ministers and the spiritual despotism practised by the courts of the Kirk over people's consciences and persons rather unchristian. It was not all that different from the intolerance of the Erastian Prelatists his father had encountered in England. In 1652 after a ministry of ten years in Newbattle he resigned from the Presbytery.

Before long, however, Robert Leighton was appointed Principal of Edinburgh University where he himself had studied classics, philosophy, and divinity, and had graduated Master of Arts in 1631, with a masterly knowledge of Hebrew and Greek, and a reputation for a wonderful facility in Latin.[5] There as well as being Principal he taught systematic doctrine. In line with the example of Robert Rollock, the first Principal of the University, he restored the Principal's week-day lecture which had fallen into abeyance, and set about encouraging the study of humane letters, philosophy and divinity in a way that would give rise to harmony and peace. David Dickson, a hard-line Calvinist, was one of the professors in the University during those years when Leighton sought to steer them away from unprofitable controversy. He objected strongly to Leighton's commendation of the *De Imitatione Christi* of Thomas à Kempis to professors and students alike.[6] In one of his theological lectures Leighton said: 'To what purpose', saith Thomas à Kempis, 'dost thou reason profoundly concerning the Trinity, if thou art without humility, and thereby displeaseth the Trinity?'[7] In another of his lectures, 'Of The Decrees of God', Leighton was unusually outspoken.

What perverseness, or rather madness, it is to endeavour to break into the sacred depositories of Heaven, and pretend

---

[4]   See the account of his life by J. N. Pearson, *The Whole Works of Robert Leighton*, London, 1830, Vol. I, p. xvii.
[5]   Thus Gilbert Burnet, *History of His Own Time*, London, 1723–34, Vol. 1, pp. 239f.
[6]   See the *Analecta* of Robert Wodrow, Vol. III, p. 452. Little did Dickson realise that John Calvin had been indebted to Thomas à Kempis! See my work, *The Hermeneutics of John Calvin*, Edinburgh, 1988, pp. 73ff.
[7]   *Works*, Vol. IV, p. 185; see also pp. 313 & 324; and Vol. III, p. 107.

to accommodate the secrets of the Divine kingdom to the measures and methods of our weak capacities! To say the truth, I acknowledge that I am astonished and greatly at a loss, when I hear learned men, and Professors of Theology, talking presumptuously about the order of the Divine decrees, and when I read such things in their works.[8]

Eventually when leaving the University he said in a Valedictory address: 'I constantly endeavoured, with all possible warmth, to divert you from those barren and thorny questions and disputes when the greatest part of divines and professors, and those of no small reputation, engaging furiously in such controversies, have split into parties, and unhappily divided the whole world.'[9]

While he himself was widely read in philosophy and engaged in its study, Leighton had little use for the growing interest in natural theology and rational arguments seeking to establish the existence of God.

I cannot help fearing, that when we endeavour to confirm this leading truth, with regard to the First and Uncreated Being, by a long and laboured series of arguments, we may seem, instead of a service, to do a kind of injury to God and man both. For why should we use the pitiful light of a candle to discover the sun, and eagerly go about to prove the Being of Him who gave being to every thing else?[10]

God cannot be known but by his own revelation of Himself … Nothing is more certain than that the doctrine which leads us to God, must take its rise from Him.[11]

After the restoration of the Monarchy in 1660, and the passing by the Scottish Parliament of the Rescissory Act in the following year restoring episcopacy, pressure was put on Robert Leighton, known for his moderate views on church order, to join the Scottish Episcopate. He agreed, although rather reluctantly, and asked to be given the see of Dunblane, the smallest see in the country. He refused, however, to take his seat in Parliament, for he resolved

---

[8] *Works*, Vol. IV, p. 242.
[9] *Works*, Vol. IV, p. 381.
[10] *Works*, Vol. IV, p. 223.
[11] *Works*, Vol. IV, pp. 310f; cf. Hilary, *De Trinitate*, 1.45 & 4.36; and Robert Boyd, *Ad Ephesios Praelectiones*, c. 59.1A.

not to mix church affairs with politics. At Dunblane he put into practice his views that the Church should be governed by presbyteries and synods with bishops acting only as chief presbyters, presidents or permanent moderators, while decisions in jurisdiction and ordination should be determined by the majority of the presbyters.[12] As his friend Gilbert Burnet has told us he refused to reordain any of the ministers, for he regarded their Presbyterian ordination to be as good and valid as any which a bishop could confer.[13] He called for the return in public worship of the Lord's Prayer, the Apostles' Creed, and the Doxology, in line with earlier practices in the Kirk. Leighton regarded his own ministry in Dunblane primarily as a shepherd of souls which he fulfilled through assiduous pastoral visitation, preaching and catechising, encouraging frequent Communion and family prayer.[14] He ministered to all alike, presbyterians and episcopalians, called for moderation and charity from the authorities, and opposed any intolerance toward ministers declining to conform to the new ecclesiastical establishment.

In 1670 a move was made to transfer Leighton to the Archdiocese of Glasgow, where it was hoped he would be able to help compose the dissensions in the Church through his conciliatory accommodation on the nature of the ministry. Once again he agreed, but again very reluctantly. There as in Dunblane he sought to persuade churchmen to move away from contentious issues and to help them reconcile constitutional conceptions of episcopacy and presbytery.[15] With the help of Gilbert Burnet, then Primarius Professor of

---

[12] Cf. J. H. S. Burleigh, *A Church History of Scotland*, London, 1960, p. 247.

[13] Gilbert Burnet, *History of His Own Time*, cited by D. Butler, *op. cit.* p. 364; see also pp. 428 & 557. Although Leighton himself had submitted, very reluctantly, to episcopal reordination he did not think of it as adding anything to his ordination by presbytery. See Robert Wodrow, *Analecta*, Vol. I, p. 133; and Gilbert Burnet, *History of His Own Time*, Vol. 1, p. 248.

[14] See the 'Charges' that Leighton gave to his fellow ministers, *Works*, Vol. IV, pp. 395–412, which reflects directly on the character of his own ministry in Dunblane; and also 'Rules and Instructions for a Holy Life', Vol. IV, pp. 413–27.

[15] See 'A Modest Defence of Moderate Episcopacy', *Works*, Vol. IV, pp. 386–92. This was in line with the remarkable work of Egeon Askew, *Brotherly Reconcilement*, which he dedicated to James I, in the hope of healing the relations between the Church of Scotland and the Church of England, London, 1605. Leighton himself, however, does not refer to this work. Cf. also Alexander Lauder, *The Ancient Bishops Consider'd Both with respect to the Extent of Their Jurisdiction, and Nature of Their Power*, Edinburgh, 1707.

Theology at Glasgow University,[16] he tried to help episcopalians and presbyterians to come together on biblical and evangelical grounds, and with a readiness for reciprocal concession on modes of church government that are not ultimately essential for the propagation of the Christian Faith, or for the building up of the Church as the Body of Christ. Leighton made it clear that he was just as opposed to the *Jure Divino* prelatists, or 'Monarchical Episcopacy',[17] as he was to Erastian Calvinists, both of whom he found held forms of political theology that were detrimental to a christocentric and evangelical understanding of the nature and mission of the Church. Ministers of the Church are properly ministers of the Cross of Christ, and ambassadors entrusted with the message of reconciliation, so that in following Christ they must do it in his livery – they must take up the Cross.[18]

In Glasgow, however, Leighton's mission of reconciliation proved very difficult, not least because many of the presbyterian ministers held themselves to be bound by the Solemn League and Covenant to reject and oppose episcopacy in every form. Leighton pointed out to them that the kind of episcopacy which he commended was grounded on the teaching of the Scriptures and of the Primitive Church, and was not contrary to the New Covenant.[19] It was not *all* episcopacy which they were against; the kind of episcopacy which they were committed to reject was the prelacy then in being in England, to which he himself was opposed.[20] The particular mode of church government, he held, was immaterial – but peace, concord, and good will were indispensable. However, Leighton's conciliating activities on behalf of a constitutional episcopacy in association with presbytery came under severe pressure from Charles II and his advisers, as well as from the Covenanters. 'All his efforts proved unavailing and negotiations were broken off,

---

[16] See H. M. B. Reid, *The Divinity Professors of the University of Glasgow*, Glasgow, 1923, pp. 155ff.

[17] *Works*, Vol. I, p. 234.

[18] Cf. *The Commentary on 1 Peter*, 2. 21, *Works*, II, p. 3; and 'A Sermon Preached to the Clergy', on 2 Cor. 5.20, *Works*, Vol. III, pp. 456–474.

[19] See the work of his friend, Gilbert Burnet, Professor of Divinity at the University of Glasgow, *A Vindication of the Authority, Constitution, and Laws of the Church and State of Scotland. In Four Conferences*, Glasgow, 1673, especially the first and fourth conferences. Cf. also the unsympathetic rejoinder by Robert MacWard, *The True Non-Conformist in Answere to the Modest and Free Conference betwixt a Conformist and a Non-Conformist, about the present Distempers in Scotland*, Glasgow, 1671.

[20] *Works*, Vol. IV, pp. 387f.

not to be resumed', Professor Burleigh remarked, 'until our own time'.[21] He resigned in 1674, and retired to live with his sister in England. There he continued to live as at Dunblane in accordance with his own *Rules and Instructions for A Holy Life*, devoted to the life of the Christian as union with God through union with Christ.[22] He died ten years later in 1684. He had earlier written in a sermon,

> The soul that is in Christ, when other things are pulled away, feels little or nothing: he cleaves to Christ, and these separations pain him not. Yes, when that great separatist, death, comes, that breaks all other unions, even that of the soul and the body, yet so far is it from separating the believer's soul from its beloved Lord Jesus, that, on the contrary, it carries it into the nearest union with him, and has the fullest enjoyment of him for ever.[23]

Leighton was the most lovable of Scottish Churchmen, and the most irenic. In one of his sermons he spoke of faith as teaching 'spiritual civility, good manners toward God'[24] – that was certainly true of himself. He was one of the most widely read men of his generation in ancient Greek and Latin works, secular as well as Christian. He gave close study to the works of the Rabbis, of which he had a considerable collection, and also of the Cabbala and Jewish mysticism. He was unusually familiar with the Hermetic philosophy, and of the scientific work of Lord Bacon of Verulam. He came rather closer than his contemporaries to understanding the *contingent* nature of the world which God has created out of nothing.[25] He was also well read in the Greek Fathers, Nazianzen, Basil, and Chrysostom particularly, and in the Latin Fathers, citing frequently from Augustine, and Bernard. At the same time he was familiar with the works of the Reformers, including Luther and Melanchthon as well as Calvin, as his many allusions to their thought indicate, apart from his specific references. In his general

---

[21] Burleigh, *A Church History of Scotland*, p. 248.

[22] *Works*, Vol. V, pp. 413–27. Cf. the impact of this on Leighton's former student and friend, Henry Scougal, evident in *The Life of God in the Soul of Man*, London, 1677. See also his *Discourses on Important Subjects*, Glasgow, 1751. Cf. D. Butler, *Henry Scougal and the Oxford Methodists, or, The Influence of a Religious Teacher of the Scottish Churches*, Edinburgh & London, 1899.

[23] *Works*, Vol. III, pp. 289f.

[24] Sermon on 'Suitable Exercises in Affliction', *Works*, Vol. III, p. 451.

[25] Cf. for example, *Works*, Vol. III, p. 228, or IV, p. 319.

theological orientation he was thoroughly Protestant, as is evident in his frequent sharp asides against Roman doctrines, and practices in worship, for example, in the use of holy water, a crucifix or of an image of the Virgin Mary.[26] Leighton was certainly a Calvinist, but a mild Calvinist horrified at the obsessive attention given to predestination as a test of orthodoxy, and at the substitution in the pulpit of doctrinal diatribes for biblical exposition and the preaching of the Gospel. He was an evangelical Calvinist of whom John McLeod Campbell once said in a letter to his father, 'I love the writings of Leighton, because they breathe so much of the spirit of an evangelist'.[27] Leighton himself preached to his congregation in direct personal terms about repentance and conversion, and spoke of the lively belief to which he called his people as 'experimental knowledge of God, and of his son Jesus Christ'.[28] This was a way of believing and knowing God with an 'inward affection towards Christ'.

> The intellective knowledge of Christ, the distinct under-standing, yea, the orthodox preaching of the Gospel, the maintaining of his public cause, and suffering for it, shall not then be found sufficient. Only that peculiar appre-hension of Christ, those constant flames of spiritual love, that even course of holy love walking in his light, shall be those characters, whereby Christ shall own his children, and admit them into the inheritance of perfect light.[29]

> Labour, then, for a more active and practical knowledge of God and Divine truths, such as may humble and renew your souls.[30]

Leighton was very faithfully orthodox in his theology, profoundly trinitarian in his thought and worship.[31] He held that the Holy Trinity, the Father, the Son, and the Holy Spirit, co-operates both in the work of creation and salvation, in election and in the

---

[26] *Works*, Vol. I, pp. 3, 24; Vol. II, pp. 25, 73f; Vol. IV, pp. 127, 133, etc.

[27] John McLeod Campbell, *Memorials of John McLeod Campbell*, edited by his son, the Rev. Donald Campbell, London, 1877, p. 43.

[28] *A Practical Commentary on the First Epistle of Peter, Works*, Vol. I, p. 95.

[29] *Works*, Vol. III, p. 149.

[30] *Works*, Vol. III, p. 151.

[31] See Leighton's own catechism 'A Short Catechism', *Works*, Vol. IV, p. 173, as well as 'An Exposition of the Creed', i.e. the Nicene Creed, *ibid.* pp. 28ff.

communion of the holy universal Church.[32] 'As to the mystery of
the sacred Trinity', however, he said in a lecture on *The Being of
God*, 'which has a near and necessary connexion with the present
subject, I always thought it was to be received and adored with the
most humble faith, but by no means to be curiously searched into,
or perplexed with the absurd questions of the schoolmen.'[33]
Leighton objected to the tedious and foreign distinctions being
drawn by current theologians 'that divide theology into *archetypal*
and *ectypal*, and again into the theology of the church militant,
and that of the church triumphant'. *Archetypal theology*, he said refers
to 'that perfect knowledge (αὐτοσοφία) which God has of himself.
And the theology of the Church triumphant ought rather to be
called θεοψία, the beatific vision of God.'[34] What Leighton was
evidently objecting to was the tendency of Calvinist theologians to
'accommodate those secrets of the Divine kingdom to the measures
and methods of our weak capacities',[35] that is, to give archetypal
force to certain truths, such as predestination, over other truths,
thereby determining the limits within which they were to be
understood.[36] This was very evident, for example, in the way in
which John Owen and Samuel Rutherford operated with logical
axioms about the ends and means determining the purpose and
limits of the atonement. Leighton probably had this in mind in a
sermon on providence when he cited Peter Martyr to the effect
that 'There is no judging of the works of God, before they are
finished'.[37]

While he was clearly well versed in current theology at the highest
level, Leighton was essentially a *scholar-preacher* who gave great
attention to careful biblical interpretation, with meticulous
attention to the Hebrew and Greek text, and was always concerned

---

[32] *Works*, Vol. I, p. 87 & Vol. IV, pp. 28f; cf. pp. 173, 228, 320, etc.
[33] *Ibid.* p. 228. This reflects the language of Nazianzen and Melanchthon. See
further pp. 320f; and Vol. V, p. 413: 'If thou think of the most blessed Trinity,
muse not too much thereon, but with devout and obedient faith, meekly and
lowly adore and worship.'
[34] *Works*, Vol. IV, p. 299. The distinction between archetypal and ectypal thought
comes from Philo (with whose work Leighton was familiar), but is found, cited
from Philo, in the *Syntagma Theologiae Christianae* of Amandus Polanus which
was used in the Presbyteries for the training of ministers. It was later taken up
by David Hume in his *Dialogues on Natural Religion*.
[35] *Works*, Vol. IV, p. 242.
[36] See again *Works*, Vol. IV, p. 242, cited above.
[37] *Works*, Vol. III, p. 123: *De Operibus Dei, antequam actum, non est judicandum.*

with the practical and devotional relevance of Christian doctrine. Although he was not an academic theologian, his theological insights were profound and directed to the really central issues of the Faith, in which he spontaneously assigned to different tenets their relative claim for attention, and avoided the kind of contentious argument that disturbed the balance of Christian belief and obedience. In determining his place in the history of Scottish theology, not just ecclesiology, we must ask how he stood in relation to the federal theology that prevailed in the Kirk.

While he admired Robert Rollock, his predecessor as Principal of the University of Edinburgh, particularly in his concern for preaching and holy living, Leighton did not follow him and his hyper-Calvinist and puritan followers in their strict federal system of thought, but returned to the teaching of John Calvin about the 'covenant of grace'.[38] He could refer to 'the other covenant, made with the first Adam', but interpreted it in the light of the 'New Covenant' made with 'A man indeed, to supply the place of the former, but he is *God-man*, to be surer than the former, and therefore it holds ... Upon this rock, the second Adam, is the Church so firmly built, that the gates of hell cannot prevail against her.'[39] Leighton thought of this New Covenant not only in relation to Adam but to Israel, taking his cue from the teaching of the Epistle to the Hebrews about the *new covenant* which God promised to make with the house of Israel, and which he established in Jesus Christ his incarnate Son with a universal range in its promise.[40] 'God in our flesh hath enlarged the nation of Israel; all that will but *look to him*, He is their *Saviour. Look unto me, and be saved, all the ends of the earth.*'[41] This is what, like Calvin, Leighton regularly spoke of as 'the covenant of grace', that is the estate of grace, the Kingdom of God, into which we are brought through the mediation of Christ, the glory of which will be fully revealed in the future. Thus in commenting upon 1 Peter 1.13: 'the grace that is to be brought unto you at the revelation of Jesus Christ', Leighton wrote:

So the grace here said to be brought to them, is either the *Doctrine of grace* in the Gospel, wherein Jesus Christ is revealed, and that grace in him; (for the whole tenor of the covenant

---

[38] Cf. Calvin's *Institute*, especially 2.10 & 2.11.
[39] *Works*, Vol. II, p. 18.
[40] *Works*, Vol. III, pp. 424ff, with reference to Hebrews 8.8f and 9.15.
[41] *Works*, Vol. III p. 400.

of grace, every clause of it, holds in him; His precious name
runs through it all;) or, it is the *Grace of salvation*, which is to
be fully perfected at the last and clearest revelation of Jesus
Christ.[42]

Leighton's brand of federal theology understood in this
Christocentric way was clearly of a mild variety, one which did not
obstruct or restrict the universal range of God's saving grace or
inhibit its free proclamation to men and women no matter how
sinful they might be. Nevertheless, he still thought of 'covenant'
as a two-way relation, involving a definite agreement contracted
between God and Christ in God's great design for the restoring of
lost mankind.

> The foundation of this plan, this appearing of Christ for us,
> and undergoing and answering all in our stead, lies in the
> decree of God, where it was plotted and contrived, in the
> whole way of it, from eternity; and the Father and the Son
> being one, and their Thoughts and will one, they were
> perfectly agreed on it; and those likewise for whom it should
> hold, were agreed upon, and their names written down,
> according to which they are said to be given unto Christ to
> redeem. And just according to that model, did all the work
> proceed, and was accomplished in all points, perfectly
> answering to the pattern in the mind of God. And it was
> preconcluded there, that the Son should undertake the
> business, this matchless piece of service for His Father, and
> that by His interposing, men should be reconciled and
> saved...[43]

This was to understand the covenant of grace as grounded in
and proceeding from God's eternal decree of election, and also as
calling for free believing response on the part of sinners. In
speaking of the establishment of the promises of the Gospel (i.e.
the covenant of grace) offered to us which we are warranted,
invited, and entreated, to receive by believing, Leighton could make
use of the current way of speaking: 'Faith closes the bargain, and
makes him ours', but he explained that this is not what we can do
of ourselves, for it is God's gift and work – 'we cannot believe any

[42] *Works*, Vol. I, pp. 102f.
[43] *Works*, Vol. II, pp. 16f.

more than we can fulfil the law'. Although he thought of those who are saved as the believing persons named by God to be saved, for whom Christ had agreed to give his life in atoning sacrifice, by which he bore the sins of all, in all ages,[44] at the same time Leighton did not think of the offer of salvation in the covenant of grace in a severely restrictive way, for by its nature it is universal in its range, as mercy and justice extended to God's enemies. It is grounded in Christ the Son of God's love. 'Therefore it is emphatically expressed in the words, *God so loved the world* (John 6.16): that Love amounts to this much, that is, was so great as *to give his Son*: but how great that love is cannot be uttered.'[45] On the one hand he could cite 'No man cometh except the Father draw him' (John vi.44). But on the other hand he could ask his brethren to consider, 'Christ is daily held out and none are excluded or excepted, all are invited, be they what they will, who have need of him, and use for him: and yet, who is persuaded?'[46]

To grasp what this actually means in respect of the precise range of the covenant of grace, we must consider Leighton's views on predestination and redemption.

Leighton undoubtedly subscribed to the Calvinist doctrine of the divine decrees as found in the *Confession of Faith* and in the *Catechisms* in accordance with which some people are elected and others are passed over, and in 'the generally received catechism' which students in Edinburgh University had in their hands.[47] His acceptance of this teaching is evident both in his interpretation of the Scripture,[48] and in the lecture devoted to the subject, 'On the Decrees of God'.[49] However, he regarded predestination as a profound truth of revelation which one should not seek to plumb. 'That prospect of election and predestination', he is reported to

---

[44] *Works*, Vol. II, pp. 21f.
[45] *Works*, Vol. II, p. 16.
[46] *Works*, Vol. III, p. 357.
[47] This was the *Heidelberg Catechism* – see *The School of Faith*, pp. 69ff. He also seems to have used the Latin Catechism composed by Patrick Adamson, a former Principal of the University for the use of students – Leighton's *Works*, Vol. IV, p. 298. This was entitled Στοιχείωσις *Eloquiorum Dei, sive Methodus Religionis Christianae Catechetica* – see D. Butler, *The Life and Letters of Robert Leighton*, London, 1903, p. 50. Adamson had earlier published a metrical version in Latin of Calvin's *Geneva Catechism* – H. Bonar, *Catechisms of the Scottish Reformation*, London, 1866, pp. 357f.
[48] E.g. his *Commentary on 1 Peter*, at 1.2, *Works*, Vol. I, pp. 8–22.
[49] *Works*, Vol. IV, pp. 239–43.

have said, 'is a great abyss, into which I choose to sink, rather than attempt to sound it. And truly any attempt at throwing light upon it makes it only a greater abyss, and is a piece of blameable assumption.'[50] He declared that especially in the *Shorter Catechism* designed for the instruction of ignorant people, it would have been 'proper to have passed over the awful speculation concerning the Divine decrees, and to have proceeded directly to the consideration of the works of God'.[51] In his *Commentary on 1 Peter* Leighton declared, with reference to the fact that while many are called, few are chosen: 'There is but a small part of the world outwardly called, in comparison with the rest that is not so, and yet the number of the true elect is so small, that it gains the number of these that are called, the name of *many*.'[52] That was not altogether unlike the way that Samuel Rutherford interpreted the biblical 'all' as a synecdoche for 'many'.

In the same commentary, Leighton revealed how he himself thought of election and effectual calling.

> We are not to pry immediately into this decree, but to read it in the performance. Though the mariner sees not the pole-star, yet the needle of the compass which points to it, tells him which way he sails: thus the heart that is touched with the loadstone of Divine love, trembling with godly fear, and yet still looking towards God by fixed believing, points at the love of election, and tells the soul that its course is heavenward, towards the haven of eternal rest. He that loves, may be sure that he was loved first; and he that chooses God for his delight and portion, may conclude confidently, that God has chosen him to be one of those that shall enjoy him, and be happy in him for ever; for that our love, and electing of him is but the return and repercussion of the beams of his love shining upon us.[53]

---

[50] See *Works*, Vol. I, p. CXXXV; cf. p. CXXX. Cf. Robert Boyd of Trochrig, *Ad Ephesios Praelectiones* cc. 58.2f *et seq.*

[51] *Works*, Vol. IV, p. 239.

[52] *Works*, Vol. I, pp. 17f. Cf. p. 233, on 2.9 : '*Choosing*, here, is the work of effectual calling, or the severance of believers from the rest: for it signifies a difference in their present estate, as do likewise the other words joined with it. But this election is altogether conformable to that of God's eternal decree, and is no other than the execution or performance of it.'

[53] *Works*, Vol. I, pp. 22f.

This was a very shrewd and important point for Leighton to make, for it cut through the problems of assurance and doubt that afflicted people due to the Calvinistic view of double predestination, and pointed them behind the divine decrees to the ultimate love of God. He returned to the point in another statement.

> The great evidence of thy election is love. Thy love to Him gives certain testimony of his preceding eternal love to thee: so are the elect here designated, *they that love God*. Thy choosing Him is both the effect and evidence of His choosing thee. Now, this is not laborious, nor needs to be disputed. Amidst all thy frailties, feel the pulse of thine affection, which way it bears, and ask thy heart whether thou love Him or not; in this way thou hast the character of thy election.[54]

The point that Robert Leighton was concerned to emphasise here is that it is because God has first loved us that we love him. That divine love mediated to us in Christ who has loved us and given himself for us is the ground and source of our love for him.[55] 'Jesus Christ is the first object of this Divine love: he is the *medium unionis*, through whom God conveys the sense of his love to the soul, and receives back its love to Himself.'[56] God creates in us the capacity to believe in him and love him which we could not do of ourselves – while he requires faith of us, what he requires he gives. Faith is the gift of God (Ephesians 2.8).[57] His love acts in a twofold reciprocal way, from him to us and from us to him. Thus when we love God we love him with the very love with which he loves us, so that our love for God is a reflex of his love for us which through the Holy Spirit he has shed abroad into our hearts. In Christ Jesus in whom God's eternal love has become flesh in our humanity we are brought to love God with the same love with which we are loved by him. It is that prevenient Love of God which in its reconciling and reciprocating movement that Leighton discerned in the heart of divine election. This means that properly to appreciate

---

[54] Cited from one of Leighton's sermons at Newbattle, by D. Butler, *Life and Letters*, p. 169.
[55] 'God doth deserve our love, not only by his matchless excellency and beauty, but by his matchless love to us, and that is the strongest loadstone of love. *He hath loved me*, said the Apostle, Gal. ii.20. How appears that? In no less than this, *He hath given himself for me.*' *Works*, Vol. I, p. 74.
[56] *Works*, Vol. I, p. 74; see Vol. III, p. 286.
[57] *Works*, Vol III p. 91.

Leighton's doctrine of election we must turn to his doctrine of atoning mediation, 'this great work of God, Christ *fore-ordained*, and in time sent for our redemption'.[58]

In his teaching about salvation and atonement Leighton could use the familiar language of current federal theology, appeasing the wrath of God, expiation, punishment, satisfaction, etc.,[59] but it was cast within a Christocentric and evangelical discourse of thought which rather altered its emphasis and slant.[60] Central to his soteriology was undoubtedly the covenant of grace by which, as we have seen, he meant salvation understood in the most concrete way, the estate of grace actually mediated to mankind by Christ and embodied in him as the Kingdom of God. Leighton did not think of the covenant of grace, therefore, in the abstract legal manner of the federal system, but in terms of its actual mediation and fulfilment in Jesus Christ. Nor did Leighton think of it, on the other hand, as grounded upon a temporal transaction in the passion of Christ, but while mediated and incarnate in Christ, as grounded in, deriving from, and flowing freely from the infinite and prevenient Love of God.[61] The covenant was an eternal agreement or transaction between the Father and the Son to effect the salvation of lost mankind through the Incarnation of the Son and his expiatory sacrifice for sin.[62] The covenant of grace rooted in eternity became embodied in time in Jesus Christ, and it is therefore, in Christ, and not apart from him, or behind his back, as it were, that we are to understand the covenant, as the covenant of grace or the covenant of salvation. God himself became man in Jesus Christ, to make all things sure.

> It was not an accidental after-device in God (for in Him there can be no such things), but was his great fore-thought project, out of the ruins of man's first estate, to raise a fairer and firmer fabric, new from the very foundation ... The purpose was bred in the Father's own breast, to give out his Son, from thence to recover and bring us back. Oh, the astonishing depth of love.[63]

---

[58]   *Works*, Vol. I, p. 140.
[59]   See *Works*, Vol. I, p. 10; Vol. II, pp. 15f, 22ff, 47, 208, 214f; Vol. III, pp. 299, 352ff; Vol. IV, pp. 9, 12, 84, 92, etc.
[60]   Cf. for example, the lecture XIV 'Of Christ the Saviour', *Works*, Vol. IV, pp. 268–72.
[61]   *Works*, Vol. II, pp. 16, 267; Vol. III, pp. 187, 203, 276, 283ff, 353.
[62]   *Works*, Vol. IV, p. 19.
[63]   *Works*, Vol. III, pp. 352f.

And so it is to the fore-ordination of God that the great work of
God in Christ is to be traced back to 'the Lamb slain from the
foundation of the world (Rev. xiii.8)'. As such the virtue of Christ's
death not only looks backward to all preceding ages, but forward,
so that 'it is of force and perpetual value to the end of the world'.[64]

> It is grace alone, the most free grace of God, that contrives,
> and offers, and makes peace, else it had never been; we had
> universally perished without it ... Jesus Christ, the Mediator,
> the purchaser of this peace, bought it with his own blood,
> killed the enmity by his own death, Eph. ii.15 ... As the free
> love and grace of God appointed this means and way of our
> peace, and offered it, – so the same grace applies it, and
> makes it ours, and gives us faith to apprehend it.[65]

> The work of redemption itself, and the several parts of it,
> and the doctrine revealing it, have all the name of Grace;
> because they all flow from Free Grace: that is their spring
> and first cause.[66]

God so loved the world that he did not spare his only begotten
Son but delivered him up for us all, and the incarnate Son so loved
us that he gave his life freely for us in order to save us. Nor did the
Son spare himself.[67] This means that the atonement was grounded
in a *joint-love* of the Father and the Son, for the Son himself was
God *co-essential with God and equal to the Father*.[68] The atonement
was, therefore, a *joint act* of Christ and God – hence the blood of
Christ shed upon the Cross could be spoken of as 'the blood of
God'![69] But, as Leighton pointed out also in his exposition of the
Creed, the Trinity participates in the work of redemption.

---

[64] *Works*, Vol. I, p. 140.
[65] *Works*, Vol. I, p. 29.
[66] *Works*, Vol. I, p. 91.
[67] 'Consider His grace, in finding a way of reconcilement, and not sparing His
own Son, His only begotten Son, to accomplish it. Nor did the Son spare
himself. O matchless love! to lay down His life, not for his friends, but for
strangers; not only so, but enemies, for unrighteous and ungodly persons, such
as be at enmity against Him.' *Works*, Vol. III, p. 203.
[68] *Works*, Vol. I, p. 235; II, pp. 21f, 265, 354; III, p. 139.
[69] *Works*, Vol. I, pp. 9 & 135: 'The precious soul could not be redeemed but by
blood, and by no blood but that of the spotless Lamb, Jesus Christ, who is God
equal with the Father; and therefore his blood is called *The blood of God* (Acts
xx).' Cf. Vol. II, p. 354.

We know that this Holy Trinity co-operates in the work of our salvation: the Father hath given us His Son, and the Son hath sent us His Spirit, and the Spirit gives us faith, which unites us to the Son, and through Him to the Father. The Father ordained our redemption, the Son wrought it, and the Spirit reveals and applies it.[70]

It was within this trinitarian and Christocentric frame of thought that Leighton gave his account of the redeeming and reconciling work of Christ in his threefold office as *king, priest, and prophet*,[71] but with special place given to the priesthood of Christ and the offering of himself in soul and in body in sacrifice for sin. 'He made his soul an offering for sin. He offered up himself, *his whole self*.'[72] The Incarnation and the atonement are to be understood together, for atonement is not simply an act done by Christ: the work and the Person of Christ are one: He is both priest and victim, priest and altar.[73] Commenting upon the clause 'suffered under Pontius Pilate' in the Creed, Leighton said: 'all his life was one continual act of suffering, from his living in the cratch to his hanging upon the cross.'[74] This means that Jesus Christ is himself the propitiation for our sins provided for us by the Love of God, and not for ours only but for the sins of the whole world. This unity of the Person and the work of Christ, together with the oneness between Christ and God, means that eternal election is to be understood as embodied in Christ and as operative in time in a retroactive and in a prospective way precisely as Christ. Hence it is to Jesus Christ and the salvation purchased by him which cannot be separated from one another, that we have to look for the reason of the Gospel and the ground of our election, not to some secret decree of God behind the back of Christ, to some unknown God of whom we are afraid. Jesus Christ is God as well as man, man as

---

[70] *Works*, Vol. IV, p. 28.; also Vol. I, p. 9.
[71] *Works*, Vol. II, pp. 114f ; Vol. III, p. 189; Vol. IV, pp. 9f, 176.
[72] *Works*, Vol. II, p. 24 – see also Vol. I, pp. 204ff, 231ff; Vol. II, pp. 24f, 208, 214f, 269f, 318, 354; Vol. IV, p. 9f. Leighton makes the point that the burden of sin laid upon Christ's shoulders in the Garden of Gethsemane was 'ten thousands times heavier than the cross which he had to bear ... it was the bitter cup of wrath due to sin, which his Father put into his hand, and caused him to drink, the very same thing that is called the bearing of our sins in his body.' *Works*, Vol. II, p. 20f.
[73] *Works*, Vol. II, pp. 24f & 208f; III, p. 459.
[74] *Works*, Vol. IV. p. 12; also Vol. II, pp. 201f.

well as God, so that the love of Christ is the love of God and the blood of Christ is the blood of God. We are therefore to interpret the election and redeeming act of God exclusively in terms of the Person and work, the life, death, resurrection and ascension of Christ. 'Christ the Mediator betwixt God and man, is God and man. A mediator not only interceding, but also satisfying (Eph. ii.16).'[75] That was the actual way in which God's eternal election was fulfilled, and it is precisely as such that it continues to operate effectively.

God's foreknowledge is his eternal and unchangeable Love revealed in Christ.[76] Leighton objected to any speculative attempt to probe behind what has actually taken place in Christ into what is hidden in the deepest recesses of the divine majesty. 'It is most absurd to seek to give any reason of the divine will without himself', apart from what he has made known of himself and his will in Christ. And so Leighton objected to any *a priori* notions of the divine decrees axiomatically and archetypically, and therefore restrictively, imposed upon the Gospel message of reconciliation with which we are entrusted as ambassadors of Christ who died for all.[77]

Let us return to the point stressed by Leighton that Christ is the covenanted Mediator of all God's love and grace to us. In commenting on the words 'through Jesus Christ' in 1 Peter 4.11, Leighton wrote:

> The Christian in covenant with God, receives all this way. And Christ possesses, and hath equal right with the Father to this glory, as He is equally the spring of it with Him, as God. But it is conveyed through Him as Mediator, who obtains all the grace we receive; and all the glory we return, and all our praise, as our spiritual sacrifice, is put into His hand as our High Priest, to offer up for us, that they may be accepted.[78]

Leighton understood this 'through Jesus Christ' as involving a relation of profound union with him. Christ is, as we have noted above, 'the *Medium unionis* through whom God conveys the sense of his love to the soul, and receives back its love to himself'.[79] In a

---

[75] *Works*, Vol. I, p. 10.
[76] *Works*, Vol. IV, pp. 242f, and Vol. I, pp. 18ff.
[77] *Works*, Vol. III, 'Sermon Preached to the Clergy' on 2 Cor. 5.20, pp. 456–74; and see also Vol. II, pp. 19 & 217; III, p. 357; and IV, p. 271.
[78] *Works*, Vol. II, p. 354. Cf. p. 365.
[79] *Works*, Vol. I, p. 74; & cf. p. 90.

fundamental sense 'Christ and the believer are one ... There is an indissoluble connexion betwixt the life of Christ and the believer. Our life is hid with Christ in God.'[80] Union with Christ probably had a more important place in Leighton's theology than that given to it in the thought of any other Scottish theologian. It was not a 'judicial union' but a real union, for, as he understood it, it lies at the heart of the whole redemptive movement of the covenant of grace, and operates in such a way that the response of the believer is itself caught up in God's redemptive activity mediated through Christ as an act of saving grace. 'This mysterious union of Christ and the believer, is that whereon both their justification and sanctification, the whole frame of their salvation and happiness, depends'.[81] Expressed otherwise, union with Christ is the result of and an expression of our election in Christ.[82]

Another way that Leighton had of expressing this redemptive union was in developing the theological concept of saving *exchange*, which he also spoke of as 'the Commutation of the persons, *He himself – for us.*'[83]

> So then, there is a union betwixt believers and Jesus Christ, by which this interchange is made; He being charged with their sins, and they clothed with his satisfaction and righteousness. This union is founded Ist on God's decree of election ... 2ndly, it is also founded in the actual intention of the Son so made man; He presenting Himself to the Father in all He did and suffered, as for them, having them, and them only, in His eye and thoughts, in all. 'For their sakes do I sanctify myself' (John xvii. 1,9) ... Again, 3dly. This union is applied and performed in them, when they are converted and ingrafted into Jesus Christ by faith ... 4thly. The consummation of this union is in glory, which is the result and fruit of all the former. As it began in Heaven, it is completed there.[84]

Leighton linked up this saving union through exchange with the biblical concept of *Goel* (גוֹאֵל) *the Kinsman-Redeemer* applied to Christ

---

[80] *Works*, Vol. I, p. 90. Leighton refers here to John xiv.19: 'Because I live, ye shall live also', and Col. iii. 3: 'Your life is hid with Christ in God.'

[81] *Works*, Vol. II, p. 38 ; cf. p. 83.

[82] *Works*, Vol. III, pp. 38 & 50.

[83] *Works*, Vol. II, p. 15; Vol. III, pp. 360f; Vol. IV, pp. 270f.

[84] *Works*, Vol. II, pp. 22f.

the Incarnate Son who is one of us as man as well as God, and precisely as such is the High Priest who represents God to us and us to God.[85]

The concept of Christ as *Goel* or Kinsman-Redeemer was particularly important for Leighton, for it helped him to emphasise the redemptive import of the oneness of Christ with God the Father on the one hand, and of the oneness of Christ with human beings on the other hand. Thus there was embraced within the compass of the one Person of Christ the hypostatic (or 'personal') union between God and man, on the one hand, and his incarnate union with man, on the other hand.[86] Hence 'Jesus ought truly to be called, the *union of unions.*'[87] Since in Christ the union of the Son of God was with sinners, even with unbelieving men who perish, it was essentially a redemptive and reconciling union, for *God was in Christ reconciling the world to himself* (2 Corinthians 4.19).[88]

> Now God Himself becomes a man, to make all things sure: that is the foundation of an indissoluble union. Man is knit to God in the person of Christ so close, that there is no possibility of dividing them any more; and this union of our nature in his person, is made the ground of the union of our persons with God. We find our own flesh catch hold in Christ of a man, and in that man may find God, and are made one with him by faith in Christ. And all this the powers of hell cannot dissolve.[89]

'Remember this for your comfort', Leighton said in his commentary on 1 Peter 3.18, 'that as you are brought unto God by Jesus Christ, so you are kept in that union by Him. It is a firmer knot than the first was; there is no power in hell can dissolve it. He suffered once to bring us to God, never to depart again. As He suffered for all, so we are brought once for all.'[90]

It was with this theological outlook that Leighton was able to help people over the insidious problems of assurance that seemed to afflict so many of them in Calvinist Scotland. He discerned that

---

85 *Works*, Vol. II, p. 17. See also Vol. III, p. 355; Vol. IV, pp. 10f.
86 *Works*, Vol. IV, pp. 10–11.
87 *Works*, Vol. IV, p. 270.
88 *Works*, Vol. IV, pp. 9ff; Vol. II, p. 83.
89 *Works*, Vol. III, p. 352.
90 *Works*, Vol. II, p. 217.

behind their difficulties lay a deficient doctrine of God, one that was not properly controlled by his self-revelation in Jesus Christ. 'All the waverings and fears of misbelieving minds', he said in a sermon, 'do spring from dark and narrow apprehension of Jesus Christ.'[91] 'There is no right knowledge of the Father but in the Son. God dwelling in the *man, Christ,* will be found or known nowhere else; and they who consider and worship God out of Christ, do not know or worship the true God, but a false notion and fancy of their own.'[92] What Leighton did above all, therefore, was to shepherd people back to 'the matchless Love of God' revealed and embodied in Jesus Christ which is freely offered to us in the Gospel. Nowhere did he do that with more effect than in his two sermons on the eighth chapter of St Paul's Epistle to the Romans from verse 33 to the end.[93]

The actual ground of assurance, the fixed kind of assurance, the proper assurance of faith, is 'Jesus Christ himself, the free gift of God's free love in Jesus Christ ... *The Love of God,* he is with us – who then can be against us?' Leighton then cited the words, '*He that spared not His own Son, but gave Him to the death for us, will He not with Him give us all things?*'[94] What Leighton sought to do was to show the relation of the love of Christ to the ultimate Love of God.

> Jesus Christ is the medium of this love, the middle link that keeps all safe together betwixt God and man, being so closely united in his personal nature, and the persons of men in and by him, to the Father, So here, it is first called the *love of Christ,* ver. 35, and then, in the close *the love of God in Christ;* the soul being first carried to him as the nearest, but so carried by him into that primitive love of God that flows in Christ, and that gave even Christ to us before [we believe]. And this is the bottom-truth, the firm ground of the saints' perseverance.[95]

[91] *Works,* Vol. III, p. 358.
[92] *Works,* Vol. III, pp. 361f.
[93] *Works,* Vol. III, pp. 275ff & 282ff. Leighton's exposition of this chapter of St Paul's Epistle to the Romans seems to reflect Hugh Binning's Sermons on this Epistle which were originally published in 1670 under the title, *The Sinner's Sanctuary.* See *The Works of the Pious, Reverend and Learn'd Mr Hugh Binning,* Edinburgh, 1735, 'The Life of the Author', p. xix.
[94] Leighton, *Works,* Vol. III, p. 276.
[95] *Works,* Vol. III, p. 286, also p. 278.

There is nothing that can separate us from that love. *Who shall accuse – Who shall condemn – Who shall separate?* It is in that 'primitive love', the ultimate aboriginal Love of God who did not spare his own Son, that there is to be discerned the hidden character of election, and the source of all the effects that flow from election.[96]

Leighton pointed out the serious mistake people make which prejudices their own comfort and darkens their spirits through a misunderstanding of election. 'They will not believe till they find some evidence, which is quite to invert the order of the thing, and to look for fruit without settling a root for it to grow from.'[97] He then turns the argument about election the other way round. 'The great evidence of thy election is love. Thy love to Him gives certain testimony of His preceding, eternal love in thee; so are they rightly designated, *they that love God*. Thy choosing of Him is the effect and evidence of His choosing thee.'[98] 'That is, indeed', he said, 'His love to us, but it is so as it includes inseparably the inseparableness of our love to Him.' Then with reference to the words in verse 37, *Through Him that hath loved us*, Leighton declared: 'His love makes sure ours. He hath such a hold of our hearts as He will not let go, nor suffer us to let go our hold: all is fast by His strength. He will not lose us, nor shall any be able to pluck us out of His hand.'[99] This is the striking point Leighton made about the reciprocating and reciprocal nature of election which we have already noted, of which Christians ought to discover about the covenant of grace and their union with God in Christ.[100]

There is 'a vast difference', Leighton pointed out, 'betwixt a Christian taken in himself, and in Christ! When he views himself in himself, then he is nothing but a poor, miserable, perishing wretch; but then he looks again, and sees himself in Christ, and there he is rich, and safe, and happy.'[101] It is when the believer looks away from himself to Christ who loved him and gave himself for him that he has, not an 'ecstatical' form of assurance,

> but the more constant, and fixed kind of assurance, the proper assurance of faith: the soul by believing, cleaves unto God in Christ as he offers himself in the gospel, and thence

[96] *Works*, Vol. III, p. 278.
[97] *Works*, Vol. III, pp. 283f.
[98] *Works*, Vol. III, p. 279.
[99] *Works*, Vol. III, pp. 285f.
[100] See again *Works*, Vol. I, pp. 22f & 74.
[101] *Works*, Vol. III, p. 282.

is possessed by a sweet and calm persuasion of his love; that being the proper work, to appropriate him, and make Christ, and in him, eternal life, ours.[102]

The *love of God*, He is with us – who then can be against us? ... He that spared not His own Son, but gave Him to the death for us, will He not with him give us all things?[103]

None can take my Christ away from me, and I am safe in Him, as His purchase. None can take me from Him, and being still in His love, and through Him in the Father's love, that is sufficient. What can I fear? What can I want?[104]

Who shall lay anything to the charge of God's elect? It is God that justifieth. Who is he that condemneth? It is Christ that died, yea, rather, that is risen again, who is even at the right hand of God, who also maketh intercession for us (Romans 8.33–34).[105]

Who shall separate us from the love of Christ? Shall tribulation, or distress, or persecution, or famine, or nakedness, or peril, or sword? &c. (Romans 8.35, etc.).[106]

Bibliography

Adamson, Patrick, Στοιχείωσις *Eloquiorum Dei, sive Methodus Religionis Christianae Catechetica*, Edinburgh, 1627.

Binning, Hugh, *The Works of the Pious, Reverend and Learn'd Mr Hugh Binning*, Edinburgh, 1735.

Bonar, Horatius, *Catechisms of the Scottish Reformation*, London, 1866.

The Book of Common-Prayer, and Administration of the Sacraments; and other Partes of Divine Service for the Use of the Church of Scotland, with Paraphrase of the Psalms in Metre by King James the VI. Edinburgh, 1637 and 1712.

Boyd, Robert, of Trochrig, *Ad Ephesios Praelectiones*, Geneva, 1661.

Burleigh, J. H. S., *A Church History of Scotland*, London, 1960.

Burnet, Gilbert, *History of His Own Time*, 2 vols., London, 1723–34.

---

[102] *Works*, Vol. III, pp. 282f.
[103] *Works*, Vol. III, p. 276.
[104] *Works*, Vol. III, p. 289.
[105] *Works*, Vol. III, p. 275.
[106] *Works*, Vol. III, p. 282.

Burnet, Gilbert, *A Vindication of the Authority, Constitution, and Laws of the Church and State of Scotland, In Four Conferences*, Glasgow, 1673.

Butler, D. *The Life and Letters of Robert Leighton*, London, 1903.

Butler, D., *Henry Scougal and the Oxford Methodists, or, The Influence of a Religious Teacher of the Scottish Churches*, Edinburgh & London, 1899.

Calvin John, *Institutio Religionis Christianae*, Geneva, 1559.

Campbell, John McLeod, *Memorials of John McLeod Campbell*, edited by his son, the Rev. Donald Campbell, London, 1877.

Cooper, James, *The Book of Common Prayer, and Administration of the Sacraments And Other Parts of Divine Service for the Use of the Church of Scotland. Commonly Known as Laud's Liturgy (1637)*, Edinburgh 1904.

Hilary, St, of Poitiers, *De Trinitate*, Eng. tr., *Nicene and Post-Nicene Fathers of the Christian Church*, Vol. IX, Oxford, 1899.

Leighton, Robert, *Praelectiones theologiae in auditorio publico academiae Edinburgenae*, London, 1693.

Leighton, Robert, *A Practical Commentary on the First Epistle of Peter*, Works, Vols. I & II, York, 1693.

Leighton, Robert, *The Whole Works of Robert Leighton, D.D.*, new edn, 4 vols., London, 1830.

MacWard, Robert, *The case of the accomodation lately proposed by the Bishop of Dunblane, to the nonconforming ministers examined...*, Edinburgh, 1671.

McWard, Robert, *The True Non-Conformist in Answere to the Modest and Free Conference betwixt a Conformist and a Non-Conformist, about the present Distempers in Scotland*, Glasgow, 1671.

Polanus, Amandus, *Syntagma Theologiae Christianae*, Hanover, 1624 & 1625.

Reid, H. M. B., *The Divinity Principals of the University of Glasgow, 1545–1654*, Glasgow, 1917.

Reid, H. M. B., *The Divinity Professors of the University of Glasgow, 1640–1903*, Glasgow, 1923.

Scougal, Henry, *Discourses on Important Subjects*, Glasgow, 1751.

Scougal, Henry, *The Life of God in the Soul of Man*, London, 1677.

Thomas à Kempis, *De Imitatione Christi, Libri Quatuor*, London, 1867. *Of the Imitation of Christ*, Four Books, Revised Translation, London, 1902.

Robert Wodrow, *Analecta*, Vol. I–III, Edinburgh, 1843.

6

The Presbyterian Tradition

James Fraser of Brae (1638–98)

James Fraser was a staunch Covenanter, a man with strong convictions which would not allow him to conform to the Erastian Episcopalian establishment under Charles II, for which he suffered imprisonment several times and then banishment. He denied the charge of schism,[1] but claimed to be acting lawfully in separating from what he believed to be a corrupt form of church government.[2] During his imprisonment he gave himself to the study of Greek and Hebrew and other Oriental languages, and, where possible, to writing. Through his experiences he learned to live, as he said,

> less and less in myself and on myself, and more and more in and on Jesus Christ, as made of God to me all my need. I less and less looked to any of my own experiences, or attainments, or feelings, or affections: but on Christ as made of God all that for me and to me. And not on him as sensibly felt and fully possessed by me and in me, but solely and always as offered to me in the Gospel.[3]

It was thus that he came to realise the real significance of faith, having learned through his sufferings to rely not on faith but on Christ in whom he believed as the personal embodiment of God's covenant of grace. Throughout his life in prison and out of prison he lived, interpreted the Scriptures and preached the Gospel in a

---

[1] *Memoirs of the Rev. James Fraser of Brea, Select Biographies,* edited for the Wodrow Society, Edinburgh, 1847, p. 343. See also the edition with an Introductory Note by Alexander Whyte, Edinburgh, 1891, p. 274. With the *Memoirs* and *Meditations* James Fraser's title is given as 'of Brea', but in *Justifying Faith* and *The Lawfulness and Duty,* it is given as 'of Brae'.

[2] See *The Lawfulness and Duty of Separation from Corrupt Members and Churches Explained and Vindicated,* Edinburgh, 1744.

[3] Cf. Alexander Whyte, *James Fraser, Laird of Brea,* Edinburgh, 1911, p. 236.

decidedly evangelical way – that is, not in such a way that he subordinated the Scriptures to the prevailing Westminster tradition, but tested that tradition before the teaching of the Scriptures themselves.[4]

According to the editor of one of his early works, 'He had more than ordinary Insight into God's Covenant of Grace, and it would seem, that the Lord had singl'd him out amongst many, that he might reveal his Son in him.' He also added, 'We would not presume to alter his Way of Speaking, which is peculiar to himself, and which any who were acquainted with him easily bear with.'[5] That applies to all the citations made from his writing here. Early in life James Fraser came across the *Marrow of Modern Divinity* from which he claimed to 'be greatly profited'.[6] Although Fraser's theology operated within the general frame of covenant theology, his Christ-centred and Cross-centred thought gave its content and substance a new and very evangelical shape.[7] He identified 'the Covenant of Grace' with the 'Free Promise of God', in which the emphasis in faith is transferred from the 'legal' to the 'personal' right to the promises and privileges of the New Covenant through Christ *in whom all the promises of God are Yea and Amen* (2 Corinthians1.20, Ephesians 1.4, Galatians 3.16).[8] 'The Promises of the New Covenant are', what he called, 'the Christian's *magna Charta*.'[9] He was certainly at odds with the prevailing interpretation of the covenant of grace in contractual terms, which gave rise to a new legalism and was a lapse back into the covenant of works, *Do this and live*, held to be universally imprinted on man's heart.[10] That

---

[4]   Cf. the 'Postscript' at the end of *Justifying Faith 1*, written as 'a Prisoner in a desolate Rock of the Sea for the Testimony of Jesus', he said that if he seemed to affect singularity, and to walk in untrodden paths in respect of some Positions, he was persuaded that he had 'not walked alone or against the Current of Orthodox, Godly, Protestant Divines.' p. 337.

[5]   *Meditations on Several Subjects in Divinity*, Edinburgh, 1721.

[6]   Reported by John Brown of Whitburn, *Gospel Truth Accurately Stated and Illustrated By the Rev. James Hog, Thomas Boston, Ebenezer and Ralph Erskine, and Others*. Occasioned by the republication of *The Marrow of Modern Divinity*, collected by the Rev. John Brown. New edn Glasgow, 1831, pp. 44 & 438.

[7]   Cf. the identity of 'God's gracious Call in the Gospel' with 'The Covenant of Grace thro' Christ as holden forth in God's Word', *A Treatise on Justifying Faith 1*, p. 10. The last few chapters are rather like a series of evangelistic addresses, VI to VIII, pp. 271–334.

[8]   This was the theme of Chapter IV of *Justifying Faith*, pp. 84–125.

[9]   *Justifying Faith*, p. 307.

[10] Fraser may have had in mind the work of Dudley Fenner, *Sacra Theologia*, 1585. See J. B. Torrance, 'The Concept of Federal Theology – Was Calvin a Federal

ran counter to the New Testament message of the free unconditional Gospel of Grace which was not a 'doing covenant' but a
'believing covenant'.[11] To link together a covenant of works with
the covenant of grace was to do damage to the freedom and
unconditional nature of the covenant of grace and the message of
the Gospel it held forth.[12] On the other hand, Fraser could use
and adapt the covenant way of thinking for evangelical use in his
own exposition of Gospel truth.[13] With reference to the freedom
of the covenant of grace, Fraser argued, 'if our Right depended
on our Faith, of if we had no interest in God's Covenant, till we
believed, then it were not a free Covenant; for that which only is
given upon a Condition, especially upon a Condition above the
Reach of our Power to perform, is not freely given.'[14] 'The promise
of Salvation is absolute, and the Covenant of Grace is absolute,
neither can this Promise depend upon another Condition.'[15] It
was thus that he was led to produce one of the most impressive
works in Scottish theology on the Gospel of grace and the
evangelical nature of faith, which he wrote in 1679 when a prisoner
on the Bass Rock, *A Treatise Concerning Justifying or Saving Faith*,
edited and published by a friend in 1722 after Fraser's death,[16]
and in a considerably expanded form, which he left in the form of
a manuscript, *A Treatise on Justifying Faith*, published in 1749.[17] In
this work he set out the objective grounds for the proclamation of
unconditional redemption and grace to the whole world, to all
men and women within and without the Church, even to the
heathen, and gave detailed attention to questions and objections
raised on all sides, in which he showed remarkable dialectical skill,
but took care to ground everything squarely on the Word of God
in the Holy Scriptures. This work was to have a considerable

Theologian?' *Calvinus Sacrae Scripturae Professor*, ed. W. H. Neuser, Grand Rapids,
1994, p. 24. There J. B. Torrance says about *Sacra Theologia*, 'This was the first
work, as far as we know, to use the phrase 'a covenant of works' (*foedus operum*),
or 'the covenant of law', and lay the basis for what we now call *federal theology*.'

[11] Cf. *Justifying Faith*, pp. 29 & 120f.
[12] *Justifying Faith*, pp. 31ff, & 40.
[13] *Meditations on Several Subjects in Divinity*, 1721, p. 15.
[14] *Justifying Faith*, p. 97.
[15] *Justifying Faith*, p. 89.
[16] See the Preface to the 1722 edition, p. viii, to which reference will be made as
Justifying Faith 1.
[17] Reference will be made to this edition as *Justifying Faith* 2, or simply as *Justifying
Faith*.

influence in the varying course of Scottish theology, from the Marrow Controversy to the deposition of John McLeod Campbell, not least in its teaching about the unconditional (or 'absolute') nature of salvation and grace, and its implications for direct personal relation to Jesus Christ, about the objective ground of justifying faith, and the inseparability of faith and assurance. Faith is to be understood in a personal way, not as an assent to information, to truths of Scripture or doctrinal propositions, but as the assent that arises in the heart and understanding as an echo of or answer to Christ's call in the Gospel. It is a 'closing with Christ', when 'the Lord speaks to the heart and draws the heart to himself'. Faith is to be understood, therefore, in accordance with the nature of its proper object, a Saviour crucified for our sins held out to us by the Love of God in the Gospel. It is not to be understood in terms of its own nature or activity as faith, but in relation to Christ its *proper object* as he is offered to us in the Gospel. Faith is 'not a giving but a receiving grace'.[18] What Fraser was concerned to stress here and all through his work was the objective basis of the confidence and assurance of faith, *in Christ himself.* 'The Ground of this Confidence is wholly in the Lord Jesus, without us, and not at all either in whole or in Part in our selves.'[19]

His great book, *Justifying Faith,* has two main parts. 1) The main part is devoted to the ground of faith in which it is shown that it is not faith itself that justifies us but Christ in whom we have faith. The ultimate grounds of believing are 'the Attributes of God, his Power, and Faith, Fulness and Wisdom', but 'the immediate grounds of believing are the gracious promises in the Gospel: But my Belief of the Truth of the Promises is founded on Christ's Faith, Fulness, the Bottom and Pillar of all Divine Faith.'[20] Of particular significance here is the correlation of our faith with the faith of God and the faith of Christ – human faith derives from, rests on, and is undergirded by divine faithfulness.[21] Great stress was laid from the outset, by Fraser, on 'Christ's all-Sufficiency', in that 'He is able also to save them to the uttermost, that come unto God by

---

[18] *Justifying Faith* 1, pp. 10–16, 72f; cf also, for example, *Justifying Faith* 2, p. 263: 'The Gospel holding out of a crucified Saviour for our Sins is the only fit Object of our Faith, and our Faith closing with this Object for salvation acts rationally.'

[19] *Justifying Faith* 1, p. 165.

[20] *Justifying Faith* 2, p. 3.

[21] *Justifying Faith,* p. 3.

him.'[22] (2) The second and longer part of Fraser's work is called an 'Appendix' devoted to the object of Christ's death. In it he shows that Christ died for all people, and not for a limited number as it was claimed in the so-called 'covenant of redemption' made between the Son and the Father. He rejected the distinction between a covenant of grace and a covenant of redemption[23] – the former, as he said again and again, is absolute in its nature and universal in its extent. Throughout his book Fraser differed at crucial points sharply with Samuel Rutherford and James Durham, as also with William Twisse the Prolocutor of the Westminster Assembly, not to mention the puritan divine John Owen. But reference is made to several others like William Fenner in connection with their support for the biblical teaching that Christ died for all men. This had to do sometimes with a subtle form of Pelagianism in their understanding of faith. 'It is an Error oftentimes in our Faith, that it is not built purely and only on the Grace of Christ, but we seek secretly other Props, and so to set some other thing in Christ's room, and this is as it is derogatory to Christ, and evidence of Distrust in him.'[24]

Fraser was not a scholastic theologian like Samuel Rutherford, but while basing his positive position on strictly biblical and evangelical grounds he used logical argument with great effect in exposing contradictions and demolishing erroneous objections.[25] He claimed that contemporary divinity was 'much altered from what it was in the primitive reformers' time'. He mourned the 'contempt of grace' by puritans like John Owen, and called theologians to return to 'the good old paths'.[26] He admitted that 'to affirm that Christ died for all is contrary to the Current of the

---

[22] Hebrews 7.15 – *Justifying Faith*, pp. 11ff. Fraser clearly had in mind current arguments put forward by those who upheld a doctrine of limited atonement which they justified by interpreting the biblical 'all men' to mean 'all sorts of men'. A succinct form of this argumentation is found in George Gillespie, *A Treatise of Miscellany Questions*, published by his brother Patrick, Edinburgh, 1646 and 1649, Chapter xxii, pp. 277–89.

[23] *Justifying Faith*, p. 170.

[24] *Justifying Faith*, p. 295.

[25] Fraser preferred not make use of logical distinctions and arguments in expounding the Truth – *Justifying Faith* 1, p. 174. 'When Divines accommodate Religious Matters to Logical Rules, it hath occasioned a diverse Manner of expressing one and the same thing, according to their different Philosophical Notions.' *Ibid.* p. 168.

[26] *Justifying Faith*, p. 43.

most godly and judicious Protestant Divines, and contrary to our Confession of Faith',[27] but with them, he insisted, 'the doctrine of the First Reformation had been overthrown and condemned, and a new notion of faith given'.[28] 'This blessed Truth shining brightly in the Days of Luther and Calvin and others whom God raised up to witness for himself and to clear his Truths, I fear is at this Day not a little obscured if I mistake not, and a Gospel Spirit is a rarer Thing than many think.'[29] Fraser claimed repeatedly that he himself adhered to the teaching of 'Luther on the Galatians and Calvin's Institutions', that book called 'Marrow of Modern Divinity' (by Edward Fisher), to Bradford, Tindal, Hamilton, Wishart, Knox, and Bruce, and a number of the French Reformed Divines, but would have nothing to do with Arminians or their notion of universal salvation which he 'abhorred'.[30] He was especially helped by reading St Paul's Epistle to the Romans.[31]

As the title of his book suggests Fraser's immediate concern was with the interrelation between faith and justification, but this was expounded within the orbit of the great mysteries of the Faith, the Trinity, the Incarnation including the atonement, the hypostatic union, and the threefold Office of Christ as priest, king and prophet, and also the union of believers with Christ.[32] While all three divine Persons have ever been active in redemption, since it was only the Son who became incarnate, Fraser's main concern was with the incarnate actualisation of the infinite Love of God in and through Christ as the one Mediator between God and man who is himself both God and man.[33] It is in the whole Christ, from his birth to his resurrection presented to us in the Gospel account of God's *philanthropia* or love for all mankind, and Christ's good-will toward sinners, that the salvation of man is to be considered

[27] *Justifying Faith*, p. 250, also p. 292.
[28] *Justifying Faith*, p. 292. He claimed to take a middle path between Arminians and Quakers on the one hand and right-wing extremists on the other hand. Cf. also Fraser's Introduction to the first edition of this work in which he wrote: 'I know and acknowledge, that in some Things I seem to step out of the common road wherein the modern Divines of our Church, in Britain and Ireland, have walked.' *Justifying Faith* 1, p. 6.
[29] *Justifying Faith*, p. 33; see also p. 43.
[30] *Justifying Faith*, pp. 147f, 207f, etc.
[31] *Memoirs*, Ch. IX.1, 1891 edn, pp. 232f. See again *Justifying Faith*, pp. 43 & 250f.
[32] *Justifying Faith*, p. 158.
[33] See the sermon by Hugh Binning on Deut. 6.4 & John 5.7, *The Works of Hugh Binning*, Edinburgh, 1735, p. 89.

rather than in the abstract with reference to divine decrees of election and reprobation.[34]

Great stress was laid throughout upon 'the all sufficiency of Christ to save to the uttermost', for it is on Christ and his all-sufficiency in his obedient life and death, and God's good-will toward sinners incarnated in him, that believing faith is grounded, but grounded in such a way that faith rests in Christ beyond itself. The absolute promise of life and salvation through Christ is the seed and ground of faith, but it is not grounded on faith.[35] 'He that believes', Fraser wrote (rather awkwardly),

> believes salvation thro' Christ's Merits, without conceiving any Thing of his own Faith, or any objective apprehension of his Faith, tho' the Object itself cannot be without this; that is, tho' Salvation doth not flow but from Faith, yet Salvation as it is objectively stated to the Act of Faith, may be considered by Faith without Faith's considering any Thing of itself which is the Condition; because Faith is not the objective Condition of Salvation, or ground that is given Faith to believe upon; for it cannot be a ground of itself.[36]

In other words, this means that faith has to 'go outside of itself' altogether without intruding itself in any way as a subsidiary prop to justification.[37] Fraser reinforced understanding of the unconditional nature of salvation and of faith, with reference to the covenant of grace, the promises of which are really made, and made equally and freely to all. The glad tidings of the Gospel do not depend on any conditions whatsoever, for remission of sins is declared absolutely and offered through Christ to faith.[38] That is the freedom of God's grace which is sealed to us in the sacraments.[39] 'The glad Tidings of the Gospel do not depend on any conditions at all.'[40] It was this view of the absolutely free and unconditional nature of grace that James Fraser was passionately concerned to convey in correction of the kind of teaching that he found to prevail in the Kirk in his times. He made a point, however, of differentiating

---

[34] *Justifying Faith*, p. 75; cf. pp. 66ff & 79ff.
[35] *Justifying Faith*, p. 92.
[36] *Justifying Faith*, p. 276.
[37] *Justifying Faith*, Chapters 1–3, pp. 1–78.
[38] *Justifying Faith*, pp. 84ff, 97ff, 117ff.
[39] *Justifying Faith*, p. 124.
[40] *Justifying Faith*, p. 127.

this view of the universality and unconditional nature of grace from
the views of the Arminians and Antinomians. In his *Memoir* he even
took exception to the dangerous teaching of 'Mr Baxter' who
regarded the utterly unconditional nature of grace as 'antinomian'.
Fraser replied that while he rejected antinomian error, it 'lay very
near the truth'![41]

The real pith of Fraser's teaching is given in the Fifth Chapter,
when after having shown how faith is grounded on the absolute
sufficiency of Christ, he went on to show that faith is grounded on
'Christ's Death for us'. Here he appealed to two passages from
St Paul, which had great significance for him. (1) 2 Corinthians
5.20, 21: 'Now then we are Ambassadors for Christ, as though God
did beseech you by us: We pray you in Christ's stead, be ye
reconciled to God: For he hath made him to be sin for us, who
knew no sin; that we might be made the righteousness of God in
him.' And (2) Romans 8.32–34: 'He that spared not his own Son,
but delivered him up for us all, How shall he not with him also
freely give us all things ... Who is he that condemneth? It is Christ
that died.'[42]

Behind this lay earlier sections of *Justifying Faith* in which James
Fraser had been concerned to speak of the *good-will of God in Christ
toward sinners*, that is of God himself, but of God in Christ.[43] His
intention here was to alter the concept of God that was steadily
being inculcated by harsh aspects of Westminster Theology in
people's minds through its doctrine of absolute divine decrees
presented apart from God's actual self-revelation in Christ. There
he showed that while God is to be thought of as Sovereign Lord
doing what he will to his creatures, he is nevertheless to be
considered 'as he hath manifested himself in Christ Jesus, in whom
he is good and gracious and hath no Fury, but is in him alone,
well pleased, *full of grace and truth*; as he sits upon this Mercy-Seat
he doth not condemn but save.'[44] This is the nature of God with

[41] *Memoir*, IX.1, p. 233, and the Editor's Preface to the first edition of *A Treatise
    Concerning Justifying and Saving Faith*, Edinburgh, 1722. Cf. Alexander Whyte,
    op. cit., p. 96. See further *Justifying Faith*, 1749, p. 295. Generations later
    H. R. Mackintosh used to say to his students in New College: 'If your preaching
    of the Gospel does not have a suspicion of antinomianism about it, you can be
    sure it is not the Gospel!'
[42] *Justifying Faith*, p. 125.
[43] *Justifying Faith*, pp. 59ff.
[44] *Justifying Faith*, p. 62.

whom we have to do in his divine decrees. On the one hand, Fraser pointed out, while God does not will the salvation of all men, 'then should all be saved', nevertheless, in spite of his judgment and damnation of reprobates, which results from justice, he does not delight in the death of a sinner. Then he told his readers how they were to think of the good-will and gracious nature of the good-will of God in Christ, by directing them to the Gospel account of how 'Christ weeped over Jerusalem.'[45] 'It was no Dissimulation', Fraser added, 'they were not crocodile tears he shed ... for this weeping and these tears did really express the tender and compassionate Nature of Christ.'

This led Fraser to made the following assertion.

> God in Christ revealed in the Gospel as gracious, in whom is no Fury, but full of Grace and Truth, wills one Thing, and such with whom only we have adoe; *God sent not his Son to condemn the world; but that the world through him might be saved*: And God as Sovereign and sitting on a Throne of Judgment wills another thing. God in Christ sits upon a Throne of Mercy, and so neither wills or issues out any Sentence of Condemnation, wills not the Death of any, but that all may be saved, and so Fury is not in him. But Christ as Sovereign wills some to be damned for their sin, and will at the Last day damn and curse Thousands: But now under the Dispensation of the Gospel we have not adoe with Christ as a Judge sitting on a Throne of Justice or as a Sovereign. These are not the garments he appears to us in, in the Gospel, but we have adoe with Christ as full of Grace and Truth, and as he sits upon a Throne of Grace condemning none, and as such he truly wills the Salvation of such as he invites, and delights not in their Death.[46]

There is some ambiguity here in what Fraser appeared to hold about a twofold will in God in regard to damnation and salvation, to which we will turn later. At this point, however, we must take seriously two points he was concerned to make about the good-will of God in Christ (in the reverse order in which he spoke of them): a) Christ did really will and desire that Jerusalem should

---

[45] *Ibid.* pp. 63f; cf. p. 75. This was to anticipate the remarkable book by John Howe, *The Redeemer's Tears Wept Over Lost Souls*, republished by Robert Gordon, Edinburgh, 1822. See below, pp. 278–85.

[46] *Justifying Faith*, p. 66.

believe. It was with a most tender affection that he wept over her, and did not dissemble. b) Believers are not to concern themselves with election or reprobation but consider themselves as fallen sinners in Adam, to whom God's philanthropy or mankind-love has appeared.[47] Consideration should be given to 'the gracious Nature of God, or God in Christ, in the Dispensation of the Gospel.'[48] Fraser went on in this section to stress the nature of God's love as an everlasting, unchangeable, unconquerable love, and of the tenderness, good-will of God toward us.

It was in following up that account of God's good-will toward sinners, that Fraser turned to direct attention to the saving truth that *God was in Christ reconciling the world to himself*, and that in his reconciling life and death Christ 'was made sin for us, who knew no sin, that we might be made the righteousness of God in him'.[49] But behind all lay the fact that God *'did not spare his only Son but freely delivered him up for us all. How shall he not with him freely give us all things?'*[50] That is to say, in the atonement the Father and the Son, the Son and the Father, acted inseparably together, for the Son was not just an organ, external to himself, used by God to fulfil an eternal decree for the salvation of the elect. In, with and through him it was the unsparing love that he himself eternally is that was the ground and source of Christ's atoning sacrifice. Of supreme importance here too, as Fraser saw it, was the fact of Christ's personal obedience and sacrifice of himself, which he through the eternal Spirit offered up to God whereby he satisfied him. On occasion he could refer to that in line with Westminster theology: 'The Satisfaction that Jesus Christ made to divine Justice is wholly bounded and ordered by the absolute decree of God.'[51] However, he actually viewed the 'satisfaction' which Christ made, rather differently from the *Westminster Confession*, not in accordance with the demands of absolute divine decrees. It was an atoning satisfaction flowing from 'God's good-will toward sinners', made not just for the elect but for all mankind in which as the Second Adam Christ substituted himself for all the descendants of the first Adam, and made restitution which they

[47] *Justifying Faith*, p. 75. This exhortation is repeated on p. 77.
[48] *Justifying Faith*, p. 76.
[49] *Justifying Faith*, pp. 132f.
[50] *Justifying Faith*, pp. 125ff; 2 Corinthians 5.20 & Romans 8.32–34.
[51] *Justifying Faith*, p. 170.

could not make, and thereby effected a redemption for all.[52] It is noteworthy that for Fraser the satisfaction made by Christ the incarnate Son was to 'the *Person* of the Father'.[53]

> The Garment of the human Nature with which the Son was clothed was indeed wrought by the three Persons efficiently, yet it was the Son only that did put it on, and not the Father and the Holy Ghost: So likewise, tho' all the three Persons did concur efficiently to the Satisfaction made by Christ, yet was it terminated only to the Father *personally considered*, for it was the *Person* of the Father that was satisfied, and not the Person of either the Son or the Holy Ghost.[54]

He did not think of 'satisfaction' as fulfilling a legal requirement on the part of God, so much as deriving from the infinite love of God the Father, which constitutes the ultimate ground of faith.

'He that did not spare his only Son but delivered him up for us all, how shall he not with him also freely give us all things?' Romans 8.32. Those were words that Fraser recalled again and again, for they expressed the 'absolute' way in which God's reconciliation is freely donated, and his promises are 'absolutely' and freely delivered. 'The glad tidings of the Gospel do not depend on any conditions at all.'[55] Because of the finished work of Christ the offer of the Gospel to the sinners for whom Christ died is not just an offer but a *donation* on the ground of which they have a title to believe. It is the conveyance of this right that is the ground of faith, so that all who believe are saved.[56] In this connection Fraser referred several times to the incident of 'the brazen serpent' mentioned by Jesus to Nicodemus. 'As Moses lifted up the serpent in the wilderness, even so must the Son of man be lifted up: that whosoever believes in him should not perish, but have eternal life.'[57] However, a distinction is to be drawn between 'if' and 'unless'. The message of the Gospel to the sinner is not that he will be saved *if* he believes, for that would throw him back upon himself as the ground of his faith, but that Christ has already died for him and

---

[52] See here *Justifying Faith*, pp. 59–70, 113, 204 & 264.
[53] Thus John Knox, *Works*, vol. 6, p. 319.
[54] *Justifying Faith*, pp. 229f.
[55] *Justifying Faith*, pp. 127ff.
[56] *Justifying Faith*, pp. 113ff.
[57] *Justifying Faith*, pp. 136, 171, 319, 321.

made satisfaction for his sins so that salvation is freely offered to him on that objective ground alone. However,

> the Death of Christ nor the offer therof in the Gospel, nor all the Seals thereof in the Sacraments, will be of any avail unto thee *unless* thou receive it and apply it and make use of it. Yea thou shalt be arraigned as Guilty of the Blood of the Son of God, if ye flight this Grace of God, and receive it in vain: Come to him therefore and thankfully receive this great Treasure.[58]

The Scripture says, 'Let us draw near in the full Assurance of Faith. But whereon is this Assurance of Faith built? Verily on the Blood of Christ by which we have boldness to enter into the Holiest of Holies.'[59]

> The Doctrine of the universal Extent of Christ's Death doth yield a clear Ground and an infallible Evidence for the strongest Faith, so as to remove all doubting, and to fill the Heart *with joy unspeakable and full of glory.*[60]

> My laying hold on a crucified Saviour doth not make him crucified for me; If therefore Christ died not for me, my laying hold of him cannot make me to have Interest in his Death, and can consequently never give me Salvation thro' his Blood; for faith doth not alter the Object, it remaineth the same whether believed or not believed.[61]

The objective ground of faith, therefore, is not faith itself, but Christ crucified in whom we have faith. Fraser referred here, as several times elsewhere, to St Paul's own faith which was founded on Jesus Christ who loved him and gave himself for him (Galatians 2.20): 'I am crucified with Christ: nevertheless I live; yet not I, but Christ liveth in me; and the life which I now live in the flesh I live by the faith of the Son of God, who loved me and gave himself for me.'[62]

[58] *Justifying Faith*, p. 139.
[59] *Justifying Faith*, pp. 135f; cf. also pp. 170, 216 & 236; and refer to pp. 40ff, where assurance of faith and assurance of salvation (grounded on Christ's atoning satisfaction) are said to belong together.
[60] *Justifying Faith*, p. 201.
[61] *Justifying Faith*, p. 133.
[62] *Justifying Faith*, pp. 131, 134, 326, etc.

In writing about Christ crucified as the reconciliation and propitiation which God has freely provided for us out of his unconditional love, and about Christ himself in his saving work as the freely given donation of God and the objective ground of faith, James Fraser was attacking the idea which had a primary place in hyper-Calvinist theology that the ultimate ground of faith is in the electing will of God. That is why he counselled sinners to set aside all thoughts about election and reprobation, and concentrate upon 'the wonderful Love and Goodness of God to poor sinners', upon 'the saving good-will of God manifested in Christ', and upon the objective 'ground of his death for us'. But there were two other issues bound up with this understanding of objectivity, which had to be faced: a) the extent of the atonement and the universality of the Gospel offer, and b) the bearing of the Gospel of unconditional grace upon the reprobate and their ultimate end. The assertion that the death of Christ was the ultimate ground of justifying and saving faith meant that election was not the objective foundation of faith, and the assertion that Christ died for all men, had the effect of questioning the distinction between the elect and the reprobate maintained by the *Confession of Faith*.[63] These were matters on which he had already had to touch, but they called for fuller and more direct treatment which Fraser gave them in *An Appendix concerning the Object of Christ's Death*.[64] In it he added powerful support for what he had already written on the unconditional nature of grace and faith, and on sufficient universal redemption through the death of Christ.[65]

Let us note right away two of Fraser's arguments, one *biblical* and one *theological*, showing that 'Christ died in some common Sort and sufficiently for all within the visible Church'.

1) The biblical argument. *The Bible tells us unmistakably that Christ died for all men and that all mankind have an interest in Christ's death.*

> The universal Strain of Scripture expresseth so frequently, clearly, and variously that Christ died for all, and that without any seeming Contradiction from other Scriptures, Isaiah liii.6. '*The Lord hath laid on him the iniquity of us all.*' 2 Cor. v.14. '*We thus judge that if one died for all, then were all*

---

[63] *Justifying Faith*, pp. 140–58 & 160f.
[64] Pp. 159–338.
[65] *Justifying Faith*, pp. 192ff, 206ff, 216ff.

dead, and that he died for all,' etc. Rom. v.18. *'By the righteousness of one, the free gift came upon all men unto justification of life.'* Heb. ii.9,10. *'That he by the grace of God should taste death for every man.'* 1 Tim. iv.10. *'Who is the Saviour of all men, especially of those who believe.'* 1 John ii.2. *'And he is the propitiation for our sins, and not for ours only, but also for the sins of the whole world.'* 2 Pet. ii.1. *'Denying the Lord that bought them,'*; and many others; and the Death of Christ is universally expressed almost whenever its Object is mentioned.

There are *four* Considerations which make me build more upon this. (1.) That these Expressions are made use of to express the Objects of Redemption, which are used, and by which we are made to believe the most universal Truths; as, that every Man is created of God, that all shall die, shall rise again, and the like: if therefore we believe these Truths because indefinitely and universally expressed; Why not, that Christ died for all and every one, which is as universally expressed? (2.) These Testimonies declaring and expressing the Extent and Universality of Christ's Death, are not contradicted plainly by other Scriptures; for there is no Scripture which testifies that there are some which have no interest in his death, nor can the same be gathered by any necessary consequences from Scripture, for any thing I could ever perceive. Hence when Christ is said to draw all Men and the like, there is Reason to restrict this universal to a certain Number of all sorts and Ranks of People, because express Scripture and undeniable experience tell us, that all are not drawn, and so in the like: But we have no such Testimonies of Scripture to be a Ground to us to restrict those universal Propositions as (if the Lord will) shall be made good. (3.) Consider the various Manner of Expressions by which the extent of Christ's death is holden out, as it would seem of Purpose, to put the Business beyond Debate, and to elide whatever our Imaginations and Unbelief might say to the contrary: Here are first as comprehensive universal Expressions in the Matter of Redemption, as there are in the Matter of Sin, Death, Creation and the Resurrection; all are said to be redeemed, as all are said to die, to have sinned; it's expressed by the Term *World*, and *whole World*. Again, lest ye should say that the *all* spoken of, is all Sorts of Men, not *each*, or every Man of Mankind; the Spirit of God meets them with Heb. ii.9, where it is said, '*Christ tasted death for every man*', (Gr. ὑπὲρ παντὸς, not παντῶν) for each particular Man: and lest ye should still say, this every Man, is every Elect man, the World of the Elect, the Lord of purpose to obviate this Cavil expresses himself partatively and distinctly, and told us that he is the Saviour of all, both the Elect and the Reprobate, especially the Elect who believe, 1 Tim. iv.10. And lest it should after all this be said, that this is a Salvation of ordinary preserving Providence, as he is said to preserve Man and Beast, he tells plainly that he is *the propitiation not only for our sins who believe, but for the sins of the whole world*, 1 John ii.2. And with what Face or Colour of Reason can it be said that such an extensive comprehensive word as the *World*, yea the *whole World*, and that as opposite to a determinate certain Sort of People should mean the little Flock of the Elect *Gentiles*, and that in this Place only, and no where in all the Scripture beside: And finally, the Spirit of God tells us plainly to put the Matter beyond Debate, that Christ *bought* Reprobates [those who denied the Lord that bought them, thereby bringing destruction on themselves] 2 Pet. ii.1,2,3, the same words used, Rev. v.9 and xiv.3,4, Gal. iii.13. not such as gave out themselves, or were thought in the judgment of Charity to be really redeemed, but designed and deciphered as such, yet brought on themselves swift damnation, these are said to be *bought*.[66]

Then Fraser asked a question of far-reaching importance. In view of these biblical statements about the truth that Christ died for all men and women, and is the propitiation for the sins of the whole world, and in view of the biblical statements which do not speak in the same universal way about election, sanctification, glorification and justification: 'Why are comprehensive Universalities used in the Matter of Redemption, when such restrictions are used in the Matter of Election and Justification?' He answered, surely this imports that 'Redemption has a larger Sphere than Election hath, and therefore that the Scripture contracts Election in Words of Speciality only, while they open and dilate Redemption in emphatical Generalities: These Considerations move me to think that there may be a general common Redemption of all Mankind.'[67]

---

[66] *Justifying Faith*, pp. 192–3.
[67] *Justifying Faith*, p. 195. Fraser added that 'the Scriptures never offer Salvation thro' Election', p. 197.

This meant that Fraser had to consider how to relate the truth of the universal extent of redemption to the reality that many people actually bring destruction and damnation on themselves.

(2) The theological argument. Like Calvin, *Fraser rejected the proposition that 'Christ died sufficiently for all, and efficaciously only for the elect'.*[68] This was a point to which Fraser had already alluded, when arguing that it is on this ground of the universal all-sufficiency of Christ's atoning sacrifice that the Gospel of redemption is rightly and freely offered to all.[69] As Christ laid down his life absolutely, and so when it is said that 'he by the grace of God should taste death for every man' (Heb. ii.2), 'this is absolutely said and meant.'[70] Christ really died for all those he is said in Scripture to die for – he tasted death for every man.[71]

When Fraser said that Christ died sufficiently, he spoke of that as 'absolute and not conditional'.[72]

> As Christ laid down his Life absolutely, even so it is said he tasted Death for very Man, is this absolutely said and really meant; what Christ purchased was absolutely purchased, tho' I grant that Christ died and purchased Grace and Glory to be conferred upon and applied to sinners thro' Faith, and this doth no more infer that he died conditionally more for the reprobate than for the elect; for salvation flows in one channel to all; there is but one door at which all must enter, whither elect or reprobate, Acts xiii.28.[73]

Fraser went on to say:

> Christ died sufficiently, that is by a naked sufficiency for all the world, i.e. his death was of infinite value, so that it might have been a satisfaction for the sins of all mankind, and in

[68] *Justifying Faith*, pp. 143f, 162ff. See Calvin, *On Eternal Predestination*, IX,5, tr. by J. K. S. Reid, London, 1964, p. 148. Fraser, however, could make use of this distinction in a modified evangelical way, while holding firmly to the truth that Christ died for all men in his one indivisible sacrifice – 'Many are called but few are chosen'. See *Justifying Faith*, pp. 256ff & 266f.

[69] *Justifying Faith*, pp. 143ff, 148ff.

[70] *Justifying Faith*, p. 183; see also p. 215.

[71] See pp. 216ff, where Fraser answers objections against a universal sufficient redemption.

[72] *Justifying Faith*, pp. 175ff, 181ff.

[73] *Justifying Faith*, p. 183.

this sense, he died for the reprobates, that is, if he had been pleased, he was able to save them, so as their perishing does not proceed from any defect or want that was in the death of Christ ... The death of Christ is sufficient to save reprobates by an ordinary Sufficiency.[74]

The fact that Christ died for reprobates means that there is no unreality in offering them divine acceptance and pardon, but in the event of their rejection of Christ, his death constitutes the ground of their judgment.[75] Fraser rejected a sharp distinction in thinking about the vicarious death of Christ, a special way for the elect, and another for the conviction of the reprobate, for '*Christ by one indivisible Action, and one infinite indivisible Price satisfied for all Men's sins*, He satisfied not for the Elect apart and for the Reprobate apart, But whatever he laid out in the whole Tract of his Humiliation, it was for both: in a diverse Manner.'[76] 'Christ by one Ransom diversely intended did satisfy for the Sins of all Mankind.'[77] Christ died for all equally, for 'there is but one Covenant of Grace or Redemption, one Redemption and not two, relating both to the Elect and the Reprobate. It's by one Covenant, one Name, that all that ever were, or shall be, shall be saved.'[78]

On the other hand, it must be said that although Christ died for all, that does not mean that he determined the salvation of all, or therefore that all are saved.[79] Fraser made a point of saying that there is 'no certain or physical connexion between the death of Christ and salvation, so as for all whom Christ died should be saved'. 'The satisfaction of Christ's death is sufficient for all, but not necessarily related to sinners, if people do not believe on Christ crucified for our sins, his blood and satisfaction shall not save them.'[80] In denying that there is a physical and necessary connection between the death of Christ and sinners, Fraser was

---

[74] *Justifying Faith*, p. 184; cf. pp. 159f, 162f.

[75] *Justifying Faith*, pp. 185ff & 264.

[76] *Justifying Faith*, p. 256.

[77] *Justifying Faith*, p. 263. It was in this way that Fraser interpreted 1 Tim. 4.10 where Christ was said to be 'the Saviour of all men, especially of those who believe'.

[78] *Justifying Faith*, pp. 170 & 262.

[79] *Justifying Faith*, p. 202: 'There is no certain connexion betwixt Christ's Death and Salvation, for all are not saved tho' Christ died for all.'

[80] *Justifying Faith*, pp. 146f, & also 219. Fraser distinguishd sharply between the material kind of causality and that of the blood of Christ. *Ibid.* p. 21.

rejecting the scholastic Calvinist way of thinking of atonement in terms of logico-causal relations, in accordance with which, it was argued, that if Christ died for all people, then all would have to be saved, so that a doctrine of limited atonement was put forward which was restricted to the elect for whom alone the saving death of Christ was held to be necessarily and causally efficacious. That was an idea that has done immense damage in Scottish theology. If Christ died only for the elect, Fraser asked, how could there be an offer of salvation through Christ's blood? In holding that Christ died for all mankind, and not for some people only, Fraser argued that this must include the heathen who are part of mankind. We cannot but hold, therefore, that Christ died for heathen people, not apart by themselves, but in his one death for mankind in general. 'He is called the Saviour of all men. (1 Tim. iv.10).'[81]

Fraser realised that the extent of the atoning death of Christ had to be thought out in light of the interrelation between the Incarnation and the atonement, and so of the saving assumption by Christ of our Adamic humanity which was comprehensive in its nature and range.[82] As the one Mediator between God and man, the man Christ Jesus embraced all mankind, and therefore what Fraser called all 'mankind sinners'. As the first Adam brought death by sin upon all flesh, so Christ came as the second Adam in order by means of death to lay a foundation of reconciliation and life for all. He did not take on himself the nature of man as elected, but the actual human nature of mankind as the object of his atoning death and satisfaction, which applies to all and every member of the human race.[83] Hence it may be said 'All men are fundamentally justified in him and by him.' 'Christ obeyed, and died in the room of all, as the Head and Representative of fallen man.' Fraser understood this incarnational assumption of our humanity in accordance with St Paul's teaching in Romans 8.2f about Christ condemning sin in the flesh, i.e. all sin in all flesh, and in 2 Corinthians 18.5f about Christ being made sin for us, that through his death and blood we might be reconciled to God, and be made the righteousness of God in him. Christ came into the world, then, as Mediator not to condemn it but to save it.[84]

---

[81] *Justifying Faith*, p. 258.
[82] *Justifying Faith*, pp. 104f & 184f.
[83] *Justifying Faith*, pp. 264–70.
[84] *Justifying Faith*, pp. 201ff, 206ff.

Woven into this understanding of redemption through Christ as Mediator and Fraser's understanding of the all-sufficiency of the death of Christ, was the place he gave to the Reformed doctrine of the active and passive obedience of Christ, his obedient life and vicarious suffering.[85] As with earlier Reformed theologians the fifty-third chapter of Isaiah about the Suffering Servant played a basic role in Fraser's thinking about the mediatorial life and activity of Jesus, prompting him to take into account 'the whole course of Christ's obedience from his Incarnation'[86] through which he united himself to sinners in an effectually saving way in order that all men might believe. Fraser admitted, however, as we have already noted, that the atoning death of Christ for sinners was 'not necessarily effectual' for all,[87] for there was no physical or necessary connection between them, although there may be one of faith.[88] It is significant that Fraser would not divorce the all-sufficiency of Christ's death from the all-sufficiency of his incarnate Person and obedient life.[89] This is very evident in the arguments he developed for 'a sufficient universal Satisfaction for Reprobates'.[90]

Quite clearly, then, Fraser held that Christ died for all people, the unbelieving as well as the believing, the damned as well as the saved, the reprobate as well as the elected. How, then, did he think that the death of Christ, not least his atoning satisfaction for sin, bears upon those who reject Christ and bring damnation upon themselves? This was one of the basic issues where James Fraser sided with the teaching of John Calvin, rather than with that of those 'Protestant Divines' who, he complained, had not followed the old road.[91] The particular point we must take into account here is that according to St Paul the knowledge of Christ is to some people a 'savour of life unto life', but to others it can be a 'savour of death unto death'.[92] In that light it may be said that while the preaching of the Gospel of Christ crucified for all mankind is meant for their salvation, it can also have the unintended effect of blinding

---

[85] *Justifying Faith*, p. 50 – associated with this was St Paul's teaching that we are saved by the *life* of Christ as well as his death, pp. 233f.
[86] *Justifying Faith*, p. 225. Thus John Calvin, *Inst.* 2.16.5.
[87] *Justifying Faith*, pp. 49ff & 225ff.
[88] *Justifying Faith*, pp. 146, 202f.
[89] *Justifying Faith*, pp. 192ff & 206ff.
[90] *Justifying Faith*, pp. 206–16.
[91] See his discussion and admissions about this, *Justifying Faith*, pp. 250f.
[92] 2 Corinthians 2.14f.

and damning people – it becomes a 'savour of death unto death'.[93]
That is how Fraser regarded what happened to the reprobates in
becoming 'the vessels of wrath'.

> The Word of the Lord goeth not in vain, but shall certainly
> accomplish that whereunto it is sent. Isa. I.5. The Messengers
> thereof being *a sweet savour unto God, in them that perish, and
> in them that are saved,* 2 Cor. ii.15. So the Blood of Christ is a
> Sacrifice of a sweet smelling Savour to the Lord both *in them
> that perish, and in them that are saved.*[94]

While the Arminians used this as an argument for universal
redemption, Fraser, like Calvin, interpreted it as indicating how
the death of Christ proclaimed in the Gospel has a 'twofold efficacy'
in which it can act in one way upon the elect and in a different
way upon the reprobate. That is to say, it is *the Gospel* that acts in
that way. Those who reject the Blood of Christ thereby become
objects of 'Gospel and Wrath and Vengeance' and bring destruction
and damnation upon themselves. It is the very condemnation of
sin in the atoning satisfaction made by Christ for all mankind, elect
and reprobate alike, that becomes the condemnation of the
reprobate who turn away from it, and thereby render themselves
inexcusable.[95] 'Reprobates by the death of Christ are made more
inexcusable ... If the death of Christ affords clear ground for all
to believe, then I think the death of Christ makes all Unbelievers
inexcusable.'[96] Fraser spoke of this judgment of the unbelieving
and the reprobate as '*Gospel wrath*' or wrath of a Gospel kind.[97]

> God's Intention, End and Purpose he designed, was indeed
> to save the Elect amongst them, but not to save the rest, but
> that they contemning and rejecting the Offer of Salvation
> might be made fit Objects to shew his just Gospel-Vengeance
> and Wrath upon them, tho' it be true that God intended
> the work should have such an End.[98]

---

[93] *Justifying Faith,* p. 279.

[94] *Justifying Faith,* p. 226. For the same point see John Knox, *On Predestination,
Works,* Vol. III, p.21. In line with this Knox declined to hold that 'God's absolute
ordinance is the principall cause of reprobation.' *Ibid.* p. 112.

[95] *Justifying Faith,* pp. 171, 204, etc.

[96] *Justifying Faith,* p. 204.

[97] *Justifying Faith,* pp. 223f. Cf. the New Testament concept of 'the wrath of the
Lamb', Rev. 6.16.

[98] *Justifying Faith,* p. 246.

According to Fraser this 'Gospel-Wrath' is a worse punishment than 'Law-Wrath'.[99]

This was rather harsher than what Fraser said elsewhere, where he was closer to Calvin. Thus in speaking of Christ as 'crucified and crucified for our sins', he wrote 'Nothing can be expected from this Saviour but *good Will*: It's by *accident* Christ condemns, but his primary end is to give life to the world.'[100] Again:

> I grant indeed Christ doth condemn many, but then consider that such as he condemns it is for flighting of his Grace offered in the Gospel; his first office is to preach Glad Tidings, to hold out the golden Sceptre that the World might believe and be saved, but when the World misbelieves Christ (for a great Part of them did) Christ secondarily condemns and *per accidens*.[101]

> If by unbelief they neglect this great Salvation, the Death of Christ will be so far from saving of them that it shall be their greatest Ditty.[102]

This was how Calvin spoke of the double force of the Word of God in a comment on Mark 4.12: 'The Gospel (*doctrina*) is not the cause of blindness properly speaking or in itself or in its nature, but only in the event (*per accidens*) ... When the Word of God blinds or hardens the reprobate, it is through their own depravity; so far as the Word is concerned, it is accidental.'[103] Again in a comment on 2 Corinthians 2.15, Calvin wrote 'the proper function (*proprium officium*) of the Gospel is always to be distinguished from what we may call its accidental function (*ab accidentali*), which must be imputed to the depravity of men by which life is turned into death.'[104] The same point was made by Fraser in regard to Christ as a 'Rock of Offence' or a 'Stone of stumbling' for the reprobate.[105]

---

[99] *Justifying Faith*, p. 254.

[100] *Justifying Faith* 1, p. 137.

[101] *Justifying Faith* 2, p. 92.

[102] *Justifying Faith*, p. 248.

[103] John Calvin, *A Harmony of the Gospels*, tr. T. H. L. Parker, Vol. II, Edinburgh, 1972, p. 67.

[104] John Calvin, *Commentary on 2 Corinthians*, tr. T. A. Smail, Edinburgh 1964, p. 35. See my *Kingdom and Church. A Study in The Theology of the Reformation*, Edinburgh, 1956, pp. 106f.

[105] *Justifying Faith*, pp. 255, 264, etc. Cf. 1 Peter 2.8.

As with Calvin, Knox, Bruce and several other Reformation theologians, this doctrine of the redemptive and justifying import of Christ's active and passive obedience was held together with a doctrine of union with Christ. It is through union and communion with him, grounded in the 'personal union' of his divine and human natures, that we come out of ourselves and partake of his fullness; we approach him empty to find all our salvation in the all-sufficient Lord Jesus. Fraser developed his teaching about this evangelical aspect of Christian life through an exposition of the Lord's Supper, in which we are bidden to feed upon Christ, through the Spirit to partake of his flesh and blood, and are admitted into the blessed Fellowship of the Father, Son, and Holy Ghost.[106]

Published only after his death, like the first edition, this work of James Fraser, *A Treatise on Justifying Faith,* was late in making its impact on the Church of Scotland. Its call to return to authentic Reformation doctrine was misunderstood by the so-called 'orthodox' Presbyterians, and its powerful biblically sustained argumentation for the sovereign act of divine forgiveness and the universal offer of salvation to all people without discrimination was resented by the hyper-Calvinist establishment. They realised that their doctrine of redemption, formulated within the logical strait-jacket of the absolute decree of God, was being called radically into question on the ground of the *sola gratia* principle of the Reformation. Being unable to meet its challenge except through reiterating the propositions of strict federalist and predestinationist theology, they set Fraser's teaching aside, but could not denigrate a saintly Covenanter who had suffered so much for his faithfulness to the Gospel and his refusal to yield to the imposition of Erastian Prelacy upon Scotland. However Fraser's work steadily bore fruit in turning people's minds back to the primacy of the nature of God revealed in Jesus Christ and his infinite Good-will toward sinners, and thereby opened the door for the proclamation of the Gospel of free unconditional grace, without yielding to Arminian universalism. This also had the effect of helping to break down the barriers against the proclamation of the Gospel to the heathen, by recalling the great missionary command of the risen Lord (Mark 16.15 and Matthew 28.19–20) to which the ancient Church had been so obedient. Very few works in Scottish theology before the nineteenth century directed the minds of people to foreign

---

[106] *Justifying Faith,* pp. 320–33.

missions in the way that was done by *A Treatise on Justifying Faith.*[107]
This it did not simply by directing attention to the heathen but by
showing that proclamation of the Gospel to the heathen could not
be restricted to the 'covenanted' or the 'elect', for by its very nature
the Gospel call is unrestricted. It was grounded in the universal
nature of the redemption which God had freely provided in Christ
for mankind: he so loved the world that he gave his only begotten
Son that whoever believes on him may not perish but have
everlasting life (John 3.16), and provided in him the propitiation
not for our sins ours only, but for the sins of the whole world
(1 John 2.2).

A citation from James Fraser published by John Brown of
Whitburn may serve as a summary of his teaching.

> That the gospel, properly and strictly, hath no moral
> conditions at all, because, as I said, it is absolute, and it is a
> declaration of the absolute right made by the Lord to sinners,
> and faith is not a condition, though it be the means, to make
> these things disponed to us beneficial and effectual. The
> Lord hath so employed faith in the covenant of grace, giving
> it such a place therein, in regard that faith doth exclude
> boasting, and holds forth the riches of grace most evidently,
> for faith goes out of itself as out of a most miserable indigent
> creature, in whom there is no help, and makes application
> to the Lord Jesus, from whose fulness and grace, which faith
> doth acknowledge, it looks to be supplied; faith is a receiving
> grace, not a giving grace; it hath beggary stamped upon it.
> Particular application of the promises to ourselves, is so much
> of the essence of faith, as it is inseparable from it.[108] Justifying
> faith believes not a Saviour in general, but looks on Christ as
> the soul's Saviour, and that either implicitly, if not explicitly,
> for as the promise holds out Christ, so faith receives him,
> but the promise holds him out particularly to the soul,
> 'Behold your God', Isa. xl.9. Faith, therefore, must
> apprehend Christ as such. There is some measure of
> assurance in all true and saving faith, and the denying or
> separating particular application from the nature of faith,

---

[107] *Justifying Faith*, cf. pp. 91ff, 161ff, 218, 257ff, 276–80.
[108] Thus also *A Treatise Concerning Justifying Faith* 1, 1722, p. 14. Cf. *Justifying Faith*
2, p. 284 where Fraser refers to faith as 'a Mother Grace, as Unbelief is a Mother
of sin' – 'what is not in Faith is Sin', p. 282.

or to say there may be faith where assurance is wanting, hath a bitter root of apostasy from God, and keeps persons at a distance from Christ, and the very fountain of all unsettledness, tossings and tormenting fears, and doubtings of the soul, and hath influence to keep souls in perpetual bondage and desperation. In order of nature we must believe Christ to be ours, (in offer and grant) ere we trust on him, and must believe the promises to belong to us, before we receive him, apply and draw comfort from them.[109]

Thomas Boston (1676–1732)

Thomas Boston was essentially a parish minister, yet a fine scholar and an influential theologian. In his two country parishes of Simprin and Ettrick he devoted himself to the pastoral care and the biblical instruction of congregations, through a ministry of the Gospel calling for personal belief in Christ as Lord and Saviour, with particular attention given to services of Holy Communion, and the cultivation of Prayer Societies. He had been deeply influenced by the preaching of Henry Erskine,[110] and by what he called 'the old ways', frequently referring, for example, to John Davidson. His main thinking and preaching were firmly set within the Westminster Tradition, and the rather strict view of the federal theology as it had been expounded by the Gillespies and Rutherford. However, in his pastoral work in which he was concerned to encourage godly piety and 'experimental religion', he was very troubled by the un-evangelical and formalist tendencies in the presentation of salvation by grace due to the legalistic and contractual frame of contemporary Calvinism which resonated with what he called 'a legal strain, a bias towards the first covenant (i.e. the covenant of works), running in the hearts of all men by nature.'[111]

---

[109] John Brown of Whitburn, *Gospel Truth*, pp. 438f.

[110] *Memoirs of the Life, Times, and Writings of Thomas Boston*, written by himself, 1852 edn, Aberdeen, pp. 11f.

[111] *Works*, Vol. 1, p. 383 & see Boston's comments in his edition of *The Marrow of Modern Divinity*, about 'the natural bias toward the covenant of works', *Works*, Vol. 7, p. 224.

Boston was aware that the concept of a covenant of grace could be and was being given in some quarters a universalist interpretation (that is, that all people will finally be saved), and he was worried about the implications of that for the spread of Arminianism. Within the Westminster tradition, now powerfully reinforced after the restoration of Presbyterianism, he fell in with the prevailing doctrine of limited atonement held by hyper-Calvinist orthodoxy along with the idea that the covenant was only intended for the elect. He regarded the idea of limited atonement as important if only to rebut a notion of justification by works, yet it continued to conflict with his ministry of the Gospel of free grace for sinners, and to feed the tension between his pastoral and evangelical concern for assurance and the teaching of conditional grace commonly being attached to faith and salvation. He wrote in his personal account of this early period in his ministry: 'I had no great fondness for the doctrine of the conditionality of the covenant of grace.'[112]

In his perturbation about current tendencies toward a conditional nature of grace and faith he came across a copy of *The Marrow of Modern Divinity*, by Edward Fisher of Oxford, first published in 1645, in which distinctly evangelical teaching about the Gospel of free grace was set forth within the federal system, with a rejection of both Neonomian and Arminian extremes. There also came into his hands a copy of Luther's *Commentary on the Epistle to the Galatians*, to which the *Marrow* was deeply indebted. Both of these helped Boston:[113] they showed him that Christian people are no longer under the covenant of works, for in Christ they are freed from the law. What appealed to Boston was the emphasis upon grace that he found in these works, and it was grace that became the supreme theme of his preaching and writing. However, as the *Marrow* taught, while Christians are saved by grace they are still under 'the Law of Christ', so that the Ten Commandments are understood and taught in a new evangelical way.

All this, however, did not affect Boston's commitment to the teaching of the Westminster Standards about the limited nature of the atonement. This meant that he had to work out a way of accommodating his evangelical preaching of the Gospel to it, without lapsing into the kind of universalism that was being taught

---

[112] *Memoirs*, p. 156.
[113] *Memoirs*, Aberdeen, 1852, pp. 155–61.

by people like Amyrald at the Reformed Academy at Saumur in France. There an understandable reaction had developed against a rationalist deviation from the teaching of Calvin. Several theologians in the French Reformed Church were then being accused by hard-lined Calvinists of being Arminian, although this was not true of John Cameron or Robert Boyd. Of them Hugh Binning once wrote: 'Many that proclaim the free grace of the gospel, their fault is not that they make it freer than it is – for truly it is as free as any Antinomian can apprehend...'[114] Boston's problem was how to hold together unconditional grace, the free and universal offer of the Gospel, with the Calvinist and Westminster tradition to which he belonged.

Boston held steadily to the doctrine of limited election and limited atonement right up to the end of his life – evidently he did not know of or take account of the teaching of James Fraser of Brae. In an exposition of Ephesians 1.3–5, he argued that in his saving grace God elected quite particularly only some people to everlasting life, and passed over others who are damned.[115] This was strengthened in his important double work on 'The Covenant of Works' and 'The Covenant of Grace'. He wrote in the latter:

> There is no universal redemption, nor universal atonement. Jesus Christ died not for all and every individual person of mankind; but for the elect only ... For if the covenant of grace was made with Christ as a representative, and the elect only were the party represented by him in it; then surely the conditions of the covenant, his doing and dying, were accomplished for them only; and he died for no other.... Our Lord Jesus has fulfilled the conditions of the covenant for those whom he represented; and it would neither be suitable to the justice of God, nor to the wisdom of Christ the party contracting with him, that he should represent, contract, and fulfil the conditions for any who shall never enjoy the benefit of the contract.[116]

On the other hand, Boston tried to take seriously the teaching of the New Testament given for example in John 3.16, which he

---

[114] Sermon on Matthew 11.28, *The Works of Hugh Binning*, 1840, Vol. 3, p. 225.

[115] *Works*, Vol. 1. pp. 149ff, 301ff. Boston rarely spoke of 'reprobation', James Walker, *The Theology and Theologians of Scotland, Chiefly of the Seventeenth and Eighteenth Centuries*, Edinburgh 1888, pp. 91f.

[116] *The Covenant of Grace, Works*, Vol. 8, pp. 404f – see also Vol. 1, p. 327.

often cited along with other passages from the Gospels and Epistles that speak of the fact that Jesus Christ is the Saviour of the world, the one Mediator between God and man, who gave his life a ransom for all. Hence he had to account, within his federal framework of thought, for the fact that in Christ the Gospel of free grace is offered to 'mankind sinners', as he referred to them, although he only died for the elect. His general approach was rather more christocentric than that of the Westminster Tradition, his doctrine of the covenant was more christological, and emphasis upon the Person of Christ became important and central in his proclamation of the Gospel and in his pastoral activity.[117] This is particularly evident in his rejection of the distinction between a covenant of grace and a covenant of redemption which had obtained currency after the Westminster Assembly, and in his complete identification of covenant of grace with Christ himself the incarnate Mediator between God and man. This meant that it is only through believing union with Christ that sinners can partake of his saving grace and redemption, and that it is only in Christ, in whom divine and human natures are united, and who is himself God and man in one Person, that we can have an 'eye to God'. This Christ-centred view of God was strengthened by *The Marrow of Modern Divinity*. With reference to John Forbes on election in which he spoke of a mutual relation between Christ and faith in justification, Edward Fisher had written: 'If faith does not eye Christ, if it be not in God as it is in Christ, it will not serve the turn: for God cannot be comfortably thought upon out of Christ our Mediator: for if we find not God in Christ, saith Calvin, salvation cannot be known.'[118]

It should be noted here that for Boston 'union with Christ' was not a figurative or merely legal union, but a real and proper union with 'the whole Christ' transformed through his death and resurrection, that is, a union of an ontological kind.[119] In federal theology and rationalistic Calvinism Calvin's own doctrine of union with Christ had been altered into a 'judicial relation' brought into line with a largely forensic notion of justification as imputation. Against this tendency Boston reacted with a doctrine of *real union* with Christ which he frequently spoke of as a 'mystical union'

---

[117] See *A Soliloquy on The Art of Man-Fishing* (1699), 1899 edition, Paisley and London, for the deeply Christocentric nature of Boston's personal faith and ministry.

[118] Boston's edition of the *Marrow of Modern Divinity*, *Works*, Vol. 7, p. 292.

[119] *Works*, Vol. 1, pp. 546 & 556.

distinguished from but resting on the 'personal' or hypostatic union in him of divine and human natures.[120] Through union with Christ all the benefits of the covenant of grace are given to elect believers. This helped to give both justification and sanctification objective and christological depth and form in line with the Reformed and patristic teaching of John Forbes of Corse and Robert Boyd of Trochrig.

In offering an account of Boston's theology it will be useful to focus upon his doctrine of the Incarnation, his doctrine of the atonement, and his doctrine of the covenant of grace.

(1) *The Incarnation.* Boston's doctrine of Christ is distinctly soteriological and incarnational in the mould of Nicene and Athanasian theology. Although he does not often cite the ancient fathers by name it is clear that he was very familiar with their teaching, and with the Calvinist theologians who followed Calvin, such as Musculus, Polanus, Ursinus and Zanchius, who made much of them. He presented his doctrine of Christ from the soteriological perspective of 'the wonderful love and grace of God in sending his Son to be the Redeemer of sinful men'. In keeping with his general framework, however, he qualified that statement by saying that in his love God freely sent his only begotten Son to be 'the Redeemer of an elect world'. At the same time he was ready to speak of 'the matchless love of the Son of God to poor sinners'.[121]

His account of the Incarnation and of the incarnate Son is really quite superb.[122] He laid great emphasis upon the truth that divine nature and human nature are hypostatically united in their entirety in the one Person of Christ without division and without change, recalling in this connection how Athanasius regarded the burning bush as a type of Christ's Incarnation. As the bush was not consumed by the divine fire, so the human nature of Christ was not consumed by his divine nature. The fullness of the Godhead dwelt bodily in Christ, and yet the fullness of his human nature with a reasonable soul subsisted in him from the first moment of conception in union with the second Person of the adorable Trinity.[123]

---

[120] *Works*, Vol. 1, pp. 398f & 544ff; also Vol. 8, pp. 177ff.
[121] *Works*, Vol. 1, pp. 396f.
[122] *Works*, Vol. 1, pp. 339–43.
[123] *Works*, Vol. 1, pp. 393–8. Cf. the *Nec tamen Consumebatur* of the Church of Scotland.

Boston clearly regarded the incarnate assumption of our human nature by Christ and its sanctification in him as necessary for our salvation and for our union with him, but he had to think together the assumption of our nature which is fallen and the holiness of Christ. 'Out of his infinite love he humbled himself to become flesh, and at the same time out of his infinite purity, could not defile himself by becoming flesh.' Hence in speaking of the end of his Incarnation, even the redemption and salvation of lost sinners, he wrote: 'that as the first Adam was the fountain of our impurity, so the second Adam should also be the pure fountain of our righteousness.'[124] In explication of this redemptive assumption Boston turned to the teaching of St Paul at the beginning of the eighth chapter of the Epistle to the Romans:

> God sending his own Son 'in the likeness of sinful flesh, condemned sin in the flesh'; which he could not have condemned, had he been sent in sinful flesh. The Father 'made him, who knew no sin, to be sin for us, that we might be made the righteousness of God in him'; which we could never have been, if he had been tainted with any sin. He that needed redemption himself could never have purchased redemption for us.[125]

Further:

> Christ assumed all, to sanctify all. He designed a perfect recovery by sanctifying us wholly in soul, body, and spirit; and therefore he assumed the whole in order to redeem it. Again he assumed our nature with all its sinless infirmities: therefore it is said of him, Heb. ii.17, 'In all things it became him to be like his brethren'.[126]

'We may be thoroughly satisfied', he said, 'that Christ had a true human body; and that though he was made in the likeness of sinful flesh, he had not merely the likeness of flesh, but true flesh, Luke xxiv. 39, Heb. ii.14.'[127] The point that Boston made here was that while Christ assumed 'the likeness of sinful flesh', that was not a seeming but a real likeness, and does not imply any docetic error.

[124] *Works*, Vol. 1, pp. 397f.
[125] *Works*, Vol. 1, p. 398.
[126] *Works*, Vol. 1, p. 399.
[127] *Works*, Vol. 1, p. 401.

This is evident in the fact that the same term 'likeness' was used by Paul when he said that Christ 'took upon him the form of a servant, and was made in the likeness of men'.[128] That is to say, in the very act of assuming 'sinful flesh', far from sinning in it, Christ condemned sin in the flesh and sanctified it, that we sinners might be sanctified body, soul and spirit, in him. 'The Father 'made him who knew no sin, to be made sin for us, that we might be made the righteousness of God in him'; which we could never have been made, if he had been tainted with any sin. He that needed redemption himself could never have purchased redemption for us.'[129]

Thus Boston clearly thought, like Calvin, of Christ as paying the price of our redemption from his very birth, and of the birth of Jesus of the Virgin Mary as itself saving and sanctifying event.

> Christ was born of a woman for us, and he was born without sin for us, that the holiness of his nature might be imputed to us as a part of that righteousness which constitutes the condition of our justification before God.

> Behold the wonderful love of God the Father, who was content to degrade and abase his dear Son, in order to bring about the salvation of sinners. How astonishing is it, that he should send his only-begotten Son to assume our nature, and bear that dreadful wrath and punishment that we deserved! See here the wonderful love, and astonishing condescendency of the Son, to be born of a woman, in order that he might die in the room of sinners. O how low did he stoop and humble himself, in assuming human nature, with all its sinful infirmities, in being subject to his own law, exposed to all manner of injurious usage from wicked men, to the temptations of Satan, and at last suffering a shameful and ignominious death! What great love to sinners, and what unparalleled condescension was here![130]

Since the Incarnation was essentially a saving event, Boston went on in that account of the Incarnation to supplement it with a general presentation of Christ's 'Mediatorial undertaking', and the offices which he executes as our Redeemer. This was the *triplex*

---

[128] Philippians 2.7.
[129] *Works*, Vol. 1, p. 398.
[130] *Works*, Vol. 1, pp. 400–2.

munus, of Christ as king, priest and prophet, 'both in his estate of humiliation and exaltation.'[131] For Boston, Christology and soteriology, Incarnation and atonement, clearly belong inseparably together. 'He cheerfully assumed our nature, that so he might be able to suffer, and thereby satisfy offended justice for his people's sins.'[132]

(2) *The atonement.* Boston expounded his doctrine of atonement in terms of the priesthood, oblation and intercession of Christ the incarnate Mediator, adapting language taken from the ceremonial law of the Old Testament about the offering of expiatory sacrifice in the satisfaction of divine justice, which he held to be figurative of the sacrifice of Christ. 'As the Mediator of the Covenant it behoved Christ to deal with both parties, in order to bring them together. God was offended with our sin and guilt; and therefore for us he behoved to be a Priest, to satisfy law and justice, and intercede for our pardon.'[133] 'God was to be propitiated that so he might pardon man.'[134] He states right away that Christ did not die for every man and woman in the world, although his sacrifice was efficacious enough, for his blood was of 'infinite value'. To hold that Christ offered himself a sacrifice with a design and intention to save all mankind, Boston claims to be absurd. Among the arguments he gives for this is that if Christ died for all, then he is an imperfect and incomplete Saviour since all men are not actually saved. Moreover, if he died for all men, he died in vain, for then his death and sacrifice had little effect for those actually perishing.[135]

In turning to show the ends for which Christ offered himself a sacrifice, Boston wrote: 'It was to satisfy divine justice, and reconcile us to God. The grand design and intendment of this oblation was to atone, pacify, and reconcile God, by giving him a full and adequate satisfaction for the sins of the elect world.' Justification is a fruit of Christ's death but it could not have been achieved, nor could grace and holiness be procured for men, 'till once divine justice was appeased'.[136] Then after stressing the affectionate

---

[131] *Works,* Vol. 1, pp. 403–11.
[132] *Works,* Vol. 1, p. 394.
[133] *Works,* Vol. 1, p. 406.
[134] *Works,* Vol. 1, p. 442.
[135] *Works,* Vol. 1, p. 447.
[136] *Works,* Vol. 1, pp. 448–9.

obedience, active and passive obedience, and humility of Christ in this transaction, in which he did not seek his own glory but the glory of God in our redemption, Boston went on to expound at length the nature of Christ's sacrifice in terms of the punishment he endured to make satisfaction to God which he could not make to himself, and thereby to 'purchase reconciliation' for us with God.[137] Christ undertook this transaction as an act of a Mediator interposing between the wrath of God and the souls of men in order to make peace with God which he could do only as man and God, as one having human nature in order that he might be able to suffer for elect human beings, and yet as one having divine nature that the satisfaction offered would be infinite.

It should be noted that Boston was concerned to emphasise the fact that Christ suffered not just in a true body but in a reasonable *soul*, thereby rejecting any element of Apollinarian as well as docetic heresy in his doctrine of atonement. 'The sufferings of his body were indeed very great; it was filled with exquisite torture and pain; but his soul sufferings were much greater.'[138] This was in line with the teaching of John Calvin, and also of Samuel Rutherford that Christ bore the infliction of divine judgment for us not just in an outward way in the sufferings of his body but inwardly in his soul, with reference to the passage from the prophet Isaiah about the Suffering Servant: 'It pleased the Lord to bruise him; he hath put him to grief ... thou shalt make his soul an offering for sin.'[139] This implies that the atoning passion takes place in the inner being of the incarnate Mediator, God and Man in one Person, but what of its bearing, therefore, upon his inner relation as man with God himself?

It is highly significant that when Boston referred to the fact that 'God spared not his own Son' (Rom. 8.32), he did not understand that to refer to the sacrifice of the Father, but took it in the opposite sense, to indicate 'the strictness and severity of divine justice, that required satisfaction equivalent to the desert of sin ... The fountain of divine mercy stopt its course, and would not let out one drop to Christ in the day of his extreme sorrow and suffering ... O the inflexible severity of divine justice!' And at the same time he could,

---

[137] Boston overlooked the fact that nowhere in the New Testament is reconciliation said to be 'purchased' from God, although it is said that *God* has bought us by his own blood!

[138] *Works*, Vol. 1, pp. 394–6.

[139] Isaiah 53.10.

say 'This doctrine affords us the strongest assurance that can be, that God is willing to pardon our sins, and be reconciled to us.'[140] And so he will never seek satisfaction for sin from those who are in Christ Jesus. There is here nothing of Calvin's teaching that the eternal love of God the Father goes before and anticipates our reconciliation in Christ, for it was not after we were reconciled to him through the blood of Christ that the Father began to love us: rather did he reconcile us to himself because he first loved us.[141] Nor is there any thought here that redemption and reconciliation flow freely from the infinite love of God the Father. However, Boston does go part way toward that, in pointing to the fact that it was God the Father who '*proposed* the covenant method of salvation', and to the fact that Christ who gave himself in atoning sacrifice for sin was himself *God* as well as man. And so Boston can say of Christ, 'He gave full and complete satisfaction to the law and justice of God for all the wrongs and injuries done thereby by the sins of men, the sufferer being God, and his divine nature stamping an infinite value upon them.'[142] 'Think not', he once preached to his congregation 'that Christ is more willing to save you than the Father is. The will of Christ, his Father, and Spirit are one ... Behold the matchless love of the Father to lost sinners of Adam's race, 1 John III.1. The whole contrivance sprang from free grace.'[143]

It is extraordinary that Boston did not see that nowhere in the New or the Old Testament was it ever held that God is the *object* of atoning or propitiating sacrifice. God the Lord is always the subject of atoning sacrifice for his people even when sacrifice is offered at his appointment by a human priest. In *propitiation* it is God himself who draws near (*prope*) to sinners and thereby draws them near (*prope*) to himself. Boston was recognised in his day as having a fine knowledge of Hebrew, but whenever he discussed the meaning of a Hebrew term for redemption, such as that of the *goel* (גֹּאֵל) or the 'kinsman-redeemer',[144] he failed to note that according to the teaching of the Old Testament it is only heathen sacrifice that is regarded as acting upon God to placate him or to induce his favour. It was undoubtedly the narrow contractual and transactional notion

[140] *Works*, Vol. 1, pp. 464f.
[141] John Calvin, *Institute*, 2.16, 3–4, with reference to Augustine.
[142] *Works*, Vol. 1, p. 467, also p. 448.
[143] *Works*, Vol. 1, p. 324.
[144] See *Works*, Vol. 8, pp. 412ff.

governing all God's relations with man, dominant in the hyper-Calvinist conception of 'covenant', together with the double decree of predestination, that blinded Boston in his reading of the Scriptures and his interpretation even of the New Testament to the truth that 'God so loved the world', that he gave his only begotten Son for our salvation that whosoever believes on him should not perish but have eternal life. And yet it was precisely this evangelical message and the Gospel offer of saving grace unconditionally to the world that Boston was so concerned to maintain and proclaim.

It seems evident that behind these tensions in Boston's thought, what was ultimately at stake here was the rather severe and inflexible doctrine of God governed, not by a notion of his infinite love and grace, but by a notion of inexorable divine law, which he had inherited in the Westminster tradition. While his rejection of the distinction between a covenant of redemption and the covenant of grace offered some help, his resort to the hyper-Calvinist federal device of distinguishing between a particular and a general application of what Christ had done, did not help him to resolve those tensions, for it gave rise to further problems tied up with the notion of conditionality, which he disliked as a subtle form of Pelagianism.

(3) *The Covenant of Grace.* It was in his conception of the covenant of grace that Boston made a signal contribution to the theology of his day, not least by rejecting the so-called 'covenant of redemption' as unbiblical, but by identifying it with the one covenant of grace *embodied in Christ.* 'The covenant of redemption and the covenant of grace are not two distinct covenants, but one and the same covenant.'[145] Behind this distinction lay the so-called 'covenant of works', a binding contract made by God with Adam and the human race. 'This covenant is sometimes called the *covenant of works,* because works or obedience, was the condition of it; and sometimes the *covenant of life,* because life was promised therein as the reward of obedience.'[146] Boston evidently realised that there is no clear warrant for this in the book of Genesis.[147] However, he regarded it

---

[145] *Works,* Vol. 1, p. 333.
[146] *Works,* Vol. 1, p. 229.
[147] See Boston's edition of *The Marrow, Works,* Vol. 7, p. 172; and Boston, *The Covenant of Works, Works* Vol. 11, p. 178.

as implied and so accepted the traditional teaching about it. If there had not been a covenant made with Adam as the representative head of the human race, there could not be a proper imputation of Adam's sin to his posterity.[148] As it is, however, the whole human race which fell in Adam is inextricably bound to the covenant of works made with Adam and is therefore under obligation to fulfil the whole law, and comes under divine condemnation for disobedience and sin against the law and justice of God the creator.

Evidently the concept of the covenant of works was *evangelically important* for Boston, for, as he understood matters, it was through the vicarious obedience of Christ in fulfilling all the conditions of that covenant with mankind, and through his substitutionary sacrifice on the Cross in bearing the punishment of our sin, thereby satisfying the justice of God and appeasing his wrath, that Christ was able to offer the Gospel freely to 'mankind sinners' *without conditions, for all the conditions have already been fulfilled completely by him.* The covenant of grace was thus held to be a 'bargain' made between God the Father and Christ as the Second Adam,[149] in accordance with which the Father promised him the salvation and redemption of the elect for whom he would make satisfaction to himself – hence the immense emphasis Boston laid upon the propitiatory act of Christ in appeasing the Father's wrath, thereby 'procuring the egress of the divine favour to man'.[150] Through fulfilling the covenant completely in himself as the Mediator, Jesus Christ embodies the covenant of grace in his incarnate person and constitutes its 'Surety', 'Trustee' and 'Testator' for the administration and fulfilment of all its promises of redemption to sinners.[151] *Christ is himself the covenant.*[152] It was because of that identification that he was able to preach the Gospel, not least in 'Action Sermons', in a more evangelical way than he could in adherence to an unmodified federal system of thought.

It is then on the ground that Christ has fulfilled all the conditions of the covenant that the Gospel of saving grace could be offered freely to sinners quite unconditionally, so that though they are summoned to believe in Christ and repent, neither faith nor

[148] *The Covenant of Works, Works*, Vol. 1, pp. 229ff, and 11, pp. 108f.
[149] *Works*, Vol. 8, pp. 396f.
[150] *Works*, Vol. 1, p. 463.
[151] *Works* Vol. 8, pp. 416–26; 519–48.
[152] *Works*, Vol. 1, p. 321; Vol. 8, p. 520.

repentance can be regarded strictly in a conditional way.[153] Properly regarded faith follows upon the offer of grace, and repentance comes after the forgiveness of sins and does not precede it. This was the doctrine of 'two forms of repentance', 'repentance of the law' and 'repentance of the Gospel', or 'evangelical repentance', as opposed to a doctrine of 'legal repentance', taught by Calvin,[154] which so many of Boston's contemporaries found hard to understand and accept. It is through 'personal inbeing' in Christ and being 'instated' in the covenant of grace made effectual through the Holy Spirit that saving faith and evangelical repentance are really possible. But this involved a powerful doctrine of union with Christ,[155] which recalls Calvin's teaching in his Genevan Catechism that it is through union with Christ *first* that we partake of all his benefits.[156]

The doctrine of the covenant of works had another importance for Boston, as for Edward Fisher in *The Marrow of Modern Divinity*, in their rejection of antinomianism. But in the Gospel the covenant of works, it was said, had to be understood in a different way, for the Ten Commandments it enshrined were taken up by Christ as the Head of the covenant, and made the expression of the kind of obedience which is due to God in the Gospel. Here we see not the impact of Luther but of English Puritanism on the *Marrow* as indeed on the Westminster Tradition, evident especially in the inculcation of a new moralism in *The Larger Catechism*.[157] There was, of course, no priority given to the covenant of works in the Gospel, for in Christ Christians are dead to the law. And so in his comments on the teaching of the *Marrow* about 'The Law as the Covenant of Works added to the Promise', Boston wrote: 'Thus there is no confounding of the two covenants, of grace and works; but the latter was applied to the former as subservient unto it.'[158] As Boston saw it, the purpose of the teaching of the Commandments, in part

---

[153] See Boston's notes on *The Marrow of Modern Divinity*, 2.3.4 – *Works*, Vol. 7, pp. 278ff.

[154] John Calvin, *Institute*, 3.3.4 – cf. also 1–3.

[155] *Works*, Vol. 1. pp. 544–56; Vol. 8. pp. 177ff, 481ff, & 565f.

[156] Thus also Boston in his edition of *The Marrow*, Vol. 7, p. 264. See also his discussion in *Works*, Vol. 1, pp. 544–56 & 561–612.

[157] See my edition in *The School of Faith*, pp. 183–234; only a relatively small portion of *The Larger Catechism* is devoted to the truths of the Gospel – the great bulk resembles the *theologia moralis* employed by the Roman Church in the Confessional.

[158] *Works*, Vol. 7, pp. 195f.

at least, was to send people back to the Gospel of unconditional grace. However, in the way in which this was pursued in seventeenth and eighteenth-century Scotland, it undoubtedly tended toward the neonomianism evident in the moral harangues of ministers about which people so often complained. This was a serious problem, especially as assurance of salvation by grace alone began to lose its objective ground, and justification by faith came to imply, in part at least, dependence on faith and obedience as prerequisite conditions.

Boston's presentation of the Gospel clearly had some unresolved tensions, particularly between the universal offer of the Gospel, and between faith and assurance.

The universal offer of the Gospel was given prominence in *The Marrow of Modern Divinity*:

> God the Father, as he is in Jesus Christ, moved with nothing but with his free love to mankind lost, hath made a deed of gift and grant unto them all, that whosoever of them all shall believe in this his Son, *shall not perish, but have eternal life*. Hence it was that Jesus Christ himself said unto his disciples, Mark xvi.14: 'Go and preach the gospel to every creature under heaven': that is, Go and tell every man without exception, that here is good news for him, Christ is dead for him; and if he will take him and accept his righteousness, he shall have him.[159]

Boston commented:

> This deed of gift and grant, or authentic Gospel Offer, is expressed in many words, John III,16, '*For God so loved the world, that he gave his only begotten Son, that WHOSOEVER believeth in him should not perish, but have everlasting life.*' Where the Gospel comes, this *grant* is published, and the ministerial offer made: and there is no exception of *any* of *all* Mankind in the grant ... This is the good old way, of discovering to sinners, their *warrant to believe* in Christ: and it doth indeed bear the sufficiency of the sacrifice of Christ, for all: and that Christ crucified is the ordinance of God for salvation, unto all mankind, in their use-making of which only they can be saved; but not an *universal atonement or redemption*.[160]

---

[159] *Works*, Vol. 7, pp. 262f; and Vol. 1. pp. 260–72, the sermon on 'yet there is room', Luke 14.22.

[160] *Works*, Vol. 7, p. 263; Vol. 8, pp. 404 & 523.

Press hard to know God by personal experience.[161]

In regard to the concluding section of the *Marrow's* account of the covenant of grace, 'the Faith of Particular Trust for Salvation', Boston laid considerable stress, very rightly, on 'the faithfulness of God in his word', for our faith and God's faithfulness go together.[162] And in speaking of the administration of the covenant of grace, Boston wrote emphatically: 'To whomsoever the gospel comes, we may warrantably say, the *promise* is to *you*, and to *you*, and *every* one of you.'[163] 'You must believe that Jesus Christ with his righteousness, and all his salvation is offered to sinners, and to you in particular.'[164]This posed a serious problem for Boston, for while the extent of the administration of the covenant of grace is determined by the sufficiency of Christ's obedience and death for the salvation of all, the *actual* extent of the atonement, he held, was determined by election.[165] That was precisely one of the ideas restricting 'the Gospel offer' to sinners, that James Fraser of Brae had tried so hard to change!

No less pressing for Boston was the tension between faith and assurance. We have already noted above that for Boston faith in the proper sense follows upon grace, and does not precede it. In understanding this, however, one must take into account that there is a passive as well as an active side in our relations with Christ through union with him and through faith.[166] In *Man's Fourfold State* Boston pointed out that it is when Christ apprehends the sinner, that the sinner is then enabled by the Spirit to apprehend Christ by faith. He goes on to discuss this twofold activity of faith as the believer is joined with Christ and is one Spirit with him. 'Hereby a believer lives in and for Christ, and Christ lives in and for the believer, Gal. 2.20: 'I am crucified with Christ; nevertheless I live yet not I but Christ lives in me.''[167]While it is certainly we who believe in Christ, our act of belief is not itself a saving act, for it is not faith that saves or justifies us but Christ in whom we believe and trust. In the proper act of faith as the older theology said, we

---

[161] *Works*, Vol. 7, p. 343.
[162] *Works*, Vol. 7, pp. 597ff.
[163] *Works*, Vol. 8, p. 540; and cf. Vol. 6, pp. 294f.
[164] *Works* Vol. 8, p. 587.
[165] *Works*, Vol. 8, pp. 523f.
[166] *Works*, Vol. 1, pp. 548f.
[167] *Works*, Vol. 8, pp. 199–200; cf. also pp. 134 & 368.

go out of ourselves and take refuge in Christ alone. It is when people think of faith as their own act, in which they subtly fall back upon themselves, as Fraser of Brae showed in his rather sharp criticism of the semi-Pelagianism of evangelical Puritans, who tended to move away from the real ground of faith and thus lose assurance.[168] This was very evident in Richard Baxter's *Aphorisms of Justification*,[169] in which he held that although Christ has sufficiently satisfied the Law, in respect of 'legal righteousness', yet in respect of 'evangelical righteousness', the believer must still perform the conditions of the Gospel, although admittedly he cannot do that without grace.[170]

This is a point on which Boston commented in his edition of the *Marrow* again and again. 'Saving faith, being a persuasion that we shall have life and salvation by Christ, or a receiving and resting on him for salvation, includes in it a knowledge of our being beloved of God: the former cannot be without the latter.'[171] He used to reinforce this by recalling John Davidson's definition, 'Faith is an hearty assurance that our sins are freely forgiven us in Christ'.[172] He also cited from Rutherford: 'The assurance of Christ's righteousness is a direct act of faith'.[173] Here Boston turned back to the teaching of the Reformation and classical Reformed theology that assurance is of the very fibre of faith in its reliance on the finished work of Christ and salvation by his grace alone. That objective emphasis was strengthened by the teaching he found in the *Marrow of Modern Divinity* about 'the free deed of gift and grant'.[174] However, in Boston's earlier preaching and teaching he had introduced an element of unease into people's assurance of salvation, not least by his preaching about 'hell', in which he exhorted them to examine themselves to find whether they were in the faith or not.[175] By asking people to test their works for

---

[168] James Fraser of Brea, *Memoirs*, 1889 edn, p. 233.
[169] Richard Baxter, *Aphorisms of Justification*, London, 1649. Cf. Fraser of Brae's Preface to *A Treatise Concerning Justifying Faith*, 1722 edn p. ii, and the 1749 edn, p. 112.
[170] See the 1655 edn, London, pp. 60–75.
[171] *Works*, Vol. 7, p. 280.
[172] Comment on *The Marrow*, *Works*, Vol. 7, p. 324.
[173] Boston's comments on *The Marrow*, *Works*, Vol. 7, p. 362.
[174] This has been well stated by Donald J. Bruggink, in his unpublished thesis, *The Theology of Thomas Boston, 1676–1732*, 1956, p. 328, New College Library, Edinburgh.
[175] See *The Marrow* on this, and Boston's comments, *Works*, Vol. 7, pp. 362ff.

evidence that they were among the elect, he undermined their assurance, for it focused their attention on the double decree of predestination, and on a subjective assurance away from the objective ground of assurance in spite of his evangelical and pastoral intention.[176] Moreover, evangelical faith and assurance sat uneasily within his attempt to incorporate the unconditional nature of grace freely proclaimed to all and every man and woman in the Gospel call with his adherence to the exclusive tenets of limited atonement and limited election.

We may conclude this account of Thomas Boston's theology by calling attention to the profound eschatological strand that ran through his preaching and teaching which struck deeply into the very heart of people's need and gripped their souls when facing up to the thought of death and the final judgment. He gave special place to this in *Man's Fourfold State*, in which he also directed his readers to 'The Mystical Union between Christ and Believers' which persists through death right into eternity. That combination made this work the most published (over 80 editions), the most widely read, and probably the most influential book in Scottish theology. In the judgment of John Macleod, 'It did more to mould the thought of his countrymen than anything else except the Westminster Shorter Catechism.'[177] It has left a lasting imprint upon Presbyterian piety, as I personally know from the old copy of it handed down in my family.

Bibliography

Baxter, Richard, *Aphorisms of Justification*, London, 1649.

Binning, Hugh, *Select Library of Scottish Divines, The Works of the Rev. Hugh Binning*, Vol. I–III, Edinburgh, 1839–40.

Binning, Hugh, *The Works of Hugh Binning*, Edinburgh, 1735.

Boston, Thomas, *The Compelete Works of Thomas Boston*, 12 vols., Aberdeen, 1848–52.

Boston Thomas, *The Crook in the Lot: Or, The Sovereignty and Wisdom of God, in the Afflictions of Men, Displayed*, London, 1791.

Boston, Thomas, *Human Nature and the Fourfold State*, Edinburgh, 1720, and edn of 1812.

---

[176] See *Works*, Vol. 7, p. 484, and cf. Vol. 11, p. 16.
[177] John Macleod, *Scottish Theology*, 1943, p. 146.

Boston, Thomas, *The Marrow of Modern Divinity, in Two Parts, by Edward Fisher, with Notes*, Edinburgh 1745, Falkirk, 1789, Boston's *Complete Works*, Vol. 7.

Boston, Thomas, *Memoirs of the Life, Times, and Writings of Thomas Boston, written by himself*, Edinburgh, 1776, Aberdeen, 1852.

Boston, Thomas, *The Mystery of Christ in the Form of a Servant*, Edinburgh, 1755.

Boston, Thomas, *A Soliloquy on The Art of Man-Fishing*, 1699 & 1899.

Boston, Thomas, *A View of the Covenant of Grace from the Sacred Records*, Edinburgh 1734, *Complete Works*, Vol. 8.

Boston, Thomas, *The Whole Works of Thomas Boston*, Edinburgh, 1767.

Brown, John, of Haddington, *An Essay Towards an Easy, Plain, Practical, and Extensive Explication of the Assembly's Shorter Catechism*, Eighth Edition, Corrected and improved by his Son, Mr Eben. Brown, Edinburgh, 1812.

Brown, John, of Whitburn, *Gospel Truth Accurately Stated and Illustrated by the Rev. James Hog, Thomas Boston, Ebenezer and Ralph Erskine, and Others*. Occasioned by the Republication of *The Marrow of Modern Divinity*. Edinburgh, 1817; new edn, Glasgow, 1831.

Brown, John, of Whitburn, *Letters on Sanctification by the late Rev. John Brown, Whitburn*, Eighth Edition, with a Memoir of His Life and Character, by Rev. David Smith. Edinburgh, 1834.

Bruggink, Donald J., *The Theology of Thomas Boston, 1676–1732*, Unpublished Thesis, 1956, New College Library, Edinburgh.

Calvin, John, *Institutio*, Geneva, 1559.

Calvin, John, *A Harmony of the Gospels*, tr. T. H. L. Parker, Vol. II, Edinburgh, 1972.

Calvin, John, *Commentary on 2 Corinthians*, tr. T. A. Smail, Edinburgh, 1956.

Calvin, John, *Concerning The Eternal Predestination of God*, tr. J. K. S. Reid, London, 1964.

Fenner, Dudley, *Sacra Theologia*, London, 1585.

Fisher, Edward, *The Marrow of Modern Divinity*, Oxford, 1646.

Fraser, James, of Brae, *The Lawfulness and Duty of Separation from Corrupt Ministers and Churches explained and vindicated*, Edinburgh, 1744.

Fraser, James, of Brea, *Meditations on Several Subjects in Divinity*, Edinburgh, 1721.

Fraser, James, of Brea, *Memoirs of the Rev. James Fraser of Brea, Select Biographies*, Wodrow Society, Edinburgh, 1847.

Fraser, James, of Brae, *A Treatise Concerning Justifying or Saving Faith: Wherein the Nature of Faith is largely handled*, Edinburgh, 1722.

Fraser, James, of Brae, *A TREATISE on JUSTIFYING FAITH, Wherein is opened the GROUND of BELIEVING, or the Sinner's sufficient Warrant to take hold of what is offered in the everlasting GOSPEL. Together with an APPENDIX concerning, the OBJECT of CHRIST'S DEATH, unfolding the dangerous and various pernicious Errors that hath been vented about it.* Edinburgh, 1749.

Gillespie, George, *A Treatise of Miscellany Questions*, ed. Patrick Gillespie, Edinburgh, 1646 & 1649.

Howe, John, *The Redeemer's Tears Wept over Lost Souls, with an Introductory Essay* by Robert Gordon, Glasgow, 1822.

Macleod, John, *Scottish Theology*, Edinburgh, 1943.

Torrance, J. B., 'The Concept of Federal Theology – Was Calvin a Federal Theologian?' *Calvinus Sacrae Scripturae Professor*, ed. W. H. Neuser, Grand Rapids, 1994, pp. 15–40.

Torrance, T. F., *Kingdom and Church, A Study in the Theology of the Reformation*, Edinburgh, 1956.

Walker, James, *The Theology and Theologians of Scotland, Chiefly of the Seventeenth and Eighteenth Centuries*, 2nd edn, revised, Edinburgh, 1888.

Whyte, Alexander, *James Fraser Laird of Brea, 'The Book of the Intricacies of my Heart and Life'*, Edinburgh, 1911.

Whyte, Alexander, *Memoirs of the Rev. James Fraser of Brea, A.D. 1639–1698 (written by Himself,) With an Introductory Note. Also, Short Sketch of Fraser*, by Gustavus Aird, Edinburgh, 1891.

7

Eighteenth-Century Presbyterianism

In the course of its development from the sixteenth into the seventeenth century deep tensions continued to manifest themselves in Scottish theology which have never been properly resolved. They were brought to the surface in two controversies early in the eighteenth century, over the alleged antinomianism and universalism of the teaching of *The Marrow of Modern Divinity* by Edward Fisher, imported from England and republished in Scotland 1717, and over the alleged rationalism and Socinianism of Professor John Simson of Glasgow.[1] These two divergent tendencies took their rise in different ways from the teaching of the *Westminster Confession of Faith* and were moving away from it. Far from being merely of passing significance, they anticipated problems which were to trouble Scottish theology for the next hundred years and lay at the root of the divisions that kept on breaking out within the Church of Scotland, in spite of the 1712 Toleration Act. It was a period of renaissance in literature, which Scotland had not experienced before the Reformation, but which now made a considerable impact. It was a century and a half marked by theological questioning, counter-questioning, and defensive reaction, when traditional hyper-Calvinist structures, centering on the absolute sovereignty of God rather than on his infinite love, were under pressure from a fuller understanding of the Gospel, and from brilliant developments in the Scottish Enlightenment, when some of the ablest minds in the Kirk engaged with advance in science and philosophy. It was not a century

---

[1]   Cf. the complaint by James Fraser of Brae, reported by John Brown of Whitburn, in *Gospel Truth Accurately Stated and Illustrated by The Rev. Messrs James Hog, Thomas Boston, Ebenezer and Ralph Erskine and Others, Occasioned by The Republication of the Marrow of Modern Divinity*, new edn Glasgow, 1831, pp. 46f. Consult, H. M. B. Reid, *The Divinity Professors of the University of Glasgow, 1640–1903*, Glasgow, 1923, pp. 207ff.

marked by outstanding theologians, although it was not without significant movements of thought.

The *Marrow* controversy

The evangelical Calvinists who recognised the good old ways of the Reformers found themselves trapped between an increasingly rigid adherence to the Westminster Theology regularly identified as 'gospel' by the 'orthodox', and a puritanised form of rationalistic Calvinism encased in a hard federal frame of thought which had become entrenched in the thinking of the Kirk and was endorsed by the General Assembly. The chief exponent of this rigid hyper-Calvinism was Professor James Hadow of St Andrews who charged the Marrowmen not only with various doctrinal errors but especially with a lapse into Antinomianism.[2] The issues at stake were already evident in the sustained dialogue in *The Marrow of Modern Divinity* between Evangelista, a minister of the Gospel, Nomista, a legalist, Antinomista, an antinomian, and Neophitus, a young Christian. Its publication in Scotland with a preface by James Hog of Carnock[3] precipitated a controversy over its teaching, as a result of which several tenets of *The Marrow of Modern Divinity* were condemned by the General Assembly in 1720, declaring them contrary to Scripture, Confession and Catechisms, and forbidding ministers to recommend it.[4] This prompted Thomas Boston and a group of evangelical Calvinists among whom were Ralph and Ebenezer Erskine to make a theological presentation of their case to the General Assembly in 1722,[5] but without avail.[6] In a sermon

---

[2]　James Hadow, *The Record of God and the Duty of Faith Therein Required*, Edinburgh, 1719, and especially *The Antinomianism of the Marrow of Modern Divinity*, Edinburgh, 1722.

[3]　See the report of John Brown of Whitburn, *Gospel Truth*, p. 44. James Hog had already made his evangelical position clear in two works, *Remarks Concerning the Spirit's Operation and the Difference between Law and Gospel*, Edinburgh, 1701, and *Some Select Notes towards detecting a Covered Mixture of the Covenant of Works and of Grace*, Edinburgh, 1706.

[4]　*Acts of the General Assembly of the Church of Scotland*, Sess. 9, May, 1720.

[5]　Sess. 9, May 20, 1720 & Sess. 10, May 21, 1722.

[6]　See the Appendix to Boston's edition of *The Marrow*, *Works*, Vol. 7, pp. 465–99; and also *A Full and True State of the Controversy Concerning the Marrow of Modern Divinity, as debated by the General Assembly, and several ministers in the year 1720 and 1721*. Glasgow, 1773.

published in 1724 on Luke 2.18, 'Christ in the Believer's Arms', Ebenezer Erskine declared:

> There is a deed or Grant of Christ made to Sinners, in the free Offer and Call of the Gospel ... Tis true indeed, the eternal Destination, the Purchase and Application of Redemption is *peculiar* only to the *Elect*; but the *Revelation, Gift* and *Offer* is common to all hearers of the Gospel, insomuch as the great Mr Rutherford expresses it, the *Reprobate* have as fair a *revealed Warrant* to believe, as the *Elect* have. Every man has an Offer of Christ brought to his Door who lives within the Compass of the joyful Sound, and this Offer comes as close to him, as if he were pointed out by Name. So that none have reason to say, The Call and Offer is not to me, I am not warranted to embrace Christ ... We have God's commission to preach this Gospel, and to make offer of this Christ to *every creature* sprung of *Adam*, Mark xvi.15, and the event of the Publication of *this Gospel* among sinners follows in the next Words, *He that believeth* this Gospel *shall be saved, he that believeth not shall be damned.*[7]

When Boston published another edition of *The Marrow* in 1728 nothing happened. 'The Marrow men', as they were called, had little difficulty in refuting the worked-up charges of antinomianism in respect of 'the commanding and condemning power of the covenant of works', but were unable to get the Assembly to retract the charge of teaching 'universal atonement and pardon' which it claimed to find particularly in the passage of *The Marrow* concerning 'a deed of gift to all mankind'. The decision of the Assembly was hardly consistent with that of 17 May, 1714, when it passed an 'Act and Recommendation in Favour of the Society for the Propagation of Christian Knowledge' which included in its charter 'the advancement of the Christian religion to heathen countries'![8]

The basic point of difference was made clear in the Assembly's condemnation of what it called 'an universal redemption *as to purchase*', which it supported with reference to question 59 of the

---

[7]   Published in Edinburgh, 1726, pp. 9f – italics and capitalisation as originally published by E. Erskine.

[8]   Andrew Walls, 'Missions', N. M. de S. Cameron *et al.* (eds), *Dictionary of Scottish Church History and Theology*, Edinburgh, 1993, pp. 567f.

Larger Catechism: 'Redemption is certainly applied, and effectually communicated, to all those for whom Christ has purchased it; who are in time by the Holy Spirit enabled to believe in Christ according to the Gospel.' 'By redemption as to purchase', the Assembly meant (to cite a phrase from James Fraser of Brae which it did not use), that 'what is purchased is absolutely purchased', that is, a redemption in which the fruit of Christ's atoning sacrifice was regarded not just as an open possibility for all but as a predetermined actuality. When applied to all people this could only mean, in the Assembly's view, a doctrine of universal atonement and redemption, which the supporters of *The Marrow* like Thomas Boston resolutely denied, for they were committed to the Westminster doctrine of limited atonement.[9] They were in fact firm believers in particular election and redemption, although they held a much closer relation between election and Christ, and a more personal relation between believers and Christ, evident in their teaching and preaching that whatever the Redeemer has done *for* mankind he has done personally for all and each of them – 'for me', and 'for you'. But this way of thinking and speaking by the evangelical divines of the sufficiency of Christ and of his redemption 'for all', was rejected by the Assembly theologians, for in their minds it carried the notion of an *actual* unlimited atonement, necessarily fulfilled for everyone outside the church as well as within it, for the non-elect as well as for the elect. In their view a concept of actual atonement made for all could not be held together with the doctrine that only some people are elected, for that would mean that Christ had died fruitlessly and in vain for many if not for most people.[10] A doctrine of 'universal redemption as to purchase', of actual atoning substitution for all mankind, was held to be universalist and Arminian, for it would mean that a sinner has a positive right to redemption. Such an idea was utterly rejected by the General Assembly in favour of a doctrine of an atonement deliberately limited by God only to a fixed number of the elect. According to Thomas Halyburton Christ's purchase of complete redemption, with all its saving blessings, was undertaken *sub termino*, that is, to be finally given to

[9] Boston's edition of *The Marrow, Works*, Vol. 7, pp. 262f.
[10] 'The argument that if Christ died for all men, and all are not saved, then Christ died in vain – and *a priori*, because God always infallibly achieves his purposes, this is unthinkable.' James B. Torrance, 'The Incarnation and "Limited Atonement"', *The Evangelical Quarterly*, 55.3, Exeter, 1984, p. 84.

the persons concerned, at a time and in an order which has been agreed upon between the Father and the Son, 'the contrivers and managers of this whole affair'.[11]

According to James Hog, what disappointed and disillusioned the Marrow Men was not only the fact that the General Assembly failed to discern that the real issue at stake was the very nature of the gospel of grace, but also the fact that 'the Assembly which condemned the Marrow with so much indignation and contempt, should yet have been very shy about the great fundamental head of the adorable Trinity of persons in the Godhead, which is the foundation of all religion, both as to doctrine, worship and walk.'[12] Thus, although it was not actually recognised either by the Marrow Men or by the Assembly theologians, the problem that had come to the surface in the current understanding of 'gospel-grace' had to do with the basic doctrine of God which had been distorted in the formulation of the *Westminster Confession* when an abstract conception of God as Omnipotent Lawgiver and Judge was given primacy over the trinitarian understanding of God's eternal Being and Nature characterised by Fatherhood, Sonship, and Communion and thus by infinite Love. That was a truth which, as we have already noted, had been clearly recognised by Hugh Binning.

Moreover, the problem had also to do with the nature and handling of biblical revelation. According to the *Westminster Confession of Faith* the Holy Scripture given by the inspiration of God is the supreme rule of faith and life, and the infallible rule of interpretation of Scripture is the Scripture itself. Actually both the Assembly divines and the evangelical divines tended to interpret the Scripture in the light of and under the guidance of the Westminster tradition, which (although they did not realise it) was a lapse from the *sola Scriptura*, and indeed, the *sola gratia* teaching of the Reformers, into a rather Tridentine conception of the relation of Holy Scripture to Church Tradition!

In some respects this was more of a problem with the evangelical divines, for their concern for the Gospel of free grace offered to all conflicted with the Westminster doctrines of the double decree and limited atonement to which they nevertheless adhered. They were afraid that any departure on their part from the Confession would be interpreted to mean that their emphasis on the universal

---

[11] Thomas Halyburton, *An Essay on the Ground or Formal Reason of Saving Faith*, 1865 edn, pp. 107f.
[12] See John Brown, *Gospel Truth*, p. 47; see also p. 51.

offer of the Gospel was but a hidden form of the concept of universal atonement or salvation held by Arminians. Their deepest trouble here was with the rather abstract Westminster doctrine of God on the one hand, and on the other hand with the kind of christological and soteriological approach to the knowledge of God which, against the trend of the *Westminster Confession of Faith*, they felt compelled to adopt in their overriding concern for the Gospel of salvation by grace alone. However, they were more concerned with the *saving Person* of Christ than formal doctrine, which was regularly nourished by 'Action Sermons' and the celebration of the Lord's Supper.[13] They were not willing, unlike Fraser of Brae, to admit that at decisive points they diverged from the *Confession of Faith*. But the theological direction which they took did lead them like Fraser of Brae to take more seriously the command of Christ to go into all the world and preach the Gospel, which was a return to the manifesto of the *Scots Confession*: 'These glad tidings of the Kingdom shall be preached throughout the whole world for a witness to all nations.' James Walker was not far wrong when he wrote: 'Boston and the Marrow men, first of all among our divines, entered fully into the missionary spirit of the Bible.'[14]

In 1758 John Witherspoon, who was later to become the President of the College of New Jersey, preached a sermon on 'The Absolute Necessity of Salvation through Christ' in which he called the Society in Scotland for the Propagating of Christian Knowledge to extend its mission to the Indian tribes. He took as his text Acts 4.12: 'Neither is there salvation in any other; for there is none other name under heaven given among men, whereby we must be saved.'[15] This was in line with his convictions about the nature and sufficiency and extent of the atoning sacrifice of Christ. In spite of the narrow view that prevailed in the Kirk he did not hesitate to draw attention to the command of Christ to preach the Gospel to all the world, and to expound the teaching of the New Testament that Christ died in propitiatory sacrifice for people in all nations. He insisted on the evangelical truth that 'Christ died for all men, even for those who perish', that 'the love of Christ to sinners, or of

---

[13] Cf. *Sacramental meditations on the sufferings and death of Christ*, by Daniel Campbell, 7th edn London, 1723.
[14] James Walker, *The Theology and Theologians of Scotland*, 1888, p. 94.
[15] John Witherspoon, *Collected Works*, Edinburgh, 1804, Vol. IV, pp. 241–79.

God in him, was from all eternity', and that 'the love of Christ is a free and unmerited love'.[16] It must not be overlooked, however, that in 1700 the Assembly sent a pastoral letter to the ministers who had joined the Darien Expedition in Caledonia, in which they expressed the hope that 'the Lord would yet honour the missionary ministers and the Church from which they had been sent to carry his name among the heathen.'[17] In 1723 Paul Millar, a predecessor of John Witherspoon at Paisley Abbey, published a two volume work *A History of the Propagation of Christianity*, followed up by another work *A History of the Church under the Old Testament*, advocating what Andrew Walls has called 'a comprehensive missionary programme'.[18] How different was the teaching of Thomas Halyburton who, although in many ways an evangelical strongly opposed to legalistic religion, nevertheless argued against the preaching of the Gospel to the heathen, for that would presuppose that they had been included within the covenant of grace through atoning satisfaction made for them by Christ![19] The inner tension in evangelical Calvinism between the doctrine of God and the mission of the Gospel remained, and was not resolved but continued throughout the eighteenth century and into the nineteenth century when a more biblical and evangelical approach to the Gospel began to bear fruit in the promotion of missionary activity. This was particularly evident in the sermons and addresses of the young Thomas Chalmers.[20]

The Simson controversy

In this controversy a very divergent movement of thought arose. It took place in an era under the increasing impact of rationalism,[21]

[16] John Witherspoon, *Collected Works*, Vol. II, Sermons on 1 John 2.2, pp.92–115 and Rev. 1.5, pp. 116–144.

[17] *Acts of the General Assembly*, Sess. 13, February 15, 1700. Refer to Henry Cowan, *The Influence of the Scottish Church in Christendom*, London, 1896, p. 32.

[18] Andrew Walls, 'Missions', *Dictionary of Scottish Church History and Theology*, p. 567. See also I. D. Maxwell, 'Robert Millar', *ibid.*, p. 562.

[19] Thomas Halyburton, *Natural Religion Insufficient; and Reveal'd Necessary to Man's Happiness in his present State*, Edinburgh, 1714, pp. 192ff.

[20] See Hugh Watt, *The Published Writings of Thomas Chalmers (1780–1847)*, Privately printed 1943, pp. 14f & 17f.

[21] Cf. Thomas Blackwell, *Ratio sacra, or, An appeal unto the rational world about the reasonableness of revealed religion*, Edinburgh, 1710.

which had the effect of bringing to light other aspects of the *Westminster Confession of Faith* and raising problems latent in its rationalist, necessitarian idea of God together with its view of nature enshrined in the notion of the covenant of works.[22] Behind the thinking of the Assembly divines lay the teaching of Robert Rollock: 'the ground of the covenant of works was not Christ nor the grace of God in Christ, but the nature of man in the first creation'[23] – a conception which had been embodied in the works of John Owen by which Scottish theologians were now being deeply influenced. John Simson, Professor of Divinity in Glasgow University, was twice accused of various heresies, mainly Arminianism, Socinianism and Arianism, and rather strange views about providence, but after subtle explanations of his ideas the charges against him could not be properly substantiated, not least in view of his acknowledged adherence to the *Westminster Confession of Faith*.[24] Although he was not formally condemned, he was rebuked and suspended, but his wider and more open view of the grace of God in creation made its mark on many minds. Simson's rather ambiguous views were not unconnected with the moralistic teaching about the light of nature, with the general framework of first and second causes in the *Confession of Faith*, and not least with the rather deterministic doctrine of God in its account of the divine decrees and what Simson called 'omnipotent grace'.[25] This seems to reflect the change in the rather determinist notion of causality found in Newtonian physics, which had the effect in some quarters of reinforcing and hardening in hyper-Calvinist thought the old Aristotelian notion of causality appropriated by the Synod of Dort, and reflected in the *Westminster Confession*. Simson's readiness to think of divine activity along such determinist lines evidently laid him open to the rationalism and determinism of the English deists like John Locke and Matthew Tindal, and rationalising theologians like Samuel Clarke.[26] Although Simson himself was not a rationalist in that sense, he stood within the Westminster tradition for a religion of reason rather than a religion of experience.[27]

[22] Cf. *Acts of the General Assembly* for May 14, 1717, Sess. 12, and May 16, 1728, Sess. ult.
[23] Robert Rollock, *God's Effectual Calling, Works*, Vol. 1, 1848, p. 343.
[24] Cf. Robert Flint, *Examen Doctrinae D: Johannis Simson, S.S.T. In Celebri Academia Glasguensi Professoris*, Edinburgh, 1717.
[25] Cf. Flint, *Examen Doctrinae*, Cap. IV, pp. 88ff.
[26] Cf. his work *Scripture and the Doctrine of the Trinity*, London, 1712.
[27] Cf. John McClaren, *The new scheme of doctrine contained in the answers of Mr John Simson, Professor of Divinity in the College of Glasgow, to Mr Webster's libel, considered and examined*. Edinburgh, 1717.

The two points that we may note here have to do: a) with a necessitarian doctrine of God and the abstract nature of his activity, an inveterate problem Scottish theology inherited from a logicalised and rationalistic Calvinism, which laid it open to sceptical attack, e.g. by David Hume; and b) a doctrine of absolute particular predestination behind the back of Christ Jesus, which opened a back door for the inroad of Arian and Nestorian views of the incarnate Person of Christ. Both of these have ever since given rise to serious problems in Scottish theology evident, not least, in recurring problems in the understanding of atonement which were later to worry John McLeod Campbell.

Before we pass on to discuss Scottish theology during the rest of the eighteenth century, it may be useful to return to the thought of Thomas Halyburton (1674–1712), who may be regarded as a transitional figure, but with 'cross-bench' sympathies. He stood squarely within the theology of the *Westminster Confession of Faith*, with its scholastic notion of first and second causes, and its hyper-Calvinist tendencies, but unlike people like Boston and Simson, who in different ways were moving away from it, he sought to bolster it up with an apologetic and eristic form of rational argumentation. That was very different from the new way of thinking theologically and philosophically which was to arise during the Scottish Enlightenment. This is very marked in his work entitled *Natural Religion Insufficient; and Reveal'd Necessary to Man's Happiness in his Present State*, 1714. It was a rational inquiry into the principles of the Deists like Lord Herbert of Cherbury, John Locke, Thomas Hobbes, but also Benedict Spinoza, whose thinking was making inroads into Scottish thought. Although Halyburton admitted that the poison of deism had not infected Scotland as much as England,[28] the main purpose of his work was clearly to demolish the claims of the deists for a religion of reason that does not have recourse to divine interaction with mankind or divine revelation, or to the doctrines of the faith, and to show that the kind of religion deists advocate grounded on 'nature's light' does not satisfy, lead to happiness, or provide us with moral motives and grounds for behaviour. Moreover it does not and cannot offer the means of pardon, or ways of overcoming sin, let alone provide any help in developing a knowledge of the Trinity or to directing us to the solemn worship of God.[29] In addition to appealing to scholastic

---

[28] *Natural Religion insufficient*, Edinburgh, 1714, p. 32.
[29] *Natural Religion insufficient*, especially pp. 45ff, 83ff, 116ff.

thinkers like Turretin, or John Owen to whose thinking he showed considerable affinity, Halyburton could refer frequently to the literature of ancient secular authors as well.

While Halyburton would not have it that faith in God can be established on external evidence, he nevertheless developed his apologetic arguments with the deists largely on their own ground, and did not hesitate again and again to appeal to 'the light of nature'. On the other hand, he insisted that faith is a supernatural gift which can arise only through spiritual relation to God as we meet him in the Holy Scriptures. It is not to be understood as mere assent to doctrine, but is a reliance upon and surrender to Christ. His taking hold of us, is the cause of our taking hold of him.[30] At the same time, however, he sought to develop grounds for reasoned belief, as he showed in his greatly lauded little book, *An Essay concerning the Nature of Faith, Or, the Ground upon which Faith Assents to the Scriptures.*[31] In it he frequently appealed to 'the light of nature', but tried through rational arguments to disclose the inner reason of faith as 'assent to propositions of truth revealed in the Scriptures'. This was developed through an analytical and logical argument with John Locke in such a way that against Halyburton's intention it opened the door, like most apologetics of this kind, to secularisation. Halyburton operated with a propositional understanding of the Scriptures, and of the formal reason of faith, rather than with the objective ground of divine revelation or basic Christian doctrine.[32] The focus of attention was more on the reasonableness of saving faith, than on Christ himself in whom we believe, and was rather less Christ-centred than the classical Reformed theology still dominant in the previous century. That way of upholding the Christian Faith was not able to stand up to the kind of thinking that developed in the Scotland of the eighteenth and nineteenth centuries, although it continued to be cultivated by reactionary circles in the Church of Scotland or in its Secessions.

---

[30] *An Essay on the Ground or Formal Reason of Saving Faith*, p. 92.
[31] Edinburgh, 1714, appended to the work on *Natural Religion*. See also the new edn, London, 1865.
[32] For another more specifically evangelical aspect of Halyburton's thought, see his *Sermons preached before and after the celebration of the Sacrament of the Lord's Supper*, 2nd. edn 1770.

Divided witness

There is no doubt that after the Toleration Act of 1712 a broader and more urbane outlook began to come over Scotland which made itself felt, albeit rather slowly, in Scottish theology, although there continued within it two main streams of thought, one carrying on the old Reformation tradition, and the other the Westminster tradition. The division between them was by no means clean cut, for they sometimes ran into each other and their characteristic emphases could cross over into each other at different points of doctrine. This was particularly the case with what came to be called the Moderates and the Evangelicals. It was the older tradition, with its emphases on worship and the sacraments, which carried forward the evangelical emphasis on the love and mercy of God. As John Witherspoon once pointed out, 'Perhaps no one circumstance has contributed more to preserve the pure uncorrupted doctrine of the Gospel, than the sacrament of the Lord's Supper.'[33] In the Westminster tradition, on the other hand, there developed a more puritan notion of worship and a more legalist understanding of the sacraments as badges of faith rather than as signs and seals of saving grace,[34] which was not too welcoming to the evangelical awakening that came with the preaching of Whitefield and later of the Haldane brothers.[35]

Throughout the eighteenth and early nineteenth centuries it was through communion seasons, action sermons, and teaching about the infinite love of God and the wonderful nature of divine mercy that the evangelical and spiritual life of the Kirk continued to be nourished and moulded. A recoil set in against legal sermonising in favour of direct proclamation of the Gospel and its practical application to sinners.[36] This evangelistic and pastoral

---

[33] John Witherspoon, *Collected Works*, Vol. IV, p. 215.

[34] This had been developed and forcefully advocated by David Calderwood in his work *The Altar of Damascus*, 1621, later issued in an enlarged Latin edition, *Altare Damascenum seu Ecclesiae Anglicanae Politia*, in 1708. In 1643 Calderwood joined with Alexander Henderson and David Dickson in preparing a directory for public worship.

[35] Cf. Alexander Webster, *Divine influence the spring of the extraordinary work at Cambuslang and other places in the West of Scotland*, Edinburgh, 1742; and James Robe, *Narratives of the extraordinary work of the spirit of God at Cambuslang, Kilsyth, etc., begun in 1742*, Glasgow, 1790.

[36] Cf. *The Practical Works of Alexander Moncrief of Culfargie*, In Two Volumes, Edinburgh, 1779.

concern gave rise to significant works concerned not so much with systematic theology, as with practical and devotional theology dedicated to the 'improvement' of Christian faith and life through 'personal covenanting', catechetical instruction, and Scripture Songs and Gospel Hymns,[37] in which not a little attention was given, as at the Reformation, to the training of children and young communicants.[38] The most impressive preacher theologian of the age was John Willison of Dundee, an Evangelical Calvinist for whom the preaching of the Gospel was 'the ministration of the Spirit'. A collection of his sermons, sacramental and catechetical writings was published under the title of *The Practical Works of John Willison*, in which considerable place was given to sacramental meditations, and guidance in personal counselling for inquirers and the terminally ill.[39] The evangelical and indeed evangelistic slant of the old Scottish view of the sacraments as 'converting ordinances', sealing the preaching of the Gospel to lost sinners was set upon on a wider basis in the congregational life of the Kirk. The practical theology that emerged in this way represents a very important stage in the development of Scottish Theology – it helped to make possible the biblical and pastoral developments in bridging the divided witness in doctrine and polity within the Church of Scotland and in mitigating the rigid legalism of the hyper-Calvinists, which were to take place in the next century. Alongside the contribution of Willison mention must be made of the great work of John Warden of Gargunnock, *A Practical Essay on the Sacrament of Baptism*,[40] which was of considerable theological importance in the eighteenth century in reaffirming and clarifying the basic theology of ministers in the Lowlands. Mention should also be made, however, of the widespread doctrinal as well as practical impact of 'Vincent's Catechism' in the Highlands.[41]

---

[37] Cf. William Geddes, *The Saint's Recreation upon the Estate of Grace*, 2nd edn Glasgow, 1753. This seems to have been in the tradition of *Hymnes and Sacred Songs*, by Alexander Hume, minister of Logie, 1599. *The Miscellany of the Wodrow Society*, Vol. I, Edinburgh, 1844, p. 568.

[38] See, for example, John Barclay, *Rejoice Evermore: or, Christ All in All, An Original Publication; consisting of Spiritual Songs, collected from the Holy Scriptures; and several of the Psalms, together with the Whole Song of Solomon, paraphrased*. Glasgow, 1767.

[39] Edited by W. M. Hetherington, London, 1844.

[40] Edinburgh, 1724.

[41] Thomas Vincent, *An Explicatory Catechism: or, An Explanation of the Assembly's Shorter Catechism*, Aberdeen, 1785. See the 1958 Report of the *Special Commission on Baptism*, pp. 58f.

Of much more importance for Scottish theology than is often recognised were the service books that were published,[42] accompanied by a revival in psalmody[43] and newly composed paraphrases which A. J. Campbell called 'perhaps the best and greatest legacy of Moderatism'.[44] By an act of the General Assembly in May 1745 there was sent down to presbyteries a collection of paraphrases, which soon saw several editions.[45] Regular doxological worship dating from John Knox's Liturgy had long been a generative source for the trinitarian theology of the parish minister after he had left the Divinity Hall.[46] These ancient trinitarian doxologies which had been appended to the Psalms had received vehement support from David Calderwood, who opposed their abolition at the Assembly of 1645: 'Moderator, I entreat that the Doxology be not laid aside for I hope to sing it in heaven'.[47]

A particularly important contribution to Christian life and thought was made by *Gospel Canticles; or Spiritual Songs* by Ralph Erskine first published in 1720, and then as *Gospel Sonnets or Spiritual*

---

[42] Apart from the editions of the Book of Common Order and the Book of Common Prayer, see *Sacramental Meditations and Advices*, by John Willison, Edinburgh 1761, *The Scotch Minister's Assistant*, Inverness, 1820. See also *A Sacramental Directory* of John Willison, *op. cit.* pp. 127 ff.

[43] Cf. *The Psalms of David in Meter. Newly Translated and Compared with the Original Text and former Translations. Allowed by the General Assembly of the Kirk of Scotland*, 1693. It was George Buchanan who initiated in Scotland metrical editions of the Psalter – see the later edition of his *Psalmorum Davidis Paraphrasis Poetica*, Edinburgh 1725. A Psalter was attached to John Knox's Liturgy or *Book of Common Order*, 1562–64, as in his Genevan Service Book of 1556, *The Forme of Prayers and Ministration of the Sacraments*.

[44] A. J. Campbell, *Two Centuries of the Church of Scotland, 1707–1929*, Paisley, 1930, p. 114. See Douglas J. Maclagan, *The Scottish Paraphrases*, Edinburgh, 1889, in which an account is given of the history, authors and sources of spiritual songs, paraphrases and hymns used from 1706 to 1781 – *Translations and Paraphrases, in Verse, of actual Passages of Sacred Scriptures*, Edinburgh, 1781. Cf. also *Scripture Songs for Zion's Travellers, A Short Christian Directory*, Edinburgh, 1761; Robert Findlay, *A persuasive to the enlargement of psalmody, by a minister of the Church of Scotland*, Glasgow, 1763; and also N. Tate and N. Brady, *A New Version of the Psalms of David ... set to Musick*, Amsterdam, 1772.

[45] *'Translations' and Paraphrases of Several Passages of Sacred Scripture*, 1745, were published after 1749 as *Scripture Songs or Translations*, 1781, with later editions. See *Remarks on the Innovations of the Public Worship of God*, proposed by the Free Presbytery of Hamilton, Edinburgh, 1854.

[46] Cf. the continued publication throughout the eighteenth century of Robert Edward, *The Doxology Approven: or, the Singing Glory to the Father, Son and Holy Ghost in the Worship of God*, 1731, Edinburgh.

[47] Cited by Robert Edward, *The Doxology Approven*, p. 78.

Songs, 1754, which by 1793 had already seen twenty-four editions.[48] In a unique form they spread through Scotland propagating the evangelical teaching of *The Marrow of Modern Divinity*, but in a way that helped to shed the remnants of legalism, and, partly under the influence of the preaching of George Whitefield, advocated the Gospel of saving grace freely offered to all. To *The Gospel Sonnets* Erskine added extensive comments which helped readers to understand the biblical basis of the evangelical truths they presented.[49]

The Enlightenment influence

During the decades known as the *Scottish Enlightenment* a new outlook in theology asserted itself, when not a few ministers became deeply interested in the scientific advance that began with Isaac Newton, and was carried on in Scotland notably by Colin MacLaurin (1698–1746) who was the son of a minister and the brother of John MacLaurin (1693–1754), another minister who was an evangelical Calvinist.[50] On Newton's recommendation Colin MacLaurin was appointed to the chair of Mathematics at Edinburgh, where he made distinguished contributions in mathematics and physics for which he was honoured by the Royal Society in London and the French Academy. He was not a theologian himself, but he adhered to the *Westminster Confession* and he cleared the way for a more realist epistemology in theology and philosophy as well as the science of human nature. This was the century of Frances Hutcheson, Adam Smith, David Hume, and James Watt, which in 1783 saw the foundation of The Royal Society of Edinburgh 'For the Advancement of Learning and Useful Knowledge'. As with the foundation of the Royal Society in London,

---

[48] Cf. the earlier *Spiritual Songs or, Holy Poems. A Garden of True Delight*, by Patrick Simson (the father of John Simson), Edinburgh, 1685–6; and also the *Spiritual Songs* of Dughall Buchanan, *Laoidhe Spioradail*, 1767 (1889 & 1913), translated into English Verse by L. Macbean, Edinburgh, 1884.

[49] See also the *Scripture Songs and Gospel Hymns* of John Willison, *Practical Works*, pp. 951–99; *Rejoice Evermore: Or, Christ ALL IN ALL, Spiritual Songs, collected from the Holy Scriptures...*, by John Barclay, Glasgow, 1768; and the religious poems of William Geddes, *The Saint's Recreation upon the Estate of Grace*, edited by George Park, Glasgow, 2nd edn 1753.

[50] See the thesis by John MacLeod, *John MacLaurin, 1693–1754, Glasgow; his life, work and thought*, 1969, New College Library, Edinburgh.

ministers joined with scientists, mathematicians and philosophers in the establishment of its counterpart in Edinburgh. From the middle of the seventeenth century to the middle of the nineteenth century Scottish thinkers in science and philosophy made an outstanding contribution to British Science.[51] It was in extension of this development that there arose the interest in the interrelations between theology and science taken up in the next century by people like Robert Flint of Edinburgh University (one of the founders of The British Academy) in his lectures on 'Theological Science', and more directly by Thomas Chalmers and Henry Drummond especially at New College where chairs in mathematics, geology, astronomy, and natural science were founded.

Consideration needs to be given to the paradoxical contribution of David Hume (1711–76) whose critical philosophy did much to undermine the rationalism of the hyper-Calvinists, and thereby helped theologians of the Kirk to break free from the non-biblical and non-evangelical presuppositions in which they had been caught up. David Hume evidently had a good knowledge of Scholastic Calvinism for he was acquainted with the *Syntagma Theologiae* of Amandus Polanus in which he expounded the teaching of Calvin with reference to the thought of Thomas Aquinas and Duns Scotus.[52] This was a classical work often used in the presbyteries for the teaching of theological students. Although he had many ministerial friends in Edinburgh, Hume offended the Kirk by his critical essay on *Miracles*. This brought reasoned replies, notably from George Campbell of Marischal College, Aberdeen, *A Dissertation on Miracles*,[53] which won him the respect of David Hume, and which revealed that Scottish theologians were very ready to engage in epistemological discussion at a very high level. These discussions, of course, were carried on still within the purview of the Newtonian deterministic conception of causal and mechanistic

---

[51] See the illuminating works by Richard Olson, *Scottish Philosophy and British Physics, 1750–1880*, Princeton, 1975, and Alexander Broadie, *The Tradition of Scottish Philosophy*, Edinburgh, 1990.

[52] This is evident in his use of the distinction between ectypal and archetypal analogy in the *Syntagma*, which Polanus took over from Philo Judaeus, and which Hume put into the mouth of 'Philo', the interlocutor in his *Dialogues Concerning Natural Religion*, who represented his own position. It was later taken over from Hume by Kant.

[53] Edinburgh, 1766. George Campbell was also acclaimed for his important book *The Philosophy of Rhetoric*, 1776.

relations, which were eventually to give way in the next century to more dynamic and open-structured ways of thinking with the epoch-making work of James Clerk Maxwell.

Another ministerial thinker of great note as a philosopher was Thomas Reid who succeeded Adam Smith as Professor of Moral Philosophy in Glasgow.[54] He laid the foundations for a realist (so-called 'common sense') philosophy which had a considerable impact on Reformed theology, not least in the United States. His ideas were developed by Sir William Hamilton in a way that was to influence the devout James Clerk Maxwell in the next century, who, according to Einstein, did more than anyone else to change the rational structure of science.[55] It is difficult to estimate the full impact of the critical attack on rationalism and the return to a realist way of thinking, which had a better reception from the Moderate than the Evangelical wing of the Kirk, but perhaps its most important effect was the way in which it made room for a reinterpretation of the Gospel by freeing it from the rigid framework of a rationalist Calvinism in which it had become trapped. Evangelical Calvinism was now more able to overcome the inner tensions which theologians like Thomas Boston or Ralph and Ebenezer Erskine had to face between their adherence to the absolute character of God's eternal decree of double predestination and the absolute sufficiency of Christ and his atoning sacrifice for sin. This gave them freedom to take a more straightforward and realist way of interpreting biblical passages about the unrestricted nature of the redemption of mankind by Christ, and the unconditional offer of the Gospel to all people even beyond the supposed limits of the covenant of grace, which had been anticipated by James Fraser of Brae.

Evangelicals and Moderates

Due to the problematic course of Scottish Theology in the eighteenth century, there were notable churchmen, but only a few outstanding theologians were found in the leadership of the Kirk, although there were several very able ministers of the hyper-

---

[54] See Alexander Broadie, *The Tradition of Scottish Philosophy*, Edinburgh, 1990, pp. 118ff.
[55] Cf. my edition of Clerk Maxwell's epoch-making work, *A Dynamical Theory of the Electromagnetic Field*, Edinburgh, 1982.

Calvinist school. Account must be taken here, however, of the enduring influence of the great John Brown of Wamphray (1610–79), carried over from the previous century into the eighteenth century, through powerful theological works published in Holland, where he lived in banishment, as well as in Scotland. One of his most formidable productions was *De Causa Dei contra Antisabbatarios Tractatus* in three Latin volumes which was heavily indebted to scholastic Calvinism.[56] In other works he helped considerably to redress the balance of teaching, giving it a more biblical and less schematic basis.[57] In discussing with the English puritans he insisted that faith was not our 'gospel-righteousness', that the righteousness of Christ, both active and passive, was not imputed to us on the ground of faith, necessary as faith was, but on the ground of union with Christ wrought by him alone. He regularly interpreted this as a taking refuge in, or a reliance upon, the faithfulness of God in Christ.[58] This was a much healthier outlook but, unfortunately, following Rutherford, Brown could see no alternative to a doctrine of universal redemption implying only a possibility of salvation and requiring faith as justifying instrument, except the doctrine of a limited atonement for the elect only. The essential relation between the Incarnation and the atonement which was so strong in the older Reformation and older Scottish tradition, was allowed to drop out of sight.[59] On the other hand, Brown continued the strong tradition in the Kirk upon searching soul examination, although with much greater emphasis upon the promises of God extended to his people in all ages as the ground of confidence.[60]

John Brown also produced other works that had their mead of impact on Scottish theology. His writing on the nature of the Church and its divinely endowed ordinances kept alive the rigid tradition of the Westminster Divines like Samuel Rutherford and George Gillespie: as there is only one King and Head of the Church,

---

[56] John Brown of Wamphray, *De Causa Dei contra Antisabbatarios Tractatus*, 3. vols., Rotterdam, 1674–76.
[57] Refer to *An Exposition of Romans, with large practical observations*, Edinburgh, 1655 & 1766.
[58] Cf. *The Life of justification opened*, 1695; and *Christ the Way, the Truth, and the Life*, Rotterdam, 1677.
[59] Brown of Wamphray, see again, *The Life of Justification Opened*, Edinburgh, 1695; and also *The Mirror or Looking-Glass for Saint and Saviour*, Glasgow, 1793; and *Christ the Way, the Truth, and the Life*, Edinburgh, 1677.
[60] See again *A Mirror or Looking-Glass for Saint and Sinner*, Glasgow, 1793.

so there can be only one Church – the old principle 'na uther face of kirk', together with a rejection of Erastian prelacy.[61] His important work on the Reformed doctrine of the Church was given in a Preface to a powerful work *Libri duo contra Volzogenium et contra Velthusium*,[62] in which he operated with a distinction between the Church Invisible and Church Visible, corresponding to the twofold Kingdom of Christ, as Second Person of the Trinity and as Mediator, and advocated the concept of the Catholic Visible Church endowed by Christ with the ordinances of Ministry, Word and Sacraments. This was acclaimed by John Macpherson as 'perhaps the very best book written by any of our Scottish divines on the ministry, church government and ecclesiastical discipline. It embraces in one treatise a full review of the topics discussed separately in many volumes of Gillespie and Rutherford.'[63]

This work of John Brown should be read in tandem with the work of Thomas Ayton, Minister of the Gospel at Alyth, *The Original Constitution of the Christian Church wherein the Extremes on either Hand are Stated and Examined. To which is added an appendix containing, The Rise of the Jure Divino Prelatists, and an answer to their arguments by Episcopal Divines.*[64] It is a work remarkable in the Post-Revolution Kirk for its unusual balance and lack of rancour! The book owed much to the Westminster divines, Scottish and English, Presbyterian and Anglican, as well as Continental writers such as Blondel, but it also revealed considerable knowledge of patristic literature. Its outstanding feature is that in it, Ayton not only examined and rejected extreme positions on either side of the Presbyterian-Anglican debate, but distinguished the ground common to the main body of belief on both sides, and sought to provide a positive and constructive account of the Church and Ministry, in a remarkably ecumenical way.

Rather different from John Brown of Wamphray were the theologians of the Secession, the Erskine Brothers, Ebenezer

---

[61] Cf. *An Apologeticall Relation, of the particular sufferings of the faithful ministers and professors of the Church of Scotland since August 1660*, 1665.

[62] Amsterdam, 1670.

[63] John Macpherson, *The Doctrine of the Church in Scottish Theology*, Edinburgh 1903, pp. 49f. For a clear account of this work by John Brown, see the essay by Ian B. Doyle, 'The Doctrine of the Church in the Later Covenanting Period', in *Reformation and Revolution, Essays presented to the Very Rev. Hugh Watt*, ed. Duncan Shaw, Edinburgh 1967, pp. 212–36. Cf. also James Walker in *The Theology and Theologians of Scotland*, Edinburgh 1888, pp. 107f.

[64] Edinburgh, 1730. See my account of this in Duncan Shaw, *Reformation and Revolution* pp. 273–97.

(1680–1754) and Ralph (1685–1752), who with James Hog and Thomas Boston had led the revolt against the Assembly's rejection of the teaching of *The Marrow of Modern Divinity*.[65] While rejecting a doctrine of universal atonement, they held firmly to their belief that 'Christ had taken upon himself the sins of all men', and that 'the Father had made a deed of gift and grant unto all mankind, that whosoever of them all shall believe in the Son shall not perish.'[66] Ralph Erskine expressed the issue strikingly:

> Let Arminians maintain at their peril their universal redemption; but we must maintain at our peril the universal offer. Necessity is laid upon us, and woe unto us if we preach not this gospel to every creature. Christ is so far given to all people that hear the gospel, that it is warrantable for them to receive the gift.[67]

Moreover, in their understanding of the nature of evangelical faith in its correlation with 'free sovereign grace ... without any consideration of any condition or qualification in us', they pointed to the way in which 'the Confession of Faith and the Catechisms exclude the very act of believing, as well as the fruits of faith, from the matter of our justification before God...'[68] They insisted, therefore, that this was both in accord with the teaching of Calvin, and with the articles of the authorised Standards of the Kirk. What had worried the Marrow Men and continued to worry the Erskines was the prevalence of 'legal doctrine' or 'a kind of refined Arminianism' found even in the way that justification by faith was being taught and proclaimed by men in the Church of Scotland.

What was at stake for them here was the absolute centrality of the Person of Jesus Christ as Lord and Saviour, and the very nature of the Gospel of grace as good news for lost sinners – 'the gift of God through Jesus Christ our Lord, without regard to any of our doings as a foundation of our claim or title thereunto'. They asserted the unconditional nature of the Love of God toward the world: 'God so loved the world – the whole world of mankind –

---

[65] For the following see especially the work by John Brown of Whitburn, *Gospel Truth Accurately Stated and Illustrated by the Rev Messrs James Hog, Thomas Boston, Ebenezer and Ralph Erskine, and Others*, Occasioned by the Republication of *The Marrow of Modern Divinity*, New Edition, Glasgow, 1831.

[66] Acts of the General Assembly for 1720 and 1722.

[67] John Brown, *Gospel Truth*, p. 385.

[68] Ralph Erskine, in John Brown, *Gospel Truth*, pp. 383–4.

that he gave his only begotten Son that whosoever believes in him should not perish but have everlasting life.'[69] Ultimately it was the doctrine of God, and the love that God is, that was the essential issue here. 'God offers Christ cordially and affectionately in the gospel; his very heart goes out after sinners in the call and offer thereof ... God's whole heart and soul is in the offer and promise of the gospel.'[70] Thus they believed there to be biblical ground even in the ultimate nature of God himself for the Gospel offer to all men and women without exception, not just as the elect, but *precisely as lost sinners*. 'The question', said Ralph Erskine, 'is not, Are you an elect or not? But the question is, Are you a sinner that needs a Saviour?'[71] 'The general call and offer of the gospel reaches every individual person, and God speaks to every sinner as particularly as though he named them by his name and surname. Remission of sins is preached unto *you*, we beseech *you* to be reconciled, the promise is unto *you*.'[72] Supreme place was given to the *Person* of Christ himself as he is in all his promises, and to the *true grace* of God in the daily life of believers, as also in the regular ministry of the Church, which the Erskines sought to deliver from 'the legal strain' that had been corrupting it.[73] Along with this approach went a recovery of the kind of evangelical assurance taught by Reformation theology. 'This assurance, a persuasion of the promise and appropriation (as the judicious Calvin speaks) can no more be separate from faith than light can be separate from the sun'.[74] This was the distinction which Ralph Erskine spoke of between 'the fiducial assurance', and 'evidential assurance', which corresponded to that between 'Gospel repentance' and 'legal repentance'.[75]

After the lenient way the Assembly seemed to adopt to Professor Simson over his alleged Arianism, and the prejudiced attack by

---

[69] *Gospel Truth*, p. 347. They rejected what Ebenezer called 'the Baxterian error, of an evangelical righteousness different from the imputed righteousness of Christ'. p. 349.

[70] *Gospel Truth*, p. 365.

[71] *Gospel Truth*, p. 391.

[72] *Gospel Truth*, p. 355.

[73] See the extracts from the writings of Ebenezer and Ralph Erskine, given by John Brown, *Gospel Truth*, Ebenezer Erskine, pp. 343–54, 370ff, & Ralph Erskine, pp. 387ff.

[74] *Gospel Truth*, pp. 357 & 367f.

[75] *Gospel Truth*, pp. 394ff, 406ff & 410f.

Principal Hadow of St Andrews over their convictions,[76] the Marrow Men suspected that the Assembly Establishment, in spite of their formal and even rigid acceptance of the Westminster Standards, were not clear and firm enough in their own affirmation of the Deity of Christ.[77] Even the doctrine of Holy Trinity seemed to be obscured under the logical and legal structure of their confessional standards in terms of which they interpreted the biblical witness.[78] While other questions regarding the laws of the Kirk, over patronage, for example, were to force the Erskines and their friends into secession, behind it all a deep cleft had opened up in the Kirk between two kinds of doctrine and churchmanship, the evangelically earnest and the formally Calvinistic, or expressed otherwise, between two disparate ways of understanding the Christian faith, as a way of salvation or as a system of doctrines. It represented in fact, an open manifestation between the two traditions, the older Scottish Reformation tradition and the hyper-Calvinist tradition, which had set in with the imposition of the rigid framework of an abstract federal theology upon the authorised teaching of the Kirk. The tension that brought about was already evident not only in the divergence between the outlook of James Fraser of Brae and that of Thomas Boston of Ettrick, but it was also evident in the very heart of Boston's own theological attempt to hold together his deep evangelical concern with unconditional grace and the logicalised framework of the Reformed Faith in the *Westminster Confession of Faith.* That was a tension that was accentuated by the so-called Evangelical Revival and the teaching of John Wesley and George Whitefield, which had the effect on the Erskine family and their friends of deepening their concern for Christ as personal Saviour and giving a sharper evangelical edge to their own preaching of the Gospel.[79]

---

[76] James Hadow, *The Antinomianism of the Marrow of Modern Divinity*, Edinburgh, 1722.

[77] Cf. *A Warning against Socinianism, Drawn up, and Published by a Committee of the Associate Synod*, Falkirk, 1788.

[78] But cf. James Hadow, *A Vindication of the Learned and Honourable Author of the History of the Apostles Creed, from the False Statements which Mr Simson has injuriously imputed to him in it.* Edinburgh, 1731.

[79] See *The Select Writings of the Rev. Ebenezer Erskine*, Vol. I, *Doctrinal Sermons*, Edited by David Smith, Edinburgh 1848; and *The Whole Works of Ebenezer Erskine*, 4 vols., London, 1871; *A Collection of Sermons by Ebenezer and Ralph Erskine*, ed. Thomas Bradbury, 3 vols., London, 1738–50. D. Fraser, *The Life and Diary of Ralph Erskine*, Edinburgh, 1834. Also James Fisher, *The Assembly's Shorter Catechism*, Glasgow, 1753 & 1760.

'During all this time', that is, after 1740, as John Macpherson has pointed out,

the Seceders were busying themselves as evangelists, and great spiritual quickening took place throughout the country. It cannot be doubted that their fervid evangelistic preaching did much to prepare the people for that remarkable period of the revival in the years immediately following. Strange to say these movements when they came about found in those very men whose work led up to them the most bitter and persistent opponents. Undoubtedly in giving this invitation the Secession fathers had primarily in view the spiritual reviving of the people, but, unfortunately, they sought to bind down their guest to work exclusively in co-operation with them. Whitefield after consideration, declared this impossible, and when it was found that the evangelist was ready to preach in any pulpit that would open to him, the rigid Seceders drew off from him and denounced him as a Latitudinarian in severe and altogether indefensible terms. Mr Whitefield continued his work as an evangelist throughout various parts of the Church of Scotland during 1742. The evangelical ministers of the Church of Scotland opened their pulpits to him and gave him a hearty welcome and ready assistance.[80]

Another John Brown, of Haddington, 1722–87, also played an important role in this eighteenth-century development in shaping theology in Scotland, and helped further to give a more evangelical and biblical slant to its understanding of the Westminster Tradition. Self-taught, he became a considerable scholar in Latin, Greek, Semitic and Oriental languages; he had been greatly influenced by the theology and churchmanship of Boston and the Marrow men, and of Ebenezer Erskine and James Fisher,[81] and served the Associate Synod as a Professor. His theological influence was furthered by his son, John Brown of Whitburn, who became well known for his book entitled *Gospel Truth*, a volume on the Secession theology occasioned by the republication of *The Marrow of Modern*

---

[80] John Macpherson, *A History of the Church of Scotland, From the Earliest Times to the Present Day*, Paisley & London, 1901.

[81] See his work *The Assembly's Shorter Catechism Explained, By Way of Question and Answer, In Two Parts*, Edinburgh, 1753.

Divinity,[82] to which reference has already been made. Of Fisher's Catechism John Macleod has written:

> This exposition of *The Synod's Catechism* attained a greater vogue than any other in Scotland, even than Willison's, though this was very much in use. Fisher's catechism thus exercised more of a formative influence in moulding the thoughts of religious homes and in making so many more people of Scotland skilled in theological matters than did any other single catechetical expository of the Shorter Catechism.[83]

In Fisher's exposition of the *Shorter Catechism* the doctrine of the Trinity was given a rather fuller and more integral place in faith than in the *Westminster Confession*, as necessary for our knowledge of the love of the Father,[84] even in relation to the Incarnation and the sacrifice of Christ, while it is pointed out that the sacrifice of Christ was laid on the altar 'in the first moment of his incarnation'.[85] The covenant of grace was called a covenant of *grace* because it is a covenant of eternal life and salvation to sinners, to be given them in a way of free grace and mercy. No distinction was made between a covenant of redemption and the covenant of grace, for the conditions of the covenant had been completely fulfilled in Christ.[86] However, all this was still defined in the old Westminster way through the contractual frame of a relation between God and man, in which the Father and the Son were held to be the two 'party-contractors', in fulfilment of God's good pleasure who from eternity had elected some to everlasting life. Christ himself was 'not the cause of election' (as Calvin had taught), although he was sent by the free love of God.[87] Christ is not said to be the Head of the human race, the Second Adam, but only 'the head and representative of his spiritual seed'.[88] This meant that through his death and sacrifice Christ satisfied divine justice and purchased redemption for the elect only, and not for all mankind.[89]

---

[82] John Brown, *Gospel Truth*.
[83] John Macleod, *Scottish Theology*, Edinburgh, 1943, p. 179.
[84] James Fisher, *Shorter Catechism Explained*, 6. Q., 1849 edn, pp. 42–8.
[85] Q. 23, p. 127; see also p. 357.
[86] Q. 20, pp. 98–102.
[87] *Shorter Catechism Explained*, p. 97.
[88] *Shorter Catechism Explained*, p. 100.
[89] *Shorter Catechism Explained*, pp. 96–104.

While it was allowed that in some sense Christ died for all people so that the Gospel could be offered to all, it could not be said that Christ actually took the place of all people in any real sense, as if his atonement were causally efficacious for all. It was efficient only for the elect, for those for whom there had taken place a definite transaction.[90] The rejection of anything like 'universal redemption as to purchase' left the Secession teaching with the difficulty of understanding and presenting the Gospel offer.[91]

The solution Fisher's Catechism offered was one in which the threefold office or *triplex munus* of Christ was expounded in the order prophet, priest and king,[92] which allowed him to detach the office and work of prophet from that of priest in a way that was not according to the teaching of John Calvin for whom the office of prophet derived from and was subsidiary to that of priest.[93] This allowed Fisher to state in the Catechism that Christ as a *prophet* makes all welcome to come and be taught by him 'in the outward dispensation of the Gospel, for he casts open the door for every man and woman, saying, Come unto me and learn of me'.[94] But it was otherwise with Christ as *priest*, for his saving work death and resurrection, his satisfaction on earth and his intercession in heaven, were said to avail only for the elect, and not for all

---

[90] Cf. the protest by Adam Gibb at the publication by Thomas Mair in 1740 of *A Treatise of Justifying Faith*, by James Fraser of Brae. In support of his attack on a doctrine of universal redemption he arranged for the republication of John Owen's book on *The Death of Christ*. Adam Gibb nevertheless upheld the views of Thomas Boston about *The Marrow of Modern Divinity*. See his work, ΚΑΙΝΑ ΚΑΙ ΠΑΛΑΙΑ. *Sacred Contemplations: In Three Parts. 1. A View of the Covenant of Works... 2. A View of the Covenant of Grace... 3. A View of the Absolute and Immediate Dependence of All things in God*, Edinburgh, 1786.

[91] *Shorter Catechism Explained*, pp. 359f.

[92] *Shorter Catechism Explained*, pp. 118ff. Cf. the Westminster *Larger Catechism*, 43–5, and the *Shorter Catechism* 24–6, and my account in *The School of Faith*, pp. lxxxvii–xcv, ciiif. Cf. Adam Gibb who presents the order of the Threefold Office of Christ as 'Priest, King and Prophet', *Sacred Contemplations*, pp. 2554ff.

[93] While in the *Institutio* Calvin expounded the *triplex munus* in the order of prophet, priest and King, he usually gave priority to the office of priest, often citing Malachi 2:7–9, 'The lips of the priest should guard knowledge, and men should seek instruction from his mouth, for he is the messenger of the Lord.' (e.g. *Commentaries on the Twelve Minor Prophets*, Vol. 5, pp. 27ff.). For Calvin the ministry of God's Word was a primary feature of *priesthood*, properly understood. Hence for the most part, like the Scriptures themselves, he referred only to the priestly and kingly offices. See J. F. Jansen, *Calvin's Doctrine of the Work of Christ*, London, 1956.

[94] *Shorter Catechism Explained*, p.124.

mankind.[95] This had the effect of introducing serious problems into the understanding of the Incarnation not as the incarnate Son of God in whom all humanity is taken up, but as One who has united to himself individual members of the human race only, which opened the door to Socinian and Nestorian error. And of course it also opened the door to unnatural interpretations of biblical statements about 'the authentic gospel-offer'.[96] This return to a closed deterministic way of thinking was to encase their Reformed Faith once again in the old hard logico-causal framework of a contractual federalism which restricted their evangelical outlook and mission, evident in their understanding of the sacraments. When the leaders of the Secession renewed adherence to the National Covenant and Solemn League and Covenant in 1743 (the effect of which had always been to politicise Scottish theology), the Secession moved away from the stance of the Marrow men, and became something of a faction, lapsing into a sectarian rigidity which closed the door to the influence of the evangelical revival that began to be felt in Calvinist Scotland through the preaching of George Whitefield in 1741 and 1742, and 1759.[97] This led inevitably to sad divisions in the Secession witness.[98]

In the second half of the eighteenth century, in spite of fresh theological thinking that had been taking place, it was for the most part the double contribution of moderate Evangelicals and evangelical Moderates that provided the theology of the Church of Scotland with its prevailing character. In it philosophical, theological, liturgical and evangelical concern, not least in relation to life in the parish, in spite of ecclesiastical and political

---

[95] *Shorter Catechism Explained*, pp. 128ff. This way of coping with the problem of the Gospel offer to all, may have been suggested by a passage in Samuel Rutherford's *The Covenant of Life Opened*, Part II, Ch. X, pp. 339ff, where he spoke of Christ procuring the preaching of the Gospel to reprobates, but did not undertake for them as High Priest. Rutherford, however, thought of the *triplex munus* in Calvin's more usual way as king, priest and prophet.

[96] Cf. the interpretation of John 3.16, *Shorter Catechism Explained*, pp. 359f.

[97] Cf. James Fisher's criticism of the Cambuslang and Kilsyth revivals, *A Review of the Preface to a Narrative of the Extraordinary Work at Kilsyth and Cambuslang*, Glasgow, 1743; and also the document entitled *The Declaration of the True Presbyterians within the Kingdom of Scotland concerning Mr George Whitefield, and the work at Cambuslang and other Places*, 1742.

[98] Cf. John Macpherson, *A History of the Church in Scotland, From The Earliest Times to the Present Day*, Paisley and London, 1901, pp. 324f. Note the results of this sectarianism still reflected in *Testimony of the United Associate Synod of the Secession Church, In Two parts, Historical and Doctrinal.* Edinburgh, 1827.

differences, presented a uniform face in their more urbane adherence to the *Confession of Faith* and in their concern for Christian learning in the universities and in the schools. Evangelicals of a more ardent kind continued to be evident in Secession and Relief churches, 'within the Church of Scotland' – as A. J. Campbell has pointed out, 'Evangelicalism and Moderatism were often little more than slightly different versions of the same thing.'[99]

It is perhaps in the historic Kirk of the Greyfriars in Edinburgh that we get our clearest glimpse of the relation between the Moderates and the Evangelicals, in the way in which William Robertson the Moderate and John Erskine the Evangelical shared the ministry for forty years. Both adhered strictly to the Westminster Standards, but they also shared in a common liturgical interest which Robert Lee was later to develop, and in the regular parish work with its care for the poor. There were divergences in their party adherence in the General Assembly, and while William Robertson, as Principal of Edinburgh University had wider interests in history and literature, John Erskine, though no less learned in classical and modern philosophy was more devoted to evangelical preaching of the Gospel (like the Calvinist Whitefield rather than John Wesley!), to frequent celebrations of the Lord's Supper, and in general to raising the standard of Gospel proclamation throughout the Kirk.[100] It was in preaching that the contrast between Evangelicals and Moderates was greatest, evident in the contrast between John Erskine and William Blair, but also in a more rigid adherence to Westminster orthodoxy even with its allowance for the light of nature.[101] What really divided the Moderates and the Evangelicals was not Westminster Theology, however, but the issues of lay patronage and Kirk discipline through the General Assembly, issues that were eventually to play a role in the Disruption.

Interestingly the differences between the Evangelicals and Moderates could cross over from one to the other! This was nowhere more evident after the turn of the century than when

[99] A. J. Campbell, *Two Centuries of the Church of Scotland 1707–1929*, pp. 100f.

[100] See John Erskine's *Theological Dissertations*, Edinburgh, 1764.

[101] Cf. the increasing tendency among eighteenth-century Churchmen toward appreciation of natural religion, castigated in the satirical essay of John Witherspoon, *Ecclesiastical Characteristics: or, the Arcana of Church Policy. Collected Works*, Vol. VI, Edinburgh, 1805, pp. 139–222.

the Edinburgh Town Council wanted to appoint to the Chair of Mathematics a brilliant scientist, John Leslie, who was reported to have spoken favourably of David Hume. The Moderates opposed him in their preference for Thomas Macknight, the minister of Trinity College Church, but the Evangelicals supported the Council and won the day! As Campbell remarks : 'The Evangelicals championed the man who had spoken in praise of Hume; the Moderates stood for orthodoxy and the Confession of Faith.'[102] Partisanship overrode conviction. Later on in the century, however, both Evangelicals and Moderates, Moderate Evangelicals and Evangelical Moderates, joined in deposing John MacLeod Campbell due to their shared adherence to the Westminster Standards and fear of anything that might undermine the very subscription to those Standards which, ministers claimed, 'secured them their emoluments'!

Foreign missions

William Robertson and John Erskine of Old Greyfriars were both favourable to the idea that the Gospel should be carried to the heathen world. The same was true of Colin MacLaurin's brother, John, who covenanted with several friends to pray that God would 'revive true religion in all parts of Christendom ... and fill the whole earth with his glory.'[103] On the whole the Church of Scotland was too tied to the narrow outlook upon the world that stemmed from the rigid principles of its Westminster tradition, but along with the wider horizon being opened up through colonial expansion and overseas trade, a change began to take place in the conscience of the Kirk. This was due to a large extent to a fresh approach to the Scriptures, and not least as a result of the evangelical preaching of people like George Whitefield and Robert and James Haldane, which was most notable in Secession congregations. Then in 1796 a debate took place in the General Assembly in which the whole question of missionary activity at home and abroad was raised, when the door for foreign missions was not closed but left open, with the decision that the General Assembly 'will embrace with thankfulness any future opportunity of contributing by their

[102] A. J. Campbell, *Two Centuries*, p. 162.
[103] Cited by Andrew Walls, 'Missions', *Dictionary of Scottish Church History and Theology*, p. 568.

exertions to the propagation of the Gospel'. A. J. Campbell remarked, 'Alone of Scottish churches the Burghers gave hearty official support to the missionary societies'.[104]

Undoubtedly what lay behind the reluctance of people to take seriously Christ's command to proclaim the Gospel to all the world was the old Calvinistic conception of limited atonement and the doctrine of God with which it was bound up. It was only when William Carey broke with the doctrine of limited atonement, with which the Baptist Church had been infected through Dutch hyper-Calvinism, that he embarked on his missionary enterprise in India. Such a breach in theological tradition was rather more difficult in Scotland, but it began to come about, not first through a basic change in doctrine, but through steady evangelical pressure upon the minds of ministers for evangelism at home, and upon prominent Churchmen like John Erskine and Thomas Chalmers who gave a lead to the General Assembly.[105] At last in 1825 sixty-one years after the 1796 Assembly, a decisive step was taken at the General Assembly when John Inglis, not an Evangelical but a Moderate, made the motion which led the Church to send Alexander Duff, one of Chalmers' St Andrews students, as a missionary to India.

There can be no question that the missionary activity of the Church of Scotland abroad had an evangelical impact upon the Church at home which coincided with the rapid increase of evangelical ministers in the parishes, and deepened the missionary conscience of the Church. But what of the theology of the Kirk? How far were Evangelicals and Moderates who alike resolutely and consistently adhered to the Westminster Standards, ready for basic change? How far were people in the Church ready to heed the call to discover what John Witherspoon spoke of as 'the real nature of God'? He laid emphasis upon the infinite majesty and transcendent glory of the living God, but of God as revealed in the face of Jesus Christ and in his atoning sacrifice. What of the truth 'that he spared not his own Son but delivered him up for us all' in Christ? 'How shall we sufficiently wonder at the boundless mercy of the Father, and the infinite condescension of the Son?'[106]

---

[104] *Two Centuries*, p. 155. It was from the Burghers in the next century that Dr David Watt Torrance was sent out as a missionary to the Jews in Palestine.

[105] See especially Thomas Chalmers, 'On the Universality of the Gospel', *Institutes of Theology*, Edinburgh, 1849, Vol. II, pp. 403–13.

[106] John Witherspoon, 'A Practical Essay on Regeneration', *Collected Works*, Vol. I, pp. 231ff & 304ff.

That was the great question, the question as to *the real nature of God* that faced the Kirk with the teaching of Thomas Erskine and the preaching of John MacLeod Campbell. What was undoubtedly at stake was indeed the doctrine of God.[107] It is the question whether the God whom we worship is a God of eternal inflexible necessity behind the back of Jesus Christ, or whether he is none other than the Father, the Son and the Holy Spirit, the One Adorable Trinity whom we know only in and through the incarnate self-revelation of the Father through the Son and in Communion of the Holy Spirit.

Bibliography

Acts of the General Assembly of the Church of Scotland, 1700, 1720 & 1722.

Anonymous, *The Declaration of the True Presbyterians within the Kingdom of Scotland concerning Mr George Whitefield, and the work at Cambuslang and other Places*, Glasgow, 1742.

Ayton, Thomas, of Alyth, *The Original Constitution of the Christian Church within the Extremes on either Hand are Stated and Examined. To which is added an appendix containing, The Rise of the Jure Divino Prelatists, and an answer to their arguments by Episcopal Divines*, Edinburgh, 1730.

Barclay, John, *Rejoice Evermore: or, Christ All in All, An Original Publication; consisting of Spiritual Songs, collected from the Holy Scriptures; and several of the Psalms, together with the Whole Song of Solomon, paraphrased*, Glasgow, 1767.

Beaton, Donald, 'The Marrow of Modern Divinity' and the Marrow Controversy' *Records of the Scottish Church History Society*, Vol. 1, 1926, pp. 112–34.

Blackwell, Thomas, *Ratio sacra, or, An appeal unto the rational world about the reasonableness of revealed religion*, Edinburgh, 1710.

Boston, Thomas, *The Marrow of Modern Divinity, With Notes, The Complete Works of Thomas Boston*, Vol. 7.

Bradbury, Thomas, *A Collection of Sermons by Ebenezer and Ralph Erskine*, 3 vols., London, 1738–50.

Broadie, Alexander, *The Tradition of Scottish Philosophy*, Edinburgh, 1990.

---

[107] Thus also James Orr, *The Progress of Dogma*, London, 1901 – undated new edition, p. 292.

Brown, John, of Wamphray, *An Apologetical Relation, of the particular sufferings of the faithful ministers and professors of the Church of Scotland since August 1660*, Edinburgh, 1665.

Brown, John, of Wamphray, *Christ the Way, the Truth, and the Life*, Rotterdam, 1677 and Edinburgh, 1839.

Brown, John, of Wamphray, *De Causa Dei contra Antisabbatarios Tractatus*, 3 vols., Rotterdam, 1774–6.

Brown, John, of Wamphray, *An Exposition of Romans, with large practical observations*, Edinburgh, 1766.

Brown, John, of Wamphray, *Libri duo contra Volzogenium et contra Velthusium*, Amsterdam, 1670.

Brown, John, of Wamphray, *A Pious and Elaborate Treatise Concerning Prayer; and the answer to Prayer*, Edinburgh, 1720, Glasgow, 1745, 1822.

Brown, John, of Wamphray, *The Life of Justification Opened*, 1695.

Brown, John, of Wamphray, *The Mirror, or Looking-Glass for Saint and Saviour*, Glasgow, 1793.

Brown, John, of Whitburn, *Gospel Truth Accurately Stated and Illustrated by The Rev. Messrs James Hog, Thomas Boston, Ebenezer and Ralph Erskine, and Others, Occasioned by The Republication of The Marrow of Modern Divinity*, Edinburgh, 1817, Glasgow, 1831.

Buchanan, Dughall, *Laoidhe Spioradail*, 1767 / *Spiritual Songs*, tr. by L. Macbean, Edinburgh, 1884.

Calderwood, David, *The Altar of Damascus*, 1621.

Calderwood, David, *Altare Damascenum seu Ecclesiae Anglicanae Politia*, 1708.

Campbell, A. J., *Two Centuries of the Church of Scotland, 1707–1929*, Paisley, 1930.

Campbell, Daniel, *Sacramental meditations on the sufferings and death of Christ*, 7th edn, London, 1723.

Campbell, George, *A Dissertation on Miracles*, Edinburgh, 1766.

Campbell, George, *The Philosophy of Rhetorick*, Edinburgh, 1776, 1776.

Chalmers, Thomas, *Institutes of Theology*, Edinburgh, 1849.

Clarke, Samuel, *Scripture and the Doctrine of the Trinity*, London, 1712.

Cowan, Henry, *The Influence of the Scottish Church in Christendom*, London, 1896.

Doyle, Ian B., 'The Doctrine of the Church in the Later Covenanting Period', in *Reformation and Revolution, Essays Presented to the Very Rev. Hugh Watt*, ed. Duncan Shaw, Edinburgh, 1967.

Edward, Robert, *The Doxology Approven, Or, The Singing Glory to the Father, Son and Holy Ghost in the Worship of God*, Edinburgh, 1731.

Erskine, Ebenezer, *Christ in the Believer's Arms*, Edinburgh, 1726.

Erskine, Ebenezer, *The Whole Works of Ebenezer Erskine*, London, 1871.

Erskine, John, *Theological Dissertations*, Edinburgh, 1764.

Erskine, Ralph, *Gospel Sonnets Spiritual Songs*, Edinburgh, 1720.

Findlay, Robert, *A Persuasive to the enlargement of psalmody, by a minister of the Church of Scotland*, Glasgow, 1763.

Fisher, James, *The Assembly's Shorter Catechism Explained by Way of Question and Answer in Two Parts*, Edinburgh, 1753.

Fisher, James, *A Review of the Preface to a Narrative of the Extraordinary Work at Kilsyth and Cambuslang*, Glasgow, 1743.

Flint, Robert, *Examen Doctrinae D: Johannis Simson, S.S.T. In Celebri Academia Glasguensi Professoris*, Edinburgh, 1717.

Fraser, D., *The Life and Diary of Ralph Erskine*, Edinburgh, 1834.

Geddes, William, *The Saint's Recreation upon the Estate of Grace*, 2nd edn Glasgow, 1753.

Gibb, Adam, ΚΑΙΝΑ ΚΑΙ ΠΑΛΑΙΑ *Sacred Contemplations in Three Parts. 1. A View of the Covenant of Works ... 2. A View of the Covenant of Grace ... 3. A View of the Absolute and Immediate Dependence of all Things on God: In a Discourse concerning Liberty and Necessity*, Edinburgh, 1786.

Hadow, James, *The Antinomianism of the Marrow of Modern Divinity*, Edinburgh, 1722.

Hadow, James, *The Record of God and the Duty of Faith Therein Required*, Edinburgh, 1719.

Hadow, James, *A Vindication of the Learned and Honourable Author of the History of the Apostles Creed, from the False Statements which Mr Simson has injuriously imputed to him in it*, Edinburgh, 1731.

Halyburton, Thomas, *An Essay on the Ground or Formal Reason of Saving Faith*, 1865 edn.

Halyburton, Thomas, *Natural Religion Insufficient, and Reveal'd Necessary to Man's Happiness in his present state*, Edinburgh, 1714.

Halyburton, Thomas, *Sermons preached before and after the celebration of the Sacrament of the Lord's Supper*, Edinburgh, 1721.

Hog, James, Republication of *The Marrow of Modern Divinity* by Edward Fisher, Edinburgh, 1717.

Hog, James, *Remarks Concerning the Spirit's Operation and the Difference between Law and Gospel*, Edinburgh, 1701.

Hog, James, *Select Notes towards Detecting a Covered Mixture of the Covenant of Works and of Grace*, Edinburgh, 1706.

Hume, David, *Dialogues Concerning Natural Religion*, Edinburgh, 1779.

Jansen, J. F., *Calvin's Doctrine of the Work of Christ*, London, 1956.

Lachman, D. C., *The Marrow Controversy*, Edinburgh, 1988.

McClaren, John, *The new scheme of doctrine contained in the answers of Mr John Simson, Professor of Divinity in the College of Glasgow, to Mr. Webster's libel, considered and examined*, Edinburgh, 1717.

Maclagan, Douglas J., *The Scottish Paraphrases*, Edinburgh, 1889, with an account of *Translations and Paraphrases, in Verse, of actual passages of Sacred Scriptures*, Edinburgh, 1781.

MacLeod, John, *John MacLaurin, 1693–1754, Glasgow; his life, work thought*, unpublished thesis, New College, Edinburgh, 1968.

Macleod, John, *Scottish Theology*, Edinburgh, 1943.

Macpherson, John, *The Doctrine of the Church in Scottish Theology*, Edinburgh, 1903.

Macpherson, John, *A History of the Church in Scotland, From the Earliest Times down to the Present Day*, Paisley & London, 1901.

Moncrieff, Alexander, of Culfargie, *The Practical Works, In Two Volumes*, Edinburgh, 1779.

Olson, Richard, *Scottish Philosophy and British Physics, 1750–1880*, Princeton, 1975.

Orr, James, *The Progress of Dogma*, London, 1901.

Owen, John, *The Death of Christ*, Edinburgh, 1755.

Patrick, Millar, *Four Centuries of Scottish Psalmody*, London, 1949.

The Psalms of David in Meter. Newly Translated and Compared with the Original Text and former Translations. Allowed by the General Assembly of the Church of Scotland, 1693.

Reid, H. M. B., *The Divinity Professors of the University of Glasgow, 1640–1903*, Glasgow, 1923.

Robe, James, *Narratives of the extraordinary work of the Holy Spirit of God at Cambuslang, Kilsyth, etc., begun in 1742*, Glasgow, 1790.

Rollock, Robert, *God's Effectual Calling*, Works, Vol. 1, 1848.

Simson, Patrick, *Spiritual Songs or, Holy Poems. A Garden of True Delight*, Edinburgh, 1685–6.

Tate, N. & Brady, N., *A New Version of the Psalms of David, Together with Hymns adapted for Christian Worship, and set to Musick, by J. Z. Triemer*, Amsterdam, 1772.

Torrance, James B., 'The Incarnation and "Limited Atonement"', *The Evangelical Quarterly*, 55.3, Exeter, 1984, pp. 83–93.

Torrance, Thomas F., *et al.*, *Interim Report of the Special Commission on Baptism, General Assembly of the Church of Scotland*, Edinburgh, 1958.

Vincent, Thomas, *An Explicatory Catechism: or, An Explanation of the Assembly's Shorter Catechism*, Aberdeen, 1785.

Walker, James, *The Theology and Theologians of Scotland*, Edinburgh, 1888.

Walls, Andrew, 'Missions', N. M. de S. Cameron *et al.* (eds), *Dictionary of Scottish Church History and Theology*, Edinburgh, 1993, pp. 567ff.

Watt, Hugh, *The Published Writings of Thomas Chalmers (1780–1847)*, privately printed, 1943.

Webster, Alexander, *Divine Influence the spring of the extraordinary work at Cambuslang and other places in the West of Scotland*, Edinburgh, 1742.

Willison, John, *The Practical Works of John Willison, Minister of the Gospel at Dundee*, ed. W. M. Hetherington, London, 1844.

Willison, John, *A Sacramental Directory*, contained in *The Practical Works*, London, 1844.

Witherspoon, John, *Collected Works*, 9 vols., Edinburgh, 1804–5.

Witherspoon, John, *Treatises on Justification and Regeneration*, with an Introductory Essay by William Wilberforce, Glasgow, 1830.

Wodrow Society, *The Miscellany*, Vol. 1, ed. David Laing, 1844.

Wodrow Society, *Select Biographies*, 2 vols., ed. W. K. Tweedie, Edinburgh, 1845–7.

8

Early Nineteenth-Century Theology

The outlook of theology in the early decades of the nineteenth century may be indicated by reference to two prominent Churchmen, George Hill of St Andrews, a Calvinist theologian who put law before grace, and Thomas Erskine of Linlathen, an evangelical lawyer who put grace before law. For Hill, God is reconciled only on the ground of satisfaction made by vicarious punishment to the divine Lawgiver; for Erskine God cannot be spoken of as being reconciled, but only as he who was in Christ reconciling the world to himself. For Hill the grace connected with salvation is confined only to those whom God has chosen, but for Erskine it is freely and unconditionally offered to all. The basic issue had to do with the concept of God: *What kind of God is spoken of in the Gospel?* That was the question with which the General Assembly was faced in 1831.

George Hill (1750–1819)

Hill was first Professor of Greek, and then Principal of St Mary's College, St Andrews. While he was in the succession of James Hadow, the hard-line opponent of both 'the Marrow men' and John Simson, his hyper-Calvinism was moderated by an inherent rationalism and moralism. He published in his lifetime *Theological Institutes* in 1803, in which he presented as a kind of theological manifesto the outline of his understanding of 'Catholic opinion' interpreted in accordance with 'the Calvinist System', and also 'A View of the Constitution of the Church of Scotland', in which he took up a position which he held to be a mean between Socinian and Roman errors. In line with his strict adherence to the Calvinist and federal system, he held the covenant to have its source in the grace of God, but regarded it as a covenant involving 'mutual stipulations'. This is very clear, for example, in his concept of Baptism as 'a federal act' which he failed, almost entirely, to relate

257

to the Person of Christ.[1] While the blessings of the covenant admittedly flow from 'God's unchangeable love', there are nevertheless conditions in the covenant of grace which are to be pressed upon Christians to fulfil. He admitted that this is language which some of the first Reformers thought it dangerous to hold, and which unless it is properly explained, still sounds offensive to some people in view of the question of the extent of the covenant of grace. However, 'whether God intended to make a covenant of grace with all men, or whether he intended to make it only with those whom, from the beginning, he elected, it is allowed on both sides, that they only are saved who accept the covenant.'[2]

Hill's *Lectures on Divinity*, given to students in St Mary's College on the basis of his *Theological Institutes*, was not published until 1821, after he had died, when it was edited by his son Alexander Hill of Dailly.[3] Although Thomas Chalmers differed from Hill on important points, notably on his view of divine 'necessity' and 'the extent' of the atonement, as well as on 'Laik Patronage', he was later to make use of Hill's *Lectures on Divinity* in his own teaching at New College, Edinburgh, after the Disruption. Its significance for the history of Scottish theology lies not so much for its actual content as for the way in which Hill as the leading theologian in the Church of Scotland in his day, and as an evangelical Moderate adhering closely to the Westminster Standards, enables us to grasp something of the theological mind of the Kirk in the early decades of the nineteenth century.

The general character of Hill's theology is indicated by his claim to expound 'the two great doctrines, that God is, and that he is a rewarder of them that seek him'. This allowed him to operate with a groundwork of thought in natural religion, 'the belief in God which is founded on the constitution of the human mind', 'the primary Revelation which God gave to man by reason and conscience', although he interpreted it in the light of divine revelation.[4] While Christianity was of infinite importance, that

---

[1] This was a rationalisation and moralisation of the Calvinistic doctrine of Baptism. See the *Interim Report of the Special Commission on Baptism,* presented to the General Assembly, May, 1958, p. 54.

[2] *Lectures on Divinity,* edited by his son Alexander Hill, 4th edn, London, 1837, Vol. II, pp. 317f.

[3] Ten years later Alexander Hill spoke against John McLeod Campbell at the General Assembly.

[4] *Theological Institutes,* p. 6, & *Lectures on Divinity,* pp. 2ff. Cf. John Owen, *The Reason of Faith... Causes, Ways and Means, of Understanding the Mind of God as Revealed in His Word, with Assurance Therein,* Glasgow, 1801.

importance Hill 'considered as a republication of natural religion'![5] Two of Hill's doctrines in particular are of critical interest for us here, the Trinity and the atonement.

George Hill was one of the very few Scottish theologians since Robert Boyd, Hugh Binning and John Forbes of Corse to give serious attention to the doctrine of Holy Trinity. This was rather different from what happened in England and so it is not surprising that it was to English theologians that Hill turned for help and guidance in his understanding of the 'Orthodox' or 'Catholic System of the Trinity', to which the Reformed Churches all adhered. The theologian to which he was particularly indebted was Bishop George Bull of St Davids, in Wales, a staunch high-churchman, the author of a celebrated work in defence of the Nicene Creed and the trinitarian teaching of the Post-Nicene Fathers.[6] The long chapter in Hill's *Lectures on Divinity* is undoubtedly very competent in his handling of the teaching and technical theological terms like ὁμοούσιος and περιχώρησις used by the Greek Fathers.[7]

This calls for two comments. a) Hill's doctrine of the Trinity was one of modified subordinationism due to his acceptance of causal concepts and terminology in his account of inner trinitarian relations.[8] Thus while he held that the three divine Persons are inseparably and eternally joined to one another without losing their distinctiveness, he understood the expression 'God of God' to imply a distinction between the uncaused Deity of the Father and the caused Deity of the Son (and of the Spirit). He was apparently unaware that the expression 'God of God' had been dropped from the Nicene-Constantinopolitan Creed in order to avoid that very mistake! Full emphasis was laid at the Council of Constantinople upon '*True* God of *true* God', for the whole Being of God belongs to each of the divine Persons as it belongs to all of them, which is how John Calvin understood it.[9] Hill's use of 'God of God' enabled him to lay a rather Latin subordinationist emphasis on the Father as the *Principium Deitatis* in such a way as to retain unmodified his

5   *Institutes*, p. 31.
6   George Bull, *Defensio Fidei Nicaenae*, 1685.
7   Vol. 1, pp. 442–71.
8   *Institutes*, p. 64; Lectures, pp. 456, 465, 469. Cyril of Alexandria had actually rejected as 'monstrous' the use of causal terms to describe the relations between the three persons of the Trinity.
9   Cf. my account of Calvin's doctrine of the inner trinitarian relations, *Trinitarian Perspectives*, Edinburgh, 1994, pp. 54ff & 73f.

preconceived concept of God as Lawgiver, Judge, and Governor of the moral universe – thus the latter retained priority in his thought of God over the Fatherhood and Love of God. Unlike Calvin he did not think of the one God only and exclusively as Father, Son and Holy Spirit, or think that it was precisely as Father, Son and Holy Spirit that God is the omnipotent creator and ruler of the universe.[10] b) Hill's rather rationalistic account of Christian doctrines was one in which the truth of the truths he advocated lacked spiritual resonance in the mind and heart thereby establishing itself in the understanding of faith in an internal evidential and spiritual way. The latter was in line with Calvin's doctrine of 'the internal testimony of the Spirit'. That helps to explain why Hill's formal handling and presentation of Christian doctrine failed in the end to have much of an evangelical and revolutionary effect on his own ultimate concept of God derived from the federal system. Although he expounded his doctrine of the Holy Trinity only after his account of Christ and the Spirit, it apparently had little actual relation to Christian experience in Christ as the incarnate Son of the Father sent by him to be the Saviour of the world.[11]

Hill's doctrine of critical interest to us is undoubtedly that of the atonement, and its extent. In line with his rigid adherence to the 'federal system' with its concept of God as Lawgiver, Judge and Omnipotent Governor of the world, Hill was attracted to and heavily influenced by the *De Satisfactione Christi* of Hugo Grotius, the Dutch Arminian theologian,[12] who offered a 'governmental' account of atonement in strictly jurisprudential terms as satisfaction made by vicarious punishment to the Divine Lawgiver. Nevertheless, Hill's Calvinism, while strict enough in the tradition of the *Westminster Confession of Faith*, was of a milder type than that of some of his colleagues in the Kirk, for he had moved away from a rather harsh doctrine of God toward one more directly influenced by the teaching of Jesus 'the Messenger of the Divine grace, who declares that God is merciful'.[13] He spoke of the concept of vicarious substitution, in which an offering made to God and accepted by him 'in place of that which he was entitled', was

---

[10] John Calvin, *Institutio*, 1.13.2–5 & 17f.
[11] Contrast the work of Jonathan Edwards, *Treatise Concerning Religious Affections*, Edinburgh, 1772, a theologian whom George Hill admired on other grounds.
[12] Cf. *Institutes*, p. 78, and *Lectures*, Vol. II, p. 50.
[13] *Institutes*, p. 73.

understood as magnifying the mercy of the Lawgiver.[14] Hence with Hill we find some place given to *the love of God* for the human race which led him to accept the sufferings of a substitute.

> When we behold the Son of God descending from heaven, that he might bear our sins in his body on the tree, and the forgiveness of sins preached through the name of a crucified Saviour, we read in the charter which conveys our pardon, that there is a deep malignity in sin, and we learn to adore the kindness and love of God which at such a price, brought us deliverance.[15]

Hill justified these views by appealing to the passages in the New Testament about reconciliation with God through the sacrificial sufferings of Christ which he interpreted with reference to the ceremonial law of atoning sacrifice in the Old Testament understood in terms of expiating the wrath of God and gaining his favour.[16]

When it came to discussing the extent of the atonement Hill presented his understanding of it within 'the Calvinistic system', in support of a doctrine of 'particular redemption' and with extended refutation of the views of Arminians and Socinians. The question at issue was whether 'Christ died for all men, or only for those who shall finally be saved by him'. There is no problem, he said, about the sufficiency of Christ's death for the world, for 'the sufferings of Christ have a value sufficient to atone for the sins of all the children of Adam, from the beginning to the end of time, yet only those shall be saved by this atonement who repent and believe in him.'[17] This was followed up by a discussion of opinions on predestination,[18] in which he took his stand squarely within the Calvinist System.[19] 'Calvinists consider the Grace connected with

---

[14] *Lectures*, Vol. II, p. 56.

[15] *Lectures*, Vol. II, p. 63.

[16] *Lectures*, Vol II, pp. 64–114. Contrast the view of his contemporary George Stevenson, minister of the Gospel at Ayr, who held that the doctrine of atonement is 'in no way inconsistent with the gratuitous nature of forgiveness', and wrote: 'God is nowhere in Scripture represented as moved, or inclined by the death of Christ to save sinners.' *A Dissertation on the Atonement*, 2nd edn, Edinburgh 1817, p. 209. At the same time he objected to 'the immoral doctrine of universal restoration', p. 223.

[17] *Lectures*, Vol. II, p. 142.

[18] *Lectures*, Vol. II, pp. 151ff.

[19] *Lectures*, Vol. II, pp. 142ff, 224ff.

salvation as confined to those whom God hath chosen.'[20] Of crucial significance here for Hill was the old argument adapted from the ninth Chapter of St Paul's Epistle to the Romans, 'Jacob have I loved, but Esau have I hated', which he did not interpret in the context of St Paul's argument about the remnant. The point that Hill was concerned to make is that while divine election was aboriginally general in Adam, it took a progressively discriminating and restrictive form in the Old Testament account of God's relations with Israel, which Hill adduced in justification for the Calvinist doctrine of the double decree of 'preterition and condemnation', according to which out of the whole body of mankind God chose certain persons determined before hand by divine decree.[21]

Hill seemed to have no idea of the biblical teaching about the *election of one for the many* found both in the Old Testament and in the New Testament, and of the idea that the redemptive purpose of God for all nations of the earth was narrowed down to Israel, to a *remnant*, and then in the most intensive way to Jesus in the midst of Israel, and was fulfilled in and through him in a universal way for *all mankind*. Thus in respect of the people of Israel St Paul pointed to the fact that from the remnant of Israel the universalising purpose of God will lead to the point when '*all Israel shall be saved*'.[22] Instead, Hill limited the universal sufficiency and extent of Christ's atoning redemption by a notion of specific 'destination', governed by God's eternal degree, of only certain individuals for ultimate salvation. Regarded from the end result, therefore, the penal satisfaction offered by Christ in his sacrificial death was held to be actually and finally effectual only for *particular* people. Thus even for George Hill, this evangelical moderate who sought to restore, in some measure at least, the place of the love and mercy of God to its primary place in redemption, the atonement was essentially and rigidly limited in its nature and extent. The question had to be asked, therefore, as indeed it was by Thomas Chalmers, *what kind of God does this imply?* That was the great question with which the General Assembly was faced in 1830, with McLeod Campbell's revolt against the idea of God that lay behind the doctrine of predestination and limited atonement in

---

[20] *Institutes*, p. 98.
[21] *Lectures*, Vol. II, pp. 228ff; and *Institutes*, p. 95.
[22] Romans 11.26.

what George Hill regularly referred to as 'the Calvinistic System' that prevailed in the Kirk.

Thomas Erskine of Linlathen (1788–1870)

With Thomas Erskine the evangelical Calvinism of the Marrow men mediated through the Secession theologians, Ebenezer and Ralph Erskine especially, was taken out of its particular field in the Secession Churches and thrown into the midst of the theological thinking in the Kirk. He was also one of those who were familiar with the *Treatise on Justifying Faith*, by James Fraser of Brae.[23] Thomas Erskine was the nephew of the Evangelical Leader, John Erskine of Greyfriars, and was one of the most prominent and respected lawyers in Edinburgh who as a layman was not fettered by formal submission to the *Westminster Confession of Faith*, but was nevertheless completely faithful to the Nicene Creed and the catholic theology of the Orthodox Church Fathers and of the great Reformers.[24] He was not himself an academic theologian, but his concern for 'theological science'[25] and the saving relevance of Christian doctrine for daily life which he shared in personal and epistolary contact with Thomas Chalmers forced him into public theological discussion in the publication of his book *Remarks on the Internal Evidence for the Truth of Revealed Religion*.[26] This was followed by others: *An Essay on Faith*,[27] *The Brazen Serpent, or Life coming through Death*,[28] *The Doctrine of Election, and its connection with the General Tenor of Christianity, illustrated from many passages of Scripture, and especially from the Epistle to the Romans*,[29]

---

[23] See *Extracts of Letters to a Christian Friend by A Lady, with An Introductory Essay*, by Thomas Erskine, Greenock, 1830, with an Appendix, pp. 59–71, devoted to lengthy citations from *Justifying Faith*.

[24] See the balanced and sympathetic account of Erskine's theology by Trevor A. Hart, *The Teaching Father, An Introduction to the Theology of Thomas Erskine of Linlathen*, Edinburgh, 1993, pp. 18–53, published with selections from his writings.

[25] Cf. *The Spiritual Order and Other Papers*, Edinburgh, 2nd edn, 1876, p. 31.

[26] Edinburgh, 1820.

[27] Edinburgh, 1822.

[28] Edinburgh, 1831, 3rd edn, 1879. The title of this book may well have been suggested by Erskine's reading of *Justifying Faith*, by James Fraser of Brae, pp. 136, 171, 319ff. See also William McEwen, *Grace and Truth, or the Glory and Fulness of the Redeemer Displayed*, Edinburgh 1811, pp. 125–31.

[29] Edinburgh, 1837, 2nd edn, 1878.

The Spiritual Order and Other Papers selected from the manuscripts of the late Thomas Erskine.[30]

His object was to raise questions about the bearing of Christian doctrines on the character of God and to show the intelligible and necessary connection between them. What worried him was the fact that there was a serious discrepancy between the content of the Gospel of the saving love of God and the rather stern notion people entertained about God which had little moral influence on their lives. The atonement was severely misunderstood through what he held to be moral fictions, salvation and justification were held to depend partly on people's own obedience and partly on the atoning efficacy of Christ's sacrifice – in fact there seemed to be such a separation between the views and character of the Son and of the Father that it undermined the divinity of Christ as much as Socinianism![31] 'I feel that to separate the work of Christ and the character of God is Socinianism.'[32] Erskine protested that this was not in accordance with the message of the Bible about the nature of God as Holy Love who is at once just and merciful, about the Fatherhood of God and the intrinsic relation between the incarnate Son and the Father, and about the true Gospel offer of free unconditional pardon through the forgiving love of God. It was above all the understanding which people had of the character of God that was the crucial issue.

> The surpassing kindness and tenderness demonstrated in the cross of Christ, and the full satisfaction there rendered to his violated law, when understood and believed, must sweep away all doubts and fears with regard to God's disposition towards him [the sinner], and must waken in his heart that sentiment of grateful and reverential attachment which is the spiritual seed of the heavenly inheritance. 'If, when we were enemies, we were reconciled to God by the death of his Son, much more being reconciled, we shall be saved by his living love.'[33]

---

[30] Published posthumously in Edinburgh, 1871.
[31] *Internal Evidence*, pp. 16ff & 116–20.
[32] *Letters of Thomas Erskine of Linlathen*, ed. William Hanna, Edinburgh, 1878, p. 194. Socinianism was a heresy levelled by Andrew Thomson against Erskine and his friends! Cf. *The Doctrine of Universal Pardon Considered and Refuted in a Series of Sermons, with Notes, Critical and Expository*, Edinburgh, 1830, pp. 257 & 414.
[33] *Ibid.* pp. 136f.

It was the personal relation between God and man and God's personal dealings with man through Christ and his reconciling work that were of paramount importance for Erskine.[34]

Undoubtedly what roused Erskine was the persistent teaching in the Kirk about divine predestination and the limitation of the atonement it involved, for they put severe question marks in people's minds about the nature of the love of God and undermined their assurance of salvation.[35] 'What view does this doctrine give of the character of God? And what influence is the belief of it fitted to exercise on the character of man?'[36] This made him question and think through the currently held doctrine of election.

> The doctrine of election generally held is that God, according to his inscrutable purpose, has from all eternity chosen in Christ, and predestinated unto salvation, a certain number of individuals out of the fallen race of Adam; and that, in pursuance of this purpose, as these individuals came into the world, He in due season visits them by a peculiar operation of His Spirit, thereby justifying and sanctifying and saving them; whilst He passes by the rest of the race, unvisited by that peculiar operation of the Spirit, and so abandoned to their sins and their punishment.

He held this doctrine for many years, 'modified, however inconsistently, by the belief of God's love to all, and of Christ having died for all.' He had not so much believed it as submitted to it because he did not see how the language of the ninth chapter of the Epistle to the Romans and a few similar passages could bear any other interpretation.[37] And yet he realised that to accept the current view of double predestination the meaning of many other passages of Scripture had to be forced to bring them into agreement with it. 'I could not help feeling that, on account of what appeared to be the meaning of these few difficult passages, I

---

[34] *The Spiritual Order*, p. 49.
[35] For a moderate view of assurance, cf. Thomas Watson, *A Body of Practical Divinity, Consisting of Above One Hundred and Seventy-Six Sermons on The Shorter Catechism*, Vol. I, pp. 257ff & Vol. II, pp. 284f. New edn, London, 1807.
[36] *Internal Evidence*, p. 116.
[37] *The Doctrine of Election*, pp. 1f. See the *Letters of Thomas Erskine of Linlathen*, pp. 554f; and also H. F. Henderson, *Erskine of Linlathen. Selections and Biography*, Edinburgh, 1899, pp. 251f.

was giving up the plain and obvious meaning of all the rest of the Bible.'[38]

However, when he examined more carefully the teaching of St Paul about election in the light of related passages from the Old as well as the New Testament, not least the ninth chapter of the Epistle to the Romans in the light of the eighteenth chapter of Jeremiah to which it refers, he found it could not bear the usual Calvinist interpretation of it in terms of the double form of election as predestination and reprobation, but found it to be consistent with the 'unforced natural meaning' of passages in the New Testament about the Gospel of the redeeming love of God for all mankind.[39] As a result he concluded on *biblical grounds* that the doctrine of election was 'just another name for the doctrine of free grace. It teaches that all men are under deserved condemnation, and therefore can have no claim on God for pardon; and that this, and all other mercies, are the gifts of his *own free bounty and choice*.'[40] Election has to do with the objectivity of saving grace. 'The ground on which pardon is proclaimed is a thing independent altogether of our believing in it, because it is firm and sufficient of itself, whether we believe in it or not.'[41] That does not mean that the response of faith may be set aside, but that the response of faith is not itself part of salvation. It is Christ who saves, not faith, for it is the object of believing not the act of believing that is saving and justifying.[42]

This teaching brought against it the same charge of 'antinomianism' levelled against the Marrow men in their rejection of a legal strain in the preaching of justification which undermined the Gospel. According to Erskine 'We are not called on to obey, in

---

[38] *The Doctrine of Election*, p. 3.
[39] See the Extracts from *The Doctrine of Election*, in Hanna's edition of Erskine's Letters, pp.533–67; and Erskine's thoughts on the Epistle to the Romans, Chapter IX, *The Spiritual Order and Other Papers, Selected from the Manuscripts*, Edinburgh, 1876, pp. 213–29.
[40] *An Essay on Faith*, Edinburgh, 1822, 5th edn, 1829, p. 11.
[41] *An Essay on Faith*, p. 115.
[42] *An Essay on Faith*, pp. 19f & 142. See 'The true meaning of Justification by Faith', *The Unconditional Freeness of the Gospel*, pp. 62–92. And cf. Erskine's exposition of the Epistle to the Romans, 3.22ff, in which he understood justification by faith as justification through the faithfulness of Christ. 'Although the propitiation cannot profit us spiritually except through believing it, yet surely it is not *our* faith which makes the propitiation; he himself made it, and by his own faith'. *The Spiritual Order*, pp. 156f.

order to obtain pardon; but we are called on to believe the proclamation of pardon, in order that we may obey ... I do believe that many people preach a different doctrine, from a notion that the true Gospel offer of free unconditional pardon is unfavourable to practical obedience and holiness.'[43] Hence Erskine retorted to the repetition of the old charge of antinomianism: 'Many clog the freeness of the Gospel from a fear of antinomianism; but this is itself a most dangerous spirit of antinomianism. The law of God is written in the heart by no other instrument but the free mercy of the Gospel.'[44]

The really basic point involved here which Erskine set himself to clarify was the bearing upon one another of the sufficiency of the atonement and the justness and mercy of God as he is revealed in the Incarnation and sacrificial death of Jesus Christ his beloved Son. He did not try to minimise the role of divine justice or the condemnation of the sinner, but pointed to the fact that divine justice is the justice of the *Father*, and that divine condemnation is the condemnation of God's holy love. This brought from him several books, *The Unconditional Freeness of the Gospel*,[45] *The Brazen Serpent or Life Coming Through Death*,[46] and *The Doctrine of Election*.[47] In them he tried to set the doctrine of God as 'Just and a Saviour' free from the legalist slant of federal Calvinism, and linked the doctrines of the Incarnation and atonement together in such a way as to allow a more faithful and natural interpretation of the Gospel message of salvation through God's unreserved and unrestrained love for the world in the gift of his only begotten Son.

What is very impressive was Erskine's penetrating theological analysis of traditional tenets and his deeply spiritual and evangelically coherent account of the saving doctrines of the Christian faith. That he should have emancipated understanding of the Gospel from its traditional presentation of God as Lawgiver and Judge set out in the arid legalist forms of so-called Calvinist

---

[43] *Internal Evidence*, p. 128.
[44] *Internal Evidence*, p. 117. 'Self is the great antinomian' – *The Unconditional Freeness of the Gospel*, p. 62.
[45] Edinburgh, 1828, republished in 1870 & 1873. This work received a very warm welcome from Thomas Chalmers, See W. Hanna, *Memoirs of Chalmers*. Edinburgh, 1849–52, vol. 3, see pp. 245 ff.
[46] Edinburgh, 1831, 3rd edn, 1879.
[47] Edinburgh, 1837.

orthodoxy, and done that precisely as an eminent advocate, did much to move ordinary people in the Church to a readier reception of the Gospel message of free grace and pardon for sinners.

> We are no longer under the cold eye of a Judge, but under the loving and encouraging eye of a Father, who 'willeth not the death of a sinner, but that he should turn from his wickedness and live'; and the assurance of daily forgiveness, as well as the blotting out of all past offences, imparts its own loving character to all the circumstances of our lot, even to the punishments and sufferings which our Father sees fit to send.[48]

'In God mercy and justice are one and the same thing.'[49] People learned from Erskine that 'Love is the great principle revealed in the Gospel, which reveals the union of an infinite abhorrence towards sin, and an infinite love towards the sinner'.[50] 'The Gospel reveals to us the existence of a fund of divine love, containing in it a propitiation for all sin, and a promise to destroy all the works of the devil – the sin – the misery – the death, which he has introduced.'[51]

The heart of Thomas Erskine's theology is nowhere better disclosed than in the 'Fragments' that were added to his last book *The Spiritual Order*, which reveal the profoundly Christocentric shape of his doctrine of God. Three New Testament passages cited there were very special for him. 'If God spared not his own Son, but gave him up to the death for us all, how shall he not with him also freely give us all things?' 'God so loved the world that he gave his only begotten Son, that whosoever believeth on him might not perish, but have everlasting life.' 'God commendeth his love toward us, in that whilst we were yet sinners Christ died for us.'[52] He cited these to show that Jesus was one with the Father, and that his giving by the Father was the measure of the Father's love. As such Christ is the revelation of God's paternal relation to us, and of *his* self-sacrificing love. Erskine was overwhelmed by the revelation that the sacrifice of Christ was grounded in and derived from *the sacrifice*

---

[48]   *The Spiritual Order*, p. 65.
[49]   *The Spiritual Order*, p. 72.
[50]   *The Unconditional Freeness of the Gospel*, new & revised edn, Edinburgh, 1873, p. 9; cf. pp. 44f.
[51]   *Unconditional Freeness*, p. 49.
[52]   Romans 8.32; John 3.16; Romans 5.8.

of the Father.[53] That is the supreme fact which opens up the spiritual world, and must be allowed to govern all our understanding of God, and of the Gospel. If the coming of Christ into our 'sinful flesh', in order to redeem and sanctify it, is in itself a declaration of the forgiveness of sin, that is supremely true of the self-sacrifice of the Father in giving up his Son in atoning sacrifice for the sin of the world. The realisation of that supreme truth had the effect of transforming Erskine's whole theological outlook, so that he could not think of God primarily as Judge but as Father whose infinite love was embodied in the Incarnation of his Son, and whose Law was and is the Love that God is as God, in terms of which all things in heaven and earth are to be understood, not least the doctrines of forgiveness and justification by grace.[54] 'The Lawgiver is our Father.'[55]

It was the way in which he understood the unqualified Deity of Jesus Christ, in utter rejection of all the Nestorian and Socinian slants that lurked in the traditional exposition of Calvinist theology, and above all his understanding of God manifest in the sacrifice of Christ, that transformed Erskine's spiritual apprehension of the *mind and character of God*, and therefore his attitude to the federal framework in which the contemporary Scottish doctrine of God was moulded and cramped.

> If there really be in the Divine nature an only begotten Son, one with the Father, who is also the Beginning or Head of the spiritual creation, the necessary inference is, that the relationship of fatherhood and sonship are the fundamental principles which regulate and harmonise that creation ... Thus love is the universal living law, originating with the Father and received by the Son, that it may by him be propagated to the whole spiritual family.[56]

Highly significant for Erskine's understanding of the Gospel was the profound interrelation between the Incarnation and the atonement, which made him realise that it was as the organic Head of all humanity that Christ partook of flesh and blood and died in atoning sacrifice, and became the propitiation for the sins of the

---

[53] *The Spiritual Order*, pp. 231f.
[54] This is what Erskine called 'the true *natural* religion', *The Spiritual Order*, p. 246; see also pp. 258f.
[55] *The Spiritual Order*, p. 207.
[56] *The Spiritual Order*, pp. 243f.

whole world. 'The appearance of Jesus Christ on the earth was the expression of an infinite love already existing in the Father's heart.'[57] Of considerable theological importance for Erskine was the teaching of St Paul 'about God sending his own Son in the likeness of sinful flesh, and for sin condemned sin in the flesh.'[58] This is not to say that Christ was a sinner, far from it, for the very contrary was the case: he condemned sin in the flesh he assumed from us, our flesh, the flesh of sinners, that he might redeem it from sin, and lift it up to God. 'It was a fallen nature, a nature which had fallen by sin, and he thus condemned sin in the flesh. He came into it as a new head, that he might take it out of the fall, and redeem it from sin, and lift it up to God.'[59] That is to say, Erskine held strongly to the truth that in assuming flesh from fallen and sinful humanity, far from being contaminated by it, Christ redeemed and sanctified it at the same time – the very assumption of Adamic humanity was essentially redemptive from the moment of its conception in the Virgin Mary.

Hence, in regard to the atonement, Erskine made a point of asserting that

> when Christ offered his blood in an atonement, he offered the blood of the offender, for 'God had made *of one blood* all nations that dwell on the face of the earth' (Acts xvii.26); and Christ offered that one blood, and here was the mighty marvel, although it was the blood of the offender, yet it was blood unstained by sin. It was in virtue of his taking part of the one condemned flesh and blood that he could meet and fulfil the condemnation, and could by death overcome him that had the power of death, even the devil (Heb. ii.14). The whole nature is as one colossal man, of which Christ continues the head during the whole accepted time and day of salvation (1 Cor. xi.3; Rom. v ; John x); and according to this head is the whole at present dealt with. The doctrine of the human nature of Jesus Christ is not merely that he is of the *same nature, of the same flesh and blood* with every man; but that he has *part* of that *one nature*, that *one flesh and blood*, of which, as a great whole, all are partakers. Unless the first Adam had been truly the root and head of the nature, his

---

[57] *The Spiritual Order*, p. 152.
[58] Romans 8.3.
[59] *The Brazen Serpent, or Life Coming Through Death*, Edinburgh, 1831, p. 34.

fall could not have involved and embraced all the rest; he could not have fallen for every man. Thus if Cain only had fallen, his fall could only have involved his posterity. And unless Christ had been truly the head and root of the nature, he could not have tasted death for every man, and his resurrection could not necessarily have involved that of every other man. For he was truly the head of the offending nature, and in his suffering the offending nature suffered the righteous sentence of God. It was no fiction of law. He suffered as the condemned head, he rose as the righteous head.[60]

It was in similar terms that Erskine wrote elsewhere:

The virtue of Christ's sacrifice is intimately connected with his being the root of the humanity he assumed. He did not take hold of a branch, he took the very root. He came into the place which Adam occupied ... He took part of the same flesh and blood of which the children partook, but he sinned not. He fulfilled all righteousness.[61]

The incarnate Life of Christ in which divine and human natures were united was thus redemptive from beginning to end. 'His whole life from the manger to the tomb was a sacrifice for sin – a suffering of the curse, sorrow and death; and in it a continual condemnation of sin in the flesh, of which he was not only a real partaker, but the head and representative.'[62] However, it was in the climax of the incarnate life of Christ in his atoning death that the redemptive import of the Incarnation became fully revealed. 'Jesus Christ was God, taking human nature into union with himself – and *he* made atonement.'[63]

It was in terms of this close bearing of the Incarnation and the atonement on one another, and of their relation to the oneness between Christ and our human nature that he assumed, that Erskine set out his understanding of the doctrine of the atonement. He held firmly to the fact that in his sacrifice on the Cross Christ tasted death for every man, and that in our room he bore the

---

[60] *The Brazen Serpent*, pp. 43f.
[61] *Letters*, pp. 184 & 185.
[62] *The Brazen Serpent*, 1831 edn, p. 54.
[63] *The Doctrine of Election*, p. 231.

penalty inflicted by God on sinful humanity.[64] However, he declined
to regard that in an individualist and forensic way, as in the concept
of 'substitution', which he held to be unbiblical.[65] 'When we hear
of God so loving the world, we hear of his so loving each man of
the world. Remember Christ came into Adam's place. This is the
true substitution.'[66] 'I am aware', he wrote, 'that the doctrine of
expiation through the vicarious death of Christ is sacred and
precious to the hearts of many, nevertheless I am compelled to
regard it as a human invention opposed to the character of God.'[67]
However, he regarded the *penal* suffering of Christ as a work of
atoning self-sacrifice in which all humanity was the object of God's
redeeming love.[68] Thus he regarded propitiation, not just as a
propitiatory act done by Christ *merely* in our place and in our stead,
but as identical with Christ himself the embodied holy love of God,
for he *is* the propitiation set forth by God.[69] In taking upon himself
the nature of man, and as our Head, elder brother and
representative, 'Christ acknowledged the justice of the sentence
pronounced against sin, and submitted himself to the full weight
of wo, in the stead of his adopted kindred. God's justice found
rest here; his law was magnified and made honourable.'[70] 'God set
forth his Son to make a propitiation through his blood. This is the
God with whom we have to do. This is his character, the just God
and yet a Saviour.'[71] 'The Lawgiver is our Father.'[72]

   While Erskine could use the classical language of satisfaction
and punishment in his account of atonement, he rejected the idea
that God's justice and his mercy are opposite to each other, and
rejected equally the idea that it was through the satisfaction of his
law that God is free to love and save us. God did not have to be

---

[64] Cf. the early edition of *The Unconditional Freeness of the Gospel*, pp. 18f, 28f, 37,
   & 58.
[65] See Chapter II of *The Brazen Serpent*, 1879 edn, pp. 40–83, and the extended
   note, pp. 279f.
[66] *The Brazen Serpent*, 1879 edn, pp. 117f.
[67] *The Spiritual Order*, p. 151.
[68] Cf. *The Spiritual Order*, pp. 62ff; and *Letters*, pp. 203ff. On Erskine's view of the
   penal ingredient in the atoning work of Christ see Trevor A. Hart, *Thomas
   Erskine*, Edinburgh, 1993, pp. 37ff.
[69] See especially Erskine's expository account of this in 'Thoughts on St Paul's
   Epistle to the Romans', *The Spiritual Order*, pp. 151–61.
[70] *Internal Evidence*, pp. 102f.
[71] *Internal Evidence*, pp. 103f.
[72] *The Spiritual Order*, p. 207.

appeased in order to extend his saving mercy toward sinners. Thus God is always spoken of as 'reconciling' – not as 'being reconciled'.[73] The Law of God's Being is his Love, for God is Love, and it was in the outgoing of his Love that the atoning propitiation which he set forth in the blood of his beloved Son, is the satisfaction of the Law of his Love. It is precisely as just that God is merciful and as infinitely loving that he came in Jesus Christ his Son to make atonement for sin, and do that in such a way that it is his *Holy Love* that is satisfied.

> It is God in our nature standing on our behalf as our elder brother and representative, bearing the punishment which we had deserved, satisfying the law which we had broken, and, on the ground of this finished work, proclaiming sin forgiven, and inviting the chief and most wretched of sinners to become a happy child of God for ever and ever.[74]

> In this wonderful transaction mercy and truth meet together, righteousness and peace embrace each other. It was planned and executed, in order that God might be just while he justified the believer in Jesus. It proclaims glory to God in the highest, peace on earth and good-will toward man.[75]

It is understandable that Erskine regarded the doctrine of atonement as the great subject of revelation. 'All the other doctrines radiate from this as its centre' – including the doctrine of the Holy Trinity, for it is in the atonement that 'the distinction in the unity of the Godhead has been revealed.'[76] The Cross is the revelation of the very heart of God, of his innermost being and nature. It is in the atonement above all, that we learn that fatherhood and filiation belong to the essential being of God. It is in the atonement that the *Mind and Character* of the One God, the Father, the Son, and the Holy Spirit, the 'living Love' of God, is made known to us, and made known in such a way that it shapes true understanding and faithful formulation of Christian truths, and cannot but govern our personal and moral life.[77]

---

[73] *The Unconditional Freeness of the Gospel*, p. 93, & see p. 80. On one occasion, however, Erskine lapsed into speaking of God as 'reconciled Father', *The Brazen Serpent*, 1879 edn, p. 156.

[74] *An Essay on Faith*, Edinburgh, 1825, p. 128.

[75] *Internal Evidence*, p. 105.

[76] *Internal Evidence*, pp. 101f, also pp. 7f & 94; *Letters*, p. 194.

[77] Cf. the chapter 'The Divine Son' in *The Spiritual Order*, pp. 18–46.

It was with his grasp of the Mind of God and of his unlimited Love that Erskine laid such strong emphasis on the gratuitous and objective nature of divine pardon and the unconditional nature of grace.[78] That was a theme he took over from the Marrow Men, and Ebenezer and Ralph Erskine, but he freed it from the way in which they tried to expound it while holding on to the decrees about double predestination enshrined in the *Confession of Faith*. Deriving from the triune nature of God as revealed in Christ, and objectively grounded in the atoning propitiation embodied in Christ, this proclamation of the Gospel of grace could not but be utterly free in its nature and universal in its range. It was not for believers that Christ died and rose again but for sinners, so that the pardon extended to them freely in the Gospel is independent of their repentance or belief, and is not conditioned by anything on their part, although it is only by believing it that they may have saving knowledge of God as revealed in Christ. It appeared to Erskine 'that this view of pardon, as being a manifestation of the Divine character in Christ Jesus, altogether independent of man's belief or unbelief, is a view much fitted to draw the soul from self to God.'[79] On the other hand, he understood that 'the very gratuitousness of the Gospel may lead to its rejection; because the gratuitousness is, in fact, a declaration on the part of God that man can do nothing for himself, and is thus an offence to his pride.'[80]

Writing in *The Brazen Serpent* about 'The union of two natures in Christ, the union of Jehovah with our fallen flesh', in connection with the teaching of St Paul in the first and eighth chapters of the Epistle to the Romans, Erskine declared:

> This is the gospel; this is the great truth of the fallen humanity of Jesus, the truth that he who was Jehovah should have consented to be made of that one blood of which God made all nations on the face of the earth, in order that he might shed that one blood, and thus make atonement for the sins of every man (Acts 17.26; Hebrews 2.14; 1 John 2.2) – the truth that he should have become one flesh with us, that we might become one spirit with him; this is the gospel hope,

---

[78] *The Unconditional Freeness of the Gospel*, Edinburgh, not published till 1870; see Trevor A. Hart, 'God's arms are always open', *The Teaching Father*, pp. 25ff.
[79] *The Unconditional Freeness of the Gospel*, p. 89.
[80] *Ibid.* p. 67.

in the prospect of the coming kingdom of him who has thus loved us and given himself for us. I do not wonder that Christianity withered away when this glorious truth was let slip. It contains all – the universal love of God, and the atonement for every man, as the ground of personal assurance, and the indwelling of the Spirit; and it contains also the glorious personal advent and reign of Jesus Christ upon this earth, because it connects him by an eternal bond, with the very substance of this earth.[81]

Later in life, Erskine pressed his doctrine of the organic Headship of Christ over all humanity, and universality of pardon to the point where it passed into the idea of 'final salvation of all' and 'final restitution of all men'.[82] There is certainly consistency between present forgiveness and future judgment,[83] but what Erskine did, however, was to move from the objectivity of pardon once and for all enacted in the death of Christ on the Cross to an objective necessity. That is to say, he logicalised the relation between unconditional grace or universal pardon and the sinner to mean that all people will necessarily be saved at last, even those, apparently, guilty of final unbelief! It was a great pity that Erskine did not learn from John Calvin and from James Fraser of Brae, whose work on *Justifying Faith* he knew, that it is the Gospel itself, the objective truth that in the Cross the final judgment of God against sin has been enacted, that becomes the judgment and even the damnation of those who reject it. This was what Fraser spoke of as 'gospel wrath'.[84] In this he followed the teaching of our Lord about the judgment of Light upon those who blind themselves to it, and about the fact that while God sent his Son not to condemn the world but to save it, those do not believe are condemned already.

Erskine was fiercely and relentlessly attacked in a series of sermons by Andrew Thomson, the outspoken leader of the Evangelical Party in the Kirk, who equated the idea of 'universal pardon' outright with 'universal salvation', thereby in his own way

---

[81] *The Brazen Serpent*, p. 150.
[82] *Letters*, pp. 422f; consult 'Reminiscences of Thomas Erskine by Principal Shairp', *ibid.* pp. 526f. See also, pp. 71, 82, 237, 286, 305, 547.
[83] See *Unconditional Freeness*, pp. 150ff.
[84] James Fraser of Brae, *Justifying Faith*, pp. 223f, 246, 254.

confounding objectivity with logical necessity.[85] Thus he said to the congregation of Free St George's in Edinburgh: 'If the principle of universal pardon is such as to establish the principle of universal salvation, or necessarily to infer it, and if you are satisfied that the principle of universal salvation is false and inadmissible, then you cannot possibly or consistently adopt the principle of universal pardon.'[86] Here in addition to his adherence to the doctrine that Christ died only for the elect, Thomson operated with the idea that in determining the ends of his eternal decrees, God determines at the same time the means by which he wills to bring them about. Thus, to borrow the language of Archibald Hodge (with which he was doubtless familiar), 'God's purpose with respect to the end necessarily, in the logical order, takes precedence of and gives direction to his purpose with respect to the means.'[87] Hence the idea that in the end all men will not actually be saved made Thomson insist that when the New Testament Scriptures use 'universal' phrases as 'the world, the whole world, all, all men',[88] they have to be understood in a way modified by other passages which speak of final judgment, thereby limiting their reference. This was to inflict what Thomas Chalmers was later to call 'unnatural violence' upon them.[89]

There is no doubt about the fact that Thomas Erskine's thought did move from *universal* pardon, understood unconditionally, to a universalist notion of the final salvation of all people, irrespective of faith, which did give Andrew Thomson a handle against him. At the same time, however, it hindered Thomson himself from discerning the evangelical nature of the fact that Christ died for all men in atoning sacrifice, really and objectively, and of the

[85] Andrew Mitchell Thomson, *The Doctrine of Universal Pardon Considered and Refuted in a Series of Sermons, with Notes, Critical and Expository*, Edinburgh, 1830. Thomson did not hesitate to caricature what his opponents meant. 'The doctrine that they teach is that of universal pardon, – meaning by it, that unbelievers, impenitent persons, hardened profligates, have all their sins, including those they may hereafter commit, already and actually forgiven.' *Ibid.*, p. 238.

[86] Andrew Thomson, *The Doctrine of Universal Pardon*, p. 96.

[87] A. A. Hodge, *The Confession of Faith*, 1961 reprint, p. 72.

[88] Thomson had in mind the following: 'The grace of God hath appeared unto all men bringing salvation'; 'God sent not his own Son into the world, to condemn the world, but that the world through him might be saved'; 'Look unto me and be ye saved, all ye ends of the earth', *The Doctrine of Universal Pardon*, p. 138 – but also 1 Timothy 2.5–6; 1 John 2.2, 2 Peter 2.1, Titus 2.11, pp. 150ff.

[89] Thomas Chalmers, *Institutes of Theology*, Edinburgh, 1849, Vol. II, p. 403.

significance of God's 'holy love directed against sin', as taught by Erskine, or therefore the heart of his doctrine of unconditional grace, and of the subtle legalism and the false notion of assurance (held by Thomson as well as others) which it overthrew.[90] It also hindered Thomson from taking into account the significance of the conception of 'gospel wrath' which he cited from Fraser, but used in a rather prejudiced one-sided way against Erskine.[91] Erskine's move from universal pardon to universal salvation was a step that the Marrow men, and McLeod Campbell later, refused to take. This did not help to commend Erskine's teaching about unconditional grace, for it emptied it at the end of the very stringency of God's 'holy love' upon which the atonement and the Gospel of grace rested, and upon which Erskine laid so much stress. Moreover, Erskine failed to take account of 'the mystery of iniquity', the abysmal irrationality of evil, which cannot be resolved away by rational means – that would mean that God need not have taken the way of the Cross in order to save us. In this connection (as we have already noted in earlier chapters) John Calvin had taught, following St Paul,[92] that preaching of the Gospel can be a savour of life unto life, but also a savour of death unto death, in which damnation and reprobation have to be regarded as an *accidental* result (*per accidens*) of the Gospel.[93] This was a point that James Fraser took over from Calvin when he spoke of the 'accidental' result of the Gospel in divine judgment and reprobation.[94] Fraser also held that the judgment of sin enacted in the atoning satisfaction for sin made by Christ on the Cross would be, and would even reinforce, the judgment of God upon all those who finally reject Christ. The doctrine of unconditional grace and universal pardon cannot be twisted into universal salvation without evacuating the Cross of its profound nature and ultimate meaning, and distorting the self-revelation of God as Holy Love.

---

[90] Andrew Thomson, *The Doctrine of Universal Pardon*, pp. 289ff, and 456; cf. also 313f & 328ff. Thomson held that 'the doctrine of universal pardon originates in the high doctrine of assurance.' pp. 328 & 499. 'It is striking', Erskine once wrote, 'that universal atonement and the personal assurance should have been the reproach at all times'. *The Brazen Serpent*, p. 170.

[91] Andrew Thomson, *The Doctrine of Universal Pardon*, p. 455.

[92] 2 Corinthians 2.14–16.

[93] See the account of Calvin's teaching regarding reprobation which I have given in *Kingdom and Church, A Study in The Theology of the Reformation*, Edinburgh, 1956, pp. 106f.

[94] *Justifying Faith*, 1722 edn, p. 137; and 1749 edn, pp. 92 & 248.

The Redeemer's Tears Wept over Lost Souls

One of the recurrent problems of Scottish theology had to do with a doctrine of predestination reached apart from the historical revelation of God in Jesus Christ, which had the effect of separating the atoning work of Christ from the ultimate nature of God uniquely revealed in Christ. And that, in turn, as Thomas Erskine pointed out again and again, seriously damaged people's conceptions of God. That was the problem of what Robert Gordon, a devout Edinburgh minister, called 'unworthy suspicions of the divine character'.[95] Passionately committed to the mission of the Gospel, at home as well as abroad,[96] he sought to counter those suspicions by directing attention to 'the effusions of divine pity and commiseration, which the Scriptures pour out over the impenitence and unbelief of an ungodly world'. He held that the indifference of many of his contemporaries to the Christian Faith was to be traced to the fact that they had no serious conviction of the *reality* of compassion on the part of God which biblical language seemed to imply. This was undoubtedly due to the hard conception of God inculcated by the legalist preaching about contractual and predestinationist relations with God. A more Christ-like understanding of the nature and will of God on the part of both Moderates and Evangelicals was much needed, not least in the interest of pastoral concern. While the Christian, Robert Gordon held, can never cease to contemplate the majesty and perfections of God, with holy and reverential awe and feel his own unworthiness to appear before him, 'all this should not interfere with his confidence toward God 'as his reconciled Father'.[97] To indulge in metaphysical speculations on the precise sense in which biblical language of the Father's compassion is to be understood, would be to withdraw oneself from its salutary influence. Hence he made a point of directing attention to the sheer compassion of God vividly revealed in the fact that our Lord is represented in the Gospel as weeping over the approaching ruin of Jerusalem, in which he was concerned not simply with the physical desolation of the city which

---

[95] Robert Gordon, 'Introductory Essay', published in his edition of *The Redeemer's Tears Wept over Lost Souls*, by John Howe, Glasgow, 1822. This was printed for the publishing firm Chalmers and Collins. C. Chalmers was a brother of Thomas Chalmers, and the founder of Merchiston Castle School in Edinburgh.

[96] Robert Gordon was to become Moderator of the General Assembly of the Church in 1841.

[97] *The Redeemer's Tears*, p. x.

he foresaw, but with the unbelief, retribution and spiritual ruin of its inhabitants. That incident recorded in the Gospel history, in which the Saviour wept over the ruin of those who lived and died in a state of unbelief, shows us the nature and extent of *God's* compassion for mankind, for Jesus Christ was no other than *God* become man.[98] The tears of Jesus are the very tears of God.[99] Hence Gordon seized upon the remarkable writing of John Howe, *The Redeemer's Tears Wept Over Lost Souls*, and republished it in Scotland in order to counter unworthy conceptions of God through a proper understanding of the love of God incarnate in Christ Jesus.

> The small still voice of the gospel, is the only melody that can expel from the human soul, the evil spirit of distrust and of unbelief. And where is this melody to be heard, if it is not in the simple, and unadorned narrative of the inspired writer when he tells us, that on our Lord's approach to Jerusalem, the place where above all others he had been calumniated and reviled ... he beheld the city and wept over it?[100]

In the reality of the Redeemer's compassion for sinners there is exhibited the unbounded mercy of God. It was to promote that truth that John Howe's 'Treatise on our Lord's Lamentation over Jerusalem' was published.[101]

In his preface to this little book John Howe had made a point of stressing the universal range of the saving death of Christ who 'offered himself to put away sin, by the sacrifice of himself', died and rose again to be the Lord of the living and the dead. The eternal Father has exalted him, given him a name above every name, that at his name every knee should bow, and all should confess that he is Lord, to the praise and glory of his name.

> Was it ever intended that men should, generally, remain exempt from the obligation to observe, believe and obey

---

[98] See Fraser of Brae, *Justifying Faith*, p. 64: 'This weeping and these tears did really express the tender and compassionate nature of Christ.'

[99] Cf. H. R. Mackintosh, *The Doctrine of the Person of Jesus Christ*, Edinburgh, 1913, p. 340: 'The words of Jesus are the voice of God. The tears of Jesus are the pity of God. The wrath of Jesus is the judgment of God. All believers confess, with adoring praise, that in their most sacred hours God and Christ merge in each other with morally indistinguishable identity.'

[100] *The Redeemer's Tears*, pp. xxii–xiii.

[101] *The Redeemer's Tears*, pp. xxviiif.

him? Was it his own intention to wave, or not to insist upon his most sacred, and so dearly acquired rights? to quit his claim to the greatest part of mankind? Why then did he issue out his commission as soon as he was risen from the dead, 'to teach all nations', to proselyte the world to himself, to 'baptize them into his name', with that of the Father and the Holy Ghost'?

To limit the universal range of the Gospel would be 'to make the whole frame of Christian religion an idle impertinacy'.[102] 'The grace of God, which brings salvation to all men, has appeared.'

John Howe took his basic cue from the words of St Luke's Gospel (19. 41,42): 'And when he was come near, he beheld the city, and wept over it, saying, If thou hadst known, even thou, at least in this thy day, the things which belong unto thy peace! but now they are hid from thine eyes.'[103] He pointed out right away than the calamity of Jerusalem was greater in the eyes of Jesus that it can be in ours, for its principal reference was to their spiritual and eternal miseries, to the eternal calamity they brought on themselves through their rejection of him as their Saviour.

'*How*', then, '*is God said to will the salvation of them who perish?*'[104] That is the question with which this work was concerned, but concerned within the all-embracing frame of the infinite compassion of God, movingly revealed in the tears of the Redeemer, as God the Father who so loved the world that he gave his only begotten Son to be its Saviour. Thus the assertion of the universal extent of redemption does not and cannot imply, as Thomas Erskine seemed finally to have held, that all men will actually be saved – that also became revealed in the Redeemer's tears for they were shed over those who would perish and did in fact perish. The 'gospel-constitution' makes the connexion between unrepentant sinners and everlasting punishment very clear. 'He that believeth not shall be damned – is condemned already; shall not see life, but the wrath of God abideth on him. If you believe not that I am he, ye shall die in your sins. Except ye repent, ye shall all likewise perish.'[105] The fact that some people will never be finally forgiven, and that ultimate judgment will fall upon them, was clearly asserted

---

[102] *The Redeemer's Tears*, pp. 44ff.
[103] *The Redeemer's Tears*, p. 51.
[104] *The Redeemer's Tears*, p. 153.
[105] *The Redeemer's Tears*, p. 39.

by Jesus in regard to those who blaspheme against the Holy Spirit. Howe devoted special discussion to this in an Appendix.[106]

The intention of this publication was to switch the minds of people over to a different perspective opened up by the Gospel record of how the Lord Jesus wept over Jerusalem, and its revelation of the incredible mercy and kindness of God. What are we to make of the persistent problems of Scottish theology since the adoption of the *Westminster Confession of Faith* when considered, not from a dominant conception of God as Lawgiver and Contractor of covenants, but from the conception of the God revealed in the tears of the incarnate Redeemer who in his unutterable compassion willed the salvation of those who perish? Here are salient truths which must surely govern our response to that challenge, expressed largely in John Howe's own words.

(1) The first point to consider is surely the *reality* of the Redeemer's tears. 'The holy Scriptures frequently speak of God as angry, grieved for the sins of men, and their miseries which ensue therefrom.' Such expressions are a human way of speaking borrowed from man, but they must be understood in a way suitable to God, for 'though they do not signify the same thing with him as they do in us, yet they do not signify nothing.' Thus 'pity' and 'mercy' when applied to God are not just names – 'it is a great reality that is signified by them.'[107]

> They signify the sincerity of his love and pity, the truth and tenderness of his compassion. Canst thou think his tears deceitful? his, who never knew guile? was this like the rest of his course? And remember that he who shed tears, did, from the same fountain of love and mercy, shed blood too! ... They signify how very intent he is to save souls, and how gladly he would save them, if yet thou wilt accept of mercy while it may be had. For if he did weep over them that will not be saved, from the same love that is the spring of these tears, would saving mercies proceed to those that are become willing to receive them.[108]

What God is in Jesus Christ he is inherently in the reality of his own divine Being.

---

[106] *The Redeemer's Tears*, pp. 153–70.
[107] *The Redeemer's Tears*, pp. 116ff.
[108] *The Redeemer's Tears*, pp. 150f.

(2) The second point for us to note is that there is no suggestion that God had to be placated in order to be propitious and merciful to sinners. The overwhelming emphasis is on the initiative and priority of God's activity in the Gospel of peace preached to us.

> That gospel lets you see 'God in Christ reconciling the world unto himself, that sin may not be imputed to them'... It tells you, 'God desireth not the death of sinners, but that they may turn and live;' that he would have 'all men saved, and come to the knowledge of the truth'; that he is 'long-suffering towards them, not willing that any should perish, but that all should come to repentance'; that he 'so loved the world, that he gave his only-begotten Son, that whosoever believes on him should not perish, but have everlasting life'.[109]

> Couldst thou think, living under the gospel, that the reconciliation between God and thee was not to be mutual? that he would be reconciled to thee while thou wouldst not be reconciled to him, or shouldst still bear towards him a disaffected and implacable heart?[110]

> If, when you were enemies, you were reconciled by the death of Christ, how much more, being reconciled, shall you be saved by his life? If God be for you, who can be against you?[111]

It is noteworthy that Howe interpreted 1 Timothy 2.1, as actually applying to 'all men, without the personal exclusion of any'.[112]

(3) Although Howe refers to the Gospel-covenant again and again, there is no talk of it being conditional on a 'holy life', although he does speak of 'the obligation of the evangelical law' for the life of believers.[113] The grace of God is free and unconditional. While the Gospel reveals our own impotence to help ourselves and even to repent of ourselves, it does tell us that 'salvation is from first to last all of grace.' While it is not possible for you to believe and repent of yourselves, 'the gospel plainly tells you that your repentance must be given you... 'By grace you are saved, through

---

[109] *The Redeemer's Tears*, pp. 73f.
[110] *The Redeemer's Tears*, p. 80.
[111] *The Redeemer's Tears*, p. 121.
[112] *The Redeemer's Tears*, p. 108.
[113] *E.g.* p. 135.

faith, not of yourselves, it is the gift of God".[114] Thus it was Calvin's emphasis upon 'Gospel repentance' or 'evangelical repentance', rather than 'legal repentance', that is inculcated.

(4) While God does not desire the death of sinners, but that they may turn and live, and while he would have all men saved, and come to the knowledge of the truth, he does not *impose* the Gospel upon people whether they believe or not.[115] 'It is unavoidably imposed upon us, to believe that God is truly unwilling of some things, which he doth not think fit to interpose his omnipotence to hinder; and is truly willing of some things, which he doth not put forth his omnipotence to effect.'[116]

> It seems out of the question that God doth constantly and perpetually, in a true sense, will the universal obedience, and the consequent felicity of all his creatures capable thereof ... He doth not efficaciously will everything that he truly wills. He never willed the obedience of all his intelligent creatures so, as efficaciously to make them all obey, nor their happiness, so as to make them all happy.[117]

This means that in the case of those who perish, as Howe pointed out, 'their destruction came not from God's first restraint of his Spirit, but their refusing, despising, and setting at nought his counsels and reproofs.'[118] Hence, while there is no divine decree of reprobation, God allows his will for the salvation of all for whom Christ died, to be frustrated, so that in view of the tears of the Redeemer for the lost, it may be said that God wills the salvation of those that perish.

(5) This is not to be taken to imply that God's holy condemnation of sin in the atoning sacrifice of Christ is of no ultimate significance. That Christ died for all, both those who believe and those who perish, effects those who believe and those who do not believe in different ways. Here the word of St Luke's Gospel (2.34) is cited: 'This child Jesus was set for the fall, as well as the rising of many in Israel'. In explanation it is the teaching of John Calvin that is followed with reference to 2 Corinthians 2.16, about the fact that

---

[114] *The Redeemer's Tears,* pp. 81f.
[115] *The Redeemer's Tears,* p. 84.
[116] *The Redeemer's Tears,* p. 115.
[117] *The Redeemer's Tears,* pp. 167f.
[118] *The Redeemer's Tears,* p. 87.

while the preaching of the Gospel is to one a savour of life unto life, to another it is savour of death unto death.[119] That is to say, it is precisely because Christ died for all, the unbelieving well as the believing that the wrath of God's holy love, the enactment of his righteous judgment upon sin in the atoning sacrifice of Christ, becomes the actualisation of divine judgment upon those who refuse to believe. Reference is made here to 1 Peter 2.8; 'The stone which the builders refused, is made a stone of stumbling, and a rock of offence even to them which stumble at the word, being disobedient, whereunto also they are appointed'. And to the word of the Saviour himself, John 10.39: 'For judgment, I am come into this world, that they who see might not see, and they which see, might be made blind.'[120] That is also how one must understand the tears of the Redeemer wept over lost souls, and so how God is said to will the salvation of them that perish.[121] 'To how many hath that gospel been a deadly savour, which hath proved a savour of life unto you!'[122]

In line with this teaching was that of Thomas Chalmers on the need to proclaim the Gospel equally to all people, and on the different reactions of people to Christ, the believing and the unbelieving.

> God, in the gospel of Jesus Christ, holds forth the very same overtures to both; and the only distinction is, that it is not responded to in the same way by both ... The application of a free pardon held out for acceptance to them both – the assurance of God's readiness in Christ Jesus to forgive, coupled with the call to repentance to them both – the declaration of a blood that cleanseth from all sin, and that will most assuredly cleanse them from their sin if they only will put their trust in it, made equally to them both ... the minister is untrue to his commission who does not bear it indiscriminately round, and cause it to operate with equal freeness and importunity at every door. We are aware that the effect within will not be the same, but the application from without ought to be the same.

> It is the obvious duty of the minister to bring the message of the gospel alike to every man, and the obvious duty of every

[119] *The Redeemer's Tears*, pp. 100f & 120f.
[120] *The Redeemer's Tears*, pp. 98.
[121] *The Redeemer's Tears*, p. 121.
[122] *The Redeemer's Tears*, p. 153.

man to prize that message as worthy of his special acceptance, and to proceed upon its truth.[123]

Thomas Chalmers made a point of reinforcing that exhortation by recalling his statement made earlier that 'there is nothing in the doctrine of predestination which should at all limit the universality of the gospel offer.'[124] It was not a doctrine of predestination by itself, however, which had that effect, but what Robert Gordon called 'the unworthy suspicions of the character of God' that went with it, which he did so much to allay in directing people back to the infinite compassion and love of God incarnated and revealed in the Lord Jesus Christ. It was a happy and significant act of the Free Church of Scotland to place a fine marble bust of Robert Gordon in their Presbytery Hall in Edinburgh.

Bibliography

Brown, John, of Haddington, *An Essay toward an Easy, Plain, Practical and Extensive Explication of the Assembly's Shorter Catechism*, Edinburgh, created and greatly improved by Mr Eben. Brown, Edinburgh, 1812.

Bull, George, *Defensio Fidei Nicaenae*, 1685; *Works*, 6 vols., Oxford, 1827.

Calvin, John, *Institutio*, Geneva, 1559.

Chalmers, Thomas, *Institutes of Theology*, Edinburgh, 1849.

Cheyne, A. C., *The Transforming of the Kirk. Victorian Scotland's Religious Revolution, Edinburgh*, 1983.

Edwards, Jonathan, *Treatise Concerning Religious Affections*, Edinburgh, 1772.

Erskine, Thomas, of Linlathen, *The Brazen Serpent, or Life Coming Through Death*, Edinburgh, 1831 & 1879.

Erskine, Thomas, of Linlathen, *The Doctrine of Election and its connection with the general tenor of Christianity, illustrated from the pages of Scripture, and especially from the Epistle to the Romans*, London, 1837, & Edinburgh, 1865.

Erskine, Thomas, of Linlathen, *An Essay on Faith*, Edinburgh, 1822 & 1825.

Erskine, Thomas, of Linlathen, *Extracts of Letters to a Christian Friend by a Lady, with An Introductory Essay*, Greenock, 1830.

---

[123] Thomas Chalmers, *Institutes of Theology*, Vol. II, Edinburgh, 1849, pp. 410ff.
[124] *Institutes of Theology*, Vol. II, pp. 404f and 418.

Erskine, Thomas, of Linlathen, *The Letters of Thomas Erskine, From 1840 Till 1870,* 2 vols., edited by William Hanna, Edinburgh, 1877, 2nd edn 1878.

Erskine, Thomas, of Linlathen, *Remarks on the Internal Evidence for the Truth of Revealed Religion,* Edinburgh, 1820 & 1821, revised edn, 1873.

Erskine, Thomas, of Linlathen, *The Spiritual Order and Other Papers, Selected from the Manuscripts,* 1871, 2nd edn, Edinburgh, 1876.

Erskine, Thomas, of Linlathen, *The Unconditional Freeness of the Gospel,* Edinburgh, 1828, new edn, 1870, and revised edn, 1873.

Hart, Trevor A., *The Teaching Father, An Introduction to the Theology of Thomas Erskine of Linlathen,* Edinburgh, 1993.

Hill, George, *Lectures on Divinity,* edited by his son Alexander Hill, Edinburgh, 1821, 4th edn, London, 1837.

Hill, George, *Theological Institutes,* Edinburgh, 1803.

Hodge, A. A., *The Confession of Faith,* 1869, Reprint, London, 1958, 1961.

Howe, John, *The Redeemer's Tears Wept Over Lost Souls, and, Two Discourses on Self-Dedication, and On Yielding ourselves to God,* with an *Introductory Essay,* by Robert Gordon, Glasgow, 1822.

Mackintosh, H. R., *The Doctrine of the Person of Jesus Christ,* Edinburgh, 1913.

Needham, Nicholas R., *Thomas Erskine of Linlathen. His Life and Theology 1788–1837,* Edinburgh, 1990.

Owen, John, *The Reason of Faith; Or, An Answer Unto That Enquiry, Wherefore We Believe The Scripture To Be The Word of God? Together with Causes, Ways and Means, of Understanding the Mind of God as Revealed in His Word, With Assurance Therein,* Glasgow, 1801.

Stevenson, George, *A Dissertation on the Nature and Necessity of Atonement,* Edinburgh, 1817.

Thomson, Andrew Mitchell, *The Doctrine of Universal Pardon Considered and Refuted in a Series of Sermons, with Notes, Critical and Expository,* Edinburgh, 1830.

Torrance, T. F., *Kingdom and Church. A Study in the Theology of the Reformation,* Edinburgh, 1956.

Torrance, T. F., *Trinitarian Perspectives, Toward Doctrinal Accord,* Edinburgh, 1994.

Torrance, T. F., *et al.,* 'Interim Report of the Special Commission on Baptism', *General Assembly Reports,* Edinburgh, 1958.

Watson, Thomas, *A Body of Practical Divinity, Consisting of Above One Hundred and Seventy-Six Sermons on the Shorter Catechism,* new edn, 2 vols., London, 1807.

9

John McLeod Campbell (1800–1872)

Like Thomas Erskine, John McLeod Campbell was influenced by the doctrine of free unconditional grace held by the Marrow men, but they reached their main theological positions independently of one another. They met for the first time in the Spring of 1828 shortly after Erskine had published *The Unconditional Freeness of the Gospel.* It was shortly after Erskine had heard McLeod Campbell preach in an Edinburgh Church, when he said: 'I believe I have heard today from that pulpit what I believe to be the true Gospel.'[1] When McLeod Campbell was taken by a friend, A. J. Scott, to see Erskine he found him to be 'one who knew the love of God in which we were both seeing eye to eye.'[2] In spite of their differences they came to appreciate one another in their common problems with traditional Calvinism and were linked together in the minds of their opponents.[3] McLeod Campbell, one of the profoundest theologians in the history of Scottish theology since the Reformation of the Church of Scotland, was charged by the General Assembly in May 1831 with teaching doctrines 'contrary to the Holy Scripture and to the *Confession of Faith* approven by the General Assemblies of the Church of Scotland.'[4] In point of fact 'contrary to the Holy Scripture' meant contrary to the Westminster Standards for it was in their light that the biblical passages adduced by McLeod Campbell were rigidly interpreted. He was deposed from the ministry on account of his belief in 'the doctrine of universal atonement and pardon, as also the doctrine

---

[1] See Henry F. Henderson, *Erskine of Linlathen. Selections and Biography*, Edinburgh, 1899, p. 106.
[2] *Memorials of John McLeod Campbell, D.D.*, edited by his son, the Rev Donald Campbell, London, 1877, Vol. 1, pp. 61f.
[3] Cf. Andrew M. Thomson, *The Doctrine of Universal Pardon Considered and Refuted*, Edinburgh, 1830.
[4] *Memorials of John McLeod Campbell*, Vol. 1, pp. 70f.

that assurance is of the essence of faith and necessary for salvation'. By 'universal atonement', however, McLeod Campbell meant that Christ died for all people, not that all people would actually be saved.[5] And by assurance he meant confidence in the atonement as the finished work of Christ.[6] In its judgment the Assembly relied on the Act of the General Assembly in 1720 which had condemned the teaching of *The Marrow of Modern Divinity* and its supporters.[7] In spite of his appeal to the teaching of the New Testament, and also to the *Scots Confession*, it was not really on biblical grounds that the teaching of McLeod Campbell was condemned: it was held to contradict statements of the *Westminster Confession* which was the basis on which ministers took their solemn ordination vows. It was on the same grounds that the charge of heresy laid against McLeod Campbell at the General Assembly had been pursued through the Presbytery of Dumbarton and the Synod of Glasgow and Ayr. The position adopted then, and sustained by the General Assembly, is very clear from the following statements: 'We must not go back to any Confession before the Westminster Confession, for to it we must bow. By my subscription, I am bound to receive the Bible in the sense of the Westminster Confession.' 'We are far from appealing to the Word of God on this ground; it is by the Confession of Faith that we must stand; by it we hold our livings.'[8]

It is significant that the Moderates and the Evangelicals combined to condemn McLeod Campbell. In a letter of March that year McLeod Campbell reported that Thomas Chalmers had told him 'the Moderation was not half so excited against me as the Evangelicals', and had added that 'he hoped I might be got

---

5   Cf. his 1830 Sermon on 1 Thessalonians 1.2, 3: 'It is an awful error to feel that if God loves a man therefore a man must be saved and it is a prevailing error at this day, and it shows itself when it is said, "If Christ died for all men then how is it that all men are not saved?"' *Notes of Sermons by the Rev. J. McL. Campbell, taken in Short Hand*, Vol. 1, Sermon IV, p. 11 & Vol. 2, Sermon 24, pp. 9–36, Lithographic reproduction by John Vallance, Paisley, 1831.

6   See Sermon 5 on 1 Peter 1.7, p. 10f, and Sermon 7 on Acts 17.22, *Notes of Sermons*, Vol. 1, p. 17.

7   See the 'Speech of J. M. Campbell to the Synod of Glasgow and Ayr', in which he showed that the Act of the Assembly in 1720, which had not been sent under the Barrier Act, was not entitled to take the place of the Confession of Faith, published by R. B. Lusk, Greenock, 1831; also reproduced in *The Whole Proceedings Before the Presbytery of Dumbarton and Synod of Glasgow and Ayr in the Case Of the Rev. John McLeod Campbell, Minister of Row*, R. B. Lusk, Greenock, 1831, pp. 174ff.

8   *The Whole Proceedings*, pp. xxvii & xxix.

through'.[9] However, Thomas Chalmers took no part in the trial at the General Assembly in Edinburgh, but remained silent. He declined to vote against McLeod Campbell. He realised, as he wrote later, that in regard to the Kirk's attitude to 'the universality of the Gospel', 'there must be a sad misunderstanding somewhere'.[10]

The act of the 1831 Assembly was undoubtedly of crucial importance for Scottish theology, for it had to do with the deep internal tensions and contradictions which had entrenched themselves in the established theology of the Kirk owing to its adoption of a rigid legalistic framework of thought which made it difficult for people to interpret many passages of Holy Scripture without unnatural violence. That was regularly done with some of the great Gospel passages in the New Testament such as John 3.16, 1 John 1.2, 1 Timothy 2.4f, Hebrews 2.9 and 17–19, in order to bring them into line with logical Calvinism and its conception of particular redemption. This is what worried McLeod Campbell, for it conflicted with his view of evangelical Calvinism and with his understanding of the Reformation (of Luther as well as Calvin), but his explanations were not helped by his rather obscure periphrastic style, and by some of his attempts to find new expressions to help him break away from hardened forms of speech which now failed to carry their original evangelical intention. Hence to do justice to his theology today we need to get behind some of his peculiar terms and idiosyncratic statements and restate them as faithfully as possible in accordance with their evangelical intention which is clearer to us now after the debates that followed. Already, however, it was said, the discerning Clerk of the General Assembly, Principal John Lee remarked that 'those doctrines of Mr Campbell would remain and flourish after the Church of Scotland had perished and was forgotten'![11] And that is certainly the case, for although he was banished from the ministry of the Church of Scotland, his teaching has had the effect of opening the door wide to fresh biblical and evangelical understanding of

[9] *Memorials*, Vol. 1, p. 78.
[10] See his *Institutes of Theology*, 1849, Vol. I, Chapter VII, 'On the Universality of the Gospel', p. 404.
[11] Cited by Thomas Erskine, who on hearing it whispered to a friend, 'This spake he not of himself, being the High Priest – he prophesied.' Henry F. Henderson, *op. cit.* pp. 107f. Refer also to A. J. Campbell, *op. cit.* p. 191; and see McLeod Campbell, *Thoughts on Revelation, With Special Reference to the Present Time*, 2nd edn, London, 1874, p. 187.

cardinal truths of the Christian Faith.[12] McLeod Campbell accepted the verdict of the General Assembly with deep sorrow but with remarkable grace. This was very evident in the address he delivered to some of his Rhu (or Row) parishioners, in which he refreshed their memory of the doctrine of the saving Love of God and the universal forgiveness of sin that they had heard from him, a doctrine, he said, 'which I know has cost me much'. 'I bless God', he said, 'that in respect of any other who may have found fault with me on account of what I have taught I can only feel this regret that it was not spoken more frequently and with more power. I do not wish to recall a single word I have ever spoken to you on these subjects.'[13]

What had gone wrong? McLeod Campbell tells us that it was during his parish ministry at Rhu that he awoke to the problem.[14] What worried his congregation were questions relating to their assurance of the love of God and the nature of forgiveness and repentance, particularly in view of the current doctrines of election and atonement, according to which only some people were chosen to be saved, which undermined their trust in God and the Gospel of salvation by grace.[15] Hence he felt that he had to give careful consideration to the *mind* and *character* of God the Father revealed in his incarnate Son, and to the nature and extent of the atonement and pardon through the blood of Christ in view of current concepts of predestination.[16] There was, he realised, an evident conflict between the authorised teaching of the Kirk about these doctrines and the presentation of the Gospel. On the one hand it was said,

---

[12] This was already apparent to McLeod Campbell in 1847 when he wrote to Thomas Erskine: 'As respects the *extent* of the atonement – its bearing on the whole human race – the Calvinism of Scotland seems breaking up fast; but this in connection with teaching, which is not light but darkness as to its *nature*, and I feel that the word for this time, if it were so uttered as to command attention, is a word supplying this great want.' (*Memorials*, Vol. 1, p. 207) This is what McLeod Campbell set out to do in his great work, *The Nature of the Atonement*, Cambridge, 1856. It has since accomplished much more than he hoped.

[13] Delivered to a few of the Parishioners of Row, at Helensburgh, August 1831, reproduced in *Notes of Sermons*, at the end of Vol. 2.

[14] John McLeod Campbell, *Reminiscences and Reflections*, London, 1875, p. 132.

[15] See the 'Extract of a letter from the Rev. John McLeod Campbell, Minister of Row', *Notes of Sermons*, Greenock, Vol. 1, pp. 1–12.

[16] Cf. Thomas Chalmers who warned that teaching about election or predestination could damage the preaching of the Gospel. *Institutes of Theology*, Edinburgh, 1849, Vol. II, p. 409.

'Believe in the forgiveness of your sins, and they will be forgiven.'
On the other hand it was said, 'Believe in the forgiveness of your
sins because they are forgiven.' Again the alternative could be
expressed thus: 'Believe that Christ died for you, and your faith
will be an evidence to yourself that you are one of those for whom
Christ died.' Or: 'Believe that Christ died for you because he died
for all mankind.'[17] What seemed to be the problem was the very
foundation upon which the Gospel rested, the wonderful love and
unconditional grace of God which, according to the New
Testament, are to be freely proclaimed to all nations and to every
person without exception. What was ultimately at stake here was
the very nature of God as Love, who loves all whom he has created,
as opposed to the kind of God who does not love all people even
though they are created by him, the kind of God whose 'love' is
partial, and not really love.[18] He was never tired of preaching that
it is in Jesus Christ that the character of God as Love is revealed.[19]
Later on McLeod Campbell was to write:

> If love be of God's character; if it be of His very Substance; if
> God is love, then of necessity God loves every man; yea, those
> who limit his love to some do actually deny that there is love
> in God at all, for this would not be love but mere partiality,
> and, however beneficial to those who are its objects, yet in
> respect of Him whose choice it is it can be no manifestation
> of *character* at all.[20]

Looking back on the problematic situation that faced him in
1827 McLeod Campbell wrote:

> The controversy in which I was constantly engaged in almost
> all my intercourse with my brethren urged me to examine

---

[17] *Reminiscences and Reflections*, London, 1873, p. 27. See also McLeod Campbell's
speech before the Synod of Glasgow and Ayr, *op. cit.* pp. 10ff; and *Memorials*,
Vol.1, London, 1877, see pp. 78ff.

[18] See the remarkable Sermon, contrasting God and Baal, delivered in 'the
Floating Chapel', Greenock, on June 9, 1930. *Notes of Sermons*, Vol. 1, Sermon
3, Paisley, 1832. See also his stress in Sermon 1 on 2 Thessalonians 3.5, on the
truth that God is Love, and Sermon 9, in which he expressed horror at the
apathy of the Church to the teaching of the New Testament that Christ died
for all – this was a question according to which people would be judged at the
last day.

[19] E.g. Sermon 1 on 2 Thessalonians 3.5 or Sermon 5 on 1 Thessalonians 1.2–3,
Notes of Sermons, Vol. 1, Paisley, 1831.

[20] *Responsibility for the Gift of Eternal Life*, London, 1873, p. 88.

narrowly the foundation furnished by communications made in the Gospel for *Assurance of Faith.* This led directly to the closer consideration of *the extent of the Atonement,* and the circumstances in which mankind had been placed by the shedding of the blood of Christ; and it soon appeared to me manifest that unless Christ died *for all,* and unless the Gospel announced Him as *the gift of God to every human being,* so that there remained nothing to be done to give the individual a title to rejoice in Christ as his own Saviour, there was no foundation in the record of God for the Assurance which I demanded, and what I saw to be essential to true holiness. The next step therefore was my teaching, as the subject-matter of the Gospel, Universal Atonement and Pardon through the blood of Christ.[21]

McLeod Campbell made the problem he had with the Kirk very clear a little later in a letter to his father in May, 1833.

When a *great thing* is going on, a controversy concerning the name of the Lord, which this about *atonement* and *assurance* is – the question about atonement being the question, "Is God Love?" and the question about assurance being, "will those who know the name of the Lord put their trust in Him?"[22] It is only when people believe the Gospel message that Christ has already come and made atonement for our sins, that by one sacrifice which he has offered for sin and has put away sin, that they can have confidence in coming to God.[23]

The basic situation has been clearly analysed by James B. Torrance in his introduction to a reissue of *The Nature of the Atonement.*

Whereas the New Testament rings with the note of assurance, and the imperatives of the Gospel flow from the Apostles' understanding of the indicatives of the Gospel, among his

---

[21] *Reminiscences and Reflections,* p. 24. See McLeod Campbell's defence of his doctrine of assurance as 'of the essence of faith', 'Speech before the Synod of Glasgow and Ayr', *op. cit.* pp. 18ff, 43ff.

[22] *Memorials,* Vol. 1, p. 109. See also *Reminiscences and Reflections,* Chapter V, 'Assurance of Faith' and 'Universality of Atonement', pp. 152–7.

[23] Sermon 5 on 1 Peter 1.7.

people he found little evidence of peace and joy and confidence in God. The more he thought about this, the more he became convinced it was due to a 'legal strain' in their thinking that led to a want of true religion in the land.[24]

That legal strain derived from the fact that teaching about the atonement was shaped by an overall perspective governed by 'the reign of law' whereas the nature of the atonement, like divine revelation itself,[25] ought primarily and properly to be regarded and understood *in the light of itself* – and that was what McLeod Campbell set out to do.[26] In doing so, however, he found that a decisive shift had to be made away from the logical framework of double predestination and rigid law in federal Calvinism, and a narrow conception of the nature of the atonement which implies that God loves and that Christ died for the elect alone. A move had to be made away from that traditional framework of thought to one that was appropriate to the atonement itself which properly must be interpreted in its own light and in accordance with its own intrinsic nature, and not from external considerations. This was a methodological decision of quite immense importance, not to separate method and content,[27] which his contemporaries did not appreciate, for they still tried to understand his theology within the brackets and abstract definitions of their own rationalistic Calvinism, and their customary belief that the *Westminster Confession* was an exact and complete transcript of Scriptural doctrine. 'In Evangelical practice', as A. J. Campbell pointed out, 'its authority was equal to the Scripture.'[28] That was why evangelical people failed to appreciate what McLeod Campbell was trying to say, as indeed many of them still do.

McLeod Campbell's problems were not only with troubled people in his congregation at Rhu but with his ministerial brethren

---

[24] See James B. Torrance, 'Introduction' to the 4th edition of John McLeod Campbell's great work, *The Nature of the Atonement*, Edinburgh, & Grand Rapids, 1996, pp. 2f; and also his Foreword to the work of George M. Tuttle, *So Rich A Soil. John McLeod Campbell on Christian Atonement*, Edinburgh 1986, pp. 6f.

[25] This was the main subject of his striking book, *Thoughts on Revelation*, 2nd edn London, 1874. See especially pp. 14ff, 26ff.

[26] *The Nature of the Atonement*, 6th edn pp. xviiff. The citations that follow are made from this edition.

[27] This is made very clear in the Introduction to the second edition of *The Nature of the Atonement*, reproduced in the 6th edn, pp. 199ff, 214, 236ff, 252.

[28] *Two Centuries of the Church of Scotland 1707–1929*, Paisley, 1930, p. 192.

who too often thought of justice and mercy as opposites, and
regarded Christ as 'more tender-hearted' and 'more merciful' than
the Father,[29] so that instead of thinking of the atonement as flowing
from the Love of the Father they thought of it as placating the
wrath of God and reconciling him to mankind. It was their doctrine
of God that troubled them for they tended to think of God as loving
mankind only because of what Christ has done, and could not
understand how in God mercy and justice, love and holiness, grace
and judgment, belong intimately and inseparably together. And
so in his sermons McLeod Campbell found that in preaching the
Gospel of saving grace he had to correct people's basic conception
of the character of God and align it again with Christ: God and
Christ, the Father and the Son, are one in their being and nature
– there is no God behind the back of Jesus Christ. As the one
Mediator between God and Man who is himself both God and Man
Christ cannot be thought of in some intermediate way, as coming
in between us and the wrath of God, or as changing God or making
him merciful. Jesus Christ is God incarnate; what God is in Christ
he ever was and is in himself. Christ's coming among us in the
likeness of sinful flesh, in the likeness of flesh as it is in us sinners,
in order to condemn sin in the flesh and reconcile us to God, is
the very movement and expression of the Love of God.[30] 'The mind
of God' and 'the mind of Christ', 'the mind of Christ' and 'the
mind of God' are completely one. The forgiving Love of God for
the world and the forgiving Love of Christ for all men are one and
the same, the Love of God in Christ Jesus for the world and for all
men.[31] That is the ground of the sinner's trust in God and the
basis of the believer's assurance of salvation.

As J. B. Torrance (to cite him again) has pointed out,

> Campbell saw that fundamental to the whole issue was the
> doctrine of God. Instead of thinking of God as the Father,
> who loves all humanity, and who in Christ gives us the gift of
> sonship and who freely forgives us through Jesus Christ, they
> thought of God as One whose love is conditioned by human

---

[29] See Sermon 27 on Psalm 89.14–17, p. 23, *Notes of Sermons*, Vol. 3.
[30] See especially the sermons on Romans 8.1–4, *Notes of Sermons by The Rev. J. M.
      Campbell*, Vol. 1, Greenock, 1831, pp. 328ff & 357ff; and also the unpublished
      Sermon 8 on Galatians 2.20, taken in Short Hand, Vol. 1, Paisley, 1831.
[31] See, for example, sermons 27, pp 10f; 30, p. 2; 32. p. 3; 34, p. 6, *Notes of Sermons*,
      Paisley, 1831; and McLeod Campbell's speech before the Synod of Glasgow
      and Ayr, *op. cit.*, pp. 12f.

repentance and faith, and whose forgiveness had to be purchased by the payment of the sufferings of Christ on behalf of the elect. 'Instead of resting in the character of God as revealed in Christ, they looked upon the death of Christ as so much suffering – the purchase money of heaven to a certain number, to whom it infallibly secured heaven.'[32] They saw a contract-god who needs to be conditioned into being gracious.[33]

McLeod Campbell unquestionably held firmly to 'the Catholic and Reformed' doctrine of the atonement. In Jesus Christ his incarnate Son God himself has come among us as the one Mediator between God and man, to be one with us and one of us in such a way as to appropriate our actual human nature, and make our life and death under divine judgment his own, in order to pay our debt and make restitution which we are unable to do, to substitute himself for us (on our behalf, as well as in our place) in such a way as to bear upon and in himself the righteous wrath of God against our sin, to suffer the penalty of death which is the wages of sin, and through offering himself in body and soul without spot or blemish in sacrifice to God to make atonement for our sin and thus in our place, in our name and on our behalf to satisfy the holiness and righteousness of the Father.[34] We shall have to ask what McLeod Campbell meant by the terms 'penalty', 'substitute' or 'satisfy'.

It must be noted right away, however, that he expounded the nature of this atonement not in abstract legal terms, as though it were the acting out of a plan, but in *personal* terms, and in particular in terms of the *filial* relation between the Son and the Father.[35] Atonement has to be understood in recognition of the fact that *God* sent his Son to be the propitiation for our sins, that *God* was in Christ reconciling the world to himself, and therefore in recognition of the fact that 'if God provides the atonement, then forgiveness must precede the atonement; and the atonement must be the form of the manifestation of the forgiving love of God, not its cause.'[36] This was in line with the statements of Augustine and

---

[32] McLeod Campbell, *Reminiscences and Reflections*, p. 25.

[33] *Reminiscences and Reflections*, p. 4.

[34] See particularly *The Nature of the Atonement*, London, 6th edn, 1895, pp. 98ff, 122ff, 248ff, 258ff.

[35] *The Nature of the Atonement*, pp. 59ff, 139ff & 150ff.

[36] *The Nature of the Atonement*, p. 15.

Calvin that God does not love us because we are reconciled to him; rather was it was because God first loved us that we are reconciled to him. While the ultimate ground of atonement – its ultimate foundation in God[37] – is in God's immense love toward us, evident in the fact that he did not even spare his beloved Son, it is in the sacrifice of his beloved Son incarnate in our humanity that God's atoning love is actively and actually embodied: Jesus Christ is himself the atonement. 'He *is* the propitiation. Propitiation for us sinners – reconciliation to God – oneness with God abides in Christ.'[38]Jesus Christ is himself *Propitiation.* 'Propitiation' means quite literally that in his infinite love and free grace God draws *near* to us in such a way as to draw us *near* to himself. In his sermons McLeod Campbell could at times speak of 'the reconciled God', but never with the idea that God had to be reconciled in order to be propitious, for reconciliation is what God the Father has himself freely provided in Christ out of his unbounded love.

A change had to be made in the controlling framework of thought. Hitherto it had been one of fixed law of a severely contractual kind which had long been supplied by federal theology, but McLeod Campbell returned to one governed by the mind and will and love of God as he is revealed in the Gospel. That is what the New Testament speaks of as the Kingdom of God, not of God conceived in the abstract but of God as he is in his beloved Son, and as he is seen to be in the relation between Jesus Christ and God the Father. 'The Kingdom of God as it seeks our faith is seen in Jesus Christ. The conception of God as a Father, and of a relation to him which is sonship, is seen realised in Christ. The Son of God is seen revealing the Father as the Father, by being in our sight the beloved Son in whom the Father is well pleased.'[39] It was within this framework that McLeod Campbell set himself to give an account of the nature of the atonement *as it is seen in its own light* and in fidelity to the teaching of the New Testament. This had to be one in which traditional forms of doctrine would be reinterpreted in such a way as to bring to light their deepest evangelical truth, and at the same time be one, he felt, which would

---

[37] Cf. *The Nature of the Atonement*, pp. 152 & 286.

[38] *The Nature of the Atonement*, pp. 16f & 170f. See Calvin, *Inst.* 2.16.3–4; Augustine, *St John's Gospel*, Ch. 6. McLeod Campbell unfortunately tended to interpret the teaching of Calvin too much in the light of traditional Calvinism rather than of Calvin himself.

[39] *The Nature of the Atonement*, p. xxx.

allow for the personal appropriation of the atonement as of the very essence of faith. Faith has to do with *realities* revealed in God's Word.[40]

Instead of beginning, then, with the eternal decrees of God and the reign of law,[41] McLeod Campbell turned to the Incarnation in which God has revealed himself in his Son Jesus Christ as the God who *is* Love, for what he is toward us in the Gospel he is eternally in himself – indeed as Luther held 'there is no other God besides this man Christ Jesus'.[42] It was not just to the Incarnation itself that McLeod Campbell turned as his starting point, but to the Incarnation in its relation to the atonement, and thus to the atonement as developed in the Incarnation.[43]It is in that indissoluble interrelation that we learn that God *is* Love, and that since he is Love he loves all people without exception, for he is, and indeed cannot be as God, toward them other than he is in himself.[44] *That is the ultimate ground of atonement.*[45] That ultimate ground, however, has been made known to us in the Sonship of Christ, for as Jesus said, 'He who hath seen me hath seen the Father', which is explained by his words 'I am the way and the truth and the life, no man cometh unto the Father but by me.' The primary revelation we have of God, then, is as *Father*, whom the Son reveals to us precisely as being the Son of the Father.[46] That essentially biblical note struck deeply into the forensic concept of God in the federal tradition, and evangelised it. This did not mean that for McLeod Campbell there was no room for the conception of God as Judge (a biblical conception which abounds in his sermons particularly), but rather that it was held in conjunction with the conception of God as Father, and understood

---

[40] 'Faith', he once said in a sermon, 'is expressive of the conviction of the mind when the things which God has revealed in his word are before the mind as realities.' Sermon. on 1 Thess. 1.2, 3, *op. cit.,* p. 2.

[41] Cf. pp. xxxiii & xxxix: 'the reign of law as such offers no place for an atonement, even as it offers no place for prayer'.

[42] *The Nature of the Atonement*, p. 37.

[43] *The Nature of the Atonement*, pp. xviff. Cf. *Christ the Bread of Life*, 2nd edn London, 1869, pp. 162f & 177f.

[44] 'If love be of God's character; if it be of his very substance; if God *is* love, then of necessity God loves every man; yes, those who limit his love to some do actually deny that there is love in God at all...' *Responsibility for the Gift of Eternal Life*, 1873 edn, p. 88.

[45] *Responsibility*, p. 286; cf. p. 152.

[46] *Responsibility*, pp. xxx & xxxixf.

in the light of his transcendent holiness. It is as *holy* Father that God is Judge, and it is as *holy* Love that he is the Judge of all mankind. 'It is only by the *revelation* of the *Father* that God succeeds in realising the *will* of the Lawgiver in men. How much more can he thus alone realise the *longings* of the *Father's heart!*'[47]

Accordingly, since the highest teaching in the Kingdom of God is the life of Christ as Sonship toward the Father, McLeod Campbell took as his guide for an understanding of the atonement the *Father-Son relationship*.[48] This meant that he had to take with the utmost seriousness the incarnate constitution of the Son of the Father as Mediator, as God and man indissolubly united in one Person, and think out the nature of the atonement as the judging and propitiating Love of God the Father actualised within the life and death of Christ through whom we are given access to him as God the Father. This is an atonement which God in his grace freely provides in order to reconcile us to himself, not one which *makes* God gracious.

> The Scriptures do not speak of such an atonement; for they do not represent the love of God to man as the effect, and the atonement of Christ as the cause – just the contrary – they represent the love of God as the cause, and the atonement as the effect. 'God so loved the world, that he gave his only begotten Son, that whosoever believeth in him, might not perish, but have everlasting life.'[49]

Quite evidently, then, McLeod Campbell does not place the Sonship of Christ in opposition to law, but asserts the primacy of the filial relation over the legal relation, of grace over law. Properly regarded, however, 'God's law is God's own heart *come out in the shape of a law.*'[50] It is the law of Love.

Thus conceived in the indissoluble relation of the atonement to the Incarnation and of the Incarnation to the atonement, and in the depths of Christ's sinless life, the intrinsic nature of the atonement is be understood as essentially *moral and spiritual* as well as physical.[51] It was not just an external transaction (which would involve a form of Nestorian dualism between the divine and human

---

[47] *The Nature of the Atonement,* p. 62.
[48] *The Nature of the Atonement,* pp. 59ff.
[49] *The Nature of the Atonement,* p. 17.
[50] *Responsibility,* p. 106.
[51] See the note to Chapter VI of *The Nature of the Atonement,* pp. 342–4.

natures of the Saviour), but the unitary divine-human movement of propitiation, between God and us, and yet taking place within the mediatorial Person and obedient Life of Christ under law from his birth of the Virgin Mary to his death and resurrection. McLeod Campbell could not forget that Christ is God and man, God himself come among us as man, and acting personally in our human existence precisely as God and man, so that he thought of atonement as taking place at once within the filial relations of the incarnate Son to the Father, and in the depths of Christ's divine humanity. Hence he thought of Christ as vicariously bearing in himself the holy wrath of God and his righteous judgment against sin, not in disjunction from God, and not just physically but spiritually and morally, in which he, the one Mediator between God and man who is both God and man, bore *in himself* the righteous wrath of the Father and confessed our sin – it was an expiatory confession, made *with his whole incarnate Being in perfect oneness with the Father,* which Christ rendered to him in our name.

> That oneness of mind with the Father, which toward man took the form of condemnation of sin, would in the Son's dealings with the Father in relation to our sins, take the form of perfect confession of our sins. This confession as to its own nature must have been *a perfect Amen in humanity to the judgment of God on the sin of man.* Such an Amen was due in the truth of things. He who was the Truth could not be in humanity and not utter it...[52]

In one of his early sermons McLeod Campbell had already anticipated this, when he said: 'Christ was in the world the great Confessor of sin – he was in the world as condemning sin in the flesh. Above all he died and suffered – he expressed his Amen to God's righteous sentence upon sin. Now this is to have the mind of Christ, that we should confess the sin that is in mankind as he confessed it', although of course he had no sin of his own to confess.'[53] In another of his sermons he spoke of the objective ground to this vicarious Amen:

> Christ condemned sin not only by being the opposite of sin, but by giving himself as a sin-offering to God. By submitting

---

[52] *The Nature of the Atonement,* pp. 116f – see the whole section pp. 115–18.
[53] Sermon 24 on 1 John 1.8–9, p. 28. He defined confession in that sermon as 'to stand on God's side ... it is joining God against myself', *Notes of Sermons,* Paisley, Vol. 2, p. 5.

in his death to undergo the curse of God upon sin, he gave his testimony to the righteousness of God's curse upon sin. He gives up his human nature in which he stood to the law of death, and this though he himself was holy and without spot of sin; and in so doing he confesses the justice of the penalty which that human nature (humanity) had incurred by transgression.[54]

As McLeod Campbell used to tell his congregation, it was essentially an *amen* of the sinner to the righteous *judgment* of God in being righteously condemned and justly forgiven.[55]

It is important to note that the 'perfect Amen' in which Christ confessed our sin, and in which he yielded himself in body and soul to the inflictions of the Father, was yielded out of the ontological depths of his sinless humanity and in his inseparable relation to sinners, thereby acknowledging and receiving in our place and on our behalf the judicial condemnation of God upon us and absorbing it in himself.[56] As James Orr pointed out,[57] it would be a serious error to think of this 'Amen' as a mere ideal realisation of what God's wrath to sin is, for it was yielded 'under the actual pressure of the judgment which that wrath inflicts'. It was not a subjective but a real Amen yielded out of the midst of Christ's vicarious *death* as well as his life.

> In Christ's honouring of the righteous law of God, the *sentence of the law* was included, as well as *the mind of God* which that sentence expressed ... It was not simply sin that had to be dealt with but an existing law with its penalty of death, and that death as already incurred. So it was not only the divine mind that had to be responded to, but also that expression of the divine mind which was contained in God's making death the wages of sin.[58]

McLeod Campbell took seriously the teaching of St Paul in the opening verses of the eighth chapter of the Epistle to the Romans:

---

[54] *Responsibility*, p. 101. See also the Sermon 24 on 1 John. 1.8–9, pp. 16ff, *Notes of Sermons*, Vol. 2.

[55] See, for example, Sermon 28 on 1 Peter 3.16–21, p. 13f & 24f, and Sermon 29 on the same text, pp. 14f. *Notes of Sermons*, Paisley, Vol. 3.

[56] *Notes of Sermons*, Greenock, Vol 1., pp. 117 & 118.

[57] James Orr, *The Christian View of God and the World*, Edinburgh, 1897, p. 313.

[58] *The Nature of the Atonement*, p. 260.

'What the law could not do, in that it was weak through the flesh, God sending his own Son in the likeness of sinful flesh, and for sin, condemned sin in the flesh.'[59] By this McLeod Campbell did not of course mean that in becoming one with us and one of us in our fallen humanity Christ himself became a sinner, but the very reverse, that in assuming what was ours he sanctified and redeemed it, and so began to pay the price of our redemption from the very beginning of his incarnate entry into our Adamic existence and all through his incarnate life among sinners. Thus in being made in the likeness of sinful flesh Christ brought his own holiness which he shared with the Father to bear upon it in such a way that 'he condemned sin in the flesh, that the righteousness of God might be fulfilled in us'.[60] As St Paul wrote elsewhere: 'God made him to be sin for us, who knew no sin, that we might be made the righteousness of God in him.'[61] Following the great Athanasius who thought of the incarnate mediatorial and priestly office of Christ as one in which he ministered the things of God to man and the things of man to God,[62] McLeod Campbell thought of Christ as *dealing with men on the part of God, and as dealing with God on the part of men*, not as two activities but as one seamless activity within his incarnate person, which he spoke of in terms of what he called the retrospective and the prospective aspects of atonement.[63] Like Athanasius, therefore, he thought of atonement as taking place within the incarnate constitution of the Mediator who is of one and the same being as God the Father. It was in this twofold atoning relation of Christ to the Father, that is, his dealing with God on the part of men and his dealing with men on the part of God, within the unity of his incarnate Person and life as the one Mediator between God and man, which called for a recasting of the traditional notion of 'penal suffering' lodged in current Scottish Calvinism. *The penal element as infliction under the wrath of God, which Christ as Mediator fully experienced, was by no means rejected*

---

[59] *The Christian View*, p. 109; & Romans 8.3. See his Sermon 34 on Hebrews 2, pp. 12f, *Notes of Sermons*, Paisley, Vol. 3.
[60] Cf. McLeod Campbell's later exposition of this truth, *Responsibility*, pp. 97ff.
[61] 2 Corinthians 5.21.
[62] Athanasius, *Contra Arianos*, 4.6 – McLeod Campbell does not actually cite this passage.
[63] *The Nature of the Atonement*, pp. 111ff, 130ff, 139ff & 150ff.

but discerned in a deeper dimension, but it could not be considered as 'complete in itself as a substituted punishment'.[64]

McLeod Campbell never hesitated to speak of the divine punishment of sin or of Christ as dying and suffering as the Just for the unjust, in which 'substitution' is distinctly implied – 'one bearing something *for* others'[65] – but he could not accept the legalist and quantitative way in which suffering and substitution were connected with one another in the rationalist Calvinism of his day, in terms of the Father punishing the Son, rather than in terms of what took place in Christ as God and Man in one incarnate Person. This is brought out very clearly in his Sermon on Psalm 89.14–17, which may be cited at length, as it represents the way in which he actually presented to his congregation at Rhu the Gospel message that it is through the atoning sacrifice of Christ that we are brought back to God.

> The error that has most prevailed is that of thinking of the sufferings of the Lord Jesus Christ as a certain quantity of misery suffered by one being for other beings, *for the purpose* that they should never suffer misery for themselves – which makes the atonement have for its direct object the delivering us from sufferings: and from this arises the not seeing the consistency of the fact that Christ died for all men with the other fact that all men are not saved. If he suffered so much just as a substitute for men's final sufferings that they should not take place, then it is impossible to see how these sufferings should have been endured for any who shall themselves suffer. But this is an error. For Christ died the just for the unjust *not* that sinful men might be happy, but that they might be taken out of their sins, and so delivered from the wrath to come – it is not in any other way. This is a

---

[64] *The Nature of the Atonement,* pp. 130–1. See his Sermon 27 on Psalm 89.14–17, pp. 5ff, where McLeod Campbell distinguishes between a right and a wrong way to regard the sufferings of Christ as substitutionary: although he suffered as the just for the unjust, his sufferings took their character from what Christ was in our nature, and not from some conception of what would have been the lot of every man. *Notes of Sermons,* Paisley, Vol. 3. What McLeod Campbell rejected was a notion of the atoning suffering of Christ 'as the suffering of that punishment which men would have had to endure throughout eternity if he had not suffered for them.' Sermon 36 on Hebrews 10.31, pp. 13f – *Notes of Sermons,* Vol. 3.

[65] Sermon 27, on Psalm 89.14–17, *Notes of Sermons,* Vol. 3, p. 5.

very vital error because it leads to all the other errors of limiting the atonement – of having a false ground for assurance – and of feeling as if the Son were more merciful than the Father. All these errors are to be referred to this root, that they don't know what atonement is – but they take a carnal, mercantile, and an arithmetical view of it – they calculate as it were by figures, and think, in this way, to measure the value and sufficiency of that sacrifice which Christ offered for the whole world. The error on the other side is the feeling as if there were no substitution – as if the just did not suffer *for the unjust* – the error of not looking to Christ as coming from the bosom of the Father: but rather looking to him as a man – the Son in human nature who because he was in this condition was to be made perfect through suffering. This error is inconsistent with seeing how a personal place can be given to us different from that we deserve, and how we should have a footing before God different from that which, in strict justice, we should receive.[66]

In other words, the difference between McLeod Campbell's understanding of substitutionary atonement and that of those opposed to him in the Church of Scotland had to do with 'the *character* of Christ's agony – it was the holiness of the blood that was shed – it was the *character* of the sufferings that were endured.'[67] It was the profound kind of suffering in which God and man were one and undivided in the atoning mediation of Christ – to think of the sufferings of the Son without the participation of the Father in the atoning sacrifice, simply in terms of the judgment of the Father inflicted externally upon the Son in our stead, was a serious lapse into Nestorian heresy which McLeod Campbell abhorred.

It must be emphasised that because of the profound way in which he thought of the 'divine humanity' of Christ, and of the indivisible oneness of God and man and divine and human activity in the incarnate Person of the Son, McLeod Campbell could not think of the atonement in a merely forensic or instrumentalist way external to Christ. Nor correspondingly could he think of justification merely in external forensic imputational terms, for he regarded that as 'often representing our relation to Christ in a

---

[66] *Notes of Sermons*, Vol. 3, pp. 23ff. See also Sermon 36, pp. 13f for a similar statement, *Notes of Sermons*, Vol. 3.

[67] *Notes of Sermons*, Paisley, Vol. 3, p. 15.

way that has been artificial and forensic – a mere arrangement, and not what affects the manner of our being to its inmost depths.'[68] Rather must atonement be regarded as the movement of divine reconciling and justifying love within the Incarnation as developed in the atonement. It was the divine life incarnate in Jesus Christ which made atonement for our sins, united to which through 'the Spirit whom Christ has for us' we are really, not just externally, imputationally, justified before God.[69] This was why Calvin, here following Cyril of Alexandria, linked justification and union with Christ closely together. Within this strictly christological and soteriological frame of thought the classical notions of penalty and satisfaction have a much deeper and fuller meaning than they often had in a federalistic Calvinism. Thus the term 'penal' which McLeod Campbell used sometimes rather ambiguously, and yet frequently, not least in his sermons, has to be understood not in crude terms of some quantitative equivalence in suffering,[70] but in an essentially spiritual and moral way, not simply in a physical way as the external infliction of divine judgment which Christ bore as our substitute in life and death. His vicarious penal sufferings were certainly physical in his death on the Cross, but they had to do above all with what he bore for us and on our behalf agonisingly in the depths of his 'divine humanity' – 'the sorrows of the Man of Sorrows'.[71] As John Calvin used to insist we must think of the sufferings which Christ endured for our sakes not just in his body but in his *soul.* 'Thou shalt make his *soul* an offering for sin.'[72] This was a frequent emphasis in earlier Scottish theology, but never more wonderfully expressed than by Samuel Rutherford in his deeply moving book, *Christ Dying and Drawing Sinners to Himself, Or A Survey*

---

[68] See *The Nature of the Atonement*, p. 351, but also pp. 114 ff.

[69] It was in this connection that McLeod Campbell like Fraser of Brae and the Marrow men cited the words of St Paul: 'I am crucified with Christ: nevertheless I live; yet not I, but Christ liveth in me: and the life which I now live in the flesh I live by the faith of the Son of God, who loved me, and gave himself for me.' (Gal. 2.20). See, for instance, *The Nature of the Atonement*, p. 347.

[70] See Sermon 4 on 1 Thess. 1.2–3: 'It has been an awful mistake just to take these sufferings as a certain amount of agony and not to know what the character of that agony was.' p. 12f. *Notes of Sermons*, Vol. 1, Paisley, 1831.

[71] *The Nature of the Atonement*, pp. 111–18; see also Sermon 23 on Hebrews 12, *Notes of Sermons*, Greenock, Vol. 2, pp. 9ff.

[72] Cf. Calvin's Commentary and Sermon on Isaiah 53.10; cf. *The Nature of Atonement*, pp. 102, 120, 122, 135, & 218ff. Cf. McLeod Campbell's Sermon 8 on Galatians 2.20, pp. 15f, *Notes of Sermons*, Paisley, Vol. 1.

of our Saviour in his soule suffering, his lovelyness in his death, and the efficacie thereof. His understanding of the sacrifice of the Father in giving up his Only Begotten Son for us, and its incarnate counterpart in the 'soule-trouble' of Christ 'rational and extremely penall ... sinneless and innocent', 'made heavie even to death, for sinne, as sinne, and as contrary to the Father's love ... Christ did more than pay our debts; it was a summe above price that he gave for us.'[73] That is surely what John McLeod Campbell discerned in the fearful unfathomable sorrow which Christ bore in the depths of his soul for our sakes, the vicarious sorrow which lay in the very heart of his atoning sacrifice. Moreover, in anticipation of McLeod Campbell, Samuel Rutherford also thought of Christ as *repenting* for us in his passive obedience: 'Christ weeped for my sinnes, and that is all the *repentance* required in me.'[74]

It is in this light also that we must understand what McLeod Campbell meant by his expression '*perfect repentance*' (suggested by a passing reference of Jonathan Edwards' to 'equivalent sorrow and repentance'[75]), which expositors have often (sometimes misleadingly), rendered as 'vicarious repentance', or 'vicarious penitence'.[76] McLeod Campbell himself never actually used these expressions.[77] 'Repentance' as he used the word in this connection evidently does not mean what we commonly mean by it.[78] What he was feeling after may perhaps be made clear, in some respect, by the terms *poena* and *poenitentia* as used in patristic Latin, which although they had different roots could be correlated with the meaning of penalty or satisfaction, and repentance or penitence. Thus *poena* could be used of external infliction, but *poenitentia* of

---

[73] *Samuel Rutherford, Christ Dying,* London, 1647, pp. 17 & 21f.
[74] *Christ Dying,* p. 79.
[75] See *The Nature of the Atonement,* pp. 118f, 123, & Notes to Chapter VI, pp. 343f; and Jonathan Edwards, *Satisfaction for Sin,* ch. ii, pp. 1–3, to which McLeod Campbell referred.
[76] See *The Nature of the Atonement,* p. 117. Consult the chapter on 'The Vicarious Penitence of Christ' in H. R. Mackintosh, *Some Aspects of Christian Belief,* London, 1923, pp. 79ff.
[77] This has been rightly pointed out recently in a superb book by Leanne Van Dyk, *The Desire of Divine Love. John McLeod Campbell's Doctrine of the Atonement,* New York, 1995, pp. 112f.
[78] For the following cf. the chapter on 'Repentance' in *Responsibility for the Gift of Eternal Life,* in which McLeod Campbell spoke of repentance as giving God the place which God always ought to have in the heart, which the sinner cannot do on his own. Is that not what Christ does for us?

its internal counterpart in the soul. Christ endured both *poena* and *poenitentia*, for the penal infliction which he endured in our nature, for us and in our place, he endured in his *soul* as well as his body. In that sense the notion of vicarious penitence is understandable, but what is not understandable is that perfect repentance offered within the divine humanity of Christ, and therefore by God as well as man, in Amen to God's righteous judgment, could be said *simpliciter* of God.

On the other hand, something else must be said. All the redemptive activity of Christ in our place and on our behalf was fulfilled in his inseparable oneness with God, in such a way that the Father did not hold himself aloof from the humiliation and passion of Christ but identified himself with it, and took it upon his own heart and shared it to the full. Behind the sacrifice of Christ was the sacrifice of the Father, who did not spare his own Son but delivered him up for us all. The Cross of Christ is to be seen as the heart of God unveiled in his feelings toward man.[79] That ultimate oneness between the Father and the Son must surely obtain even in Christ's atoning identification with us in our sin and in his expiatory bearing with us God's (and his own) righteous judgment upon our sin. It is that identification of *God incarnate* with us which was inexpressibly present in the *Amen* to God actualised in the Saviour's vicarious submission, contrition and confession which McLeod Campbell sought to express by the term 'perfect repentance'. This is not essentially different from the point made by John Calvin that as the incarnate Mediator Christ made himself 'answerable for our guilt', and that it is in this way that we are to understand the *Pater Noster.*[80] While sinners we are unable to pray to the Father as we ought, yet the Lord Jesus Christ in his self-submission and self-offering to the Father, has put his prayer, *Our Father*, into our unclean mouth so that we may pray through him, and with him, and in him to the Father, 'Forgive us our trespasses as we forgive them who trespass against us', and be accepted by

---

[79] 'If we carry with us continually the conviction that Christ is God, then we see in his sufferings, not what was felt by God for a short time when he appeared on earth, in our nature; but we see what is continually felt by God in regard to sin...' Sermon 15, on 2 Peter 3.15, *Notes of Sermons*, Vol. 3, p. 8.

[80] See Calvin's *Commentary on Isaiah* 53.7–12, and his *Sermons on Isaiah* 53.4–6, 9–11. McLeod Campbell himself, however, did not follow Calvin in this vicarious way of understanding the Lord's Prayer. See, for example, his Sermon 26 on Luke 11.1–3, *Notes of Sermons*, Vol. 3, pp. 17ff.

the Father through, with and in him. Thus, as McLeod Campbell expressed it, when we pray the *Our Father* which Christ puts on our lips, it is the *Abba Father* of Christ himself which cries in us through the Spirit to the Father.[81]

We may express McLeod Campbell's point in still another way: the older theologians, like Thomas Boston, thought of God as providing the means whereby his justice was satisfied, but in McLeod Campbell's thought those means were not just external but primarily internal to God incarnate, in that 'he made his *soul* an offering for sin.'

> Unless we contemplate His sense of our sin and His desire to accomplish for us this great salvation as livingly working in him and practically influencing him, we cannot understand how truly He made His soul an offering for sin, when, receiving into Himself the full sense of the divine condemnation of sin, He dealt on behalf of man with the ultimate and absolute root of judgment in God, presenting the expiation of the due confession of sin, and in so doing at once opening for the divine forgiveness a channel in which it could freely flow to us, – and for us a way in which we could approach God.[82]

While the ultimate objective ground of the atoning self-offering of Christ lies in God himself who so loved us that he did not withhold his Only Begotten Son but gave him to be our Saviour, and in him gave us himself, it was in the actualisation of that atoning propitiation in the human nature which Christ assumed from us, in the inner depths of his soul, that our answer to God the Father has been provided.

Writing about 'the vicarious penitence of Christ' advocated by some of McLeod Campbell's interpreters, H. R. Mackintosh remarked: 'Vicarious penitence, however unsatisfactory as it stands, is suggestive of the truth that at the heart of the Lord's atonement is the perfect acknowledgment made of the righteous judgment

---

[81] See *The Nature of the Atonement*, pp. 214ff; also pp. 199f, 236ff, 252, 344. Mention is to be made here of McLeod Campbell's frequent reference to Galatians 2.20: 'I live, yet not I, but Christ in me, for the life which I now live in the flesh I live by the faith of the Son of God who loved me and gave himself for me.' See, for example, *Memorials* I, p. 249, and II, p. 83.

[82] *The Nature of the Atonement*, p. 199.

of God as embodied in his pain.'[83] It is that objective confession of
our sin which Christ offered and his objective submission to the
wrath of God, which constitutes the vicarious ground on which
our confession of sin and our repentance rest. For McLeod
Campbell, full and proper repentance includes real sorrow and
contrition for sin and indeed expiatory confession in acknow-
ledgement of the holiness and love of God, which we are unable
to offer but which Christ Jesus offers in our name and in our place.[84]
Thus 'perfect repentance', in McLeod Campbell's deeply spiritual
sense, means that when the sinner confesses his sins, all too
unworthily, the Gospel tells him that *Christ has already answered for
him*, and that *God in Christ has already accepted him*, so that the sinner
does not rest on any repentance of his own, but on what Christ
had already offered to the Father not just in his place but on his
behalf. McLeod Campbell speaks of this as 'the voice that is in the
blood of Christ, viz. Christ's confession of our sins. In the faith of
God's acceptance of that confession on our behalf, we receive
strength to say Amen to it – to join in it – and, joining in it, we find
it a living way to God.'[85] That was surely the evangelical intention
in McLeod Campbell's notion of 'perfect repentance'. Behind it
also lies the truth and importance of John Calvin's distinction
between 'legal repentance' and 'evangelical repentance', which
had already been playing a role in Scottish theology.[86]

It must be noted that while McLeod Campbell did not hesitate
to speak of Christ as bearing the wrath and judgment of God, he
declined to speak of Christ being 'punished' for our sins,[87] at least
in the Anselmic sense given to that expression by many of his
contemporaries. Here he was true to the teaching of the New
Testament which *never* speaks of the judgment that Christ bore for
our sake as 'punishment'. For McLeod Campbell, God can no more
be thought of as 'punishing' Christ than of being 'angry with him
personally'.[88] This does not mean that there was no penal element

---

[83] Mackintosh, *Some Aspects of Christian Belief*, pp. 96f.
[84] See 'Notes of an address to an Elder', Sunday, 9th May, 1830, after preaching
on 1 Thessalonians 1.2, 3, *Notes of Sermons*, Paisley, Vol. 1, 1831.
[85] 'Notes of an address to an Elder', pp. 156f.
[86] John Calvin, *Institute*, 3.3.4. For the biblical basis of evangelical repentance
see John Colquhoun, *A View of Evangelical Repentance from the Sacred Records*,
Edinburgh, 1825.
[87] *The Nature of the Atonement*, pp. 47ff, 70, 101f, etc.
[88] *Ibid.* pp. 49 & 348. 'Though God's wrath against sin was not felt by the Son of
God as coming forth against him personally, as if the Father saw him as a sinner;

in the substitutionary sacrifice, but that it is of a fuller and profounder kind than can ever be expressed in terms of legal and logical equivalents as in the notion of 'penal substitution'. The more McLeod Campbell tried to see the atonement 'by its own light', he found himself forced to 'distinguish between an atoning sacrifice for sin and the enduring as a substitute the punishment due to sin – being shut up to the conclusion, that while Christ suffered for our sins as an atoning sacrifice, what he suffered was not – because from its nature it could not be – a punishment.' Thus in faithfulness to the New Testament teaching about the intrinsically spiritual nature of the Christ's atoning sacrifice for sin, McLeod Campbell felt himself 'obliged to recognise a distinction between an atonement for sin and substituted punishment.'[89] He asked:

> The sufferings of Christ in making his soul an offering for sin being what they were, was it the pain as pain, and as a penal infliction, or was it the pain as a condition and form of holiness and love under the pressure of our sin and its consequent misery, that is presented to our faith as the essence of the sacrifice and its atoning virtue?[90]

That is to say, Christ's atoning sacrifice did not have to do with a penal infliction coming on Christ *from without*, but one which he received and endorsed in the depths of his vicarious life and divine humanity. Christ really bore in his own Person the penal inflictions which are the expression of the wrath of God against the sin of the world.[91] It is, McLeod Campbell held, only in connection with what he called a 'lower moral region' that the notion of punishment arises.

> But if we will come to the atonement, not venturing in our own darkness to predetermine anything as to its nature, but expecting light to shine upon our spirits from it, even the light of eternal life; if we will suffer it to inform us by its own light why we needed it, and what its true value to us is, the

yet must that wrath in the truth of what it is have been present to and realised by his spirit...' p. 249.

[89] *The Nature of the Atonement*, pp. 101 & 104. Cf his early sermon on Hebrews 10.31, Sermon 36, pp. 13f, *Notes of Sermons*, Paisley, Vol. 3, pp. 13f.

[90] *The Nature of the Atonement*, p. 102.

[91] *The Nature of the Atonement*, p. 314.

punishment of sin will fall into its proper place as testifying to
the existence of an evil greater than itself, even, *sin*; from
which greater evil it is the *direct* object of the atonement to
deliver us, – deliverance from punishment being but a
secondary result.[92]

The usual criticisms of McLeod Campbell over the question of
'penal substitution' in his own times and since appear rather
shallow for they fail to appreciate the profound soteriological,
moral, and spiritual dimension in which his thought moved in the
interrelation between the Father and the Son in the one divine-
human Person of the Mediator. Their critique regularly implies
the very kind of Nestorian dualism in Christ, and external
instrumentalist notion of atonement, which McLeod Campbell
studiously avoided. As he understood it the penal suffering which
Christ bore in our place and on our behalf was one which he bore
in the indissoluble oneness as God and man in one Person, not
just in his human nature but in the union of his human nature
and divine nature, and thus in the innermost relation of the
incarnate Son and God the Father, inexplicable as that may be.
He was deeply aware that the atonement is a profound mystery
which cannot be understood or expounded in accordance with
our preconceived notions of 'rectoral' government, let alone
expressed, in simplistic logical and legal terms.

This way of thinking of the vicarious death of Christ in spiritual
and moral terms applies not least to the notion of 'satisfaction'
first introduced into theology by Tertullian, developed by Anselm,
and appropriated by Calvinists. As McLeod Campbell used the
term, it did not have to do with the kind of satisfaction of legal
requirements or preconditions, such as were expressed in the
covenants of works and redemption, or with the satisfaction of
inexorable divine justice in order to pacify and reconcile God to
sinners. With reference to 'the assumption that his sufferings were
penal', McLeod Campbell wrote

there is still seen in this great peace-making an awful coming
together in the inner man of the Son of God of moral and
spiritual elements; the harmonising of which in the result of
peace between man and God – a peace in God realised in
humanity for man to know and partake in, a peace to be

---

[92] *The Nature of the Atonement*, pp. 163f.

preached to the chief of sinners – has been a work of love in which the Son of God is seen bearing the chastisement of our peace; suffering for us, the just for the unjust, to bring us to God.[93]

It was in that connection that McLeod Campbell spoke of *satisfaction* as essentially a moral and spiritual rather than a legal matter, which must be understood in accordance with the nature of God as he has *actually* revealed himself to us in Jesus Christ.

The wrath of God against sin is a reality, however men have erred in their thoughts as to how that wrath was to be appeased. Nor is the idea that satisfaction was due to the divine justice a delusion, however far men have wandered from the true conception of what would meet its righteous demand. And if so, then Christ, in dealing with God on behalf of men, must be conceived of as dealing with the righteous wrath of God against sin, and as according to that which it was due.[94]

Without the assumption of an imputation of our guilt, and in perfect harmony with the unbroken consciousness of personal separation from our sins, the Son of God, bearing us and our sins on his own heart before the Father, must needs respond to the Father's judgment on our sins, with that confession of their evil and of the righteousness of the wrath of God against them, and holy sorrow because of them, which were due, due in the truth of things, due on our behalf though we could not render it, due from Him as in our nature and our true brother;- what He must needs feel in Himself because of the holiness and love which were in Him – what he must needs utter to the Father in expiation of our sins when he would make intercession for us.[95]

Whatever be supposed to have been the nature of the link between Christ and our sins, it was needful that he should on our behalf deal with the righteous wrath of God against sin in that way which accorded with the eternal and unchanging truth of things.[96]

---

[93] *The Nature of the Atonement,* p. 250.
[94] *The Nature of the Atonement,* p. 116.
[95] *The Nature of the Atonement,* p. 129.
[96] *The Nature of the Atonement,* p. 269.

The holy one of God, bearing the sins of all men on his spirit
– in Luther's words, 'the one sinner' – and meeting the cry
of those sins for judgment, and the wrath due to them,
absorbing and exhausting that divine wrath in that adequate
sense of confession and perfect response on the part of man,
which was possible only to the infinite and eternal
righteousness in humanity.[97]

By that perfect response in Amen to the mind of God, in
relation to sin, is the wrath of God rightly met, and that is
accorded to divine justice which is its due, and could alone
satisfy it.[98]

It should be clear from these citations that far from rejecting
the notion of *expiation of our guilt* and *atoning satisfaction* for our
sins, McLeod Campbell thought of it in a rather different and richer
way, not just in terms of the satisfaction of the righteous law of
God, but in accordance with '*the demands of the Father's heart*',[99] and
thus at a deeper level, at which Christ received it into the bosom
of his divine humanity,

responding to it out of the depths of that divine humanity –
and *in that response he absorbs it*. For that response had in it all
the elements of a perfect repentance in humanity for all the
sin of man, – a perfect sorrow – a perfect contrition – all the
elements of such a repentance, and that in absolute
perfection, all – excepting the personal consciousness of sin;
and by that perfect response in Amen to the mind of God in
relation to sin is the wrath of God rightly met, and that is
accorded to divine justice which is its due, and alone could
satisfy it.[100]

As such the Lord Jesus Christ was the Father's beloved Son in whom
he was well pleased. 'We feel', McLeod Campbell wrote, 'that such
a repentance as we are supposing would be the true and proper
satisfaction to offended justice, and that there would be more
atoning worth in one tear of the true and perfect sorrow ... than
in the endless ages of penal woe.'[101]

---

[97]   *The Nature of the Atonement*, p. 125.
[98]   *The Nature of the Atonement*, p. 117.
[99]   *The Nature of the Atonement*, pp. 158f.
[100] *The Nature of the Atonement*, pp. 118f.
[101] *The Nature of the Atonement*, p. 125.

We must return again to the indissoluble relation between Incarnation and atonement upon which McLeod Campbell laid such stress, for the atonement cannot be adequately understood apart from the fact that it was through union with us in which he made our sin and our death, our poverty and our misery, our indebtedness to God, and our condemnation, his own, that Christ engaged in atoning expiation with the roots of sin and guilt in our fallen existence – 'not only the expiation due to the righteous law of God, but also the expiation due to the fatherly heart of God'[102].It was through this profound union and indeed oneness with us that the incarnate Son of God penetrated into the inner depths of our alienation from God, and brought his holy condemnation and atoning activity to bear upon us at the very root of our sinful existence, thus even of our original sin. That is what the atonement conceived as an external legal transaction could not do – at the best it could only deal with actual sins. As McLeod Campbell understood it, the atonement developed naturally and compellingly out of Christ's inner relation to men and women as the incarnate Son; or expressed the other way round, the incarnate activity of Christ in his oneness with us in our fallen human existence reached forward into the atonement with both retrospective and prospective effect, retroactively penetrating into the depths of our sin and guilt and undoing them, but prospectively in translating us from imprisonment in our mortal existence into the new life of the risen Jesus. This understanding of the inner ontological relation between the Incarnation and the atonement, and the atonement and the Incarnation, reinforced the message of the Gospel that the forgiving love of God precedes the atonement, and that the atonement is the supreme manifestation of the *love* of God in which it is ultimately grounded. It was precisely because God so loved the world that he gave his only begotten Son to be the Saviour of the world. It was this biblical and evangelical conviction that radically altered the fundamental conception of God which McLeod Campbell had inherited from his Calvinist tradition, and led him to say calmly and frankly to the General Assembly 'I hold and teach that Christ died for all men.'[103] Hence in accordance

---

[102] *The Nature of the Atonement*, p. 158.

[103] This was, of course, also the teaching of John Calvin himself, that Christ died for all, for every creature. He pointed out that the biblical expression 'many' sometimes denotes 'all' – see *Comm. on Isaiah*, 53.12, and *Comm. on Romans*, 5.15.

with its nature this universal message of salvation and reconciliation
is proclaimed freely and unconditionally – that is what many people
found, and still find, so difficult to understand and accept.[104]

The free unconditional nature of the Gospel was a regular theme
in McLeod Campbell's sermons.

> Christ the Son of God, God in our nature, God over all
> blessed for ever, and made of the seed of David according to
> the flesh; this Lord Jesus Christ, did, as the head and
> representative of the family of mankind, offer himself without
> spot to God, as a living sacrifice, wherewith God was well
> pleased; and God, in acceptance of this sacrifice, this holy
> offering of Christ, did remove *absolutely, unconditionally,*
> without waiting for us to say whether we desired it or not,
> the barrier between Himself and us, and gave us Christ, on
> the ground of whose work the barrier was removed, to be to
> us a living way of access, having the Holy Spirit for us, for
> that end; so that he is revealed to us, as one in whose strength
> we are to draw near to God to whom we are free to come.
> These are the facts concerning the work of Christ for all and
> every human being. The humble and contrite man, is the
> man who knows these facts.[105]

Years later Thomas Chalmers, who was glad that he had never
cast his vote against John McLeod Campbell, published a lecture
entitled 'On the Universality of the Gospel'.[106] 'I cannot but think',
he began, 'that the doctrine of Particular Redemption has been
expounded by many of its defenders in such a way as to give an
unfortunate aspect to the Christian dispensation.' In coming out
strongly in support of the truth that Christ died for all people,
and that Christ is set forth in the Gospel a propitiation for the sins
of the world, he went on to complain about 'the infliction of an
unnatural violence on many passages of Scripture' in the way in
which they were being interpreted, and castigated the 'narrow
sectarianism', 'artificial theology', and 'partial gospel' of some
theologians who limited the range and proclamation of redemption

---

[104] Cf. *The Nature of the Atonement*, pp. 181f.

[105] From McLeod Campbell's 'Sermon on Isaiah 57.15'; reproduced in Michael
Jinkins, *Love Is Of The Essence. An Introduction To The Theology Of John McLeod
Campbell*, Edinburgh, 1993.

[106] *Institutes of Theology*, Edinburgh, 1849, Vol. II, Chapter VII, pp. 403–13. See *The
Nature of the Atonement*, pp. 52f.

through a misunderstanding of the doctrine of predestination. 'If the efficacy of Christ's blood be only commensurate to the salvation of a chosen few, how can they expatiate on the virtue and peace-making power of that blood in the hearing of the general multitude; and more especially, as might lead all or any of that multitude to venture their reliance upon it?' Although Chalmers did not refer by name to McLeod Campbell, it was clear that he wanted his theological message to be taken seriously. This is an issue of supreme importance today which all Presbyterian theologians and ministers in Scotland, in both the Church of Scotland and the Free Churches of Scotland, must take to heart in a united Reformed witness to the great evangelical truths of the Faith.

Bibliography

Athanasius, St, *Against The Arians*, 4.6, *A Select Library of Nicene and Post-Nicene Fathers of the Christian Church*, Second Series, Vol. IV, p. 435, Oxford, 1892.

Bell, M. C., *Calvin and Scottish Theology*, Edinburgh, 1985.

Calvin, John, *Institutes of the Christian Religion*, tr. Henry Beveridge, Edinburgh, 1845.

Calvin, John, *Commentary on the Epistle to the Romans,* tr. Ross Mackenzie, Edinburgh, 1960.

Calvin John, *Commentary on Isaiah*, Eng. tr., Edinburgh, 1854.

Calvin, John, *The Gospel According to Isaiah, Seven Sermons on Isaiah 53 Concerning the Passion and Death of Christ*, tr. Leroy Nixon, Grand Rapids, 1953.

Campbell, A. J., *Two Centuries of the Church of Scotland*, 1707–1929, Paisley, 1930.

Campbell, John McLeod, *Christ the Bread of Life, An Attempt to Give A Profitable Direction To The Present Occupation of Thought With Romanism*, Glasgow, 1851, 2nd edn, London, 1869.

Campbell, John McLeod, *Memorials of John McLeod Campbell, D.D., Being a Selection from his Correspondence*, in two volumes, edited by his son, the Rev. Donald Campbell, London, 1877.

Campbell, John McLeod, *The Nature of the Atonement and Its Relation to Remission of Sins and Eternal Life*, 1st edn, Cambridge, 1856.

Campbell, John McLeod, *The Nature of the Atonement,* With Introduction and Notes, 2nd edn, London, 1868.

Campbell, John McLeod, *The Nature of the Atonement,* 4th edn,

London, 1873; republished with an Introduction by Edgar P. Dickie, London, 1959.

Campbell, John McLeod, *The Nature of the Atonement and Its Relation to Remissions of Sins and Eternal Life*, 6th edn with An Introduction and Notes, London, 1895.

Campbell, John McLeod, *Notes of Sermons by the Rev. J. McL. Campbell*, Taken in Short Hand, 3 vols., lithographic reproduction, Paisley, 1831 & 1832.

Campbell, John McLeod, *Notes of Sermons of the Rev. John McL. Campbell*, 2 vols., Greenock, 1831.

Campbell, John McLeod, *Reminiscences and Reflections, Referring to his Early Ministry in the Parish of Row, 1825–31*, edited, with an Introductory Narrative, by his son, Donald Campbell, London, 1873.

Campbell, John McLeod, *Responsibility for the Gift of Eternal Life*, Compiled by Permission of the late Rev. John McLeod Campbell, D. D., From Sermons Preached Chiefly at Row, in the Years 1829–31, London, 1873.

Campbell, John McLeod, *Sermons and Lectures*, Taken in Short Hand, 2 vols. Printed, R. B. Lusk, Greenock, 1832.

Campbell, John McLeod, *Thoughts on Revelation, With Special Reference to the Present Time*, Glasgow, 1862, 2nd edn, London, 1874.

Campbell, John McLeod, *The Whole Proceedings before the Presbytery of Dumbarton, and Synod of Glasgow and Ayr in the Case Of the Rev. John McLeod Campbell*, R. B. Lusk, Greenock, 1831.

Chalmers, Thomas, *Institutes of Theology*, Edinburgh, 1849.

Henderson, Henry F., *Erskine of Linlathen. Selections and Biography*, Edinburgh, 1899.

Howe, John, *The Redeemer's Tears Wept Over Lost Souls: and Two Discourses on Self-Dedication, and on Yielding Ourselves to God, With an Introductory Essay*, by Rev Robert Gordon, Edinburgh. Glasgow, 1822.

Jinkins, Michael, *Love Is Of The Essence. An Introduction To The Theology Of John McLeod Campbell*, Edinburgh, 1993.

Mackintosh, H. R., *Some Aspects of Christian Belief*, London, 1923.

Orr, James, *The Christian View of God and the World*, Edinburgh, 1897.

Rutherford, Samuel, *Christ Dying and Drawing Sinners to Himselfe*, London, 1647.

Thomson, Andrew Mitchell, *The Doctrine of Universal Pardon Considered and Refuted*, Edinburgh, 1830.

Torrance, James B., 'The Contribution of McLeod Campbell to Scottish Theology', *Scottish Journal of Theology*, 26.3, Edinburgh, 1973, pp. 295–310.

Torrance, James B., 'The Incarnation and "Limited Atonement"', *The Evangelical Quarterly*, 55.3, Exeter, 1984, pp. 83–93.

Torrance, James B., 'Introduction' to the reprint of the fourth edition of John McLeod Campbell, *The Nature of the Atonement*, Edinburgh & Grand Rapids, 1996.

Tuttle, George M., *So Rich A Soil, John McLeod Campbell on Christian Atonement*, with a foreword by James Torrance, Edinburgh, 1986.

Van Dyk, Leanne, *The Desire of Divine Love, John McLeod Campbell's Doctrine of the Atonement*, New York, 1995.

Index

Printed in the United States
141619LV00003B/7/A